Camelot

The True Story

by Michael D. Miller

Copyright 1997 by Rideout Publishing Company
4118 Montrose Ct., Orlando, Florida 32812 USA
Tel: 407-859-8638, Fax: 407-826-9524

First Edition

Cover by: Transphoto, Inc., Orlando, Florida

Edited by: Edith A. Cooper

Library of Congress Catalog Card Number 98-091276

ISBN No. 0-965148-41-6

The story of Camelot and King Arthur as seen through the eyes of 102 people who were regressed to their past lives with King Arthur and Camelot. Hear the story as related by Guenivere, Merlin, Arthur, Morgana, Lancelot, Galahad, Gawaine, Percival, and other members of the Round Table, their wives, and children.

Table of Contents

	Introduction	vii
	Prologue	x
1.	Who Am I?	1
2.	My Healing Continues	12
3.	A Knight's Story	18
4.	Camelot and the Church	32
5.	I Do My First Regression	50
6.	My Regression Technique	54
7.	Cathy Channelling Raziel, April 1994	58
8.	Laurie as Guenivere, April 1994	71
9.	Susan as Marlinda, April 1994	86
10.	Multiple Reincarnations	97
11.	Barb as Guenivere, May 1994	100
12.	Linda as Morgana, May 1994	112
13.	Bill as Frederick, June 1994	130
14.	Barb as Guenivere, July 1994	138
15.	Greg as Arthur, August 1994	146
16.	Jerry as a Page, August 1994	167
17.	Fran as Guenivere, September 1994	181
18.	Tad as Sir Kay, September 1994	196
19.	Jackie as Arthur, September 1994	208
20.	Brenda as Sarah (wife of Lionel), September 1994	223
21.	Angela as Merlin, September 1994	236
22.	Richard as Bedivere, September 1994	245
23.	Candice as Guenivere, October 1994	256
24.	Earl as Lancelot, November 1994	260
25.	Jake as Galahad, December 1994	275
26.	Mike as Percival, January 1995	286
27.	Doreen as the Bird Woman, April 1995	293
28.	David as Gawaine, April 1995	310
29.	Peter as Gawaine's Son, April 1995	323
30.	Stephanie as the Red Knight, April 1995	337
31.	Thomas as Lancelot, February 1996	349
32.	About Time	357
33.	Dana as Lancelot, February, 1997	360
34.	The Camelot Connection	375

Introduction

I began to meditate in 1985. I meditate daily. Since 1992 my spirit guide has been Merlin. He comes to me while I am in meditation. I have been blessed with the ability to speak with, and sometimes see him. Over the next few years we developed a pretty good working relationship. Then, in 1994, he asked me to work with him to reconstruct the true story of Camelot.

It seems that King Arthur lived around the year 500AD. Nothing was written about him until the year 1200AD. This 700-year gap caused much of the true story to be lost. Most of what has been written about him has been conjecture, guesswork, or reconstructed legend. "It is time for the real story of Arthur to be told," said Merlin.

We then embarked on a fantastic journey which still has me amazed. Merlin has brought to me 102 people who were reincarnations of persons who had lived during Camelot. I regressed each of them, and each told his or her story. I captured 82 of the regressions on tape. This collection of tapes tells an amazing story, a story which is more beautiful than anything yet written.

Galahad stated the following to me during one of his regressions:

"Camelot was never meant to be a constellation in the sky. A constellation is permanent. Camelot was never meant to be permanent. It was instead meant to be a shooting star. It was meant to flash briefly across the sky. Camelot was meant, in its brief sojourn on earth, to give us a glimpse of what mankind could aspire to. It set an example for us, just as the shooting star shows us for a brief instance the beauty and glory of its existence. But just as we remember the beauty and magnificence of the shooting star long after it has vanished, the concepts and ideals established by King Arthur's Round Table were remembered long after Camelot was no more.

The ideals of Camelot are still remembered. They will always be remembered. There are periods since Camelot when these principles have once again surfaced as guiding beacons for mankind's struggle to regain his oneness with God. But again, mankind was not ready, and so they were again extinguished. But never forgotten. They live on in the breasts and hearts of men. And they will continue to resurface as mankind progresses in his spiritual evolution. One day they will surface, and mankind will be ready. Then Camelot can be permanent. In the meantime, we keep these ideals kindled in our hearts, waiting for that magic and wonderful day."

Galahad was right. A few of the highlights of the story are as follows: Camelot was about love, honor, and nobility. Merlin and Arthur established the Round Table as a movement to set the example for man of what he could achieve when he recognized his own godliness; when he let his natural qualities of nobility and honor guide his actions. The Round Table was round because it represented the earth. Just as when a pebble is dropped into a still pool of water, and it creates a series of circular ripples which eventually reach out and cover the entire pool, so was the Round Table meant to represent the first ripple of a concept which will expand until it has covered the earth.

As Arthur selected young men and trained them to be great martial warriors, so did Merlin at the same time train them to become great spiritual warriors. This balance was their magic. They knew that when they had purity of heart, innocence, and God's blessing for the nobility of their purpose, they could not be defeated. Merlin also taught them many protective magic rituals. They could, for example, make themselves invisible, shape-shift into other forms, or make one man appear to be many. Thus armed with Arthur's and Merlin's training, these warrior-priests could single-handedly defeat large groups of the enemy.

Camelot was love. All of the knights adored their king and queen. Merlin was greatly loved and admired. Great camaraderie existed among the knights. Even the great sword Excalibur was about love. When Excalibur was forged, Merlin arranged a special ceremony where Jesus and St. Michael appeared and placed their hands in the molten metal, thus permanently imbuing it with their energies of love. This gave Excalibur its famous powers. For when someone held Excalibur in their hands, they were enveloped with love. When enveloped in love, you cannot be harmed. This is only one of the messages which Merlin seeks to rekindle within us: love is the greatest protection of all.

As the following stories tell, Camelot was a beautiful experience. Quite possibly it is mankind's most beautiful experience yet. But built into the fabric of this experience was tragedy; tragedy which would bring the dream of Camelot to its end.

What sort of tragedy? The tragedy of two sets of soul mates who could never be together. One set of soul mates was the king and his sister. The other was the king's best friend and the king's wife. Fate cast them into this difficult situation, quite possibly so that Camelot would end when it was supposed to end. Another tragedy was that Arthur's idealistic genius, which created the magic of Camelot and the Round Table Movement, did not know how to comprehend or defend against treachery. Believing that all around him shared his purity and idealism, he did not respond when his kingdom was threatened by the darker sides of men's ambitions.

It was Arthur's destiny to bring Christianity to Britain. This threatened the existing druid religion. To ease their concerns, Arthur promised to protect the druids. He promised them that they would always peacefully coexist with the Christian church. Ironically, years later when the church had lost its memory of Arthur the benefactor, church leaders mounted a campaign in Europe against Arthur because he protected the heathens (druids) from persecution. A large Christian army came to Britain, and in Arthur's 57th year, he and his knights and his movement were destroyed in a last dramatic battle. And Camelot was no more.

Prologue

How Can It Be?

One question often asked of me is how I was able to regress so many people who had lived during Camelot. How is it that, given the millions of souls on earth at this time, so many Camelot figures showed up at my doorstep? "The probabilities of such a thing happening are such that it couldn't happen," is a comment I have heard more than once.

At first I was unable to answer this question to my satisfaction. So I turned to my spirit mentors with the same question. Merlin replied, "It is simple. The people who are meant to hear this story will know in their hearts that everything you print is the truth. No further proof for them is needed." Then one day while in meditation, to my great joy and pleasure, I received a message directly from God himself. "As far as my ability to bring so many Camelot personalities to you, do you doubt that I can do such a thing?" No, I do not doubt that God can do such a thing!

One great effect on me personally from this whole affair is that it has firmly impressed on me the realization that the events in our lives and worlds are not as random as we usually think they are. I find myself quite often now saying to others, "Nothing is this world is random. Nothing is by chance."

As for you, dear reader, I leave it to you to decide about my book. In your heart will lie the truth.

Who Am I?

They say that the word "History" is actually made up from a joining of the two words "His-Story." This suggests that history began with the collection of "his stories." I would like to relate to you a bit of history which is My-Story.

I am an unlikely person to be writing a story such as this. It is 1997, and I am 57-years-old. Here is my story: I was raised on a small farm on the outskirts of Tulsa, Oklahoma. My Dad was a struggling small contractor, my Mom a secretary. I was a shy and skinny kid. I was a very normal and average kid. But somehow when I got to high school things really began to click into place for me. I distinguished myself. I was elected president of my class each year. There were 840 students in my high school class. I graduated in 1958. In 1958, my school, Will Rogers High School, was chosen by *Look* magazine as one of the top ten high schools in the nation. So I was the president of the graduating class of one of the top high schools in the country.

Following the principles of "self-fulfilling prophecy" I naturally, with this accomplishment under my belt, knew that I would do well in life. I went out and got myself accepted into West Point. My Dad had a third-grade education, and no male member of my family had ever gone to college before. I was flying high! And my family was very proud of me.

Was West Point ever an experience! I loved and hated the place. That was okay, because I think that is the way the system at West Point was set up. You were supposed to both love and hate the place. It was wonderful; the education was great, the camaraderie and idealistic atmosphere very expanding for a bunch of ambitious middle-class American dreamers. It was brutal; the system was designed to break you, then ruthlessly mold you into a perfect leader and statesman. Most of us busted our guts trying to fit this mold. Half of us made it.

Approximately 1100 of us started out; 565 of us graduated. I graduated in 1964, ranking 202 out of my class of 565.

Then, suddenly I was an Army officer. I had never given much thought as to whether or not I really wanted to be an Army officer. I had spent all of my energy in surviving the "system" at West Point. Graduating had been my goal. Now I was graduated, and was Second Lieutenant Michael D. Miller. My Mom and my Dad were so proud of me that they thought I could walk on water. Perhaps I also thought that I could walk on water.

I then became a Paratrooper and a Ranger (these guys *know* that they can walk on water!) In 1968 I went to Vietnam. Up to this point in my life, at the age of 28, I was a typical middle-class American success story, and I was a typical "left-brain" type of thinker. I was molded, trained and educated to have a scholarly, engineer-oriented, military-leadership approach to life. Vietnam was the beginning of the end of my being such a type of thinker.

Vietnam was a magical and mystical experience for me. I was a Captain in the Corps of Engineers. Through a unique series of events, I ended up as the commander of a small engineer task force in the Mekong Delta. "Task Force Builder" was set up as an experimental program to have American engineer troops build schools and medical clinics in rural hamlets, in the process helping the local struggling Viet-namese infrastructures establish their authority over an area which had been under Viet Cong control. In many cases, the villages and hamlets in which we built schools were still being fought over by the Americans and the Viet Cong. We were to also be a demonstration of American good will and intention toward the Vietnamese people.

Within ten days of setting up the task force base camp in the village of Rach Kein in Long An Province, one of the engineer soldiers was killed and eleven were wounded in Viet Cong attacks. The higher echelons who had planned this experimental program were aghast. Careers were on the line should this program become a fiasco. The engineer brigade staff looked about for a quick fix to this problem. They decided that they needed new leadership for the task force.

So guess which Airborne Ranger Captain arrived in the 46th Engineer Battalion about this time? I was almost immediately offered the opportunity to take over Task Force Builder. I was taken by helicopter to visit the task force. From the moment I stepped off my Battalion Commander's helicopter at one of their jobsites, I somehow knew that I had arrived at my destiny. Two days later, I took over as the Commanding Officer of Task Force Builder, 46th Engineer Battalion, 159th Engineer Group.

I, to this day, still don't understand everything that happened. It was magical. I led Task Force Builder to greatness. We built 22 schools, numerous medical clinics and other facilities. Our project became famous. We were visited by one VIP group or another almost every week. We were a legend in our own time. A combat command was six months. After my six months were up, no one in the battalion could be found to volunteer to take my job. It was too dangerous. So I stayed on as commander for the full year. When I left the country, the task force was disbanded with our mission successfully completed. We were a model of success. Great pride and recognition was given to our work.

During this year I had complete focus on one objective: to get the job done without losing any of my men.

I did it! I never lost a man who was under my command. I had 13 wounded, none seriously. We went through 42 base camp attacks and three road ambushes. I was blown out of my jeep, had an artillery shell go through my breakfast table, had everyone in the five vehicles in front of me killed, had everyone in the vehicle behind me killed, had enemy mortar shells explode within 15 feet of me, had the local VC place a price on my head, had a man standing next to me killed by enemy fire. I could not be touched. It was magical.

At one time I was recommended for four Bronze Stars. I received the "Legion of Merit", which was the nation's second-highest award for meritorious service. At that time I was the only Captain in the Army Corps of Engineers to have the Legion of Merit.

I had walked on water. I had done it. I had the medals to prove it. But, somehow I knew that I hadn't done this thing alone. I knew that I had been guided and protected by some unseen spiritual forces. For one thing, my left-brained engineering mind knew that the probabilities of me having survived unscratched through all of what I had experienced were nil. For another thing, the sight of dead bodies had an unsettling effect on me. I somehow knew that those dead bodies were not the persons who had been there. Some years later, I wrote a short poem to describe my feelings:

Are you dead?
I think not

I viewed your body
sprawled and cold

Youth cut down
in battle
The fallen warrior

But
You were not there
That shell
was not you

Something
way deep
within me
cried out
He has gone on
To Heaven

Thus I learned
It exists
And I am eternal

In short, my Vietnam experience left me with a gnawing thought in the back of my mind that there was a spiritual element to life that should not be ignored.

I left the Army at the age of 29 to pursue my dream of being an international businessman and developer. I ignored those gnawing thoughts about an unseen spiritual side to life. I also stuffed way down deep within myself the terrible memories of death and suffering which I had observed. I stuffed way deep that I had killed in order to keep from being killed.

You no doubt have heard the expression "You can run but you can't hide." I could run from my memories, but I could not hide from them forever.

In 1978, at the age of 38, I owned a small construction company in Abu Dhabi. There was a lot of political instability in this small, but wealthy, Arab country. It had affected my business. I was under great pressure to keep my company going.

One night I awoke with a start to find a spirit presence in my dark-ened bedroom. It was my deceased grandfather. He had come to give me comfort. I had an immense love for him. His visit was very special to me.

His visit also shook the hell out of me. Once again, this left-brained thinker was confronted by a truth which was not even recognized or accepted by his society: there is an unseen spiritual element to life. Had it been anyone but Grandpa who had visited, I might have once again ignored the experience. But this time I sought answers.

On my next trip home to the United States I searched several book-stores, thereby discovering the works written about Edgar Cayce. I read everything I could get my hands on about this clairvoyant and his amazing revelations. Thus began my spiritual odyssey, which contin-ues to this day. I hope that it never ends.

Eventually, my Abu Dhabi construction company failed. I could no longer walk on water. As a matter of fact, I got really dunked! I had apparently reached that point in my life where God had decided to take me in a different direction. I entered that period of my life when failure began to plague me. His message to me was simple. I would never be able to again walk on water until I recognized Him, and realized that He was the one all along who had kept me from sinking.

I was a slow learner. It took two divorces, numerous business failures, a health crisis or two, but then I began to catch on. As my spiritual path began to bring me closer to God, my life began to straighten out. Happiness and prosperity slowly returned. This time it was built on the solid foundation of my connection to God.

In 1991, at the age of 51, I was dating a very nice lady who was a college instructor. Her name was Lisa. We meditated together quite often. Lisa was gifted with the ability to occasionally see spirits. One morning as we sat in her bedroom meditating, Lisa calmly announced to me that a spiritual presence was in the room with us. It was Merlin. I was very unimpressed. Had Jesus, an Archangel, or someone important been there, well then I would have been impressed. But Merlin? All I knew of him were some fuzzy images of a guy in robes with a crystal mounted on his forehead who did magic for King Arthur. I did not identify with him at all. I certainly did not believe in magic.

I knew almost nothing about the King Arthur and Camelot legends. I had never read a book about them or gone to the theater to see a King Arthur movie. I had seen several old movies on television about King Arthur. I vaguely had some recollections about the mystical adventures depicted in those movies. But I had not identified or "connected" with those TV shows at all. I would have preferred viewing a good Western. In short, I was not a King Arthur buff, and had very little identification with, or interest in, those old, musty legends.

So for Merlin to appear to us was not a big deal to me. He came back the next day to visit us. Lisa seemed intrigued by him. I was not. Then he became a regular visitor, coming to Lisa almost every day. He began to give her messages about the King Arthur period. Some of them were interesting. For instance, he explained that as King Arthur trained a young man to become a knight, Merlin also trained him to become a priest. As each young warrior learned his martial skills, he was also given the spiritual skills he would need in order to have perfect balance as a warrior-priest. It was the spiritual nature of the Round Table's knights that made them so exceptional. It was their connection to the God force that made them so successful in battle. Hey, this was getting interesting! Maybe there is something to this Merlin after all!

Then, after a period of several weeks of this, I began to see Merlin also. Sometimes he would appear to me as the wizard, the fellow in long robes. Other times he showed himself as an oriental magician, or as Britannica (a female goddess), or as a tree. Merlin then explained to us who he really was.

Merlin explained that when Earth was first formed as a planet, God assigned several powerful spiritual forces to assist it. One of these forces became in charge of all of the plant and animal life above the oceans. This is the force that we would refer to as Mother Nature. This force, at various times and places, has been worshipped by mankind as mankind slowly began to reawaken to his connection to God. The early inhabitants of the British Isles worshipped this force of nature, which they referred to as the "Green Man". Their "churches" were sacred groves of oak trees. They were known as druids. There was always one druid priest who was considered the supreme priest of this religion. His title was Merlin. Merlin was a title, not a given name. It had been held by many people prior to the arrival of our Merlin.

Jesus came to earth. Christianity was born. Christianity began to spread throughout the earth. It was time for Christianity to supplant or replace the other, shall we say, "incomplete" religions of the day. Christianity spread far and wide. Then it was time for Christianity to arrive in the British Isles. The spiritual force then being worshipped by the druids, being completely dedicated and subservient to Lord Jesus, knew that it was time for it to be replaced by Christianity. To help you understand this, Merlin has explained that it is somewhat akin to our own concept of the chain of command, or organizational chart. On God's organizational chart, the force of nature being worshipped by the druids "reported" directly to Jesus. So, Merlin, the loyal executive, agreed to step aside so that the people could worship his "boss" directly.

Anyway, it was time for the druid religion to be replaced by Christianity. So the "Green Man" incarnated as a man who would become the Merlin, the leader of the druid religion. He would then create King Arthur who would, under his guidance, bring Christianity to the British Isles. In short, Merlin came into existence to bring about his own downfall.

In doing all of this, Merlin and Arthur would also create Camelot and the Round Table Movement. This would show mankind its potential for greatness, nobility and purity. They would establish a movement which would live forever in the hearts of mankind until the day when we have reached a point of spiritual growth and evolution when Camelot will once again exist. But this time Camelot will exist for all, and will endure. Every man will be a knight. Every woman will be Guenivere.

Hey, this information was interesting. I was hungry for this kind of knowledge and information. Now I really began to like Merlin! I looked forward to his visits. After several months, Merlin asked me if I would let him train me. He explained that he would take me on a spiritual path similar to the spiritual training path which he had taken the knights of the Round Table so long ago. I agreed and off we went. It was amazing. One time I had read in a book about indian shamans that many of the shamans received their spiritual training directly from the spirits of deceased shamans. This seemed pretty far-fetched. Now I was being trained by a spirit. The same thing was happening to me.

Over the next six months, I was tutored by Merlin in many things. It changed my life completely. He taught me about the power in certain symbols. How certain symbols, especially many which have been worshipped for many centuries, have special vibrational power which can be harnessed. He taught me about the power of ritual. I attended Catholic church services in order to study certain aspects of their rituals. I learned to incorporate some of their ritual into my own worship. He showed the power of gemstones, pyramids, certain liquids, and colors to affect reality. He taught me that many of the powerful dark forces on earth at this time use some of these principles to attempt to dominate and exploit us. He taught me how to express a desire so that the universe can best utilize it. He taught how to empower a thought so it would more readily manifest. He showed me how the knights could make themselves disappear, or to appear in another form. He showed me how they used special rituals for their personal protection. Finally, at the end of my training period, he very patiently waited for me to ask him why he had taught me all of this.

One Sunday night I sat in my circle meditating. Merlin appeared. I began to question him about a seminar I had attended that weekend. It had been given by William Cooper, a retired Naval intelligence officer who tours the country speaking about some of the various conspiracies and efforts that are presently underway in our country to undermine our democracies and freedoms. I rather casually asked Merlin if I could use some of the techniques and practices which Merlin had taught me in order to offset the dark forces which were behind these conspiratorial forces.

Suddenly, fireworks went off behind Merlin. The sky behind him was lit up with bright starbursts. He got very excited. He actually began to jump up and down. He waved his arms in the air. I had never seen Merlin behave so. I had never seen him show such emotion.

"Yes, yes!" he said. "This is why we taught you the powers. It is so that you can use them to do God's work. But we couldn't tell you to use them so. You had to offer, which you have now done. You can use your newfound powers to help others increase their awareness. You can use your powers to offset the energies sent out by the forces of darkness." The dictionary defines magic as the act of making things happen. Prior to my friendship with Merlin, my distaste with anything associated with the term magic was typical. Merlin changed my stereotypical belief. He explained that every time you pray, every time you recite a mantra (such as the rosary), every time you practice creative visualization, you are practicing a form of magic (you are making something happen). Jesus explained that he taught many things to the people which are no longer mentioned in the Bible. He said that as a youth he attended the ancient mystery schools at the pyramids in Egypt. There he learned many things which he incorporated into his teachings. He also learned much from the Essenes which he practiced. When he said, "All these things that I do, ye shall do also," he had meant it. He had intended that we would evolve spiritually to the point where we too could manifest at will. Just as Jesus had fed the multitudes with five fishes, we were meant to be able to draw upon God's powers to manifest at will.

It was not too many years after Jesus's death that the church began to delete this sort of information from the teachings of the Master. Such information tended to empower the individual, and not the church. The leaders of the church, seeking to increase the power of the church over its flocks, eventually removed almost all of this information from the Bible. Jesus and Merlin explained that it was time for this information to again be told to the people. As we evolve spiritually we will find that it cannot be denied us.

Merlin pointed out how he has been incorrectly portrayed as a non-Christian. Modern stereotypes reflect him as a magic-wielding heathen. But as the following story of the King Arthur odyssey points out, Merlin is the one who orchestrated events so that Christianity could be brought to Britain. Merlin was a druid. Then King Arthur announced that Christianity was to be accepted throughout the land, and was to be his religion. From this point on, Merlin was both a Christian and a druid. As a matter of fact, Merlin was widely hated and schemed against by many of the druid elements throughout the kingdom. They believed that he had betrayed them. There were many plots and schemes launched against him.

Likewise Merlin pointed out to me that magic has been maligned. Usually any association with the word magic involves images of "black magic" and witches, etc. Magic can be explained very simply. When you pray to God, you are speaking to God and his minions. And when you ask God for assistance, God, Jesus, the Archangels and angels, etc., will go to work for you and your request, inasmuch as it is compatible with the lessons which your God-path indicates for you at that time. As an example, should your particular path in life according to God's plan require that you experience a certain level of poverty until a certain lesson or lessons have been learned, then any prayers to God requesting prosperity in your life cannot be answered for you at that time. These prayerful petitions will be stored up, held in abeyance, and given to you at a later date when it is appropriate to God's plan for you to receive these blessings.

Any such petition to God I prefer to refer to as "white" magic, or God magic. However, should someone through a prayer, or through ritual, request assistance from the dark forces of the unseen spiritual world, then they have entered into that realm commonly referred to as black magic. Since their request is most certainly probably not compatible with the God plan for their life, any manifestation given to them in answer to their supplication usually leads to tragedy or misfortune for them. Merlin stated that many weak people resort to black magic as a short cut to get what they want. The resulting backlash from God's universe is usually not long in coming. Should any person be successful in using the dark forces to manifest something, they will end up paying a terrible price for their transgression. "God is not mocked."

Merlin taught me a simple and steadfast rule to follow to make sure that every request through prayer or ritual is compatible with God's plan. The rule is simply to include the statement "God's will be done" in your request. Then you cannot go wrong.

But I digress from my story. Let us return to my adventure. Eventually Lisa and I went our separate ways. Then Teresa came into my life. A depth of love exploded about us which we could not handle. Neither of us was ready for the love we had found. We had both waited our entire lives to find a love this deep. Then we both ran from it. Our relationship lasted six wonderful months, and then it was over. During this time Merlin and I began to get closer. He suffered along with me as I struggled to deal with a broken heart. There were nights when he cried along with me. I began to feel a deep love for Merlin, as I also began to realize the depth of his love for me. We were definitely becoming emotionally attached.

He is a very witty man. We got to the point where we joked with each other a lot. He teased me about the fact that he had been unlucky in love when he was on the earth plane as Merlin. Now, he said that I "was guided by a spirit guide like him who was so unlucky with his own loves, I was probably doomed to the same fate." This was in reference to the fact that many old legends portray Merlin as a man with some difficult romantic experiences. He showed great love and compassion and understanding for me. I began to consider him a great friend. The relationship was to me as real and as special as the relationship you would have with your best friend.

All this while, I always felt very flattered by the attentions of this so great spirit force. But why me?

In August of 1993 I visited the home of a friend named Noreen. It was midmorning. I had gone to her house to discuss some of my personal problems. We sat in her kitchen drinking a cup of coffee. Suddenly Merlin appeared to both of us. To our amazement he began to tell Noreen that she had lived during the time of Camelot, and that she had been a handmaiden to Arthur's half-sister, Morgana La Fay. Feeling a bit left out of the conversation, I asked Merlin if I had also been there at Camelot. With an impish smile, he grinned, thought a moment, and stated, "Why yes, I believe that you were there. I see you as the man who swept up around the castle." He then went on to discuss with Noreen how her life then had impacted her present life as a nurse in Orlando, Florida. She was given quite a bit of information. I was left with only the cursory observation that I had been a janitor during the reign of King Arthur.

Both Noreen and I were elated by this experience. Imagine that! We had lived during Camelot. That I had lived during Camelot might explain some of the attention which Merlin had given to me. But as a janitor, had I really deserved such special recognition from such a great one?

Two days later I attended an evening class led by a healer from Sedona, Arizona named Tim Heath. In the course of the evening he led us through a rebirthing session. I had been rebirthed a number of times before, so I was quite comfortable doing this. Briefly, Rebirthing is a technique of controlled breathing relaxation which opens up the doors to your subconscious mind. This allows memories, fears, anxieties, etc. which are buried in your subconscious mind to come up so they can be released. This rebirthing was very different for me. As I felt myself opening up, I was overwhelmed with a feeling of grief. I began to shout, "They took my king, they took my king!" I felt this tremendous sense of loss of someone whom I loved immensely. I was sweating, drooling at the mouth. I was lying on the floor, and I began thrashing around. Several of my friends rushed over to comfort me and to assist me through this emotional experience. After the rebirthing had ended, and I had recovered, I was left with the fascinating question, "What the heck is going on here?"

The very next day I went to visit my good friends Cynthia and Lawrence Ferguson. Cynthia is a very gifted clairvoyant and medium. Lawrence is an expert at hypnotic regressions. We had quite an animated discussion, as they explained to me their own discoveries about past-life connections to the Camelot experience. Lawrence volunteered to lead me through a past life regression; we would check out my Camelot connection.

Lawrence regressed me back to the King Arthur period. I was there. I was not the janitor (shame on Merlin for teasing me!) I saw myself seated on a green lawn. It was after a tournament. King Arthur and his Queen sat on two straight-back chairs in the center of this lawn. About them, sprawled and sitting in the grass, were their knights. I was one of the knights. I felt this incredible love. I was filled with an incredible feeling of peace. I have never felt any emotion in

10

this lifetime as strong as the feelings of love and peace which I felt with them. I somehow knew that they were my family. I somehow knew that this Camelot experience was the standard by which I have compared every experience since. I somehow knew that, unknowingly, I had been searching my entire life to find the same level of love and peace which I had known then. It explained the emptiness in my stomach which I never understood, and it explained my constant searching throughout this lifetime for something which I didn't even know I was looking for. I just knew that something was missing. Now the mysteries of my life were being explained. I began to sob, great emotions of love long-lost filled my being. After a while, my beloved Jesus appeared to me. I was filled with his incredible love for me. I began to sob even more uncontrollably. Lawrence was handing me kleenex sheets as I wiped away the flood of tears, struggling to regain control of myself. Then Jesus spoke to me. Here is his message to me, as close as I can recant it:

"Please do not be sorrowful. It is time for you now to know who you really are, just as it is time for many others to be reawakened to their past-life identities as participants in Camelot. Many of you, those that are ready, are being once again drawn together. It is our desire that this be done. You are very special to us. For you see, many of you walked with me during my Jesus sojourn on earth. You were called together again for the Camelot experience. Just as a coach calls for his favorite team in the starting lineup of his biggest game, so we called on many of you again. The King Arthur period was an important time: it was the ushering in of a new era, the birth of Christianity in that part of the world. So we called in our favorite team to accomplish this. But in order to usher in Christianity, most of you had to be sacrificed. It is now our pleasure to bring you back together again. We are doing so in order that we may receive the enjoyment of watching you have a happy ending this time. You see, we also like to see a happy ending. It is our gift of love to you. This time, you will once again usher in a new era. But this time you will have a happy ending, with many smiles for all of you."

I was overwhelmed by this message. My life has not been the same since.

2

My Healing Continues

It was August of 1993. I awoke in the middle of the night. I sensed that there was an extraordinary presence in the room. I lay there in bed trying to determine the nature of this presence. I sensed that it was gentle and sincere, and then sensed that it was the spirit of a Vietnamese soldier. I quickly got up, went to my altar spot which is set up in my bathroom, and lit a candle and incense. I quickly prayed for God's forces to surround me and protect me, and then invited the unknown visiting spirit to be with me. He was there.

He instructed me to go to my dresser and get "the medallion." I asked myself, "What medallion?" Then I remembered. I was stunned. How could he have known? It had laid in the bottom of the old cigar box where I had placed my Army medals and uniform insignia some 23 years earlier when I had taken off my officer's uniform for the last time. I had always kept the box in a top drawer of my dresser. But I did not remember that the old medallion was in the box also.

Back in 1968, in the Mekong Delta, I had obtained this medallion. My Mess Sergeant, Raymond Barajas, was a coin collector. Knowing that I visited a lot of small Vietnamese villages which were seldom visited by Americans, he had asked me to keep on the lookout for rare old coins. Consequently, I sometimes would ask the merchants of small villages if they had any old French, Indochinese or other old coins stored away which they might like to sell. On several occasions, I was able to locate valuable old coins for Sergeant Barajas.

We were building a new village market in Can Guoic. I had spoken to the merchants there about old coins. The word spread. Over the next several days a number of villagers approached me to show me their old coins. I managed to purchase several nice ones. One day a small boy about nine-years-old ran up to me and held out a coin. I could tell that he was very nervous. I think that he was scared to death to approach me. Can Guioc was a center of Viet Cong strength, so not everyone there loved us. I understood his nervousness. I was very busy and preoccupied at the moment. But I stopped my activity long enough to look at his coin. It was not a coin, but a round medallion of some sort, made of a pewter-like metal. I was not interested in cheap Vietnamese medallions. I shook my head "no" and handed the medallion back to him. I returned to my pressing business. I looked down a few moments later. He was still there. Although scared to death, he held the coin out to me again, as if to say that he would not take "no" for an answer. He looked very determined. There was something about his manner that struck a chord within me. And I was still very absorbed in dealing with the pressing jobsite matters at hand. So I reached for my wallet, more to get rid of the kid than anything else. I held out the Vietnamese equivalent of five US dollars. He grabbed the money, dropped the medallion in my hand, and ran off.

That was it. I had never really paid any attention to the medallion. I don't ever really remember keeping it. But I had apparently stuck it in amongst my Army insignia in the cigar box. There it had lain all these years. Until now.

I went to my dresser, found the cigar box stuffed in the back of a top drawer, and retrieved the medallion. I returned to my altar and sat in my meditation chair. The Vietnamese spirit asked me to hold the medallion in my left hand. I did. I sat there holding the medallion. A scene materialized in front of me. There was a simple wooden shack located at the edge of a large river. River water actually lapped in on the dirt floor at one corner of the one-room shack. An elderly Vietnamese woman lay ill on a pallet. She was alone with her son, who was still a small boy. She said goodbye to him, and handed him the medallion. It was her parting gift to him. I sensed great love between them. I also sensed that she would soon be dead.

The Vietnamese spirit then spoke to me, saying that his name was Nguyen Nghuoc. He then showed me another scene. Now he was a young man of about twenty-four-years old. He was very tall for a Vietnamese, was slender, and was a very handsome young man. He wore the dark khaki uniform of a Viet Cong. He was a Lieutenant. He was with a group of about two dozen Viet Cong soldiers. It was daytime, and they were walking in the open across a rice paddy. It was the dry season, and the surfaces of the rice paddies were dry and firm, which allowed them to walk directly across the paddies. They were attacked by an American jet fighter which dropped several bombs at them. The jet was I believe an F-86 US Air Force fighter.

He then showed me another scene. It was dark. He was dead. He had been struck at the base of his neck by a large piece of shrapnel from one of the bombs. Several of the VC soldiers were digging into the side of a river bank levee. They were digging a makeshift grave,

13

one that would be easily concealed as part of the levee. There he was buried.

He then told me that the small boy who had brought me the medallion was his son. After his death, his few belongings, including the medallion, had been returned to his wife. She lived in Can Guioc with their two children. Without her husband, she lived a precarious life. The Viet Cong had no "survivor's benefits" for the families of those lost fighting for their cause. So she and the children lived in poverty. She heard that there was an American captain in the marketplace buying old coins. She had no old coins. But in desperation, she had sent her son to me with her deceased husband's medallion. Thus it had passed on to me.

Nguyen Nghuoc then told me that he wished to be my spirit brother. The crystal which I wore on a chain around my neck had finished its work. It was now time for me to wear his medallion. I looked closely at the medallion. There were several oriental letters engraved on one side. I asked him what they were. He stated that they were Chinese symbols which stood for health, prosperity and happiness. Then he said goodbye, and was gone. I returned to bed, placing the medallion on top of my dresser, with my mind still stunned and amazed by the experience.

When I awoke the next morning I was a bit doubtful about the whole event. I shoved it out of my mind. It was pretty weird. I didn't want to deal with it.

By coincidence (*that* word again!) I had a luncheon date that day at "Little Saigon", a quaint Vietnamese restaurant. As I finished dressing for my date, my eyes fell on the medallion laying on my dresser. I thought to myself, "I'll take it along to the Vietnamese restaurant. Maybe someone there can help explain the engravings on it." As I picked it up off the dresser, a voice very clearly said to me the word "Phuoc." Or that is how I visualized it as the voice said it. Actually it was pronounced "fook."

My date was late. As I sat there waiting in the restaurant, I remembered the medallion in my pocket. With not much else to do, I thought that I would show the medallion to the manager of the restaurant. He was a young Vietnamese man about thirty-years old. I explained to him that I had gotten the medallion in Vietnam. I asked him what the engraved symbol meant. He looked at it closely, then said, "Wait a minute, I will show it to some elderly men in the rear of the restaurant. Maybe they can help." I watched as he respectfully approached three older Vietnamese who were dining at a table in the rear of the restaurant. I watched as they examined the medallion, chatting among themselves. Then the restaurant manager returned to me. He handed the medallion to me, saying, "The symbol is Chinese. It represents their symbol for Happiness." I thanked him, very pleased with this confirmation of the information given to me by the spirit Nguyen Nhuoc. As I walked away, I heard the manager say the word "Phuoc." I spun around. "What did you say?" I gasped. He said, "That is how it is pronounced. The Chinese symbol on your medallion is pronounced Phuoc." I was stunned. I returned to my table, almost in a daze from this strange but wonderful confirmation of my visit the night before with Nguyen Nhuoc. Then, as if right on some cosmic schedule, my date arrived.

So that is how I got to know my spirit brother Nguyen Nhuoc, who had been my enemy in real life. Now a great bond of love and fellowship had somehow, for some reason, drawn us together. And somehow we knew that we had never really been enemies. We had simply played different roles in this lifetime.

Two weeks later it happened again. I was awakened from a deep and comfortable sleep by a presence in the room. There were a number of Vietnamese soldiers in the room with me. But this time it was different. These men were in great distress. I saw them standing there in their khaki uniforms. It was very dark around them. They wore pith helmets. They had fresh vegetation fastened to their helmets and uniforms as camouflage. It was raining. They were streaked with wet mud. They wore the same attire which they were wearing when they were killed. They were very sad. With a start, I jumped from bed and quickly hurried to my altar. After saying my prayers, lighting the candle, etc., I turned to them. There were eight of them. They were part of a twelve-man Viet Cong mortar squad which had the assignment of attacking the American soldiers in Rach Kein. Nguyen Nhuoc had brought them to me. I had killed them.

This mortar squad was well known to me. It was incredibly effective against the 3/39th Infantry battalion (of the Ninth Infantry Division) which was located adjacent to our base camp. This VC mortar crew had killed many Republic of Vietnam soldiers who were stationed in Rach Kein, and had caused many of my task force casualties. But their main target had been the 3/39th Infantry. Most of their mortar attacks had been at night. One night they killed or wounded over two-hundred infantrymen. In total, they had probably inflicted over six-hundred casualties on the Americans. Not bad for a twelve-man squad.

But they apparently did not feel so. They stood side-by-side in a line in front of me. They communicated to me that they were stuck. They did not go to the Light because they felt disgraced. They felt that they had failed their cause by getting killed. With their oriental sensitivity about respect, they felt that they had lost their respect when they failed their mission. They were ashamed.

I felt great love for them, as perhaps only one warrior can feel for another warrior. For these were true warriors with purity of heart and dedication second to none. I felt their grief and shame. I began to speak to them. I told them that I loved them for the great soldiers they truly were. I explained to them the great respect, we, the Americans in Rach Kein, had felt for them and their ability to so successfully thwart the most powerful Army in the world. I told them of my great respect and admiration for their army which had proven itself to be so tough, resourceful, and undefeatable. I opened myself up to absorb their grief, and to at the same time, radiate out to them the love I felt for them. As I spoke to them, their demeanor began to change. Their grief and sadness began to dissipate. They looked at each other, as if saying, "It is going to be okay now."

I saw something appear over my left shoulder. It was a foot. I suddenly sensed that I was being joined by some of my West Point classmates who had died in Vietnam. They descended behind and on both sides of me, making a U formation. They wore the West Point parade dress uniform, and carried their parade rifles at "present arms." The Vietnamese looked startled. Seeing this, one of my classmates, Bob Serio, said, "Hey fellahs, we are scaring them with these fancy uniforms." Instantly they were changed. Now they wore the olive drab jungle fatigue uniform which was worn in Vietnam, and they now carried M16 rifles, again at "present arms" to honor the Vietnamese. Now the American soldier at each end of the U formation held out his hand to the Vietnamese soldier standing at each end of their lineup. The two Vietnamese at the ends of their lineup looked uncertain as to what to do. They both glanced at an older Vietnamese who stood in the center of the line. I guess that he was their leader. He slowly smiled, and moved his head slowly up and down in the universal sign of approval. The Vietnamese soldier on the left end of their line was very young, perhaps twelve or thirteen, and had a cowlick of black hair which stood up prominently on his head. He slowly held out his hand. The Vietnamese at the other end of the line did likewise. Now the soldiers, American and Vietnamese, joined to form a square. They slowly began to rise. My classmates were taking the Vietnamese to the Light. As they rose past me, Marty Green, a good friend of mine, glanced over his left shoulder and quipped, "Mike, you're getting to be an old fart!" Then they were gone.

I laughed at Marty's humor. Then I realized that they were all still young. All of my classmates had appeared just as they had been during our Vietnam years when we were in our twenties. I was in my fifties. I had aged. They had not. Good for them!

These experiences ushered in a period of great healing for me. I was finally able to shed all of my anger, rage, and hurt that I had carried about the war. I also discovered that I felt guilt that I could not have saved the many other Americans who I saw die. I shed this guilt also. It allowed me to openly feel and acknowledge the great love and respect for the Vietnamese people which I held in my heart. And I am very grateful that I got to become friends with Nguyen Nhuoc, and that I got to speak with and assist the Viet Cong mortar squad. I know that they are very happy now. In a way, we all got healed.

Editor's note: The combat incident leading to the death of the eight Vietnamese is described in the following citation:

CITATION
BRONZE STAR MEDAL

By direction of the President, under the provisions of Executive Order 11046, 24 August 1962, the Bronze Star Medal with "V" Device is awarded to:

Captain Michael D. Miller, OF101610, Corps of Engineers, United States Army, for heroism, not involving participation in aerial flight, in connection with military operations against a hostile force in the Republic of Vietnam. Captain Miller distinguished himself as the commanding officer of Task Force Builder, located at Rach Kein in the Mekong Delta. At 0145 hours on 18 February 1968, the Viet Cong launched a sustained and concentrated mortar attack on the Rach Kein compound. The attack came at a time when the majority of fire support normally available was deployed elsewhere. The attack was so intense that it destroyed all wire communications and the infantry unit located at Rach Kein was unable to initiate counter mortar fire. Recognizing that the mortar attack had to be suppressed as rapidly as possible in order to reduce casualties, Captain Miller left his secure mortar bunker and, with complete disregard for his own personal safety, climbed to the top of the District Military Headquarters to man a 50 caliber machine gun in an exposed tower. Throughout this period over 200 mortar rounds were received in the compound, several of them impacting within 15 feet of Captain Miller's position. Undaunted, he continued to direct a heavy volume of accurate fire at the mortar emplacements causing the Viet Cong to reduce the intensity of their attack. By suppressing the enemy attack, he undoubtedly reduced greatly the number of friendly casualties. Captain Miller's courage and devotion to duty exemplified by his deliberate disregard for his own safety in exposing himself to the deadly mortar fire to reach the roof of the District Military Headquarters, and his continued efforts to suppress enemy fire in spite of the incoming rounds landing around him, is in keeping with the highest traditions of the military service and reflect great credit upon himself, his unit, and the United States Army.

3

A Knight's Story

This portion of my story is a collection of past-life memories which I garnered from the following sources:

1. My own past-life regressions.
2. Messages given to me by Merlin, Jesus, and Mother Mary.
3. Messages channelled to me by others.
4. The past-life regressions of others.
5. Memories which surfaced during rebirthing sessions.

I was born in an isolated area of the British Isles. I sense that we lived in the Southwest portion of the Isle. It was wooded where we lived. We lived alone, almost in total isolation. We were not wealthy. Perhaps we were poor, because we did not have much. We did not feel as if we were poor. Our situation, living alone in the woods, sometimes seemed a bit mysterious to me. I had two younger sisters.

My mother was a pretty lady. She was a person of class and distinction. She had the bearing and composure of a respectable and graceful woman. We may have been living a poor existence, but we were not of the peasant class. I loved my mother and my sisters very much. I was very happy. Most of my childhood, as I remember it, was wonderful. I spent all of my free time playing alone in the woods. I never seemed to realize that our isolation deprived me of having other childhood friends and playmates. I had the trees as friends. I was always at home, and I always felt comfortable and among friends when I was playing in the forest. It seemed that the forests were more "enchanted" in those days. To me, the trees were alive. They were my friends. I felt the warmth and protection as I played amongst them. It was as if they watched over me. They were my guardians and protectors. I loved them and they loved me.

Although my sisters loved me very much, and looked up to me, I greatly preferred playing alone in the woods. My mother was a priestess.

18

She spent most of her time doing what priestesses do. She was always busy preparing herbs as potions and medicines, or was in solitude practicing her religion. Preoccupied with her own matters, she did not seem to mind our isolation. She seemed quite content with it. Nor did she seem to mind that I was always off in the woods somewhere. She did mind it when I was late for supper. But otherwise, she gave me plenty of freedom.

I was told that my father, a mounted soldier, had been killed in battle somewhere. My mother had sought seclusion at our isolated cottage in the forest. Finding great peace of mind there, she had remained. However, the fact that we were poor and lived alone in the forest did not mean that I was not somebody. I had a claim to fame. As my mother explained to me, I was a distant nephew to King Arthur. King Arthur was the famous and powerful king who had united all of Britain. Some day I would claim my birthright. King Arthur would recognize my heritage. I would become somebody.

When I was fourteen-years-old, the time came for me to leave our enchanted forest. It was time for me to claim my birthright. Mother packed up my clothes. I was dressed in my finest, which was still somewhat ragged. She put me on a horse. It was our only horse. He was old and worn out. Standing proudly, but wiping away the tears, my mother sent me off alone to find my way to Camelot, the home of King Arthur. I, too, choked away the tears as I glanced back at my mother standing there crying for me.

I had no idea where I was going. But that was okay because there was only one trail to follow. After several days travel, I came to a castle. I was amazed at its size. The stone structures of the castle fascinated me. They seemed so powerful and dominating. Had I been less innocent, I might have been completely overwhelmed by this sudden and abrupt change from my cottage in the woods. My cottage was all that I had ever known. Now this! But, being innocent and thus without fear, I proceeded on and entered the castle grounds.

The castle belonged to the local king who reigned over our area of Britain. My presence was announced to him. I was very appreciative when he quickly acknowledged me, and invited me to stay with his family. What would I have done had he ignored me?

I explained my situation to him. The king took me under his wing. I stayed with him about six months. The king fattened me up (I was quite skinny and gangly). He dressed me in better clothes. He gave me a good horse to ride. His soldiers began to train me in swordsmanship. The king was, as he explained, making me presentable for my arrival at Camelot. I dined with his family. The whole episode was an amazing and wonderful experience for me.

The king had a daughter who was about my age, perhaps a year or two older. She was incredibly beautiful. I had not known any girls

19

other than my sisters. Being fourteen, and being exposed to the first girl other than my sisters that I had ever known, the obvious happened. I immediately fell completely in love with her. My crush on her was complete. I could not keep my eyes off of her. I got flushed whenever I was in her presence. My feelings for her were quite obvious to all. The king was amused. Everyone was amused. The king enjoyed watching the interactions between his daughter and myself at the dinner table. My awkwardness and complete adoration of his daughter led to many amusing moments during our mealtimes together. Everyone at the castle was aware that this skinny, awkward and unschooled country boy was smitten with the king's daughter.

His daughter was very gracious about the whole thing. She was very gentle and kind to me. She, as a young lady, was flattered by my attentions. She was a bit flirtatious also. I recall being alone with her in a hall, and how completely zapped I was by her presence. I recall her kind and gentle face, and her sweetly flirtatious smile which seemed to say that she appreciated my attention, but she would be careful not to lead this lovestruck boy too far. She would not let him get hurt, understanding how vulnerable and open I was. We never touched. Her name was Guenivere.

After my six-month preparation period, it was time for me to proceed to Camelot. The king sent me on to my destination. Arriving at Camelot, I was not as intimidated by the massive stoneworks and grandeur, now that I knew all about castles.

I announced my presence to the guard at the gate. Peering at me through a small grated window, the guard told me to wait, and then left. I waited. Nervously. Certainly, as a nephew to the King, I would be taken in. But what if not? He returned shortly, and without speaking, opened a wooden door. I stepped in. I was immediately ushered off into the bowels of the castle. King Arthur did not meet me, nor did he pay me much attention during those first years. He was too busy. But I was well cared for by others. I was given lodging in a large second-story room occupied by other young men about my age. They were at Camelot seeking to become knights. It seemed that everyone, myself included, knew that I would enter the training program to become a knight. I had arrived at Camelot at that time when Arthur was just consolidating his new empire. He had great need for more knights to help him control and protect his expanded kingdom. This was just fine with me.

I took to the program like a duck takes to water. I had found my home. I found the father I never had; Camelot became my father. But it was more. Camelot became everything: it was my mother, father, sisters and brothers. I prospered. I grew big and strong. I trained hard, and I grew into a good warrior. I was among other big and strong men.

I was not exceptionally big or strong in comparison to them. But I had focus. My determination and concentration gave me the edge. I became known for my fighting abilities. Although not bigger or quicker than my training opponents, I almost always won. Since in our business, which was battle, you either won or were dead, winning was important! After several years, I became a knight of the Round Table. My name was Percival.

Most knights excelled with one or more weapons. They were famous for prowess in one form of warfare or another. Some were exceptional swordsmen, others great at jousting, etc. For instance, Geoffrey of Monmouth was a great warrior with the lance. On horseback, wielding his lance, he was unbeatable. But as a swordsman he was only an average fighter. Accolan was a great fighter with the broadaxe; this was his specialty. Lancelot was a great swordsman, either on foot or mounted. Not so for Percival. I was good with all weapons, great with none. But I always won in battle. Some said that it was my intense stare. Others said that it was my focus, my complete dedication, which brought me out alive from all of my forays and battles.

Our training consisted of two facets: martial and spiritual. A knight's greatness derived from great martial skill backed up with great spiritual strength. In short, he was a spiritual warrior as well as a martial warrior.

Our military training was led by the older, more experienced knights. They were battle tested. Most were famous and had accomplished great deeds for King Arthur. Lancelot, Gawaine and Galahad were among these leaders. We had a reverential respect for them that bordered on worship. They passed on to us the wisdom and knowledge they had accumulated in their many battles and adventures. To be trained by these great men was a tremendous honor. We strived to please them. To receive praise from Lancelot, or one of the other older knights, was a great honor. Our training was, as we believed, the best in the world.

And oh how we trained! Hour after hour, day after day, the physical training was grueling and relentless. We stood in the sun for hours at a time swinging our swords and other weapons at practice posts; in this manner great muscles were developed. Our hands grew rough and calloused in spots from holding the weapons; these callouses were testimony to the constant grind of relentless training exercises.

Our spiritual training was conducted by the great Merlin himself. This was another great honor, to be trained by the greatest master of them all. Merlin had raised Arthur. Merlin and Arthur had together created Camelot. Merlin and Arthur were inseparable; where you found Arthur, Merlin was sure to be also. Arthur consulted with Merlin about almost everything. Camelot, everything that we stood for and believed in, was a joint creation of these two great men. So for

Merlin to take the time to school us in his crafts was another wonderful benefit for us.

Everyone knew that Merlin, as his name implied, was the spiritual head of the druids. He was the greatest druid priest. But Merlin was more than that. Yes, he taught us some things from the druid religion. He taught us some druid mystical practices. He taught us some druid magic. But he taught us other things that transcended druidism. No one knew where Merlin got his knowledge. He just had it. It was as if he had the knowledge of the universe at his disposal. He taught us rituals, magic and other mystical practices which were known nowhere else.

But please don't think that magic and such were the only things that he taught us. He taught us much more. He taught us about God. He taught us to be servants of God's work, and that as doers of God's work we were indestructible. He taught us about innocence, and that God would always look down with favor upon those of innocence. He taught us about purity of heart. With a pure heart, a knight could safely venture where no other could go. As a knight of Arthur's Round Table, each knight would many times be exposed to grave danger and peril. Merlin explained to us a secret of God's kingdom; God would always give special attention and protection to those of a pure heart. We were to be almost childlike in our purity of thought and heart. This would allow us to "enter the dragon's lair" and return safely. These were our great secrets. This is what gave us our power. This is what gave us our success in battle. This is why Arthur would send one knight out alone to put down an insurrection or revolt in a distant province, knowing that knight would return victorious. This was our real magic. God gave us our special power.

Merlin taught us leadership. Many hours were spent in his chambers. We would respectfully kneel on one knee as Merlin read to us from one of his very large Books of Knowledge. No one knew where these books came from, but they seemed to have all the answers. They were full of ageless wisdom. We listened carefully.

He also taught us powerful mystical rituals and practices. Not all knights were taught the same things. He tailored his teaching to the spiritual level of each knight. All of us were taught basic things such as how to invoke sacred word magic to make yourself invisible. Or how to shape-change, to make yourself appear as something or someone else. Or how to make yourself appear to others as if you were a much larger group of men. These practices were needed by us for our work. They were the "bread and butter" magic which was practiced by all knights. Some of us were taught more. We were taught to be able to look into the hearts of other men and know their true intent. We were taught how to protect ourselves against poisons (a common problem in those days). We were taught special powers for personal protection.

Not all knights were taught all of this knowledge, for great responsibility went along with the knowledge of some of these great powers.

Merlin's chambers also contained tables and workbenches filled with glass and ceramic containers. He did much in the way of concocting special lotions, potions and other special formulations. However, we knights were not privy to this area of Merlin's knowledge. So we could only speculate and wonder at the purpose and use of these concoctions.

We all knew that Merlin was very old. No one knew his age. It was said that he was an old man when Arthur was a young boy. Now Arthur was thirty years old, and Merlin had not appeared to age much, if at all. He was as spry, agile, and active as any of us. Among certain members of the court it was known that Merlin drank a daily herbal potion which kept him young. It was a clear liquid. That is all we knew. We knew this because occasionally one of us would be in his chambers with Merlin when he took his daily drink of the potion.

Merlin was liked and greatly respected by all of the knights. He, in turn, was like a kindly and beneficent father to us. He was devoted to all of us. Social life was quite different in those days. There was no TV, or newspapers, or radio, or movies. We talked. This was our entertainment. This was especially true during the long winter months when we were confined to the castle because of the weather. We spent many long hours visiting, talking, trading stories. During these periods, Merlin was always greatly sought after. Merlin's great wisdom, the twinkle in his eye, his spry and agile manner, his great sense of humor, all made him the ideal conversationalist. I was delighted to find that Merlin had a special liking for me. He made me one of his favorites. He spent a lot of time alone with me, explaining much of his theories and practices, telling me his personal views. He also taught me a lot, things that most of the other knights were never told. For this I was especially grateful.

It is interesting that Merlin taught us much about God long before Christianity arrived in our land. When Arthur finally made Christianity the official religion, the transition from druidism to Christianity was easy for us. We already knew much from Merlin's teachings. Merlin worshipped and acknowledged this God of the Christians long before they arrived.

My most vivid and emotional memories are of the Round Table and the movement which it represented. It was a creation of Arthur and Merlin. The table itself was not exceptionally large. It was not especially beautiful. It was made of oak. It was stained a dark color, best described as brownish-black. It did not dominate the Great Hall where we met and dined. It sat off to the side. The other tables there were regular rectangular wooden tables, just a bit longer than a picnic table of today. At mealtimes most of us sat at the regular tables. Arthur was usually seated at another rectangular table at the head of the hall. It was elevated on a dias so that it was about a foot above our tables. This way we had a better view of Arthur, and he had a better view of us. Our mealtimes were periods of great joviality. Much good-natured joking and pranksterism took place. Arthur's vantage place on the dias allowed him to readily participate in all of this humorous banter. It also allowed any of us to readily address him from our seat anywhere in the hall. Merlin and the Queen also sat at the head table.

The Round Table was a symbol. It was round because it represented the earth. The druids knew that the earth was round. The Round Table represented the first wave of a movement. The easiest way to explain this is to relate it to a pebble which is dropped into a pool of still water. When the pebble is dropped into the water, it first makes a single circular wave in the water. Then the waves begin to multiply, and they spread out in ever widening circles until they have covered the entire pool. Likewise, the Round Table represented the first ripple of wave of a movement which would spread out in concentric circular waves until it covered the entire earth.

We actually didn't use the Round Table very much. Mostly it was used for special formal ceremonies. But its symbolism was very important, and its presence in the Great Hall was a constant reminder to us of the nobility of our purpose.

The Round Table movement was to recognize the honor and nobility of mankind. This was the dream of Arthur and Merlin. This was what Camelot was all about. King Arthur and his knights set the example. By their honorable and noble conduct they showed the rest of the world what it could become. They established an awareness, a concept, which has never since been extinguished. Some day it shall complete its journey. Some day it shall cover the entire earth, and live in the breast of every person.

Camelot was also about love. Woven throughout our movement was love in its various aspects. There was romantic love, as represented by Arthur and Guenivere. But there was also the great universal love which transcends romantic love. It was everywhere. Maybe Merlin used some of his special powers on Camelot. Maybe he didn't have to. Love permeated the place. The actual magic of Camelot was its love. We all loved and adored our Arthur. Arthur loved and adored us. We loved and adored our Queen. We loved and adored our Merlin. They loved and adored us. Most of the knights loved and adored each other. Although we were very competitive, we never seemed to lose sight of the special love which bound all of us to Arthur and his movement. Our sense of camaraderie was awesome.

I had been a knight for about a year or so when Arthur left on a trip to visit another king. Arthur was to wed this king's daughter. She was younger than Arthur. Merlin had selected this young lady to become our Queen. This marriage also was politically expedient. This king was powerful and controlled a vast portion of land. Arthur's marriage to his daughter would help to consolidate Arthur's power, and would pull the king's land more securely into Arthur's realm. This was to be a good marriage also, because Merlin had carefully screened this young lady and had insured that she was pure in heart. Her purity and beauty would grace and complement Arthur's Court.

I was quite busy with my newfound responsibilities as a knight. So I didn't pay much attention to Arthur's trip to wed a queen. But I was soon taken aback by these developments. For when the queen-to-be arrived at Camelot with her entourage, I discovered that she was my Guenivere. Who I had never stopped loving. I had never gotten over my first love. Now she was to be my Queen.

In a way, this series of developments made Camelot complete for me. Camelot was my family. The other knights were my brothers. Arthur and Merlin were my father. Now the Queen was my first and true love. I placed her on a pedestal, and considered her the perfection of all womanhood. I idealized her. I still do.

Guenivere and I lived in Camelot for many years. We shared many experiences. We weathered many adventures and crises together. Yet we never spoke of my love for her. I spoke to no one else about my love for her. Only Merlin knew. Merlin knew all. She was my Queen. To me, she was the perfect Queen. She was a perfect complement to Arthur and the court. The perfection of her beauty became part of the magic of Camelot. She was wildly popular with the people. It seemed that Camelot was under Merlin's spell. Now Merlin had done it again; he had given us a queen who matched the love and purity which existed around Arthur and his knights.

One humorous incident comes to mind. At jousting matches and other tournaments I would always try to impress Guenivere by placing well in the competition. Guenivere's brother had also become a knight. His name was Segwarides. Segwarides remembered my infatuation with his sister when I had stayed with his family long ago. He suspected that I still was infatuated with his sister. So he challenged me to a jousting match. This he did in front of Guenivere. Jousting was his specialty. He and I both knew that he was much better at jousting than I. Knowing that I could not decline such a challenge issued in his sister's presence, he also in a loud voice added to this challenge that the prize for the winner of this match would be to select and keep the best horse belonging to the loser. Knowing how important it would be for me to best him in front of his sister, Segwarides had cleverly placed me in a great predicament.

I came from a humble background. My five horses were all that I owned. Therefore this was a serious challenge. I could not afford to lose such a match. But how could I refuse? I accepted. The match was set to occur in two days. After a day and two evenings of wagering, speculating, joking, and listening to Segwaride's boasting, the morning of the match arrived. Much to my chagrin, Segwarides unseated me on the first pass, all in full view of his sister. I sat, legs sprawled in the dust, as Segwarides was wildly cheered by the crowd. I was too embarrassed to glance at the King's viewing box to see Guenivere's reaction. I felt humiliated. Now the unthinkable was happening. I was about to lose one of my best mounts. Segwarides proudly walked over to my string of horses. He selected his prize. Much to my amazement, he selected the poorest of my horses, a yearling who was barely trained.

I had lost my pride. But at least I had not lost one of my precious horses. What I did not know was that Arthur, Guenivere, and the other knights had been let in on a secret. Segwarides had cajoled and bribed one of the pages. He had arranged for this page to improperly cinch the saddle on my horse so that it would come loose upon impact of the jousting lances. The match had been rigged! Segwarides had counted upon me being so nervous about this match that I would not perform the usual inspection of my horse and saddle rigging before the match. Segwarides had guessed right. I had been easily unseated. The entire incident had been great sport for everyone but me.

Now, to complete his victory, Segwarides later boasted to me of his scheme. To maximize the effect, he did this in a speech to me after supper in the Great Hall, in front of my entire family, Arthur, Merlin, the knights, and Guenivere. Everyone was greatly amused, especially at my embarrassment. Now that I knew the truth, the good natured ribbing and cajoling commenced. The ribbing that I took from this event lasted for many years. The mere mention of my jousting match was always good for a round of laughter. My blush at the mention of this story also lasted for many years. A standard greeting which met me for many months after the match was, "Percival, have you checked your cinch lately?" We all got a lot of laughs from that jousting match.

This incident reflected the jovial and friendly mood of the court. We had great respect, love and affection for each other. Joking and humor became a form of art for us. We spent much time and energy preparing jokes, humorous stories and friendly pranks which could be related as we sat together for our meals in the Great Hall. Great effort went into our preparations. We lived for this comedy and camaraderie. The entire mood at mealtimes was of festivity, joviality and kindredship.

The Great Hall had the banner of each knight mounted on a staff and suspended above us. The banners hung along the stone walls of the hall. Most were brightly colored. I seem to remember much bright color. Our clothing, our banners, and the decor were attractive and brightly colored. My coat-of-arms on my banner was a single white swan on a blue background. There was a pair of green pine boughs crossed beneath the swan.

Excalibur

Excalibur was Arthur's famous sword. As legend tells us, anyone holding Excalibur was invincible, and could not be harmed. Legend does not explain how Excalibur provided this protection. The actual design of Excalibur was copied. It was an exact replica of the sword carried by Archangel Michael. As explained to us by Lord Michael himself, one edge of his sword was Love, the other edge of his sword was Truth.

Excalibur was made under the direction and supervision of Merlin. Merlin arranged a special ceremony for the forging of the sword. The foundry was consecrated by Merlin. Then molten steel was prepared for forging into the sword blade. At that time Lord Jesus and Archangel Michael appeared. Jesus and Michael each placed one hand in the molten metal, endowing forever the metal with the power of their love. Then the metal was forged by the smiths into the famous sword blade. This is how Excalibur got its power: the power of Excalibur is Love.

Any person holding Excalibur is affected by the power of the sword. The sword is imbued with the power of love; therefore, any person carrying the sword is enveloped in love. When you are enveloped in love you cannot be hurt. This is the sword's magical secret, the power of love. In revealing this secret to us, Lord Michael and Merlin told us that it is time once again for mankind to know about Excalibur, and its secret. It is once again time for us to regain our knowledge about the power of love. You cannot be hurt when you are empowered and protected by love. You cannot fail when you are empowered and protected by love. Love is the ultimate weapon.

When Arthur carried Excalibur into battle he was protected from harm, and he could not be defeated. When you surround yourself with love, you are likewise protected. You cannot be harmed. This is the wonderful message of Excalibur. This is the message which Merlin and St. Michael wish to convey to you now: You are Arthur. You have Excalibur at your disposal, to use at any time. Simply strap this magical sword around your waist whenever you go into battle. Draw your

Excalibur whenever you are under attack. Be enveloped in its love and you cannot fail. You are protected by the ultimate weapon.

Knighthood was conferred upon men in a special ceremony led by Arthur. A special moment of this ceremony was when Excalibur was laid for a few moments on each shoulder of the man being knighted. This allowed the magical power of love to be passed from the blade of Excalibur to the new knight. He was thenceforth permanently endowed and empowered with the sword's power. It was as if Excalibur was a power wand. Each knight was empowered when he was touched by this so special power wand. This was one of the reasons why knights were so successful in battle.

The Holy Grail

The first years of King Arthur's reign were years of warfare. Eventually peace was achieved throughout the kingdom. With peace came a complication. Arthur's knights were trained for warfare. They were accustomed to the excitement and challenge of the battlefield. With peace, they lost their mission. They lost their reason for being knights. Boredom became a problem.

To deal with this problem Merlin and Arthur devised "quests" on which to send the knights. These quests were to keep the knights busy. The quests kept the knights challenged. They kept the knights occupied in knightly pursuits. One quest devised by Arthur and Merlin was the quest to find the Holy Grail.

The Holy Grail was the metal plate and the metal cup from which Christ had dined at the last supper. The Grail was hidden in a small stone castle overlooking the ocean on the Northwest coast of the British Isle. The castle was at the edge of the sea. One wall of the castle extended out into the sea.

The castle had been permanently hidden in a mist. By what magical process this mist was placed around the castle is unclear. Who placed the mist is unclear. The mist was there to protect the Holy Grail from those who should not know of its location. Most people could not see it. Many knights passed close by on their quest to find the Grail without seeing the castle hidden in the mist.

A requisite for seeing through this magical mist was absolute purity of heart. Only those of pure heart could see through the mist to the castle. Gawaine and Galahad, those great knights of purest heart, were the first to find the castle. I was the third knight to find the castle and its treasure.

After I found the Grail, Arthur terminated the quest to find the Grail. Arthur then assigned his knight Percival to guard the Grail. I was to reside in the small stone castle and protect its contents. The assignment was permanent. The magic mist which surrounded the castle was to be lifted.

I was stunned and shocked by this assignment. I was a robust, adventure-seeking knight who was accustomed to an active life on horseback roaming far and wide. My days as a wandering adventure-seeker were over. Very abruptly.

My days as a bachelor had also come to an end. Now Percival was assigned to occupy a castle. This also entailed the responsibility for taking over the control of the realm surrounding the castle. Not only did I now have to run a castle, I had to administer and protect the people who lived in the area around the castle. Perplexed by this abrupt change in my fate, I retreated to my friend and teacher Merlin for guidance. With a mischievous twinkle in his eye, Merlin delivered his sage advice: Percival needed a wife to help him with his new responsibilities. Merlin then helped me locate a wife. Using his special powers, Merlin scanned my life. Merlin was checking for "possibles." Merlin then pointed out to me that I had met a very suitable bride during my sojourn to Ireland.

It seems that Arthur had sent me to Ireland on a quest. There I had become a friend of the King of Ireland. The King had a very attractive daughter. Her name was Martha. At the time, I was not romantically inclined. I was mostly focused on my role as knight. I also had my memories of my secret true love Guenivere. I did not seek other romance, and did not show any particular interest in the King's daughter.

Martha, Merlin pointed out, would make an excellent wife. She came from a family of good breeding. Her mother was a sturdy, loyal and reliable partner for the King. She was practical and resourceful. These qualities had been well taught to the daughter. Martha was accustomed to the responsibilities of running a castle and a realm. She was not only beautiful, she was a perfect partner for someone who was raised in poverty and isolation, and had no experience in running a small kingdom.

So off I went to Ireland, in search of a bride. I returned to visit the King. This time I showed interest in Martha. It had been several years since I had last seen her. She had blossomed into an even more beautiful and mature woman. After a visit of several weeks, I made my move. I asked the King for his daughter's hand in marriage. The King was by now well aware of my intentions. The King liked me. The King considered this young knight a good catch for his daughter. He also knew that Martha was smitten with me. The King had known that she had a crush on Percival from his first visit years ago, and that she now felt very much in love with him. My request was granted.

We were wed in her father's castle in Ireland. Even though this marriage to one of King Arthur's knights meant that they might never see their daughter again, the King and Queen were truly happy for their daughter. She was radiant and happy. Percival was radiant and happy. It was a delightful marriage, and the ceremony was memorable for all. All that is, except Martha's brother. He was resentful of me. He disliked that he might never again see his sister. He loved her very much. He boycotted the wedding ceremony and pouted in a locked upstairs room.

The family, less Martha's brother, blessed me and my new bride as we departed across the sea to Britain.

With my new bride, we set up residence in the Grail Castle. I had no idea how to administer to the subjects of this new realm. Accustomed to rule, Martha knew just what to do. Martha helped me set up administration over an agricultural area that had not been governed for a long time. The peasants and other people of the area were enthusiastic about this change in governance, mainly because of the greater security and protection it would afford them. A knight-in-residence brought security in a time when much danger lurked about the land. They now had security and Martha quickly got everything organized. The people were content.

The castle was also organized and efficiently run. Martha showed the same qualities as her mother, being dependable, efficient and practical. Everyone, including myself, quickly grew to adore her. Along with her many other skills, Martha was an artist, weaving tapestries which were famous for their intricate designs of great beauty. In later years, when Christianity overshadowed our native druid traditions, Merlin and Martha got amusement and satisfaction from the many secret druid symbols which Martha cleverly concealed in her woven tapestry designs.

Family life with Martha was delightful. We grew to love each other very deeply. We had three children, two daughters and a son. Great happiness surrounded us.

Percival, the wandering knight, was now content with his new life. But there was a lot of spare time, now that my wandering days were over. I took to fishing off the castle wall which jutted out into the ocean. I got great pleasure from tossing several fishing lines into the sea, and then leisurely resting on the wall as I watched the beauty of the water, sky, and clouds. Much daydreaming took place. I looked forward to when my son would be big enough to join me in my fishing pursuits.

We had many visitors. Many knights came to visit their "stranded" brother-in-arms. With Martha the ever-gracious hostess, and with the harmony and contentment of our domain felt by all, these visitors enjoyed themselves. We became a favorite destination for our many friends. Their visits were a source of joy to us also, as we enjoyed their companionship. The visits also kept us informed about what occurred in the outside world.

As the knights approached our castle on horseback, they could see the castle a long way off in the distance. Many times, as they drew closer to the castle, they would spot me fishing off of the castle wall. Always ready to jest with another knight, one of the knights once referred to me somewhat jokingly and good-naturedly as "the Fisher King." The name stuck. This is how the legend of the Fisher King was born.

4

Camelot and the Church

The Early Christian Church in Britain

Britain was occupied by the Roman Empire for five-hundred years. During this period the Romans brought a level of organization and civilization to the Isle which had not before existed. Then, as the Roman Empire began to decline, the Romans abruptly departed.

When the Romans departed, they left behind a great political void. There was no one to take their place as a unifying force. No one person or group was strong enough to assume control. Chaos soon followed. The British Isle broke apart politically. Local kings and chieftains reclaimed dominance over their own areas. There was no cooperation between kingdoms. This invited the many enemies which surrounded Britain to exploit the situation. Soon invasions from Scotland, Scandinavia, and France decimated much of the territory. To make things worse, many of the minor kings throughout Britain began to war among themselves. Britain was in a dire circumstance.

This was the situation which faced young King Arthur when he assumed his mantle. Therefore, Arthur spent the first years of his reign at war. The Celts, Visigoths, and Saxons had to be driven back and defeated. Many warring local kings and chieftains had to be subdued and brought under his control. Arthur and Merlin literally lived in the saddle during those first years, fighting one battle after another.

Gradually Arthur defeated all of his enemies. The invaders left and did not return. The local kings all swore allegiance to him. All opposition to his throne was defeated. He had consolidated Britain into one empire, a feat accomplished only once before by the Romans.

Now came a period of relative stability and peace. Arthur's power was supreme, his popularity was immense. Only the Romans had brought such stability. But the Romans, harshly extracting a heavy tax burden for their services, were hated by many. Arthur was different. His rule was gentle and fair. The kingdom flourished as never before.

The native religion was druidism, the worship of the forces of nature. Arthur was a druid. Most people were druids. The Romans had introduced Christianity. Many people had converted to Christianity. But Christianity was a small and somewhat insignificant newcomer compared with the more prevalent and ancient practices of the druids.

Arthur was at the height of his influence and popularity, and he had great power. He chose this advantageous moment to become a Christian. He went further. He made Christianity the official religion of the court. He granted lands to the church for the construction of Christian churches and monasteries. He admitted a priest to the court as his religious representative. He encouraged his knights and the other members of Camelot to embrace Christianity. As you can imagine, the druids were aghast. The impact was tremendous. The entire kingdom was shaken by these vast changes. A less powerful king would have been pulled down by such an unpopular move. The people were content as druids. They liked their religion. Only the wildly powerful and successful King Arthur could pull this off. Even still, there was great opposition to these changes.

Ever the peacemaker, and attempting to be fair, Arthur promised the druids that druidism and Christianity were to always co-exist peacefully. Arthur the dreamer, Arthur the idealist, truly felt that these religions could exist side-by-side in a peaceful manner. In so doing, Arthur set in motion those forces which were to eventually destroy everything that he had so laboriously and valiantly created.

So it was that King Arthur fulfilled his destiny by bringing Christianity to Britain. Under Arthur's protection and support, Christianity grew quickly. As Christianity grew, the druid religion declined. Christianity grew until it was the dominant religion in the land.

One of the powerful political centers of the church at that time was Constantinople. The Christian Church at Constantinople was, as was to be expected in that Byzantine era, a hotbed of intrigue and political scheming. One ambitious and scheming bishop, finding himself outsmarted and outschemed, was disgracefully banished from Constantinople. He was banished to the farthest realms of the empire. His victorious enemies had him sent to an isolated and uncivilized (to their way of thinking) outpost. There he would most certainly wither away, never again to bother them. He was sent to Britain.

The Bishop thought otherwise. Ambition and desire for power burned deeply within him. Humiliation from his defeat in Constantinople burned deeply within him. "No," he thought, "I shall not quietly fade into oblivion. I shall wring vengeance from my new assignment. I shall use whatever situation I find in Britain to my advantage. I shall once again rise to prominence. I shall return to Constantinople victorious and vindicated." With these unwholesome motives, this bishop arrived, unannounced, unexpected, and uninvited, to the doorstep of King Arthur and the court at Camelot.

King Arthur was quite content with the priest who attended his court. This priest was a favorite of Guenivere. He spent long afternoons in deep conversation with her. The priest was equally well liked by the other members of the court. He wisely treated Merlin with respect, thus avoiding any conflict of religion or ideology which might have been embarrassing to Arthur and Arthur's longtime friend Merlin. In short, the priest fit in well at the court. Therefore Arthur was somewhat nonplussed and annoyed when this new bishop arrived unexpectedly and announced that he was to henceforth be the church representative at court. Arthur, ever faithful and loyal to his new religion, complied with the dictate of the new bishop. In this manner entered into the court at Camelot the person who would scheme, cajole, maneuver, undercut and plot until he eventually destroyed Arthur, Camelot, and the Dream.

Accustomed to the Byzantine atmosphere of intrigue and complicated political maneuvering of Constantinople, the Bishop quickly sized up Arthur and his empire as "a bunch of simple people" who he could easily outmaneuver and control. He was right. Arthur was an idealist and a dreamer. His creation, Camelot, was a reflection of his idealism and dreams. People who daily lived by high standards of honor and nobility were not accustomed to the level of skullduggery, lying, and scheming which the Bishop introduced into the court.

The Bishop had several steps to accomplish in order to achieve his objectives. First, he had to break up the camaraderie which existed between the knights. He also wished to split the knights away from their unswerving dedication and loyalty to Arthur. He would also make Christianity supreme in the land. Then, with the control of Arthur and his knights weakened, he would destroy the druids. This would bring the Bishop fame and glory. He would go down in history as the man who destroyed the heathens and championed Christianity. He would return triumphantly to the central corridors of power in the church.

Thus it was that the church began to plot the downfall of its benefactor. Arthur brought Christianity to Britain. Arthur then protected the church as it grew powerful and ambitious. The church eventually grew envious and jealous of Arthur himself. For it was Arthur who had promised the druids that Christianity would never threaten them. It was Arthur who promised that both religions would peacefully coexist. It was Arthur who protected the druids. As the church gained dominant power, it was no longer willing or able to abide Arthur's dictates. It could no longer accept co-existence with the heathen druids. Since the druids were protected by Arthur, Arthur would first have to be destroyed. Then the Christians would destroy the druids. This they did.

Thus it was that Camelot changed from the place of magical wonderment to a place of conflict and discord. It happened in a piecemeal fashion. First, Merlin began to withdraw from Arthur. Merlin, Arthur's constant companion and confidant, was the sole religious presence in the court. The first priest changed that. Merlin gracefully pulled back from his position of prominence in order to acknowledge the position of the Christian representative in the court. Then, with the appearance of the power-grabbing Bishop, Merlin began to withdraw more completely from the court. This weakened Arthur. Then the Bishop turned knight against knight. Lies, rumors, and spells were used to pit former friends against each other. Knights were turned against the King. The close relationship between the King and the Queen was damaged. Bickering and dissention became prevalent throughout the court.

Many were disappointed that Arthur stood by while the Bishop steadily increased his power. At any point Arthur could have stopped the Bishop. Many advised him to so do. Many counselled Arthur to stop the Bishop before all was lost. But Arthur, ever the idealist, could not say "no" to his religious leader.

At one point, the King himself was poisoned by the Bishop, but not fatally. Greatly demoralized by the crushing disappointment of seeing his dream torn asunder, and weakened by the poisoning, Arthur took to his sickbed for a year and a half. There he lay in the fetal position, while his Queen and a few of the senior knights struggled to ward off the ever increasing encroachment of the Bishop.

While Arthur lay sick, Guenivere ruled the empire. Sweet Guenivere, the beautiful and lovely lady, was left to try to salvage the dream. But it was not her dream. It was Arthur's dream. It was Merlin's dream. They were not there. So she carried their dream for them. She ruled until Arthur could return.

In her distress and loneliness, Guenivere had turned to the senior knights for assistance. In her distress and loneliness, she succumbed to the embrace of her beloved Lancelot. The Bishop had spies everywhere. He quickly gained knowledge of this situation. Ever vigilant to seize every advantage, the Bishop wasted no time in utilizing knowledge of Guenivere's indiscretion to spread rumors of this among the knights, and to directly inform the ailing Arthur of his wife's sinful behavior. This caused further destruction of the dream. Knight fought against knight over the matter of Guenivere's purity. Lancelot, Arthur's closest friend, found himself humiliated and dishonored. He had betrayed his King, who was also his best friend. Hastily departing the castle, Lancelot banished himself from Arthur, Guenivere and Camelot. Arthur's heart was broken; his best knight and best friend had betrayed his trust. His best knight and best friend was now gone from his side. His queen had disappointed him. Guenivere was devastated. She lost contact with her true love, the man she adored deeply. She had hurt her king, who she loved deeply.

Lancelot was devastated. He had disgraced his king, his queen, and himself. Lancelot went to the distant borders. There he remained, fighting for his king, disgraced from ever returning. Years passed. Only at the end, when word of Arthur's impending last battle reached Lancelot, did Lancelot return to be at Arthur's side. Both Arthur and Lancelot rejoiced at being together again. All was forgiven and forgotten. Joyously reunited with his beloved king, Lancelot stood at Arthur's side at the last battle. Lancelot died while cradling the mortally stricken Arthur in his arms. Lancelot, full of love and gratitude for his king, died happy. He died never again having seen his beloved Guenivere.

The End of Camelot

The Bishop relentlessly pursued his goal of destroying Arthur. Arthur and Morgana had a son named Mordred. He was Arthur's only son. Mordred became a knight. Mordred was much loved by Arthur, but he lacked his famous father's qualities of greatness and idealism. He was resentful and jealous. Mordred resented that his mother, Arthur's half-sister, had been eclipsed by Guenivere. Mordred felt that his mother should have been the queen. He felt that Arthur had somehow dishonored his mother by making another woman queen. Never mind that his mother, Morgana, could never have been officially recognized as the queen because she was Arthur's half-sister. He still hated and resented his father for this. He also very much resented Guenivere.

Mordred resented that he, Arthur's only son, had no line of ascension to the throne. Mordred felt slighted by his father because he had not been recognized for what he really was, the only male descendant to the throne of Britain.

The Bishop seized upon this opportunity. Promising Mordred that he would become the new king, the Bishop managed to recruit Mordred into his scheme to overthrow Arthur. Mordred was elated and electrified by this turn of events. His dreams had been answered. A way had been shown to him so that he could vindicate his mother and himself. He would finally get his reward. He would be the king! The pent up rage and humiliation he had borne for so many years would now be vented upon his father and Guenivere; they would pay for his bottled-up frustrations.

Lest anyone think that Morgana was behind the treachery of her son, let me explain that Morgana barely knew Mordred. Mordred, as was often done in those times, was taken from Morgana shortly after he was born. He was raised by others in a distant land, so that she had no contact with him. It was not until he was a young man that he was finally presented to her; by then his character and philosophies had already been formed. She was not even aware of the avarice which lurked in his heart. Had she known, she would have been aghast. She, Arthur's soul mate, still loved Arthur more than anyone else alive. So Morgana was unaware of her son's dangerous intentions.

Encouraged by the Bishop, Mordred scouted for means to eliminate his king. His focus was drawn to one of Arthur's pages, a young man by the name of Nottingham. Nottingham was from a good family of excellent reputation. His parents were close personal friends and supporters of Arthur. They had known and befriended Arthur when he was a young man. As such, their son was now honored by Arthur with the important and honored position of personal page to the King. This was Arthur's way of honoring the friendship and loyalty shown to him by the parents. Eventually, it was assumed, Nottingham would become a knight.

Nottingham had been selected for this important position close to the King more for his parent's qualifications than for his own qualities. The King's welfare and security depended upon the qualities of those around him. The position of page to the King was a very important assignment. He had to be discreet. A page to the King was privy to much which had to remain secret. He knew many of the King's secrets. He was privy to the private and personal details of the King's life. A page had to also be loyal and trustworthy. He was physically close to the King in a period when kings were exposed to much danger by poison and dagger.

Nottingham was an unfortunate selection to be one of Arthur's pages. Nottingham was emotionally insecure, and was unsure of himself. As such, he was a weak spot in Arthur's court. Mordred, spotting this weak spot in Arthur's armor, pointed Nottingham out to the Bishop's men and they went to work. The clergy began to woo and befriend Nottingham. The young seventeen-year-old was flattered and honored by their friendship. Over a period of time they managed, through innuendo and falsehood, to convince him that Arthur was against the church. They began to poison his mind. They slowly began to turn him against his king. Preying on Nottingham's weaknesses, they began to groom him as the assassin to kill the King.

Meanwhile, the Bishop proceeded with his plan. From his first arrival at the court, the Bishop had formulated his strategy. He would portray Arthur as a disobedient follower of Christ who sheltered the heathens (druids) from the hands of the true followers of Christ. As such, Arthur was to be seen as an impediment to the growth of Christianity. This was the message which was sent back to Rome and Constantinople in every dispatch. And, as with many lies which are told repeatedly, this lie began to be accepted as the truth. After years of receiving such messages, they began to be believed and accepted back in the power centers of the church. Forgotten was the fact that Arthur had brought Christianity to Britain. Now he was seen as the enemy of Christianity. The church only heard the Bishop's version of what was going on. There was no one to speak up for Arthur.

Eventually the years came when powerful and ambitious young church leaders began to look for new horizons to conquer. They began to concentrate on the situation in Britain. The stacks of dispatches from their bishop extolling them to intercede in Britain caught their eye. Here was an enemy right in their midst. The stormclouds of disaster began to gather as they plotted and planned to invade the Isle of Britain, destroy the enemies of the church, and release the wrath of their God upon the unrepentant heathens there.

A great armed force began to gather. Anxious to show their loyalty and their devotion to their church, the young adventure-seekers of many countries gladly and quickly volunteered for service. Forces from Germany, France, Holland, the Netherlands, Greece, Rome and Spain began to congregate in France. A great armed force, driven by devotion to God, would sweep down on King Arthur's heathen-protecting kingdom. This European army numbered five times the forces under the control of King Arthur.

Arthur was not ignorant of these events. He was ignorant of his bishop's plotting which had brought it about. Arthur did not know what to do. He was a loyal and devoted Christian. He had dedicated his life and his court to the service of Christianity. How could this not be understood? How could his bishop not appreciate his devotion and loyalty? How could the church he so loved turn on him, make him the enemy?

To compound the situation, for years his trusted knights and advisors had warned him that these events were unfolding. Arthur was no longer a young man. In his fifties, he was unable to conceive or accept the treachery which they had repeatedly warned him about. Now it was about to unleash itself upon his kingdom. Unable, or unwilling, to admit that his beloved church would betray him, Arthur had done nothing until it was now too late.

Arthur's friends and advisors had, for years, seen this coming. They had repeatedly begged Arthur to step in and curtail the ever-growing powers of the churchmen before it was too late. The church had grabbed power in an unrestrained fashion. Why? Because Arthur would never stand up to the Bishop. When the Bishop had arrived years earlier,

Arthur had complete control of everything in his kingdom. Now, just as a great oak falls as a result of many, many, small chops of the axe, Arthur's kingdom was about to fall because of the accumulated years of allowing the church many, many, small concessions.

In his idealism, Arthur had assumed that the church was pure. He had assumed that the churchmen were driven by the same levels of nobility and honor as were his own men. Therefore he had never been able to bring himself to say "no" to his religious leaders. In this, Guenivere had not helped. For she, too, was at first greatly deceived by the Bishop. He had played up to her vanity, befriending her and becoming a close confidant of hers. Thus she had encouraged and pressured her king to grant the church's every wish. Only when it was too late, did Guenivere realize her mistake. For when the Bishop no longer needed her support, he quickly dropped the role of friend and confidant. Then, in his great betrayal of her friendship, the Bishop viciously attacked her when he reported her "sinful" conduct with Lancelot to the bedridden Arthur.

In all of this, King Arthur's own weaknesses of character became apparent. The great Arthur, who had accomplished so much, was, after all, still a mortal man, with weaknesses. What weaknesses betrayed him? Stubbornness. Arrogance. Arthur, with the determined mindset of a king in his fifties who had ruled since boyhood, refused to admit that he may have been wrong about the Bishop and the church. The many knights and others who pleaded with him were ignored. They watched with growing horror as they saw everything they had struggled so hard to accomplish become threatened because of their beloved king's stubbornness and arrogance. Their subsequent demoralization led to a weakened Round Table. Knights began to bicker among themselves. Camelot began to slowly disintegrate.

Amidst all of this, there was one man who could change things. Merlin. Merlin, the man who had raised Arthur, the man who taught Arthur all that he knew, the most powerful magician of all, could make things right. Arthur would certainly listen to Merlin. Or if Arthur would not listen to Merlin, Merlin had powers to make Arthur do the right thing. So everyone, knights, queen, advisors, all ran to Merlin for help.

Remember that Merlin had withdrawn from the court when the Bishop began to assume too much power. Then, as Arthur was drawn more completely under the control of the church, Merlin had disappeared from his side. It had been a long time since Arthur and Merlin were seen together, as in the wonderful days of old when they were inseparable friends and cohorts. Now Merlin kept himself mostly confined to his chambers in the castle.

Merlin had listened to their grave concerns with patience. Then, he gave one and all the same answer; "This is the way of things." For

Merlin was the only one who knew that what was transpiring was the will of God, for God had given his earthly children free will. God would not now interfere in this situation. Neither could Merlin. He could not interfere.

The Last Battle

The great Christian army entered Britain. They were led toward Camelot, guided by men supplied by the Bishop.

Arthur gathered his forces. There was great dismay on their part. They were, for the most part, loyal Christians. They did not feel that they could, as loyal Christians, defeat another group of Christians. How could they battle forces which were fighting for their own God? This was a great dilemma for them. On the one hand, they were honor bound to fight to protect their king and his kingdom. They were honor bound to fight to defend their own honor. But, could they as loyal Christians defeat and destroy another Christian army? No, they could not.

How did Arthur feel? He also felt trapped. He was honor-bound to defend his kingdom. But he could not defeat other Christians who fought under the banners and flags of God.

That they were outnumbered five-to-one was not unusual. Arthur had many times been victorious under similar situations. But to fight other Christians was his great dilemma. Arthur knew that, unable to be victorious, he would be defeated. His knights also knew.

The last battle was fought not far from Camelot. As his scouts reported that the opposing army was drawing near, Arthur and his forces went out to meet them. On the morning of this decisive battle, Arthur's forces were lined up just below the crest of a long, sloping hill. Arthur stood at the top of the hill, where his soldiers could see him. He was about twenty yards from his lines of soldiers. Arthur was surrounded by twelve knights. They had formed a protective circle about him.

There had been some rumors about a plot to kill the King. Aware that some treachery might be afoot, security for the King was keen. Therefore, twelve knights circled Arthur to protect him from assassination during the battle.

The long sloping hillside ran down into a valley. The other side of the valley rose up into another long sloping hill. It was onto this hillside that the invaders appeared.

They began to appear on the far crest, arrayed in a long line. At the appearance of the enemy troops, our attention was naturally drawn to them. As we all turned to view the adversary, the knights surrounding King Arthur also turned to view the enemy. We watched as their lines seemed to swell, and then burst as they began to charge toward us. Their battle cries reached out to us. At this moment, while everyone looked at the enemy on the far slopes, an assassin struck. It was Nottingham the page. He was standing close to the circle of knights who were protecting Arthur. He quickly slipped to his right, slipped past two knights, and plunged a dagger into Arthur's back. Arthur was struck just inside his right shoulder blade. Arthur fell, mortally wounded. The page was immediately struck down by the knight standing to Arthur's right.

Other conspirators were interspersed among the forces near Arthur. Some of them fell on the twelve knights surrounding Arthur. A vicious fight ensued, the enraged knights slashing away at the betrayers. Arthur lay in the circle, his head in the lap of Lancelot, as the other knights slashed huge gaps in the ranks of their adversaries.

Other conspirators were in and among the fighting forces. They shouted out that Arthur was dead just as the enemy forces reached our lines. Our soldiers, confused, turned to view the top of the hill. Arthur was nowhere to be seen. Then the enemy was upon us. Great confusion reigned. With the horrible thought that our Arthur was already dead, we were thrown off balance. The assassination of Arthur had accomplished its purpose of demoralizing us just at the crucial moment of the fight.

By now many of the knights around Arthur had fallen. The others were engaged in hand-to-hand fighting, some rolling on the ground in pitched battle with daggers or axes. As Arthur had fallen, his sword had been flung to the side. Excalibur had fallen to the ground, forgotten in the melee. Another page found himself flung to the ground. He landed on top of a sword. Glancing down, he immediately realized that it was the famous Excalibur. Realizing that it should not fall into the hands of the enemy, he slipped the sword to his side. It was hidden by his large brown cape. Quickly standing, he ran down the other side of the hill. Thus Excalibur was saved. The page later hid Excalibur. There it remains hidden.

I was in the front line of soldiers. The fighting was intense. The men to my left began to fall back so that there was a bow in our line of fighting soldiers. I glanced to my left. I saw one of our knights with the enemy. It was my good friend Lionel. Lionel had always been ambitious. The Bishop had spotted this gap in Lionel's armor. Lionel had betrayed us for promises of greater power and prestige in the Bishop's new administration. He had betrayed all out of his blinding need to surpass everyone. Angered by the betrayal of this great knight, I shouted out to him. He had also seen me. He quickly dispatched the swordsman in front of him. Then he began to fight his way toward me. I likewise began to slash a path toward him. Lionel was a big and pow-

41

erful man. I had never bested him in swordfight practice. He was a great swordsman. Nevertheless, my breast was filled with indignation at his traitorous action, and I sought to destroy him. We reached each other, a mini-battle about to ensue in the midst of the great battle. He swung his great sword at me. I easily deflected it with my shield. I countered with heavy blows from my sword. All of a sudden, Lionel stumbled over a smooth stone which was about the size of a small loaf of bread. Down he went. In that instant I had a vision of Merlin looking down at me with an impish grin! I had been helped. In order to get to Lionel I had gotten myself behind the front lines of the enemy. There was no time to hesitate. I plunged my sword into Lionel's stomach, withdrew it, and barely had time to swing about to my right to thwart the intentions of two men, one with sword, one with spear, who bore down on me. Then I scrambled and slashed my way back to my lines.

The enemy was organized to strike us in five waves. The waves were timed about twenty minutes apart. All of the enemy in the first wave were struck down, while the dying and other wounded crawled back toward their rear. I wiped my brow, glancing to my left and right. Our lines seemed to have held well. Here and there were humps on the ground between the legs of our men, each hump a fallen warrior. Now the serfs and servants scrambled forward to drag the humps away. The men gasped for air, their bodies desperate for oxygen after their adrenalin-filled exertions. Those of us who were hardened by training and experience stood solidly, calm and reassuring, so that our influence would be felt by the others, steadying them for the next onslaught.

I spotted two older soldiers on my left who had been retired. Their white hair looked out of place amidst the leather, gleaming metal, blood, and youthful faces. I knew these men. Memories of battles long-past surged through me. I was young then, they in their prime. Now, they had come out of retirement in order to die with their friends and comrades. Off in the distance to my left I could see the outline of a man who stood head and shoulders above the rest of the line. There was only one man in all the realm who was that big. The Red Knight. It had been many years since Merlin had sent him back to his mountain forest home. Memories of his grizzled beard, terrifying roar, and awesome presence on the practice field with his huge sword, swept over me. Most had feared him. He and I had become friends. But I had long ago lost track of him. Now he was back with us. To die with us. A great lump formed in my throat. I am unable to properly describe the love I felt for him at that moment.

Twenty minutes was not a long time. The second wave was upon us. They did not yell as much as the first wave of soldiers had, as if sobered to the reality of the plight of the first wave. I do not know what they had been told about us, but I was ready to wager that they were not properly apprised of our fighting skills. It was much quieter this time. We were settled down, they were somber. Grunts, shouts, punctuated the stillness, as we otherwise silently went about the task at hand. We did not destroy all of the second wave. As their line weakened, many of them fled back toward the hillside on which their forces were arrayed.

Now, sweating profusely, I wiped my brow. Our lines were now thinned. In spots there were gaps. Men were waving frantically about, searching for replacements, trying to fill those gaps before the next surge. From the rear, serfs and servants, many armed with pitchforks and clubs, scrambled forward, anxious to avenge the loss of masters who had fallen. In this kind of battle, exhaustion was the key factor. It wasn't the best or most skilled warrior who lived, it was the one who could lift his sword when his opponent was too exhausted to fight back. Exhaustion would defeat us, not enemy skill, or ability. Many of the men were so tired that they could hardly stand.

Up to now I had not used any of the magic which Merlin had taught us for battle. But my arms were now heavy. It was time. The third wave approached. I intoned the chants taught to me so long ago. Now my sword took over. I held it as it swung in its wide figure eight swing. My mind went numb. Sometime during the third attack our lines crumbled.

One of my servants had insisted on accompanying me to the battlefield. He was barefooted, and dressed in plain brown pants, white shirt. He carried a spear. I had tried to run him off, to send him back to safety with the others. He would not go. So I had placed him directly to my rear. I told him that he could protect my back. After the first attack, he had a face as white as a sheet. After the second attack, he was fine, and had a red flush to his face and a gleam in his eye which I had never seen before, as if immersed in the immensity of the event in which he was embroiled. Now, our line shredded, his spear broken, he laid in an awkward pile, badly mauled and chopped up.

I do not remember much else about the battle. I was one of the few who survived. I stood in my light field armor, holding sword and shield. I was covered from head to foot with blood. Every inch of me was covered with this unwanted red badge of honor.

This is how I escaped. I was so covered with blood that I was not recognized as one of Arthur's soldiers. I was completely spent. Everyone around me was down. Many of the enemy were down out of exhaustion. There was a strange quiet, interrupted only by the soft moans of the wounded or exhausted. I have been here before, filled with the memories of similar after-battle scenes; the heaviness of my arms, the exhaustion which drags at me imploring me to lay down on the ground for just an instant, knowing that I will then not be able to rise. My senses were dulled, and I slowly looked about for any enemy who was still standing. Despite my utter exhaustion, something within me still sought to fight, to lash out at this enemy which had destroyed all that I believed in. Seeing no one left to fight, I slowly turned about and walked away. I was so tired that walking was painful and difficult. But I was not the only one feeling such utter exhaustion. The enemy forces were also exhausted. They were so exhausted, and their senses were so dulled by the shock and gruelling clash of combat, that they wandered about as if in a daze. So I was able to simply walk past them.

I caught a ride in a cart. I arrived at the castle. I went to the stables, where my servants and stewards awaited me. I collapsed in front of a small fire. While I slept, my men bathed me, and cleaned and repaired my weapons. A smith removed the many dents in my armor and helmet. When I awoke, I was so sore that I could hardly walk. Meanwhile, my men had gathered together two other knights. One was Segwarides, the brother of Guenivere. Arthur had left him behind at the castle to guard his sister. The other was Florence, a young and new knight who had returned from a mission too late to be in the battle. We sat around the small fire and talked. It was decided. All was lost. We would make a final stand. We sent one of my servants off on a horse with a white flag and a message. Camelot was no more. Therefore we chose to die a soldier's death, beneath a soldier's blow.

The next day, three knights waited, standing together on a stone rampart of an abandoned fortress. They stood with their backs against a stone wall. It was a beautiful and bright morning. Birds sang and insects chirped. The wind wafted the grasses and trees back and forth. They waited. Gradually they became aware of the sounds of an approaching mounted force. A force of about eighty men paraded into view. They rode four abreast, as if on parade. Banners swung briskly in the breeze. The mounted warriors were dressed gaily, brightly colored scarves and robes among the armor. There were even some trumpeters. "More of a parade than an attack," we mused to ourselves.

We realized that we were the last of the knights of Camelot. This was the last chance for any of the invading force to glorify themselves by slaying one of King Arthur's knights. We were a grand prize. Apparently our opponents were going to make the best of this last opportunity. We were going to make the best of it also.

They dismounted. There was some sort of parley amongst their leaders while they decided how to deal with us. At first, they came at us in groups of three. Three against three, evenly matched.

Each of us stood with sword and shield. Segwarides was on my left, Florence on my right. We inflicted great losses as the destroyers of our dream poured onto us. After a while I found myself fighting as if going uphill. The dead were stacked so deep that the enemy was standing atop a pile of their fallen warriors. The dead had formed a sort of rampart in front of us. Trumpets blew. The men facing us pulled back. Servants carrying white kerchiefs came forth and dragged off the dead.

This gave us a chance to catch our breath. Many of the men facing us were more adventurer than they were trained warrior. So we weren't particularly challenged by any of them. Now, during this recess, we began to joke about the situation. "I hope that we don't run out of enemies," said Florence, a wide smile crossing his face. He was calm. I was struck with the thought that this may have been his first big battle. "They don't seem to be smiling as much," quipped Segwarides, returning his smile. Not wanting to be left out, I replied, "I'm feeling insulted that they only sent 80 men. Perhaps they didn't know that I was here." We all laughed. We actually began to feel elated, as we stood there joking about the situation. We were calm and collected as we watched with mirth while the enemy unenthusiasticly reformed for another go at it.

This time they came at us in groups. The wisdom of our choice of battle location now came to bear. The stone wall behind us and to our sides prevented anyone from encircling us. They were, as before, channelled by the wall to approach from the front. Now the faces in front of us were full of fear and worry. We were the ones smiling. Again the dead piled up in front of us. The desperate men lunging at us were now no longer interested in harvesting honor, they were choosing death before the dishonor of retreating from three men. Again the trumpets blew. Again they withdrew. Now we were confident. They were scared. None of the men standing some 70 feet away would look at us. I knew what this meant. No more "Mister Nice Guy" from these fellows. Their thoughts of bringing home honor were now smothered with thoughts of getting home period.

Florence yelled in excitement, "Hey, I count only seventeen left." I quickly counted the now small force facing us and realized that he was right. We had been so focused during the fighting that this change in the situation had gone unnoticed. Now serious, Segwarides said, "Let's not forget why we came here." I didn't know what to say or do. I could not fathom not fighting with honesty and vigor. This dilemma was resolved for me. Quickly reassembling, the enemy came toward us again. But as they reached us, I heard the snap of arrows in the air from our left and right.

Segwarides, on my left, began to sag. An arrow was in his neck. I could not let him fall to the earth. In a flash I decided that holding him, this beloved friend, fellow knight, and brother of Guenivere, one last time was more important than living on. I could not let him die on the ground. Dropping my sword, I turned and grabbed him. I was caught across the right side of my neck and shoulder by a sword blow. My last glimpse of Florence was of him being overwhelmed by the enemy.

I died quickly, not filled with memories of my glorious days at Camelot, but instead filled with memories and visions of my beloved wife, my son, who I would now never get to see become a man, and my beautiful daughters. I died regretful that I was leaving them so.

It was a subdued group of men who returned from this battle, carrying our banners, weapons and armor back to their base camp. No parade this time. Not enough men. And little glory and honor.

Camelot

The people waiting back at Camelot agonized as they waited for word of the outcome of the battle to reach them. First, a few bloody and dishevelled stragglers ran up, shouting that all had been lost. Then nothing but silence.

The next morning a delegation from the victorious army arrived. They were led by the Bishop. Never had the ladies of Camelot seen the Bishop act so haughtily and arrogantly. This was just as well with the other members of the victorious entourage, for they were quiet and withdrawn. They were content to let the Bishop have his day. These other men were the leaders of the invading army. The had just witnessed the destruction of half of their forces on the battlefield. They were still in a state of shock. That the group of British defenders, so greatly outnumbered, had wrought such devastation to their forces was something they found to be unsettling. The British forces were labeled as heathens, yet they had fought with a courage and character never before seen by these men. These victors were, in effect, humbled with respect for the fallen foe.

The Bishop announced to the inhabitants of Camelot what they already knew. Arthur and his forces were no more. They would be given a three day "period of grace" in which they might vacate the castle and have safe passage past the victorious army. The castle's inhabitants were mostly women and children, the families of knights, and other members of the court. They had already begun to pack their belongings, so the castle was quickly vacated. Hastily bidding a sorrowful goodbye to each other, these dazed survivors of the magical days of Camelot straggled off past the portals of Camelot, down the roadway, and slowly passed from history. The corridors and hallways of Camelot were empty.

Guenivere had at first busied herself assisting her handmaidens and servants to get packed. She forcefully pressed onto each of them precious momentos of the court. Some of her favorite dresses and jewels were tucked into the clothing bundles of her beloved friends and associates. The pages and other men remaining at the court were gifted with Arthur's accumulated treasures of bejewelled weapons, decorations, and other items of personal value.

She was interrupted by word that Mordred waited outside of her chambers to speak with her. She was chilled by the mention of his name. She had long been aware of the evil intent in Mordred's heart. The skills she had been taught by Merlin had served her well, for she had for a long time "looked into his heart" and had seen the dangers posed by Mordred. Arthur, refusing to believe that his beloved son would betray him, had refused to listen to her pleading about him. Now the betrayer was outside her door.

Guenivere surmised, quite correctly, that Mordred had plans for her. Mordred was well aware that she was wildly popular with the people. It would help his transition to power if Guenivere was at his side. Mordred had also coveted his father's wife. Guenivere could serve him well.

Guenivere, summoning all of the regal bearing that she could muster in such a situation, had Mordred summoned into her chambers. Acting a bit stiff and formal in order to hide his shameful behavior, Mordred told the Queen that she was welcome to stay at Camelot. He would arrange it so that she had a wing of the castle for her private use. Without pausing, Guenivere declined his offer. "I wish to leave Camelot immediately," she heard herself saying. "I wish to reside alone and in isolation." Her wishes were granted.

What of Merlin? Merlin waited patiently in his chambers. The Bishop and Mordred knew that Merlin had to be destroyed. The Bishop wrung his hands in anticipation of destroying the man he considered his mortal enemy. None of the Bishop's or Mordred's henchmen could be convinced to kill this great magician and sorcerer. All were afraid of Merlin's powers. So the Bishop went where Merlin was not well known. He appealed among the foreign troops for volunteers to rid God's kingdom of a man described by the Bishop as "the most blasphemous heathen of them all." A band of men, eagerly responding to the Bishop's invitation to do more of God's work, stepped forward. The group was made up of fearless and reckless adventurers. Eagerly they swept into the now almost abandoned Camelot to kill Merlin. Merlin, the knower of all, awaited them. They poured down the stairway which led to Merlin's chambers in the basement of the castle. Merlin waited in the hallway. They sighted him. He dashed down the hallway, followed by these shouting pursuers. Merlin darted to his left into a tunnel, constructed of large stone blocks. The ceiling was vaulted and also made of stone. The would-be assassins suddenly ran abruptly into the end of the tunnel. There were no doors or other exits of any kind. Merlin had disappeared.

Merlin had chosen this end for himself. He had just gone. He had made his grand exit. The authorities tried to hush up word of this event but of course could not. It immediately became a great legend. Thus it was that this story was told and retold among the people for hundreds and hundreds of years. Bards sung of the wondrous exit from this life made by Merlin, the greatest wizard of them all.

Three days later Mordred was summoned to see the Bishop. When Mordred entered the room, four husky men seized him, slammed him down before a block, and he was beheaded before he could even cry out. Mordred had not realized what the Bishop had known. Mordred was the last surviving member of the lineage of King Arthur. As such, he would always be a potential threat to the church. So was Mordred's treachery rewarded with treachery. He had reaped what he had sown.

Guenivere, as she requested, was sequestered in a small isolated manor near the ocean. Accompanied by only a few people, she spent the rest of her life in isolation. There she walked the windswept dunes, roamed the woodlands, and kept to herself. Alone with her memories, she was content in knowing that her life's work had been finished. There, many years later, she quietly passed away.

What happened to Camelot? Camelot was abandoned. Who could have inhabited this place of such greatness? Who could have stood up to the legends and accomplishments of its former inhabitants? No one. The castle was left to slowly fall into decay and ruin. The lonely winds were left to wander down the halls. The rain and ice slowly reclaimed nature's own. Now no trace of it remains.

The Round Table Movement

The Round Table Movement could not be extinguished. Arthur and his wondrous knights had lit a spark within the hearts of mankind. This spark, recognizing the inherent honor and nobility within mankind, resonates deep within us. Arthur and his knights had been destroyed. But their legacy lives on.

The Round Table Movement had sought to glorify and recognize the idealistic qualities of mankind. The church recognized the strength of this movement, and the power of these ideals. The church twisted the concepts for its own purposes. Instead of glorifying and honoring man, the movement was redirected so that it glorified and honored (and enriched) the church. The church did this by eventually turning the attention and direction of the movement toward the Holy Lands of the Middle East. Thus the Crusades began. Unsuspecting Arab nations were about to receive much unwanted attention.

And Camelot was no more, except as it remained as a memory in the hearts of men.

The Destruction of the Druids

All of the druids were destroyed. They were hunted down and killed. Most druid men had blue tattoos of serpents on their arms. Druid priestesses had blue tattoos of a crescent moon on their foreheads. Thus it was easy to spot them, and they were killed on the spot. Any others of likely druid background were subject to ruthless extermination.

Saint Patrick achieved his immortality for the vigor in which he rid Ireland of its druids. This legend has been portrayed so that we now remember him as the man who rid Ireland of all snakes. This is in reference to the blue tattoos of "serpents" on the arms of the druid men. It wasn't snakes that he rid Ireland of, it was men with blue tatoos of snakelike creatures on their arms.

The druids were more than just a religion. The were the spiritual, medical, educational and cultural leadership of a society. They had all of the healing and medical knowledge. They provided the only educational facilities of the time. They owned and controlled the institutions of learning, healing and culture. When they were suddenly exterminated, a great void of learning and knowledge was created. The Christian church was unprepared and unable to replace the institutions which they had destroyed. Thus ignorance set in, and the Dark Ages began. Hundreds of years of darkness were to follow.

History is written by the victor. In the case of Camelot, the history was erased by the victor. The church, destroying all remnants of Arthur's realm, was so zealous in its effort that few written records exist confirming the existence of Arthur. It was left for the story to be carried forward in bits and pieces in the songs of bards, whispered legends, and myth.

5

I Do My First Regression

I received a telephone call from a friend who lives in Gainesville. Susan was calling to tell me that she was sure that her boyfriend Steve had lived during Camelot. Susan is a gifted sensitive, and she had picked up definite glimpses and impressions of Steve as a knight at Camelot.

I enjoyed my occasional visits with Susan, so using this event as an excuse to have a get together, I arranged for my girlfriend and I to go visit them in Gainesville. A few days later, we arrived at Susan's home. Marsha and I sat in Susan's living room with Steve while Susan served us some iced tea. As Steve explained his background to us, I became a bit skeptical. Steve was a very handsome man about 40-years-old. I did not like him at first. He did not seem to have a spiritual bone in his body, and he seemed to bristle with hostility whenever the rest of us spoke of spiritual matters. His demeanor was of arrogance and disdain for our spiritual interests.

This was interesting, because he did not have a lot going for himself. He was an alcoholic. He was a used car salesman, but was unemployed. His car in the driveway was a junker. He found occasional work as a musician at some local bars. "This unemployed alcoholic is no knight," I thought to myself. We sat in Susan's living room for about an hour, visiting and chatting. Steve continually made derisive comments about Susan's interest in his Camelot connection. As he did so, I got more and more annoyed. Finally Steve, lounging on one end of Susan's sofa, said, "Well maybe sometime I will let someone regress me." Without thinking, I snapped back, "Fine, let's do it now. Lean back on the sofa, close your eyes, and relax." This was interesting, because I did not know how to regress someone. My only experience was that I had been regressed once myself. But I was so annoyed with this joker that I was not going to let him get away with his act. I did remember the process which was used to regress me, so I began to use the same technique on Steve. Steve, caught off guard by my assertive instructions, got a scared look on his face, laid back on the sofa, and closed his eyes. Steve, not knowing that I did not know what I was doing, began to go into a light trance. I could hardly believe it. I was actually regressing someone!

It went beautifully. Steve went through "the door" back to Camelot. His story was beautiful. I did not have a tape recorder available, so was unfortunately unable to record the story. But it is a story worth retelling, so I am going to reconstruct certain memorable portions of his regression, as best I can remember them.

Mike: Where are you?

Steve: It is the summer festival. I am standing inside a large round enclosure made of stone. The stonework is about waist-high. I have just won the melee. I am the only one left standing. All of the others have been wrestled to the ground.

Mike: What is a melee?

Steve: It is the event held every year at the summer festival so that young men such as myself can have a chance to become knights for King Arthur. You see, I am the son of a peasant. I want to become a knight. Now I will get my chance. The melee is an event which was arranged by Merlin, so that young men of all classes and walks of life have a chance to become knights. Merlin has told us that it is important that knights be from all walks of life, even peasants, so he has arranged for the melee to give some of us a chance. Anyone who wishes to become a knight can jump into the enclosure. Everyone has an equal chance. I have won.

Mike: Why do you want to become a knight?

Steve: To avenge my father. When I was a little boy some men took him from the field where he was working, and he never came back. As a knight I can punish men who do this.

Mike: Now you are a knight. What is your name?

Steve: Persant.

Mike: Which is your favorite weapon?

Steve: The broad axe.

Mike: Why?

Steve: Because on horseback it gives me a great advantage. (At this point, still in a light trance, Steve jumps off the sofa, and shows me his special wrist action which he uses with his broad axe. The three of us sit there spellbound, if not a bit in shock.) You see, when the enemy charges you on horseback, you can block his sword blow like this. (Steve demonstrates, using an imaginary battle axe to block a sword blow.) Then while he is still pulling his sword back to strike me again, I use this wrist action to swing the battle axe on its thong which is attached to my wrist. By swinging the axe behind my back like this, I can catch him before he has recovered his sword to strike again. (Now I *am* in shock. An unemployed alcoholic used car salesman in Gainesville, Florida has just taught me how to fight with a medieval battle axe!)

Mike: Tell me about your favorite battle.

Steve: That would be my first one. I was the youngest knight. Arthur and Merlin selected me to go out and destroy the Black Knight. He was from a distant part of the realm. He was empowered by black magicians. He had already killed four of Arthur's knights.

Mike: Wait a minute. This Black Knight has killed four knights already, and they are sending the youngest knight out alone to get him? Why?

Steve: This is the magic of Camelot.

Mike: What happened?

Steve: Well, I traveled from village to village, asking directions to find the castle where the Black Knight lived. Someone in each village would silently point in a direction and say nothing. I proceeded in this manner. One morning I came out of a forest into a clearing. Off in the distance I could see a castle on a hill. On the other side of the clearing a solitary knight sat on a beautiful and powerful-looking black horse. This knight was in black armor. His visor was up. He lowered his visor, and his horse charged toward me.

Mike: What did you do?

Steve: Nothing. My horse was trained so that when he saw another horse coming at him, he charged forth to meet him. So my horse charged. I pulled out my small sword.

Mike: (Not knowing what a small sword was.) Why the small sword?

Steve: I don't know. It all happened so fast, I didn't have time to think. But as we got close, I saw that the Black Knight had his big sword in hand. We crashed together. He raised his big sword to strike. With his arm raised overhead, I saw an opening in his armor under his arm. I quickly plunged my small sword through this opening. He falls. It is over. The Black Knight lies dead.

Mike: What did you do then?

Steve: I got off my horse, and took his weapons. Normally we retrieve the fallen foe's armor and weapons, because they are very valuable. But because he was empowered by forces of darkness, I do not touch his armor. But I take his weapons. And his horse. This is the most magnificent horse I have ever seen. Much better than any of my few horses. Coming from a poor background, I have only a couple of horses which were given to me by the King when I became a knight. I want this horse! I tie the black horse behind my horse.

Mike: What then?

Steve: I returned to Camelot. As I passed through each village, I passed silently, the black horse trailing behind me sufficient notice of the outcome of my battle. As word spread throughout the kingdom, my return trip became famous. This is how the tradition of the riderless black horse at funerals began.

Mike: Did you ever get to avenge the disappearance of your father?

Steve: No. I didn't want to. Everything changed as I gradually became a knight. As I passed through Merlin's training, I lost my desire for revenge. Better to let God handle things.

Postscript: This session blew me away. My first regression, unplanned and spontaneous, was a wild success. Had it not happened so spontaneously, I would not have had the confidence to do it. But Wow, it has been great. And it gave me the confidence to plunge ahead and do other regressions. Which I did.

This session changed Steve completely. It was as if he had always been a knight, but no one had ever told him. In the kind of light trance he had been in during the regression, everything is remembered. So he had full awareness of this amazing experience. He and I became friends. I truly love him now. Six months after this regression, he came by my house in Orlando to visit. He was a changed man. He was off alcohol. He had a great job selling new Buicks, and had been salesman of the month for several months in a row. He and I had a great visit. He spoke with earnest of his connection to God. He drove a new car. Across the top of his windshield was labeled the word Camelot. Steve is once again a knight.

6

My Regression Technique

I believe that it is appropriate here to brief you on the type of regression I do. Most of the regressions were done in the office of my home. Some of the regressions were done solely to explore the past at Camelot. Other regressions were oriented toward healing. In such cases, the person had come to me with a problem, either emotional or physical. We then explored their past to ascertain the emotional root of the problem. Sometimes this led us to Camelot. In such a regression, we searched out the emotional issues from the Camelot experience, and attempted to resolve them. Thus we are "killing two birds with one stone" in a number of these regressions. The person is undergoing an emotional healing experience, while we also explore their Camelot adventures.

How does this work? First of all, remember that body, mind and spirit are one. They are all connected. If there is an illness manifesting in the body, factors involving the mind and spirit may just as likely be responsible for the illness, as is the condition of the body itself. I believe that this is where modern medicine has missed the boat; if you have cancer, for instance, most doctors will treat the cancer as a completely physical phenomenon. But, as I have personally learned by working with persons with cancer, sometimes emotional issues are at play as well. For instance, anger trapped in the body can contribute toward cancer. Thus it is not coincidence, for example, that a 62-year-old woman who held extraordinarily hateful feelings toward her ex-husband, developed cancer in her brain. If the hateful emotions are not released, she will probably die. But sometimes it is not this simple; sometimes an unresolved emotion from a past life will pop up in this lifetime, manifesting as an illness. Thus the 42-year-old carpenter whose low self esteem we traced back to his experience as a person who stood in the crowd at Jesus's crucifixion, filled with fear and afraid to speak out for Jesus. Subsequent feelings of guilt that he had not had the courage or bravery to try to defend or somehow rescue

Jesus, had since plagued him. By revisiting the crucifixion, we were able to let him change his behavior so that the underlying emotional turmoil was released, and his self esteem was improved.

Thus I have had noteworthy success in using regressions to go back to the experience itself which has caused harmful emotions to be locked into the body, address the experience, identify the emotions, and release them. For the most part I relied upon my psychic ability to determine where to go in order to reach the trapped emotions. But a limitation was that my work was only as good as was my psychic ability. Then I made a breakthrough. While reading Barbara Marciniak's book *Bringers of the Dawn*, I discovered her revelation that all illness can be traced back to the emotions from a particular experience in the past. It came to me that I could let the person's subconscious mind do the work! The person could lead us back to the appropriate past experience. So now, after I have placed the person in a light trance, I ask the person to: "Take us back to the point in time where you picked up the emotions which are causing you to have multiple sclerosis (as an example.)" Sometimes we end up in Camelot.

My actual procedure for the regression is quite simple. I ask the person to lie down on a sofa which is in the office. Then I ask the person to close their eyes, to breathe deeply and relax for a few minutes. I also take a few deep breaths, say a short prayer asking for guidance, and focus on the person. I then lead them through a relaxation technique which lasts for eight to ten minutes. At the end of this relaxation phase, I say: "Please imagine or visualize that you and I are standing in the basement of a castle. We are standing there looking at one of the outer walls of the basement. There is an entrance to a tunnel in this wall. The tunnel leads out away from the castle. This tunnel is very special. It is wide. It is wide enough for the two of us to walk abreast through the tunnel without our shoulders touching the walls of the tunnel. The tunnel is very brightly lit. There are torches mounted all up and down the length of the walls of the tunnel, so that it is very bright and cheerful. The tunnel itself is beautiful. The walls are made of polished stone blocks. The blocks are so perfectly fitted and polished that it appears that the walls are made of polished marble. The floor of the tunnel is made of smooth polished stone. The ceiling is vaulted, and also made of smoothly polished stone. But most noteworthy is the feelings or vibrations coming from the tunnel. The tunnel is filled with feelings of friendship, camaraderie, and love. These feelings coming from the tunnel fill us with the desire to enter the tunnel and partake of these emotions. I would like to go and explore this tunnel, to see where it goes. Would you like to accompany me?

We have now entered the tunnel. I am on the left, and you are standing on the right. We smile and laugh as we are filled with the emotions and cheerfulness which come from the tunnel. As we walk along, I reach out my left hand, and I feel the smoothness of the finely polished stone wall. Likewise, you hold out your right hand and feel the wall. You feel the smoothness of the stone, and the finely crafted joints between the blocks of stone. As we go along, we smile and laugh together.

Now I point out to you that there is a turn in the tunnel up ahead. You look up and see that the tunnel makes a sharp turn to the left. We approach this turn, and follow it around to the left. Now you look up and see that a few steps ahead the tunnel makes a sharp turn to the right. We follow the turn to the right. Now we are in another straight section of the tunnel, which appears to head in just about the same direction as the first section of tunnel, except that perhaps this section of tunnel slopes downward slightly. We walk along, again smiling and enjoying the experience of being in this so special tunnel.

After a short walk, I point ahead and state that we are coming to the end of the tunnel. You look ahead as we approach the end of the tunnel. We observe that our tunnel has run into some sort of under-ground wall. The stone in this wall is very different than the stone in our tunnel. The blocks of stone in this underground wall are very crudely carved. The stone is a much lighter gray color than is the stone blocks of our tunnel. And somehow we know that this is a very ancient underground stone wall. In the center of this ancient stone wall is a doorway. There is a door made of heavy wooden planks mounted in the doorway. It looks as if the wooden planks are of oak. The door is rounded at the top. There are two massive black metal door hinges on the left side of the door, and there is a black metal door latch on the right side of the door.

This is a very special door. We can go through this door to return to any time in the past. If it is all right with you, I suggest that we go through this door back to the time of Camelot and King Arthur. Do you approve? Would you like for me to open the door for you? Okay, I'm opening the door. With your permission, I am going to go on this journey with you. When you are ready, step through the door, and tell me what you experience or feel."

Note: Having passed through the tunnel together, we usually pass through the door into another time period; in this case, Camelot. Occa-sionally the person draws a blank, or blocks himself/herself from any feeling or observation. But on the whole, I estimate that about 90% of the time we successfully tap into the other time dimension for a mean-ingful experience.

This type of light trance allows the person to remember every-thing. This is very helpful where emotional healing is needed. Many of the people I regressed carried suppressed emotions from the Camelot lifetime which were released during or shortly after the regression. In a few noteworthy occasions, the emotions experienced during the regression were so powerful that the person could not stand or walk for some time thereafter. Many, such as Steve, had their lives profoundly changed by the experience.

7

Cathy Channelling Raziel April, 1994

Background: Cathy is a 42-year-old legal assistant. She also channels. This chapter consists of excerpts from a two-hour channeling she did about Camelot. The spirit force she was channelling identified himself as Raziel, the "record keeper."

Normally I do not put much stock in channelled information. I believe that much of it is misinformation, or is meant to misguide us. There are positive and negative forces at work in the other dimensions. It is easy for a dark force energy to identify itself falsely as an "enlightened being," and do much harm by passing information through a channelling medium who has not properly protected himself or herself from such tampering.

How do you protect yourself? Simple. Just pray to God and his angelic forces to surround you in God's white light, and to place you within a circle of God's protection. Most of the channels I have observed have failed to follow these basic procedures; they do not properly protect themselves, and I thus discount the value of their information.

But Cathy was different. She is very advanced in her spirituality. I asked my own spirit guides to review the 32-page transcript of her channelling. They selected the following from her effort to be presented to you.

Mike: How did Arthur get the inspiration for the Round Table? What was the purpose of the Round Table movement?
Cathy: It was suggested to him in his childhood as part of his teachings. As you know, the ancient Greeks knew that this planet was a sphere. And this knowledge was forgotten in the Dark Ages. However, Camelot was before the Dark Ages. Merlin was an educated person,

reading eight or nine languages, and he knew about celestial bodies. He had also fashioned himself a small . . . form of telescope. And he could go and observe the stars, and planets, Venus in particular. It being the closest. One night . . . Arthur was around ten-years old. Arthur was supposed to have been in bed because he had to get up very early and tend to the horses in the stable. But being curious, he knew when he went to sleep at night, he could look and see the light on, way up in the tower where Merlin was staying. And he wondered what Merlin was doing up so late. Why could an adult stay up when he couldn't? So, he snuck up on Merlin.

Now, Merlin, of course, is going to be snuck up on? (Laughing.) So, he calmly waited, knowing that Arthur was quietly creeping up the stairs behind him. He was looking through the telescope, and he decided to talk out loud to himself, and he said, "My goodness, there goes a shooting star right there." He said, "Oh, yes, look at that, there are seven suns together over here." And he said, "And look at this, this is not a star at all." He had Arthur so curious that Arthur didn't make any pretense of sneaking up on him any longer. Merlin said, "Come here and see, boy." So, Arthur came and looked through the telescope. He could barely see anything . . . it looked like a dot of light to him. And so Merlin taught him that if he would stare at the light, and then shut his eyes and look at the white wall, then he would see better. Then he could tell that it was a sphere, instead of flat. For the common people, they thought that these were just little pin pricks of light, something like fire flies. They had no concept of distance. But Merlin taught him about distance, movement, spheres, all in that one evening. And Arthur began to ask questions like what makes the stars hang where they are? And Merlin said, "They are not hanging, they are proceeding on their path." Arthur asked, "How can you tell they are going on any path? I do not see any woods." Then Merlin said, "Let's make a notch on the wall where we see that star. There. You come up in five days, and we'll see if the star is still there."

So Merlin showed him, and he marked it. And Arthur would sneak up every five days, and he would mark where the star went. And he said, "Well Merlin, what does all of this mean?" And Merlin said, "Well, God has put all of those things there to teach us that each star is like a person. They are all following their own paths." Now, at that time, they thought that earth was in the center, and things were running around it. And he said, "Now, since we are in the center and they are all going around us, perhaps . . . God is here. (Gestures at his heart.) Just perhaps, what we do here is very very important. And if the people don't understand that what they're doing here is important, we might just need to have a person to lead them, to be their center. We just might need to have some ideas like . . . making them stand in a circle at the maypole, or making them stand in a circle around the well. Look into the well and see the future. And they just might . . . need to sit around a table where everyone is equal. Be round, instead of straight."

So, he planted the seed in Arthur's mind, and when Arthur had the opportunity, he had the great Round Table made. And it was made in such a fashion that it was . . . it was not solid. It was in four curved sections. So that a person could go and stand in the middle and present his case before everyone. Equally. And the person that stood in the center had the right to speak without being disturbed. As soon as his allotted time was over, he was out and the next one could go in and make his case. I know there are a great many drawings showing a big solid table, but that is not how it was. For you see, Arthur was trying to make it like the heavens. And each of the knights was a star. And each had their paths, and each had their quest. And they each had a family, they each had people to protect. They all had a fiefdom. But they were always supposed to come back to center. Just as each star, each planet, had its path.

Mike: Did all of the knights sit around the Round Table when they ate, or did some have to sit at other tables?
Cathy: They were not always all present. And, this was a large enough table and it was in four pieces, that it could be stretched and little straight ones put in the middle. And made even larger. And then, others would sit at the other tables. No one was ever made to sit apart that was a knight.

Now, you see, this is where the ladies will get mad at me. But the ladies were in another room. The squires were in another room. It was only those that had the ability and the invitation. And in this case, we are talking about . . . apprentices. They are not, they haven't passed all of their . . . postings, yet. And they haven't been through the lists.

There is a great event that they used for those who wished to become knights and were not being sponsored by anybody. It was called the Melee. And all who wished would go onto the field, and the last one left standing was the next knight. Very simple, but it would allow people that had no political. . . .

Mike: Yes. Yes, that explains how serfs could become knights. . . . Some of the knights were from backgrounds of poverty.
Cathy: But they were strong. You see, Arthur wanted ALL people to be represented. Because he knew even the tiniest star had its path. And he knew that if the grooms in the stable were gone, and no one was there to take care of the horses, then the knight could not accomplish a thing. No one would be there to put him on or off of his horse. If the

armor-bearer was sick, what could the knight do? His sword would be rusty. His armor would be stiff and could not move. And of course, if the cook in the kitchen wasn't there, nobody could eat. He knew the importance of everyone.

Remember . . . Arthur was a sort of an orphan in his youth. He was taken very soon after his birth and brought, as a "foundling," to Sir Kay. Or "Sir Guy." He preferred his name to be pronounced as "Sir Guy." Arthur was raised nicely enough. But he was thought just to be a "child of the woods." A "child of the woods" is one of these children that is born to an unwed mother. Being an unwed mother wasn't bad in those days, but it was not always easy for a woman to support a child by herself. And they would sometimes leave their babies in the woods, and if someone found the baby, they were honor bound to take that baby in. Because it was a gift to them from the Great Mother. And this is how Arthur was left, in a place where he would be found by Sir Kay, and taken in. Sir Kay was not allowed to know exactly who Arthur was.

Mike: Did Arthur and Merlin use mystical ways to pick their knights? Did they pick them for purity of heart, and things like that?

Cathy: Arthur was the one who chose, but he would ask Merlin for his advice. Arthur had a way of feeling about things, that was based on his early life experiences, and the experience of his soul. For his soul, as I have mentioned, already was very sensitive to people. He could sense what they were feeling and thinking. So, he would usually give them a test based on the thing that they disliked the most. To see if they were willing to do this thing. Then they would be willing to do whatever it required to uphold . . . the vision. There are times when you will be tested to the limits of your endurance when you are trying to birth an idea. No matter how good the idea is, because people are set in their ways. Even those that are being abused, as in slavery, will uphold slavery for fear of something new.

Cathy: Arthur was very happy. And Guenivere was happy too. And when the thing happened with Lancelot, all three of them were at the same time feeling betrayed and betraying. And it was very hard on all three of them. And yet, they all understood it and they all took part in it. It is very hard to explain this.

Mike: It's okay. I can understand.

Cathy: But it was all connected, and they all loved each other and trusted each other and they were going to keep this silent. The problem is, there's always a meddler around.

Mike: Who was the meddler?

Cathy: (Big sigh.) As we have mentioned to you, Arthur had a son by his half sister. When this son was fourteen, he came to Arthur and said,

"You are my father." And Arthur was without children, and heirs. And he was wanting to take him in. Unfortunately they did not get along.

Mike: Arthur and the boy?

Cathy: Arthur and the boy. The boy could not . . . the boy couldn't fight, and he was not honest.

Mike: What was his name?

Cathy: Mordred.

Mike: M-O-R-D-R-E-D?

Cathy: Yes. And he knew by lineage that he would be the next king, because there was no other heir. And he thought that a scandal would get everybody out of his way, and he could become king. After all, he was a man, he was fourteen. That was his motive in doing what he did.

Mike: Did he later kidnap Guenivere?

Cathy: Actually, he had also a romantic attachment to Guenivere, himself.

Mike: Yes.

Cathy: And she rebuffed him, of course. And that was another motivation for what he did.

Mike: Did he use his magic on her to seduce her and later kidnap her? I want to make sure I have my stories straight.

Cathy: He had intended to do all of these things. He had some fantasies, yes. Unfortunately he did know the use of certain herbs, to make people unconscious. In fact, his own mind had been poisoned against his mother as well. Because she refused to do anything against Arthur to make Arthur take him in, or to otherwise favor him. She refused. Some of Mordred's people had poisoned his mind because they wanted to take their power back. Power that they were losing.

Mike: Who did this? Who poisoned his mind?

Cathy: Some of the druids. Not. . . .

Mike: He was raised by druids?

Cathy: Yes.

Mike: Okay.

Cathy: Not the druid holy men. The holy men would never have done this. And not the priestesses. But the other people.

Mike: Okay.

Cathy: They wanted him to be king. They wanted him to get rid of all this "new" Christian stuff.

Mike: Okay.

Cathy: So, shall we say, the conservatives poisoned his mind. By building him up and telling him what a great guy he was. You see, he was rather a weakling. And a weakling is fearful, and a fearful person is a great bully. And what he did, was that he gave her a sleeping potion to knock her out, so he could then remove her to a place where he would have her at a disadvantage. He got so far as knocking her

62

out, and had her over his shoulder, and was making for the back exit, and got confronted by someone. So he fully intended to do this. He did not complete it.

Mike: Huh. Okay. Was this someone Lancelot?

Cathy: Yes.

Mike: Did Lancelot kill him at that time?

Cathy: Would have liked to have, but no, he did not. He gave him a severe beating. During the scuffle, Guenivere got dropped. She came to and woke up. It was all brought to Arthur's attention. Lancelot would not kill a son of his friend. No matter how slimy the kid was. He was thinking that this would make Arthur see how bad this boy was, and that Arthur would kick him out. Arthur saw, already, what the boy was. But he still didn't kick him out, because he felt honor-bound. This was his son.

Mike: Has Mordred incarnated at this time? Reincarnated?

Cathy: His soul is still experiencing great weaknesses. And there is one on earth that carries these memories.

Mike: Is he here in Florida?

Cathy: Yes. We are not certain exactly where. His appearance is somewhat similar, in that he is still weak of muscle.

Mike: How were they able to convince a page to assassinate his own king?

Cathy: Well, Mordred was not the only weakling in the world! This was another, weak of physical frame, who was jealous of the other boys who could go out and become knights. He could not possibly have made it through the Melee. And no one would nominate him to be a knight. He couldn't become a knight. He did not physically have the capabilities. And he was jealous, angry. So treachery was his way of working out his anger.

Mike: What happened to Merlin after Arthur was killed?

Cathy: Merlin was not . . . Merlin was not in the battle. Merlin of course, knew everything that was going to happen. Merlin had problems of his own. You see . . . now that is another story, that will take a long time. He had great problems of his own, personal ones. And what it amounted to was that there was an upstart after his position. And it was not Mordred, it was another person. Mordred was not a threat to Merlin. Mordred was attempting to be king, not the Merlin. This other person was causing Merlin difficulties.

Mike: Did that other person eventually replace him, when Merlin left?

Cathy: Attempted to, yes.

Mike: How so?

Cathy: He did not last long, because the druids were all hunted down and killed. Hollow victory.

Mike: Okay. How did Merlin die, after Arthur's death? What happened?

Cathy: You know the term "samadhi"?

Mike: Yes.

Cathy: Where the body ceases to breathe at the will of the person.

Mike: Yes.

Cathy: And it is the state of supreme bliss.

Mike: Yes.

Cathy: He knew how to practice this. And he went to a particular spot that was his favorite spot. And he voluntarily left, in that fashion. He was about one-hundred and twenty-three years old. His job was done and he did not see a reason to stay around, it being dangerous. And, there was nothing more for him to do, except be hunted. And he did not find that very interesting.

Mike: He did not want to stay and be killed.

Cathy: They would have tried.

Mike: I believe the person who replaced him, in this lifetime, calls himself "Samadhi."

Cathy: (Laughs.)

Mike: Isn't that interesting.

Cathy: Well, that person . . . the person who was attempting to replace Merlin had been one of his students, of course. And, like the page, he was very anxious for Merlin to move on, so that he could be the Merlin. It was not unusual for a Merlin to say, "I am ready to retire from the world," pick a replacement, and go on to other things. And this person had been Merlin's student for approximately forty years, and was losing patience. He was already going out and proclaiming himself "Merlin," and performing a lot of the public functions. And Merlin didn't do anything to contradict this. Because he knew the time was short, anyway. There was no need to get into a battle over it. So, as I had said, that was a rather long story.

Mike: Concerning the Grail Castle: is it true that magic was used to keep the mist around the sanctuary, so that no one could find it? And the mist was lifted so Percival could find it?

Cathy: Actually, the area is known for its mist. However, if you wish to call it magic or if you wish to call it prayers, the person that hid it had asked that it be hidden from view. The way that it was hidden was through this mist.

Mike: Where was the cup kept after that? Where did they put the plate and the cup, when Percival guarded it?

Cathy: A special case was made for it. As you know, glass was very precious in those days, and sheets of glass were worth more than gold. So, a glass case, with the finest wood for the frame, was made. So that all could see, but not touch. For it was also believed that if someone touched it, and did not have a pure heart, they would die. This was their superstition, at that time. Percival was allowed to touch it, and his wife was allowed to touch it. But no one else.

Mike: I'd like to go to Arthur's last years. I seem to have picked up that his last years were very trouble filled. It was almost as if he was being squeezed on many fronts by the church. How did he handle that, and how did it go?

Cathy: The church, what the church did . . . they eventually wanted to have control. At first, there was one priest assigned to the castle to do all of the masses for the King and for everyone there. Arthur didn't mind that too much. Well, then the church wanted to send a bishop. Now, this is someone in authority. And, it began to look like a struggle between kings, because a bishop is someone who has all of the priests under his control. And some of these priests were warriors.

Now, this is the time when Merlin stepped back, when the Bishop came. The Bishop arrived at the court without being invited, relieved the priest of his duties, and there he was. It was like, "this is how it is." No asking. And, it was a very uncomfortable situation, because Arthur, having brought in Christianity, couldn't just send him away. On the other hand, Arthur's mentor was stepping back and gone. This priest could not help Arthur with advice as Merlin once had done. As a matter of fact, the Bishop resented the tattoos that Arthur wore on his arms. Arthur had been tattooed as a boy. The King had a special tattoo, which of course, was a dragon. A dragon with a sword in its mouth.

Mike: On the left arm?

Cathy: And on this arm, this is where the mouth and the head of the dragon is, on this arm. (Gestures to the left arm.) And on this arm, the mouth and head is here, coming in. (Gestures to the right arm.) This is the arm that dispenses and this is the arm that takes. This is the arm for battle and this is the arm for comforting. All right. Of course, you can't take a tattoo off. The dragon, of course, is in the book of Revelation. Which is not a good sign. And, every time you move your arm, it is showing. The Bishop is looking at you down his nose. People weren't being killed by the church yet, but it would happen soon enough. For less than having a tattoo. It was rather difficult. Mordred, of course, had the same tattoo on his arms. The Bishop was sent by, this will be of interest to you, not Rome, but Constantinople. This was the height of the power of Constantinople, and Rome was weak by comparison.

Mike: Yes, yes.

Cathy: And there were people in this land over there (Constantinople), and they had similar tattoos on them, and they were considered heathens. So, this Bishop was a bigot. And he came in and saw what looked to him like ruffians, because he had come from the court of Constantinople, which was the richest land in the world at that time. And he determined to do something about it. You know about the court at Constantinople?

Mike: No.

Cathy: Ah, what a story that is. Murders and intrigue and. . . .

Mike: A Peyton Place.

Cathy: No, much worse. People were being murdered over a glance . . . they knew all the poisons, they knew all of the ways. They could do a bit of sorcery themselves. Not exactly a pleasant place, but very, very wealthy. That is another story.

Mike: Were the knights trying to warn Arthur at the last? It seems as if there were many years of this intrigue.

Cathy: Lancelot, who was French, knew a bit about the court at Constantinople. He did not like the attitude of this bishop. So he went back home, and he asked the priests where he came from, about this man. If they knew him. Oh yes, they did know him. This man had murdered some people to get to his position, and he had bribed others. Not exactly a sweet person. And he came back with this information for Arthur. And Arthur's comment was, "This is the one that God has sent." He could not send him back, for he had no authority to do so. He was not a member of the church hierarchy himself, with authority to send a bishop back. At this time there was no one strong Pope, like today. There were many bishops.

It is unfortunate that the Bishop was uncomfortable with the people and culture of his new assignment. But it was an important assignment. What the church was after was control of the wool. For you see, the robes of kings were made of fine wool. And the English had particularly nice sheep, with very special, strong wool. And the church wanted to get a corner on the market. Isn't it interesting. . . .

Mike: Wow. Nothing has changed, nothing has changed.

Cathy: That people are, nations are killed, for little things like this.

Mike: Did Arthur stay lovers with his half-sister for most of his life?

Cathy: It was not physical, it was at a distance. It was . . . a tragedy, just as if you had been separated from your first, first love, as a child. They were not together, no. It was not possible.

Mike: She lived at Camelot?

Cathy: No, she did not live at Camelot. She would visit from time to time, but she did not live there. She lived on her island with . . . she was a priestess, and therefore, she lived with the women.

Mike: Was that the invisible island?

Cathy: (Laughing.) That was the magical island!

Mike: The magical island, yes. Is Avalon still there?

Cathy: Actually, physically, there is some land there. It is not, it is not any more distinguishable than what you would find elsewhere. There was a well, and there were small, adobe and stone-type buildings with thatched roofs.

Mike: Does anybody know that it is Avalon?

Cathy: There are people who have their suspicions. People who have the wisdom, that can feel it. But very few go there.

Mike: What happened to Camelot after Arthur's . . . demise?

Cathy: There were a number of things that happened. There is the old children's tale about Sleeping Beauty. Sleeping Beauty is like an allegory, okay? Where Guenivere could be thought of as Sleeping Beauty. Instead of pricking her finger on a spinning wheel, the great princess, her heart is broken. And she withdraws, almost to sleep. As you know, Guenivere went away and became as a nun. She hid out the rest of her life inside of a nunnery. And everything just went to sleep, everything just quieted down.

As for Camelot, the people had left because of the persecutions, and then there were some natural disasters, some lightning and some thunderstorms and heavy winds that demolished a great deal of structure that was there. There was some demolishing on the part of individuals, but it was not nearly as great as the demolishing done by nature. It was as if the hand of God came in and just mowed it down and smoothed it over. It was not, it was not the PLACE that was important, it was the MEMORY.

Mike: Uhhuh.

Cathy: And for a while the stories had to be told in this version, to children, at night, as bedtime stories or around the campfire. Not out in public. Whispered. And just as Sleeping Beauty is an allegory for Camelot, and Cinderella is an allegory for another . . . civilization in time, a lot of these stories are the myths, are legends of real people that existed at one time. And their civilization has fallen for whatever reason. And the good that was in the civilization lives through these stories. Even though the civilization is gone.

Mike: Did they actually have dragons back in those days? There were a lot of allusions to knights going out fighting dragons. There were a number of references to that.

Cathy: . . . Actually, there are certain species of . . . remnants of what you call dinosaurs.

Mike: They were still around?

Cathy: They did not necessarily breathe flame. However, when something that large is moving rather quickly in your direction. . . .

Mike: (Laughing.) They perhaps seem like they're breathing fire. . . .

Cathy: YOU are burning up the territory getting out of there. They tend to hide in dark areas, or in deep water. There are still some on the planet. They are very shy. They don't necessarily like the dark, because being of the lizard form of life, they do like the warmth. But they go DEEP into caves, because as you get deeper, beyond a certain point, it begins to get warm again. So they are mostly deep into the earth. At the time of Camelot, however, they were closer towards the surface.

Mike: After Arthur died, what happened to Excalibur?

Cathy: As you can imagine, Mordred was seeking it. The page who stabbed Arthur was supposed to take it. The page died on the spot. There . . . were approximately fifteen knights standing in a circle around Arthur. The page was not actually inside the circle. He was not allowed to be there. But as I've said, he was small, and slight of build. Short and small. In the commotion, he darted between the others. And his last act was to do this, this thing. As Arthur was stabbed, he fell backwards. His hand held the sword, and it was flung over his head and outside of the circle, and landed on the ground unnoticed. A scuffle immediately started. All of those who were traitors immediately began to try and kill those next to them who would not be expecting it. And so a great many fell right at that moment. It is often in such a battle and such a time, when the small and the weakest person around, generally unnoticed, because they are not seemingly dangerous, gets the prize. And there was another page present, who saw the sword, who was loyal to Arthur. He saw the light catching the sword as it whipped through the air and landed. In the scuffle, he got down on all fours and began to crawl toward the sword. Grasping Excalibur, he hid the sword in his clothing. He then fled. And he took it and buried it in an unusual place. He took the sword to a stream. Now, being steel, ordinarily steel rusts. However, this had been made in such a way that it would not rust. It had been tempered, but it also . . . it had been made in such a fashion that I can not explain. Where it would not rust. And he took stones at the bottom of this river, and displaced them. And put it under there. And put the stones back in place. And it is there to this day. For . . . it is not time for it to come back out again.

Mike: Could you explain the persecutions of the druids?

Cathy: Persecutions are never explainable. (Laughs.) However, the reason for every persecution is fear. Simply fear, that you are going to lose what you have taken, or what you had. Now, in this case they were taking something that was not theirs. And they were afraid the rightful owners would rise up against them and take it back.

Mike: Uhhuh.

Cathy: So as I have said, there were tattoos. That made it easy to identify many druids. The men had tattoos on their arms, and the women were tattooed on their forehead. These were the ones that were the "holy" people. The common people, it was less easy to identify them. Sometimes the women had just a single line here on the chin. There were certain ways of wearing the hair, certain articles of clothing that would also distinguish them as druids. The pointed hat, for example. The country people wore these hats. You had a hat like that, you were . . . gone. Or you got rid of your hat, quickly.

Mike: How long did the persecutions last? How many years?

Cathy: It was very bad for five years. And they continued the policy, strictly, for fifteen years. And by then, they pretty much had everybody killed off or completely servile. Or converted, or whatever you wish to call it. Willingly.

Mike: And how did they come up with a new king after Arthur? Did the church put someone in as king?

Cathy: They went back to city-states for a while. The church tried to appoint one of them to be the king. And he was immediately murdered. They appointed another one who went crazy and jumped off a cliff. (Laughs.) It was . . . a very rough time. It was the beginning of the Dark Ages. It went back to chaos for hundred of years. These times are the times of, also, St. Patrick in Ireland. You'll read the legends of St. Patrick, and what he went through too. You'll read how he got rid of the "snakes." They are referring to the tattoos, which were often of serpents, or snakes.

Mike: Ohhhhhh.

Cathy: St. Patrick slaughtered all of the druids. Not exactly what an Irishman would want to hear today.

Mike: I'll be darned.

Cathy: He was getting rid of the "temptor." The temptor is the old way, the pagan way.

Mike: He was a bad dude.

Cathy: He was a warrior. And, not the same one as this bishop I have mentioned, but similar.

Mike: Has that bishop popped up in our lives, in this lifetime?

Cathy: This one was present fifty years ago, in Germany. In which time he attempted to remove his "debts," by being Jewish. He died in a concentration camp. So he is currently not in body. He was a religious persecutor, and so he tasted that himself in this lifetime.

Mike: Why has Camelot and Arthur become such an enduring legend?

Cathy: Because there were a great many people that found freedom in that time that were not given freedom before, or after, for many centuries. As I have said, the feudal system, which started out everyone being pretty much equal, had separated to where there were a bunch of serfs and a few powerful families.

Mike: Yes.

Cathy: Ruling and running these serfs. They all owed something . . . everybody owed something to everybody else. If you wanted your neighbor to stop beating you up, you started bribing him off. (Laughs.) That's what it was. So it had gotten pretty bad. Only the chief bully, and he always had to watch his back . . . only the chief bully had anything, and he didn't have any peace. So it was a bad time.

But when Arthur came, he taught people to trust each other. He taught people to like each other. He taught people they could work together. He taught them they could actually make a deal in trade, instead of beating each other up. Instead of taking wool, why not take some of your flax over and trade it for the wool? Why do you have to beat each other up all the time? So he brought peace. Something that wasn't there before or after. And he brought equality. Everyone had an opportunity to speak that wished to at his court.

8

Laurie as Guenivere
April, 1995

Background: I met Laurie the day of our regression. She was 34-years-old. She was a physical therapist. Her boyfriend was an acquaintance of mine. He was curious about a possible past-life connection between them, and requested that I regress them both. She went to Camelot. He, to his dismay, did not.

Mike: May I open the door for you?
Laurie: Yes, please do.
Mike: For some reason or other, I want to do that for you. Okay, good. Have you gone through the door?
Laurie: Uhhuh.
Mike: Where are you?
Laurie: I'm in a meadow.
Mike: Okay. Tell me about it.
Laurie: It's warm and it's . . . I think it is springtime. And there are wildflowers all around. There are wildflowers everywhere. And it's outside the castle.
Mike: Which castle?
Laurie: It's Camelot.
Mike: Okay. And what are you doing?
Laurie: I'm picking wildflowers. Skipping and dancing around.
Mike: And who are you? Are you a boy or a girl?
Laurie: I'm a girl.
Mike: How old are you?
Laurie: I'm nineteen.
Mike: What color's your hair?
Laurie: It's long and brown, with gold highlights.
Mike: Are you married or single?

Laurie: I'm single, and I'm about to be married.

Mike: Who are you going to marry? Tell me about your husband-to-be.

Laurie: I don't know if I like him.

Mike: Why? Why do you say that?

Laurie: I don't know if I love him.

Mike: Who decided for you to marry him?

Laurie: Someone else decided. It was arranged.

Mike: Okay. Is he nice to you?

Laurie: Yes.

Mike: Do you miss your home?

Laurie: Yes I do.

Mike: Have you been in Camelot very long?

Laurie: No, I just arrived. I came to meet my husband.

Mike: Would you like to go to the wedding? . . . Does that make you uncomfortable?

Laurie: It scares me.

Mike: Okay. Isn't he nice to you?

Laurie: Yes. It's just that I don't know if I want to marry him.

Mike: Okay. Have you met a man named Merlin?

Laurie: Yes.

Mike: What do you think of Merlin?

Laurie: I like him.

Mike: Did you spend any time with him?

Laurie: Some.

Mike: Are you able to discuss this with him?

Laurie: I haven't yet. I think he knows.

Mike: Yes, he seems to know a lot, doesn't he?

Laurie: Yes.

Mike: What does he look like?

Laurie: He looks wise and ancient. He's very wise.

Mike: What color are his eyes?

Laurie: They're dark, but they're also bright . . . they're piercing.

Mike: Okay.

Laurie: Sometimes they're just full of light.

Mike: Do you sense that you two will become very good friends?

Laurie: Yes.

Mike: Yes. Could it be that he's one of the people who helped choose you . . . to marry your husband?

Laurie: Possibly. Yes.

Mike: Have you been to the Great Hall yet, during the mealtimes, where everybody gets together?

Laurie: Yes.

Mike: What do you think of that?

Laurie: It's huge. It's noisy.

Mike: You like that?

Laurie: Yes.

Mike: They have a lot of fun together, don't they?

Laurie: Yes.

Mike: It's great love there.

Laurie: Yes.

Mike: What do you think of this Round Table Movement, and everything else that's going on there?

Laurie: It's a wonderful idea.

Mike: So you relate to it very easily?

Laurie: Yes.

Mike: Who has explained all of this to you, and what it is that you are about to enter into?

Laurie: The King.

Mike: The King explained it?

Laurie: Yes.

Mike: Okay. Does he spend much time with you?

Laurie: He has been, yes.

Mike: Where would you like to take me now?

Laurie: To the fair.

Mike: Okay, let's go to the fair.

Laurie: I enjoy all these people.

Mike: Tell me what you're seeing.

Laurie: People everywhere, hawking their wares.

Mike: Uhhuh.

Laurie: A lot of fun and laughter.

Mike: Do you go by yourself?

Laurie: No.

Mike: Who's with you?

Laurie: My ladies, and the knights.

Mike: Are you married now? Must be, if they're your ladies.

Laurie: Yes. They watch over me.

Mike: They watch over you? How does it feel to be the queen?

Laurie: A little frightening.

Mike: Okay. Several years have passed. How do you feel about your husband now?

Laurie: I love him, but he still frightens me.

Mike: Why?

Laurie: Hummmmm. He's loud sometimes. He speaks loud.

Mike: And you're very quiet and gentle.

Laurie: I don't know if he loves me.

Mike: Why do you love him?

Laurie: I'm supposed to love him.

Mike: Okay. Kind of a duty thing?

Laurie: Yes.

Mike: Okay.

Laurie: I respect him.

Mike: Have you become better friends with Merlin now?

Laurie: Yes.

Mike: Has he started to teach you things?

Laurie: Yes.

Mike: He has told me that he likes to sit with you every afternoon on a bench in the garden. . . .

Laurie: Uhhuh.

Mike: And teach you things?

Laurie: Uhhuh.

Mike: What does he teach you?

Laurie: He teaches me some of the things that he taught Arthur. Mystical things.

Mike: Yeah . . . what we call magical things?

Laurie: Yes . . . very magical.

Mike: Can you tell me the kind of things he taught you?

Laurie: He taught me how to fly.

Mike: Wow! Neat.

Laurie: Uhhuh.

Mike: Did he ever teach you how to be invisible?

Laurie: Yes. He's the wisest person I know.

Mike: Yes. Did he ever teach you how to shapeshift?

Laurie: Yes.

Mike: Among other things?

Laurie: Yes.

Mike: He did teach you that?

Laurie: He taught me how to be an eagle.

Mike: Wow.

Laurie: A bird.

Mike: Okay. Neat.

Laurie: And I can fly all over the kingdom.

Mike: Okay. Neat.

Laurie: Uhhuh.

Mike: Did he teach you anything about herbs and healing?

Laurie: Yes.

Mike: Aromatherapy?

Laurie: Yes. He taught me all about the flowers too. Flower essences.

Mike: Flower essences. Okay. Did he ever read to you out of his big books?

Laurie: Yes.

Mike: Where did those books come from?

Laurie: I think from maybe the crystal city.

Mike: Okay.

Laurie: From another place.

Mike: Did Merlin ever take you to his chambers? Did you ever get a chance to see where he lives and does his work?

Laurie: Briefly.

Mike: What do they look like?

Laurie: I saw a room that was like . . . I think he was doing something with . . . chemistry. He was . . . what did he say? He was doing some kind of test. Mixing things.

Mike: Uhhuh.

Laurie: Potions.

Mike: Does he drink any kind of potion?

Laurie: Yes.

Mike: What does he drink?

Laurie: There was something . . . he drank it out of this . . . clear flask.

Mike: Okay. What did he take that for?

Laurie: To keep him forever young.

Mike: Okay. Good. Did he ever give you any of that?

Laurie: Yes.

Mike: He did? Oh neat. Did he ever tell you how he made it?

Laurie: I think he did . . . I think he did, but I don't remember.

Mike: Yes. I think he's here and I think he's blocking that. He knows that I will be a mischievous boy and ask the wrong questions. . . . (Laughter.) I sense he has great love for you and great affection for you.

Laurie: Yes. He does. I love him.

Mike: Yes, you have great love for him. You sense his gentleness and his sincerity.

Laurie: Uhhuh. He's always there when I need him.

Mike: Yes. Yes.

Laurie: He gives me great comfort.

Mike: Yes. Well, what is it like to be the queen and be adored by all these knights?

Laurie: Humm. . . . It's fun.

Mike: You like that?

Laurie: Yes.

Mike: Who are some of your favorite knights?

Laurie: Humm. . . . His name is . . . (Long pause.)

Mike: How about Galahad?

Laurie: Humm. . . . Yes, I like Galahad.

Mike: How about Gawaine?

Laurie: Gawaine. . . . That's the one.

Mike: What do you like about Gawaine?

Laurie: He's very strong. They watch over me.

Mike: Yes, he's very loyal to you, isn't he?

Laurie: Very protective.

Mike: Yes, very loyal to you, and Arthur.

Laurie: Yes.

Mike: How about Gaharis?

Laurie: Humm. . . . I like him, but not as much as Gawaine.

Mike: There's a knight that comes along, I think his name is Seg-warides. Does that ever ring a bell?

Laurie: Yes.

Mike: Do you like him?

Laurie: Not particularly. I don't think so. Not as much.

Mike: Is it true that he's your brother?

Laurie: Humm. . . .

Mike: Does that ring a bell?

Laurie: Humm. . . .Yes.

Mike: Okay. But you're not very close to him?

Laurie: No.

Mike: Do you think that Arthur made him a knight just because he was your brother?

Laurie: Probably.

Mike: Okay. Let me mention some other knights. Let's see. How about Lancelot? What do you think of Lancelot?

Laurie: Humm. . . . Yes.

Mike: Do you like him?

Laurie: Yes.

Mike: What's nice about him?

Laurie: He's beautiful.

Mike: Uhhuh.

Laurie: He's kind. He's very, very pure in his love.

Mike: Good. Did you ever . . . there's a younger knight, Percival. . . .

Laurie: Uhhuh.

Mike: What about him?

Laurie: He's very nice.

Mike: Okay. Did you eat in the Great Hall with the knights very often?

Laurie: Sometimes.

Mike: Did your ladies eat with you, or did you just eat by yourself?

Laurie: No, I ate by myself. With Arthur and the men, the knights. I like their laughter.

Mike: Yes, a lot of joking and good-natured. . . .

Laurie: Camaraderie. . . .

Mike: Yes, the camaraderie.

Laurie: They're all like one family. One big family.

Mike: Yes, exactly. Umm, where is the Round Table? Where do they keep the Round Table?

Laurie: It's in this great big room.

Mike: Okay.

Laurie: Large room. Lots of stone walls.

Mike: All right. As the years go by, as you're married to Arthur and enjoying your life there at Camelot, how do your feelings for Arthur develop? Are you beginning to love him more?

Laurie: I'm trying to.

Mike: Is he loving you more?

Laurie: Ummm. . . . I don't think so.

Mike: You don't think so?

Laurie: No, I think he tries maybe.

Mike: Why is it that he doesn't love you? You're very beautiful . . . all the knights love you.

Laurie: He's too busy doing his things.

Mike: Are you saying that he ignores you?

Laurie: Yes.

Mike: Okay. Would you describe yourself as happy now?

Laurie: No.

Mike: You're not happy?

Laurie: No. Very lonely.

Mike: Very lonely. Do you sit in your room a lot alone?

Laurie: Yes.

Mike: What do you do then?

Laurie: I daydream, and I read. I sew. I paint. I do sketching.

Mike: Are you artistic?

Laurie: Yes, somewhat.

Mike: Are your handmaidens able to keep you entertained and happy?

Laurie: No. They try though.

Mike: I sense that you like to be by yourself sometimes.

Laurie: Yes, I do. There I don't have to pretend to be happy.

Mike: Yes. What's happening inside of you as this unhappiness settles into you?

Laurie: I'm very sad. I want to be loved.

Mike: Very unfair, isn't it?

Laurie: Yes. I didn't want to marry him.

Mike: Are you able to discuss this with Merlin?

Laurie: Yes.

Mike: What advice is he able to give you?

Laurie: He said I came to do this.

Mike: That is good advice.

Laurie: Yes. . . . He said I chose to do this.

Mike: He told me, he's explained to me that in his wisdom he knew that he could not interfere.

Laurie: No. It was destined.

Mike: Yes, and he could not interfere in Arthur's free will, as much as he loved Arthur.

Laurie: No.

Mike: I also get the feeling that as you're becoming very sad about Arthur, Merlin is also.

Laurie: Yes, he is.

Mike: And he's also becoming disappointed.

Laurie: Uhhuh.

Mike: In the way that Arthur is developing. And that it's almost as if you two share that grief.

Laurie: Yes, we do.

Mike: And there's a great love there between both of you.

Laurie: Uhhuh.

Mike: He also told me one time that much of the healing he taught you in your earlier years. . . .

Laurie: Uhhuh.

Mike: He taught to you because he knew the future. He could see the future.

Laurie: He knows the future.

Mike: And he knew that you would need to know this healing, in order to heal yourself. Because he wouldn't be there to help you heal. He could not be. Later when the church became very strong.

Laurie: Yes.

Mike: He couldn't. He lost his connection with you.

Laurie: Uhhuh.

Mike: And this was also very sad for both of you.

Laurie: Uhhuh.

Mike: And he missed you very much.

Laurie: Uhhuh.

Mike: Do you have any children?

Laurie: No.

Mike: Is that a source of disappointment?

Laurie: Yes.

Mike: Is that a source of disappointment for Arthur?

Laurie: I think so. Yes. I think that's the only reason he wanted me.

Mike: Is there any possibility that Arthur is being unfaithful to you now?

Laurie: Yes.

Mike: Do you know that?

Laurie: Yes.

Mike: How do you feel about that?

Laurie: Very sad. (Begins to cry.)

Mike: You know, I have some Kleenex here, and I'm going to put some Kleenex in your hand. Because, one of the reasons we do these regressions is so we can feel those old emotions that we're carrying and we can let them out. And I've done a lot of crying myself, reliving my Camelot experience. So, don't feel embarrassed if you want to cry. Because it sounds as if you're still carrying a lot of sadness. We can let it go now.

Laurie: Okay.

Mike: And as you know, Merlin is ageless. And he's still around.

Laurie: Uhhuh.

Mike: And he still loves you as much as he always did. And he would like for you to release that unhappiness and heaviness in your heart. Tell me about Lancelot.

Laurie: I love him.

Mike: How did that happen?

Laurie: We were just together a lot, and it just happened.

Mike: Aren't you worried what this might do to . . . things?

Laurie: Yes. But we can't help it.

Mike: Your need to be loved is so strong?

Laurie: Yes.

Mike: Is he as sincere in his love for you?

Laurie: Yes. He loves me.

Mike: Do you think anybody else has found out about this?

Laurie: I don't know. I hope not.

Mike: Is he able to make you feel loved now?

Laurie: Oh yes.

Mike: So you're happy?

Laurie: Yes. I love being with him. It's very dangerous.

Mike: How does Arthur handle all of this?

Laurie: I think he ignores it.

Mike: Yes. Why are you having difficulty breathing in your chest? Describe your feelings.

Laurie: My heart is beating so hard.

Mike: Yes. Why do you think that is?

Laurie: I think because of my love for him . . . but I'm also frightened. They might find out.

Mike: I would like to take you to a point in time where your fears manifest and Arthur finds out. I'd like you to tell me about it.

Laurie: I'm very sad.

Mike: Yes. Does the Bishop have anything to do with Arthur finding out?

Laurie: I think so.

Mike: What do you think of the Bishop?

Laurie: I think he's evil.

Mike: I thought you were one of his best friends?

Laurie: I think he planned this.

Mike: Okay. Was he your friend initially?

Laurie: Maybe he pretended to be.

Mike: Okay. Would it be safe to say that he, like, tricked you?

Laurie: Yes.

Mike: But you since have decided that he is not good?

Laurie: Yes, not good.

Mike: Okay.

Laurie: I think he's deceptive.

Mike: There was a time when you had to run the kingdom when Arthur was sick. . . .

Laurie: Uhhuh. . . .

Mike: For like a year-and-a-half.

Laurie: Uhhuh.

Mike: How did you feel doing that?

Laurie: I liked it.

Mike: You liked it?

Laurie: Uhhuh.

Mike: Who were your advisors and helpers during this period?

Laurie: Merlin.

Mike: Okay. Oh, you were able to. . . . Yes, you could make the old contact again. You two had an excuse to be together again.

Laurie: Um-hummm.

Mike: Which knights helped you, advised you?

Laurie: Sir Galahad.

Mike: Yes, okay.

Laurie: Lance helped me too.

Mike: Uhhuh. How does Galahad feel about you?

Laurie: I think he loves me.

Mike: Yes, in a very standoffish way.

Laurie: Yes.

Mike: A very shy way.

Laurie: Uhhuh.

Mike: Yes.

Laurie: He's always there.

Mike: He seeks your approval?

Laurie: Yes. Just like a very, very sweet boy.

Mike: Yeah. How is the Bishop doing while you're running the kingdom? Do you find the Bishop helping you, or is he a problem?

Laurie: I think he creates problems in subtle ways.

Mike: Uhhuh. Why is it that Arthur is sick? What's wrong with Arthur?

Laurie: . . . Maybe consumption, or. . . .

Mike: I wish to suggest something to you. Is it possible that Arthur has been poisoned?

Laurie: Humm. . . . Yes.

Mike: Is it possible that the Bishop had him poisoned?

Laurie: There's an evil around the Bishop. There are some that don't like the King. They want him out of the way.

Mike: Oh, they want Arthur out of the way. Arthur has a son who is a knight. I think his name is Mordred.

Laurie: Uhhh.

Mike: How is he?

Laurie: I don't like him.

Mike: You don't like Mordred? He's quite taken with you, I understand.

Laurie: Maybe.

Mike: Okay. You don't like that?

Laurie: I don't think he is nice.

Mike: Why don't you like Mordred?

Laurie: There's a side of him I don't like. I think he wants his father out of the way.

Mike: Why would he want his father out of the way?

Laurie: So that he can become king.

Mike: Ohhhh, okay. That's an old plot, isn't it? Son overthrows father. . . .

Laurie: Mordred creates problems.

Mike: Okay. Why do you think the Bishop does this scheming and plotting? What do you think his objectives are?

Laurie: I think he wants a higher position.

Mike: In Camelot?

Laurie: With Mordred. Yes, in Camelot.

Mike: Yes, go ahead. With Mordred?

Laurie: I think he works along with Mordred.

Mike: How about Mordred's mother, Morgana? How do you feel about her?

Laurie: I don't really know.

Mike: Did you two used to be good friends?

Laurie: I don't feel close to her.

Mike: You don't feel close?

Laurie: No.

Mike: Do you see her very often?

Laurie: Not too often, no.

Mike: Is it possible that she is one of Arthur's lovers? Do you know that?

Laurie: Yes.

Mike: Does that cause you pain?

Laurie: Yes.

Mike: Okay. Where would you like to take me now? Oh, let's go back to the part where Arthur found out about you and Lancelot.

Laurie: Yes.

Mike: What happened?

Laurie: He seemed angry, but he seemed sad.

Mike: Yeah.

Laurie: He's losing both of us.

Mike: How is he losing Lancelot?

Laurie: He loves Lance too. He knows that it's over.

Mike: What does Lancelot do?

Laurie: Lance is very sad. Very saddened by the whole thing.

Mike: Uhhuh. He loves Arthur very much doesn't he?

Laurie: Yes. He wanted to do right.

Mike: Uhhuh. And yet his love for you has caused him to betray Arthur.

Laurie: Yes.

Mike: How are you feeling about this?

Laurie: My heart is breaking.

Mike: Are you feeling guilty?

Laurie: Yes.

Mike: Have you caused a lot of harm?

Laurie: Yes. (Several big sighs.)

Mike: What does Merlin say about this? Have you talked it over with Merlin?

Laurie: He said that it's not my fault.

Mike: Do you believe that?

Laurie: I don't know. He said it was all meant to happen.

Mike: You know that in many of these regressions, Jesus comes down and talks to the people.

Laurie: Uhhuh.

Mike: And I've been asking him to come down and visit with you and explain things, and he's playing some kind of trick on me, because he's up there smiling, saying, "No, you handle it." So, I'm going to talk to you. . . .

Laurie: Okay.

Mike: So that you can release your guilt. You've been carrying it for so long now, it's time for it to go.

Laurie: Yes.

Mike: It's part of the Photon Belt experience, and all that. It's time to cleanse yourself of old harmful emotions. We don't want to go into the new millennium carrying any grief and guilt and sadness. And . . . the message is very simple. Merlin is right. It is not your fault. Arthur betrayed you; you didn't betray Arthur. Arthur betrayed Lancelot.

Arthur betrayed all of the other knights when he did not live by the same code of honor that he set up for his knights.

Laurie: (Crying.)

Mike: Yeah. That's okay. Go ahead and let it out. That is your love for Arthur. And you know what? Because of your love for him, you didn't want to blame him. So you took the blame yourself. Now you can let it out and release it. It's not to be carried anymore. Go ahead, cry it out. Your beloved Arthur, who you all loved so much. The terrible weight in everyone's heart is there because they didn't want to accept the fact that Arthur brought about his own downfall. He was unfaithful to you, and that's what brought about your great loneliness and despair. And as you said earlier, you deserved to be loved. . . .

Laurie: Yes.

Mike: You needed to be loved. And it's Arthur's fault. Had he lived by the same code of ethics as he had given his knights, he would have given you the love you needed. Had he given you this love you sought, as he should have, none of this would have happened.

Laurie: No.

Mike: Had any of his knights behaved the way he behaved. . . .

Laurie: He would have killed them.

Mike: Yes. So it's all okay with you, isn't it?

Laurie: Uhhuh.

Mike: And you know what?

Laurie: What?

Mike: You are the light, pretty little butterfly that you saw in the meadow, the butterfly Merlin loved so much. And your heart can be just as light now as it was in the meadow when you were looking at the flowers, and the sun, and the birds, and the beauty. And it's all okay. The one who most of all wants for you to understand that it's okay and that you shouldn't have any guilt, is Arthur. Arthur's not a bad person.

Laurie: I know.

Mike: That's why you all loved him so much.

Laurie: Uhhuh. I know that.

Mike: Arthur made a little mistake. He got caught up in his power.

Laurie: Yes.

Mike: And that was part of his lesson.

Laurie: Uhhuh.

Mike: But the other thing that's really important, and something that Merlin understood, and he would like for you to understand now, is that it was all meant to happen.

Laurie: Uhhuh. I know that now.

Mike: Yes. Camelot was not meant to last forever. The world wasn't ready for Camelot.

Laurie: No, but we'll have it someday.

Mike: Yes, it's coming again.

Laurie: Yes.

Mike: You did your job. You did your job so well that, some fifteen-hundred years later, everyone dreams of Camelot. So, you know what? Camelot was perfect.

Laurie: Yes.

Mike: You should be like one of those butterflies in that meadow. Very light and very happy about it.

Laurie: I understand.

Mike: Yes. And that heaviness in your chest.

Laurie: Uhhuh.

Mike: Let's just let it go.

Laurie: It's gone.

Mike: Yes. Some angels came down with a big hook, with a chain, like a winch, and they hooked into it and they just hoisted it up and they've taken it off to the light. It was almost like an anvil. A big, heavy weight.

Laurie: Yes.

Mike: And Merlin's smiling very broadly now, and says to me that he always knew he chose well when he picked you to be "his queen." And he says that he wants you to understand how much love you gave to him. His job at Camelot got to be very lonely.

Laurie: Uhhuh.

Mike: Especially when Arthur, his beloved creation, turned his back on him.

Laurie: Uhhuh.

Mike: And you filled the gap. In the love that you gave to him, and the love he held for you.

Laurie: I loved him.

Mike: It was very, very important to him.

Laurie: Yes.

Mike: And he will always appreciate and thank you for that. And he's going to always be around.

Laurie: I appreciate his love.

Mike: Anything else you'd like to visit?

Laurie: I'd like to go to the meadow again.

Mike: Good, let's go back there.

Laurie: And make crowns of flowers.

Mike: Okay. Merlin told me he searched far and wide for the perfect queen. And it was not only external beauty, but he was looking for internal beauty in the heart and purity of heart. Because he needed a queen who matched the idealism and the nobility of the movement. Of their Round Table. And you did a magnificent job.

Laurie: Thank you.

Mike: You were a great blessing for them. You were God's blessings for them at Camelot.

Laurie: We were happy for a while.

Mike: Yes, and now you can be happy again.

Laurie: Yes.

Mike: You did your job perfectly.

Laurie: Will I see Lance again?

Mike: Sure . . . especially now that the guilt is gone.

Laurie: I'm glad it's gone. It feels like a weight has been lifted.

Mike: He will be coming back into your life. So you two can take another plunge into exploring your love for each other.

Laurie: I look forward to that.

Mike: Yes, and you can help him deal with his guilt that he still carries. And you can help him a lot.

Laurie: Umhum. I will.

Mike: Yes. Are we in the meadow?

Laurie: Yes.

Mike: Would you like to stay there a while, or are you ready to come back?

Laurie: We can leave.

Mike: Ok. You can come back any time now.

9

Susan as Marlinda
April 1994

Background: It was at Susan's house in Gainesville that I regressed Steve. On my next trip up to Gainesville, I showed off my new-found prowess at doing regressions by regressing Susan. What a delight and amazement to find out that she was Percival's sister, and was also Persant's wife at Camelot. The insight she gave into Percival's childhood was helpful to me. Also, her close connection with Guenivere gives an interesting perspective about the Queen. That she did not ever know that her father was Merlin is also interesting.

Susan: I'm sick as a child. It's a fever.
Mike: Is it an epidemic?
Susan: (Big sigh.) I'm a little girl. Mother has these herbs, and she has these wet cloths. And she has these herbs, and she keeps putting them on my body and she is making me drink herbal teas. And I'm having delusions. I'm not in my body and I'm not in my mind, because of the fever.
Mike: What are you experiencing?
Susan: Actually, it's very peaceful. Very white and light. I'm not in pain. This is very peaceful.
Mike: Go past that period of illness to some other point in your childhood. Get away from that fever.
Susan: You were there. You've been observing mother at work, and you're a little older than I am. You're my brother.
Mike: What do I look like?
Susan: You appear to be around perhaps eleven- or twelve-years old, and I see you with brown hair. And you're certainly not sickly at all. You do not have a large build, but you're certainly not thin either. Just a medium build.
Mike: Uhhuh.

Susan: You are puzzled, and concerned. You've just been observing this time of illness and watching your mother at work and being very quiet. Lots of depth with you, but I also sense a longing. Something missing. Wanting to, it's like you're being pulled. There's a restlessness. And I know the time's growing near that you are leaving. It's almost like I see this energy field that's pulling you.

Mike: Yeah, I'm about a year away from leaving home.

Susan: Yes. And there is a . . . I sense a younger sibling.

Mike: Yes, another sister.

Susan: Okay. Yes, and she's younger than I am. Again, she is just observing everything. Very sensitive child.

Mike: What does your mom look like?

Susan: Oh, she's got such a sweet face. Her features are real soft. And warm, and her hair is long, and she has it pulled back. And I'm seeing it like a light-brown color. And there's no face that I'd rather see on the face of the earth than her face. I mean, it's that kind of face. It's very gentle and loving. Not a beautiful woman, but very attractive woman. And VERY disciplined and focused, and VERY strong in her faith. Nothing takes her off this beam. I mean, she knows what her mission is; she's very clear. And she's made quite a sacrifice to be alone and raising us three kids. And knowing that she's going to have to let us go soon. You being the first.

Mike: Uhhuh.

Susan: Uh, the third child is somewhat frail. She doesn't have the strength that you do. And although I got the fever, I was not a frail, sickly child. Like this one is a little more frail and needs Momma's care and attention more than we do. And mother teaches us about herbs. And there's a ritual that we have in our home. And there's symbols, and I'm seeing the two inverted triangles, or pyramids, come together to form like, what do we call that?

Mike: It's a hexagram.

Susan: Yes. And it's contained in a circle. And then I see the cross, like a Maltese Cross, but it's even more rounded. There's a lot of circles. There may be things in the circles, but everything seems to have a circle to it.

Mike: Where's your dad?

Susan: He's not there.

Mike: Does he come to see you?

Susan: It's been a very long time, and I really don't remember him. There's simply the sense of a man on a horse leaving, and I can only see the back of him.

Mike: Okay. Tell us about when you left home.

Susan: I was a teenager, mid-teens, I would think. Fifteen, sixteen. And I was sent to a castle, because I had cousins there. There were relatives there. And I was sent there to continue my education. Mother had done the best that she could, with the limitations that she had. And certain schools, schooling us in . . . when I say the "Arts," I mean the Cosmic Arts. These were not "arts" as we know them today. The Art of Divining, and the Art of Herbs, and Potions and Rituals. But anyway, we were sent, and we learned how to read. But we were also sent there because mother thought it would give us opportunities and we needed to interact with other people. And she knew it was time. But there was much that she knew that she didn't tell us kids. She also felt it her duty to protect us. And there were certain things that we were too young to know. And we would find out when the timing was right. And so we were sent to this castle. . . . I seem to be assigned to serve or to help an older relative, who was introduced as something like a cousin. A woman. A young woman. And she wasn't married yet, but she was waiting. Like a "Lady in Waiting."

Mike: What was her name?

Susan: It was Guenivere.

Mike: I see you two talking.

Susan: We talked a lot. I was her best friend.

Mike: Had she met the man she was going to marry?

Susan: You know, it's not clear, because the strength of her heart, it was so strong. Whether she'd met him or not, she already knew him in her heart, and she literally pined away for him day and night. And I don't know if she'd met him at that point, or seen him in a dream. But I can almost see the energy streaming from her heart, drawing this man, like a magnet, to her. It's almost like she knew that she had a destiny, and that it was big. And she held, this is interesting, because again she held such a focus of energy for this man. Well, we might call it an obsession today, but it wasn't. It was perfectly natural and wonderful.

Mike: It was focus.

Susan: It was focus. And I can remember asking her if she would help me hold a focus to bring mine also to me. Because I was beginning to long for that companionship that she already had in her heart. Whether she had met him at that point or not, I'm not clear.

Mike: So. . . .

Susan: You know, he was literally in her head and her heart, twenty-four hours a day. Even when she was painting. She was an artist, you know. She painted fine canvas. And she would go out into the gardens and the courtyard, and I would watch her. I'd go with her. I was like a shadow in many ways, with her. Attending her and all. But also, like a sister. Very close. Even when she was painting, and she was concentrating, cause she would paint like beautiful. . . .

The gardens, she would paint that, within the walls. She painted him, also. He was never out of her head and her heart. . . . And he came, and we left, and I went with them.

Mike: Where did you go?

Susan: Humm. . . . A much larger castle. And much lighter. The one we were at before was smaller and very gray. This seemed to be made of lighter stone. And she became his queen. . . . (Laughs.) And she helped me trap my knight.

Mike: Tell me about it. I see you two plotting, checking him out.

Susan: (Laughing.) Uhhuh. Oh dear, I'm a little embarrassed.

Mike: She was very protective of her ladies-in-waiting, wasn't she?

Susan: Oh yes, but she was also extremely sensitive and psychic. And, she also knew that maybe the situation . . . maybe he needed a little encouragement. So, we just worked out some potions and things and ritual. . . . (Laughing.)

Mike: You wouldn't happen to have those formulas, would you? (Laughing.)

Susan: Oh, my goodness.

Mike: (Jokingly.) Careful, don't tell me about any potions. I might concoct them.

Susan: And it worked.

Mike: Like, you slipped it in his beverage?

Susan: He didn't know what hit him; he didn't have a clue. It was a secret we took to our grave.

Mike: Why did you have to use potions on him? Was he too shy? Did he lack self-confidence?

Susan: Right.

Mike: Yeah. He was probably so focused on being a knight.

Susan: Right. You see, people were much more focused then. Much more focused on what they were doing than we are now. We're so distracted now.

Mike: How did you get the potion to him? Can you share your secret with me?

Susan: Well, I had friends in "high places." (Laughs.) The people in the kitchen who prepared the grog.

Mike: I'm seeing that. I'm seeing the tray with one cup off to the side, and I'm seeing the steward or somebody making sure that that one got placed in front of your man.

Susan: And we watched. We had our location where we could see what was going on.

Mike: I see that, yes.

Susan: And we also devised a formula, and it's what we call perfume, but it's much more than that. It was an aphrodisiac. And she put it on me. He didn't have a chance.

Mike: I see you two laughing and joking about what's going to happen if the wrong person gets that cup.

Susan: Yeah. But it wasn't the wrong person at all.

Mike: (Laughter.) How long, how many months later were you married?

Susan: You know, I'm not sure. The first thing that came to me was nine months, but I'm not sure. It seemed like he had to leave, and there was a period of being away. I don't know, though, I'm not sure.

Mike: What was your wedding like?

Susan: It was beautiful. There was a lot of . . . there was a lot of blue there. And beautiful . . . there was a lot of celebration. (Laughter.) Let's see, I slept with him before the wedding.

Mike: Okay.

Susan: (Still laughing.) That was fun. He didn't forget me when he went away. See, that was the thing. That helped keep his focus where it needed to be, on me.

Mike: So you slept with him before he went away?

Susan: Yes, yeah.

Mike: What was the court like? What was it like, being part of the court?

Susan: It was wonderful. Not that everyone there was wonderful. And there were many people there. You know, the first thing that I'm seeing, it's a huge, round room. That we only went into for special occasions. And the men more so. I mean, the women knew it was there, but we didn't really go in there very much. But we were developed enough within our own God Presence, within our own female intuition. And Guenivere was a very wise woman. I learned a great deal from her. And she learned from my energy as well. It was not just me taking from her, but there was a mutual benefit there. So we were very close. But there were those there, in the court, that were not trustworthy. And, fortunately, we knew who they were for the most part. We were able to devise our ways of being better at their game than they were, just because we had an edge because of knowing some of the finer arts. I'm talking about spiritual arts now. It was always such excitement preparing for the men coming. It was a very happy time. There was much to keep us busy. There would be people visiting from other countries, which was always exciting because they would bring news and goods. New oils, new cloth. It was a happy time.

Mike: Let's move ahead in time.

Susan: There's a female child. She's mine.

Mike: Are you still living at Camelot?

Susan: I don't think so.

Mike: How do you feel about your little child?

Susan: There's a great loneliness. I think I've moved ahead here. Having left that happy period, maybe I'm not in Camelot. I'm just feeling . . . I've got this female child and we're very alone. And I worry for the safety of her father, and I wonder if he's going to come back. And that is really taking a lot from me. I must be in a different place now. I'm not feeling that protection that I felt when I was in Camelot.

90

Mike: How do you feel in the house?

Susan: I'm in a different place. I'm alone. This is not a comfortable feeling for me. . . . There was only one child. (Big sigh.)

Mike: What is it?

Susan: . . . She died. (She starts crying.)

Mike: What was it?

Susan: It was like a fever. And I felt so guilty, cause I couldn't save her like my mother had saved me. And I couldn't save her . . . and I was alone. I mean there wasn't anyone, my husband wasn't there, there wasn't anyone who had any greater powers to help me. And I felt guilty because I wasn't able to save her. That I should have been able to do more.

Mike: Do you live near to Camelot?

Susan: I don't know. . . . I'm older and have been alone for sometime. I'm in a totally different place now, and I'm with other women. Women like myself. Some could have called us witches, but we weren't. We were practicing the arts, more like the druids. But we found solace and protection with one another. And that's how I died. I was killed. We were all killed there.

Mike: How were you killed? Who killed you? Did you kill yourself?

Susan: Uh uh. . . . There were those sent out to seek us out and destroy us. Arthur was not in rule anymore, and we were seen as a threat to Christianity because of our practices and beliefs. And the men were sent out to destroy us. They called themselves knights, but they weren't. And they were sent out to spy on us, and they killed us. With swords.

Mike: What had happened to King Arthur's knights?

Susan: They were all gone. But these who came to seek us out, there were three with no hearts, and one with a heart. And the one with a heart, when he realized that they should not do this, it was too late. He wasn't able to stop them.

Mike: Where was your husband?

Susan: I don't know.

Mike: Had he died?

Susan: He just never came back.

Mike: Did you ever have any recollection of him dying in battle, or otherwise leaving?

Susan: I'm not sure.

Mike: What I'm sensing is that your husband died. And when your husband was killed, you asked to leave Camelot. And you went out and ended up living alone, out of solace. But then, eventually the loneliness got very oppressive, and you were sorry that you had isolated yourself so. You kind of had repeated the pattern of your mother. That's what you saw your mother do, so you went and did it also. But it wasn't a really good thing to have done. She had done it for a specific purpose. There was no reason to do it again.

Susan: Hummmm.

Mike: Could we now go back to the time when you did live in Camelot?

Susan: Uhhuh.

Mike: What kind of room did you live in? What were your quarters? What did they have for you to live in?

Susan: Well, at one time when I first went there, I was sharing a room with other ladies. And then that changed when I married, I had my own quarters then. And they were smaller, but they were very nice.

Mike: You and your husband lived there?

Susan: Uhhuh.

Mike: Tell me what the colors were like. The uniforms they wore, what you wore, the kind of dresses. Let's go to one of the festive occasions, one of the balls or festivals. When you're dining with the knights.

Susan: Such pretty clothes. I always dressed pretty, but this was special. And this would be a time when we would put things in our hair. Flowers, if they were available. And the veil-like materials, like silks. And the men wore the brighter colors, the women wore more, what for me was more pastel. And they all had their coat of arms, their symbols. And they were sooo beautiful, so powerful.

We had the understanding what those symbols meant. And you see, the women would do so much more. First of all, we held a focus for the men. Not only did we pray for their safety, but we held a focus. But also, there were certain candles we would light, and certain recitings that we would do for them, for their protection. And then there would be certain oils that we would use for anointing. Even when they were away our protection helped, because of the level of work that we were doing. We knew in our minds that there was no such thing as distance. And we would work to create a force field of protection around them. That would make them invisible when they needed to be.

God knows why it didn't work for my husband when he was killed. But I know that it worked for a number of years, very well. The men honored us so much, they knew the importance of our work. They believed it. Though we didn't talk a lot about it, there was no need to. But they knew, and honored the help that the women were doing. It wasn't like we were just back in the castle, learning how to cook, or you know, how to look beautiful and take care of the babies. Our work was so much more important than that. And we were much more honored than many of the women are today.

Mike: Did you ever see your brother at the castle?

Susan: Oh yes. Oh yeah.

Mike: How was he doing?

Susan: Absolutely wonderful.

Mike: Did he marry?

Susan: Yes, yeah.

Mike: Did they live in Camelot?

Susan: Yes, they did for a while. They had boys, you know.

Mike: Uhhuh. How were things with Guenivere and Arthur when you left the castle? Was it still a storybook romance?

Susan: There was a depth of love like none I have ever known. Storybook? No, it was much greater than any story that people know now. It was like a twin flame. It was deep, very deep. See, she had love for so many people, not just women and not just for her husband. But for the knights as well, and sometimes this was misinterpreted by those in the court who were not of the consciousness, or not of the fabric she was. I understood her because I knew her so well. But others didn't. And even then there were jealousies of those who were less evolved. That would create problems. . . . And there were some problems.

Mike: Tell me about them.

Susan: There were those there who were practicing what we would call the black magic. And, because there were enough people there that they had won over, it was beginning to put a niche into things. And things were beginning to unravel.

Mike: Who was doing this, what kind of people? Church people, or just people in the court, or knights?

Susan: At that time, it was more the people in the court. They were jealous, they were not as evolved. The knights were really too busy to be involved in such chicanery. And later, there was that element that we call the Christian, coming in. But then, once that wedge had been put in through the misuse of the energy, what we call the practice of the black arts. . . . Now, Merlin, I see him at a distance. And I don't know why, but his presence was not there all the time. And I see, the more that he was away, the more that the other came in. It's like, you know, when he was there, he was able to keep a check on it. But there were times when, for whatever reason, he wasn't there, cause I'm seeing now, the back of Merlin at a distance. And, as that energy was not there as much as he could have been, that was one reason, but not the total reason. But there was just the jealousies of those people in the court, and the lack of spiritual evolution they did not have. And they caused problems.

Mike: What are you seeing now?

Susan: I'm praying for Guenivere and for Arthur, and for all that I know that are for the good of the kingdom. I just feel myself doing a lot of praying because there's a need. There's a feeling; it's an ominous feeling. It's like, kind of like a dark cloud. Even when there are no clouds in the sky, it was kind of like that feeling of a dark cloud coming over. For those of us that were sensitives, we could feel it and sense it. But then I was also dealing with my own dark cloud energy of loneliness. And I felt that perhaps I could do more good by playing the role that my mother had, of going off to almost like an asylum. And yet, you know, it wasn't really the thing for me to do.

Mike: Tell me your recollections of Merlin. Do you ever remember talking to him? Or what does he look like? How did he dress?

Susan: His eyes would dance when he talked, always filled with light and wisdom. And for me, he was always so kind. Like the father I never had. I mean, he always was so loving and always had time for me, even though he was very busy. I never felt that busyness. Yes, I did have interactions with him, and he was very helpful to me in perfecting the arts that my mother had been teaching and sharing. And some of the potions and things that we'd get ourselves involved in. He was . . . delightful.

Mike: Did he take a special interest in you?

Susan: Absolutely. Very special. I was always so honored. You know, there were so many there that would have loved his time, and yet, when you were with him, you never felt that he was in a hurry. He never gave you that impression. And he loved animals. He always had an animal somewhere on his being, like a bird or an owl or . . . he really liked birds a lot. And he had wonderful rings that were fascinating to me. He didn't always wear a cape, but I always remembered seeing him in a lot of white. Like white, always a white . . . I don't want to call it a shirt; it's more like a blouse. Like a poet's, you know. It had the ruffles, and not the buttons but the tie here. And then he'd wear darker colored pants. But there would always be color on color. On his pants, he always wore a velvet-like stripe going down the side of the leg of his pants. There was a lot of grey, as we've seen pictures and all. His hair was long, and had a lot of grey in it. And yet he never seemed to age. I mean he always seemed to remain the same age. He didn't seem to age like others did. And even though it seemed that he was kind of ageless, there was like a spryness to his step. He never walked as if he were out of energy. There was always a little bounce to his step. He was delightful for me.

Mike: You said he was almost as if he was your father. Could he have been your father?

Susan: I didn't know it at the time, but I think he could have been.

Mike: Do you sense it now?

Susan: Uhhuh.

Mike: That's why he had the special time for you.

Susan. Yeah.

Mike: It was your mother's great secret.

Susan: (Big sigh.)

Mike: What are you doing now?

Susan: I was just aware that my decision to leave Camelot was made in haste, and I did not take him into my counsel. For some reason, he wasn't there when I left Camelot. And I don't remember seeing him after that.

Mike: And you don't remember exactly what happened to your husband? He just went off and didn't come back from one of his trips?

Susan: That's right.

Mike: Your husband's armor, his weapons and his breastplate and helmet and all of that. Who took care of that? Did he take care of that, or did you take care of it, or did he have people do that?

Susan: There were others who did that, who took great honor in doing so. There were young men.

Mike: And he had horses?

Susan: Yes.

Mike: How many horses did he have, do you remember?

Susan: There were three, but his favorite . . . the dark one.

Mike: Was it a stallion?

Susan: Absolutely.

Mike: Was it black?

Susan: Yes.

Mike: How did he get the stallion?

Susan: He earned it. He won it.

Mike: What was his favorite weapon?

Susan: Well, I see several. First, there's a shorter sword. And then a longer one, and then there's this thing that looks like an anchor. Not an anchor, what do you call that? That you throw? And the javelin. There were several, and he was good at all of them.

Mike: What did he look like?

Susan: Oh, he was the most handsome man on earth to me.

Mike: You had a happy marriage?

Susan: Oh yes. I wanted no other. He was it.

Mike: Do you recall how many years you were married?

Susan: The only figure that comes to me is six.

Mike: What are you doing now?

Susan: I'm just in a place of peace. It's all light, maybe in the afterlife, the next dimension.

Mike: Are you back with your husband?

Susan: I don't feel anything but light around me.

Mike: I never did ask you what your name was.

Susan: What was my name? . . . You know, I'm not getting anything clearly, but the interesting thing is, it's like a "M-A-R" energy. I'm not saying it's Mary. It's not Mary. But it has that same vibration to it, the

"MAR" energy. It could have been Maranda, it could have been . . . you know, something like that.

Mike: How about Martha?

Susan: Yes, it could have. . . .

Mike: Marsha? . . . Pretty close?

Susan: But it's the same "M-A-R" energy.

Mike: It's almost like your name was a takeoff on "Merlin."

Susan: It could have even been M-E-R.

Mike: Marlinda seems to come to mind. I'll dowse later and get your name correctly.

Susan: Yes. Marlinda sounds right.

Mike: What else would you like to be remembered about your experience?

Susan: I was very devoted to the cause. To Camelot, to the cause, to the knights. To all they represented. It was a very high energy, and I was a part of that. And in my own small but significant way, I held a focus of light for that. So that it can continue, even now, and in an even higher form. Even higher energy. And ultimately, the whole thing is about ascension. I don't know if that is what you asked me or not, but that's just what it feels like it was all about.

Mike: Anything else you'd like to say, or are you ready to come back?

Susan: I'm ready to come back.

Mike: Okay, thank you very much for a nice visit.

Susan: Thank you.

10

Multiple Reincarnations

One of my first regressions was a lady who was Guenivere. It was a great regression, with a wonderful message. About a week later, another lady came to me for a regression. We regressed her and she was Guenivere. It was another great regression, great message, and a very fulfilling experience for her. But this regression left me quite confused, if not in a bit of shock. How could there be two Gueniveres? Well, as I was to find out over the next few years, there are many Gueniveres out there. Just as there are many Lancelots, and many Arthurs, etc. What I had run into was the situation of multiple reincarnations.

Since I ran into this phenomenon, I have discovered that it is discussed in a number of metaphysical texts. There are a number of various ways to explain it. For instance, let's take Guenivere. My understanding is that during this present lifetime, Guenivere, the original Guenivere, is operating as an "Oversoul." That's Oversoul with a capital "O." The Oversoul is sometimes referred to also as the Higher Self. The Oversoul Guenivere is in charge of the lives of a number of people who are living on the earth today. They are all fragments of Guenivere. Each of these fragments is seeking certain lessons, or is working on specific issues. This allows the Oversoul Guenivere to deal with multiple issues at the same time, or to resolve many issues at the same time. As an example, for purposes of this discussion, let's say that the Oversoul Guenivere is directing the lives of fifteen people who are alive on this earth right now. That means that the Oversoul Guenivere could be dealing with fifteen separate issues.

I use Guenivere as an example because I regressed more Gueniveres than any other person at Camelot. There were some clearly defined issues that were easily recognizable among all of these various Gueniveres:

1. Guilt about the betrayal of Arthur
2. Guilt about the betrayal of Camelot

3. Authority and Responsibility
4. Greed (desire) to possess Lancelot
5. Failure to have children
6. Not being loved and honored by Arthur
7. Being abandoned by Arthur
8. Love (soul connection) for Arthur

By Guenivere operating as an Oversoul during this life period, she is able to deal with all of these issues at the same time, and is therefore able to progress much faster in her own soul's development than would be the case if she were here as one person.

Another analogy that I use is a squad of soldiers. Picture if you will, a squad of soldiers. If the squad of soldiers stays together, it is able to go out and perform one task. However, if the squad leader (the Oversoul) directs each individual soldier to go on a separate mission, and then to return to the squad after he has accomplished the mission, multiple missions may be completed. As an example, this squad needs to forage for food. The squad leader might send one soldier out for water, another soldier out to hunt meat, another soldier out to dig for roots, and one out to a nearby cornfield to pick corn. He might send another soldier down to the river to fish, and another soldier to climb trees and look for birds' eggs. In this way, the squad leader would be able to have each of those individual soldiers perform separate missions, and then return to the group when the missions are complete, thereby greatly increasing the scope of the squad's mission. This basically is the same thing that seems to have been done during this life period, when so many of the Camelot figures are split into multiple segments or fragments.

There's another analogy I can use. Picture, if you will, the Oversoul as an octopus, an octopus which is up in heaven. But it has many arms extending down onto the Earth plane. An octopus has many arms, and picture if you will, that at the end of each of these eight arms there is a person. So the octopus is able to gather eight separate experiences at once, but it is still one octopus. That's another way that I can grasp and understand the concept of multiple reincarnations.

As I began to get more comfortable with this concept of multiple reincarnations, I began to see a certain wisdom and beauty to this system of soul fragmentation. During a number of the Guenivere regressions, I took the person being regressed back to the first time when Guenivere saw Arthur. And in each experience, the setting was the same. Guenivere was standing in a second-story window of her parent's home and saw Arthur through the window. Arthur was arriving on horseback in the courtyard below. He was with his entourage, and he was coming to court her and seek her hand in marriage. In each of these regressions, the physical setting was the same, but the perspective of each individual Guenivere was different. Each Guenivere saw the situation in a different context or a different light. The Guenivere who had the soul connection to Arthur felt immediate love for the young man she viewed through the window. The Guenivere who was dealing with the darker issue of guilt saw Arthur as just an attractive young man with long hair. The Guenivere who was dealing with responsibility and authority viewed Arthur in terms of someone who was coming to take her away to a new lifestyle with greater responsibility. Each soul fragment saw the experience from her particular perspective.

11

Barb as Guenivere May, 1994

Background: I had not met Barb until the day of the regression. She was a 34-year-old beautician from Palatka, Florida. She had driven two hours to Orlando to have this regression with me. She already had a belief that she was Guenivere. Normally I prefer subjects who have no preformed beliefs, as this assures me of getting information that has not been "contaminated" by prior influences (books, movies, etc.). But the intensity of her regression left me with no doubt that we were dealing with truth. This was probably the most emotional experience I encountered in all of the regressions. Barb was so emotionally drained at the end of the session that she could not rise from the sofa for 45 minutes. Then it was another hour before she could walk well enough to get to her car.

Mike: Let's go to the castle where you grew up. Can we do that?
Barb: Okay. I'm in the kitchen having breakfast.
Mike: You say it's breakfast time in the kitchen? I see the kitchen people scurrying around, fixing some kind of porridge. Cooking some meat. I see a little girl, helping and watching, joking with the cook. A lot of love, a lot of friendship in that kitchen. Good energies. Do you pick that up?
Barb: Uhhuh.
Mike: Tell me what it's like.
Barb: I . . . it's like I'm talking to them about why we have to kill the animals to eat them. I don't want to do that. I don't want to eat the animals.
Mike: Okay. What are they telling you?
Barb: Well, they're trying to explain it to me. That it's okay. That is what the animals are for. But it doesn't matter to me.

100

Mike: Who all is there with you?

Barb: I'm not really aware of any particular person, just . . . seems like there is one woman who's in charge of the kitchen. And there's several other women and girls there who are just workers. And I'm basically there under foot. But there's no problem with me being there. I'm just asking a lot of questions and following them around and that kind of thing.

Mike: How are you dressed?

Barb: I seem to have a loose shift on. It's warm. It's like summertime.

Mike: How do the people in the kitchen feel toward you? Do they like you? Do they love you?

Barb: Yeah, they do. It's like I'm, yeah, they really seem to care a lot about me. I'm not aware of their love as I'm there. But, as I'm looking back, I see that they seem to mother me. It seems as if I had a lot of maternal type energies around me.

Mike: Are you a boy or a girl?

Barb: I'm a girl. My hair is naturally wavy or curly, kind of like it is now. But it's lighter in color, it's not as dark as my hair is now. But I have a lot of hair and it's in tight waves, curls.

Mike: Why don't we leave the kitchen now and go out to the dining room, and see who is out there. They are fixing breakfast, aren't they?

Barb: They're preparing some meal.

Mike: Yeah, okay. Let's go out to the dining room and look at your family. And tell me who's out there.

Barb: I'm not really getting any information about that.

Mike: Do you see anybody?

Barb: No.

Mike: All right. Let's go look at your mother. I'd like to see your mother. Let's go to wherever your mother is. Go see your mother and tell me what she looks like.

Barb: Well, she's . . . sitting in front of an opening. I guess we'd call it a window. But it's not really a window, it's more like an opening. And she's doing some kind of sewing.

Mike: What does she look like?

Barb: Well, her hair is a little darker than mine as a child. Well, maybe she's got something on her head.

Mike: Is she pretty?

Barb: Uhhuh. She's beautiful.

Mike: Does she seem to be happy?

Barb: Yeah, she's alone in the room there. Oh, there's another girl in the room with her, helping her do whatever she is doing with the sewing. This other girl kind of has a reddish cast to her hair.

Mike: Do you sense that you're the only daughter?

Barb: I'm not feeling any other children around.

Mike: How about a brother?

Barb: Well, if there's a brother, it's an older brother. I'm not sure, seems like there might be an older brother.

Mike: Okay.

Barb: I don't know.

Mike: What kind of house do you live in?

Barb: Well, I'm seeing . . . it's made out of stone and it's quite large.

Mike: Could it be a castle?

Barb: Yeah, cause I run and play in it. In the halls, and in and out, up and down the stairs and the stones. I'm barefoot a lot. When I can be barefoot, I'm barefoot.

Mike: Could we go visit your father now?

Barb: He seems to be gone. He seems to be gone a lot, like he comes and goes. But it's a busy place. There's a lot going on.

Mike: How do you feel towards your father?

Barb: I love him. It feels like maybe there's a real special connection between us. But yet, he's not there a lot.

Mike: What does he do for a living?

Barb: I don't know what he does for a living. There's land. He rides a horse.

Mike: Do you know what your father's name is?

Barb: No.

Mike: Do you know what your name is?

Barb: (Big sigh.) Well, I think my name's Guenivere, but I'm not sure. It's not said exactly the way I just said it. And I'm also called different things.

Mike: How is it said? How is it pronounced?

Barb: I don't know. I just know it's not pronounced the way I pronounced it. I'm hearing. . . . Sometimes there are those that call me, like, "Vera." And I also hear something like "Wen" something. I just don't know.

Mike: Are you a happy little girl?

Barb: Uhhuh.

Mike: Do you have other little girls to play with?

Barb: Yes. I like it as a child, there doesn't seem to be any problems. It's a very carefree childhood. I'm just oblivious to worry. If there's any problems or anything going on around me, I'm totally oblivious to it. Seems like it's very secure. I feel loved and secure and just unaware. If there's any problems, I'm unaware of them.

Mike: I'd like to move on in your life to when you're about fifteen-years-old. Can you do that? Can you see yourself as a fifteen-year-old young lady?

Barb: Well, I think I see myself. And I'm in a bed chamber. The bed sets up higher on a stone ledge. The floor where the bed sits is higher than the other part of the chamber. And there are furs on the bed and around on the floor. Skins or something, but with fur on it. I'm sitting, and someone is plaiting my hair, doing something with my hair.

Mike: How are you dressed?

Barb: I'm wearing a shift again. I haven't gotten dressed yet, I'm just wearing a shift.

Mike: Do you have a boyfriend?

Barb: It seems like there's someone.

Mike: What's he like?

Barb: Uh, seems like he's coming to where I live to visit. Or else I'm getting ready to go down where he is. And there's a lot of excitement and anticipation in me.

Mike: Do you think this is the man that you'll marry?

Barb: Feels like it.

Mike: Have you ever met him before?

Barb: The first thing that comes to me to say is that I've seen him before.

Mike: Okay.

Barb: But I don't feel like I really . . . I'm not sure if I really know him. But I know I've seen him before. It seems like I've probably led a very sheltered life. I. . . .

Mike: Didn't you have a visitor to the castle a year or two before? A young boy who was really quite taken with you, and had quite a crush on you? Do you remember that? (Here I am referring to Percival's visit.)

Barb: Seems like maybe, yeah. I'm not sure.

Mike: Do a lot of boys have crushes on you?

Barb: I'm not aware of it. May have been, but I wasn't probably aware of it in that way.

Mike: How does your mother feel about you meeting this young man who is perhaps going to marry you?

Barb: It seems to be okay with her. It seems as though maybe she . . . she's not really unsure, but she is like a mother that just doesn't really want to see her daughter have to leave. But it seems like that the decision has already been made.

Mike: Made by whom?

Barb: I assume my father.

Mike: How does your father feel about your being married?

Barb: Well, it seems to be what I'm supposed to do.

Mike: Why don't we go ahead in time now to when you do meet this man, when you are with him. Tell me what it's like.

Barb: Well, the first thing that comes to me is that he brings out shyness in me, and I'm NOT ordinarily shy. I have sort of a wild streak in me, an independent streak I should say. But now I'm unsure. I'm more shy around him. I'm happy, I'm real happy to be with him. It feels like it's something that I'm real glad to be doing.

Mike: What does he look like?

Barb: I'm not getting any really clear images.

Mike: Can you sense how old he is?

Barb: Not really, he may be a year or two older than I am. I'm not sure.

Mike: Okay. Can we go to your wedding?

Barb: Well, I see springtime. I don't know if it is the wedding, but that's the first thing that comes when you say wedding. I see springtime. And I see lots of flowers. And I'm riding on a horse, that has a beautiful type of blanket, only it's really not a blanket. I don't really know what it is.

Mike: Is your father next to you on a horse?

Barb: Uhhuh. . . .

Mike: Where's your mother?

Barb: I don't see her. I know she's there, but I don't know where she is.

Mike: Where's the ceremony held? Inside or outside?

Barb: I don't see the ceremony. It feels like maybe it was held outside, but I. . . . It feels like maybe there was something going on outside and something going on inside, too. And I think that I really wanted. . . . I like to be outside. I like to be outside. I'm really not getting anything real clear.

Mike: Okay. Why don't you tell me what your marriage is like. What's it like being married? Tell me whatever you want to share with us, so we'll know how you felt during those days.

Barb: Well, it feels like there's a lot of responsibilities that I have that I . . . I'm not really sure I'm prepared for. Like overseeing a household, and I . . . I can't run barefooted anymore. And I have to keep my hair, and I have to do my hair differently. I can't let it just fly like I would like to. I have to do other things with it.

Mike: What does your husband do?

Barb: Well, I see horses. I know he rides a horse. And people come and go, men come and go. And he talks to them a lot. I don't really think about. . . .

Mike: About that.

Barb: Yes, he talks to me, but I. . . . In my home before this, before I was married, I was very protected from what was going on in the world. It seems as though in many ways, that that is the same. There are times that I'm aware that things are taking place, but I. . . .

Mike: Are there men around your husband all the time? Does he have business friends or associates?

Barb: Yeah, I guess. Yeah. There's lots of people around all the time.

Mike: Is there an older man who is always advising him named Merlin?

Barb: Seems like, yeah, seems like there is. Kind of like a father to him, but it's not his father.

Mike: How is Merlin's relationship with you?

Barb: It feels fine. I don't feel any negative energies at all.

Mike: Does he spend time with you, teaching you things?

Barb: It seems as though he does. It seems sometimes the bird comes. . . . Sometimes the bird comes and sits on the window ledge, and sometimes it comes and sits on my hand, my arm.

Mike: What color's the bird?

Barb: It's black, kind of bluish black.

Mike: It's Merlin's bird?

Barb: I think so.

Mike: Does Merlin teach you things that you need to know?

Barb: I think that he probably does, yes.

Mike: Do you have any children?

Barb: You know I feel that there was early on a child lost, that I didn't carry.

Mike: How long have you been married?

Barb: About two years, I think.

Mike: Okay. Are you happy?

Barb: Yes.

Mike: Does your brother ever come to visit you?

Barb: I'm not sure. He may be one of the people that's around. I don't seem to be able to really connect with that.

Mike: Okay. You think he may be one of the people there?

Barb: Yeah.

Mike: Could we go to one of the banquets when they all get together and you're seated with your husband? Can you tell me what that's like?

Barb: Well, it's noisy.

Mike: What kind of noise?

Barb: Laughing, and talking and . . . boisterous is the word. Boisterous!

Mike: How is everybody dressed?

Barb: Well, sometimes, it's just the way we usually dress, it's no fancy dress. And then sometimes, more time is taken to dress, and . . . it's more formal.

Mike: Tell me what it looks like when everyone is dressed up in their fancy clothes. Is there a lot of bright colors?

Barb: Yes. Lot of bright colors.

Mike: Yellow?

Barb: Yellow. Different; all different colors.

Mike: Is it like a banquet hall that you're in?

Barb: Yeah, I guess it is.

Mike: All right. Are there banners hanging around the ceiling of the hall?

Barb: There are banners on the walls, that hang down, like they cover the walls.

Mike: Is each banner on a pole, or are they just hanging from the walls?

Barb: Well, some are wall hangings that hang over the wall, and then some stick out on poles. It's like different ones are different family banners.

Mike: Family crests?

Barb: Crests, or coat of arms, or something like that. And so it is an honor, when they come in and they bring their coat of arms, or their crest to be displayed. They are hung to show who is there at the time.

Mike: Ohhhh, so they get changed all the time?

Barb: They could, yes.

Mike: Okay, how many women are eating in the banquet hall?

Barb: There are some. Sometimes more than others.

Mike: Look around the hall. Do you see your friend Susan there? Is she in the banquet hall at this time?

Barb: I'm sure she is. I don't see her, but I feel like she's there.

Mike: What is her relationship to you?

Barb: I think she's a little younger than I am, and . . . feels like we're friends. Feels like we've become better friends, but we're friends. I feel like she's a little younger than I am.

Mike: How did she happen to come live in your husband's castle?

Barb: I think her husband brought her. I'm not sure.

Mike: Could she have come to live with you as your friend?

Barb: Yes, she could have. I just, I feel that she's there, but I'm not. . . .

Mike: All right. I'd like to jump forward, oh, about ten or fifteen years. Is there a spot where you can jump forward to within this time frame that you feel comfortable with?

Barb: Well, things are a lot different. Seem to be a lot different than they were. Seems to be trouble. Seems to be . . . it's not as peaceful. Seems to be conflict in places.

Mike: Can you tell me about some of that? What's going on?

Barb: I'm just getting a headache with it.

Mike: When you go to worship God, how do you worship? Do you worship as a Christian, or as a druid?

Barb: Seems like I do both.

Mike: Okay. Is there a priest in the court, or is there a bishop or someone like that who you talk with and visit with and discuss God?

Barb: I prefer to talk to Merlin.

Mike: Uhhuhhh. How do you talk to Merlin? Do you go to his chambers, or does he come to your chambers, or do you sit in the hallway, or. . . .

Barb: Well, both, and we're outside sometimes.

106

Mike: Do you feel close to God?

Barb: Uhhuh, yes.

Mike: Does Merlin have a lot of wisdom to share with you about God?

Barb: Yes, and it makes sense.

Mike: I feel that Merlin has become your good friend.

Barb: It feels as though he's very dear to me.

Mike: How is your relationship with your husband?

Barb: Well, I love him very much, but he's not always here. He's gone.

Mike: Do you have any children?

Barb: You know, I saw myself earlier with child, but I don't have a sense of whether or not there are children.

Mike: And you can't put your finger on exactly what the problems are that are causing everybody to be unhappy?

Barb: I'd say it's some sort of, just strife on the land. Conflict, people are in conflict.

Mike: Does it have anything to do with the Christian church?

Barb: It may. I'm not sure, but it seems like there is someone in the castle that has to do with the strife. I don't like him very much. I'm not sure, maybe I don't trust him. There seems to be. . . .

Mike: Is that the Bishop?

Barb: It may be. I'm not sure, it's just not a comfortable feeling. It's just not comfortable for me for some reason.

Mike: Does your husband discuss these matters with you?

Barb: At times, yes.

Mike: Is your friend Susan still around?

Barb: Seems as though she is. I'm just not getting anything really clear. The thing that is the most clear is when the bird comes, that's real clear. And my relationship with Merlin is real clear.

Mike: Why don't you tell us in detail some of those things that seem real clear to you. Tell us about some incidents, and tell us everything that you feel or see.

Barb: Well the things that Merlin teaches me are . . . sometimes are, I guess, magic. And the word alchemy comes to mind. And herbs. I have a herb garden, and Merlin teaches me about the herbs. And about different kinds of plants and different things to be done with the plants. (Big sigh.) He teaches me to focus my mind, and he teaches me to ask questions and to look around and to see, to see beyond what appears to be. And he teaches me to look into the heart of the people around me because they're not all trustworthy. That helps me to protect myself, and at times, even protect my husband.

Mike: What else would you like to tell us about your marriage with your husband and your friendship with Merlin? In all of those years, what would you want us to know, to remember you by? And to remember about the time period.

Barb: (Crying.)

Mike: Here's some kleenex. What are you feeling?

Barb: I'm feeling several things. I'm feeling an overwhelming love for many of the people around me. But I'm feeling a great sense of sadness and loss.

Mike: Why's that?

Barb: (Big sighs.) . . . Oh. . . .

Mike: What's happening?

Barb: It's like I'm just in blackness. I'm not seeing anything, I'm just feeling the feelings.

Mike: Is Arthur, is your husband still alive?

Barb: Maybe not, maybe that's the loss I feel. It's like a part of me is dead. It's like half of me is gone. It's just. . . .

Mike: Where do you go? Do you just continue living where your husband lived, or do you go someplace else? Let's go ahead like about five years into the future. Show me where you're living now.

Barb: I don't see where I'm living, but I see myself outside of a cave. And I'm wearing a long cape. I don't see what I'm wearing but I'm wearing a long cape with a hood up over my head. And I've come there on a horse, and it . . . seems like there's no one there now. It seems like a place I used to go to and it was significant to me. But it's like, I've just gone there because I'm lonely and I want to just go someplace where I. . . . (Crying.) Someplace where there were happier times.

Mike: Okay. We don't really want you to feel a lot of grief, we just kind of want to see what happened. So could you get on your horse and go back?

Barb: Well, it's a castle of some sort. I don't know if it's the same one as where I lived before. Maybe not as big, I just can't tell. Maybe I'm coming to it from a different direction.

Mike: Let's go up to the building and see who runs it. Are there like monks or nuns that run it? Is it run by the church, or run by your husband, or your family or. . . .

Barb: Well, it's probably. . . . Seems like maybe the church has something to do with it, I'm not sure.

Mike: Could it be that they run the place as a home for you?

Barb: It could be. It seems as if that is where I'm supposed to be.

Mike: Is it near the ocean?

Barb: Seems like the sea is nearby, yes. There's trees on one side, and the sea. . . .

Mike: Could it be that the church has set that up as a home for you? So you can live out your life in peace?

Barb: Possibly, yes.

Mike: Okay.

Barb: (Crying.)

Mike: Want to come out now?

Barb: Yes.

Mike: Tell me what you're feeling. Tell me.

Barb: (Crying harder.) I'm not sure.

Mike: Let it out. Merlin's here right now. Your beloved friend. He says, "The reason we're doing this regression this afternoon is so that you can let it out. Let out your unhappiness, your grief. You can't carry that anymore."

Barb: (Sobbing.)

Mike: Anything you want to let out of yourself, let that go right now. Feel those emotions.

Barb: It seems like I had to just . . . be . . . so. . . .

Mike: I know, you couldn't show your grief.

Barb: So, just. . . .

Mike: You had to put on a facade, you wouldn't let those people see. . . .

Barb: I know. . . .

Mike: They had destroyed your husband, and you wouldn't let them see your grief. So you carried that grief with you. Just let go of it now.

Barb: (Big sighs. Big sobs.)

Mike: Want to tell your husband you love him?

Barb: Oh, I do. (Deep sobs.)

Mike: Tell him.

Barb: I do. I do. (Sobbing.)

Mike: Tell him. Tell him, say, "I love you now. I love you and I will always love you."

Barb: (Sobbing.) I love you, I love you and . . . I will . . . always . . . love you . . . so. I can't go on without you. . . . My heart is gone, it's . . . empty. It's like my soul is just drained from my body. . . . (Racking sobs.) I can't continue, and I have to. . . . I don't have any choice. . . . Ohhhh. . . . Ohhhhh. . . .

Mike: I'd like to do something. I'd like for you to close your eyes again. There. Please go to the white light. . . . Who is there waiting for you?

Barb: (Had been beginning to calm down, but began sobbing again when asked who was waiting for her.)

Mike: So you didn't lose him. It is Arthur. He's smiling, isn't he?

Barb: Yes, but it felt as if it was so long.

Mike: But you're back together again. So, now you know you didn't lose him.

Barb: (Beginning to calm down.) Yes.

Mike: So, let's let all that other emotion out. Let your grief go.

Barb: (Big sighs.) Oh. . . .

Mike: And your beloved friend Merlin's coming down now with some magic dust. He says that he knows when to use it. He's making a circle around you out of golden dust.

Barb: I need some in my heart. I need some in my heart.

Mike: You have to make room for it. You have to let that other emotion out. You have to let go, let go of a lot of grief.

Barb: It feels like that may take me a while. (Talking between big sighs.) I think if I let . . . it all go at once, my heart would burst. . . . Oh . . . but I know I can let it go now. Ohhhhh. . . .

Mike: You see, I also carried grief about my loss of Arthur and the movement, the loss of my family. The movement was my family. And I had to learn to release all that grief because, as they explained to me, Camelot was meant to be, and then it was meant to go away.

Barb: (Crying softly again.)

Mike: And so . . . what we created was magical, and will live forever. The beauty of Camelot is forever in men's hearts. And so it doesn't serve anybody for us to carry that old pain. And it is all okay, and it is all eternal. Now, Camelot is eternal. We did our part and we should be joyous instead of sad. We have to let go of those old emotions. I loved dear Arthur also.

Barb: I know. I loved you.

Mike: And I loved Merlin. And I loved you. And we have very intense pain and joy . . . and we just have to let go of the pain now. And understand the beauty of the fact that Camelot is with us forever.

Barb: Yes. Oh . . . that's the pain that I've been feeling in my heart, and I didn't know what it was.

Mike: And it's blocking you from getting what you want now in this life. So it's time to let go of it. You can't carry that pain into the ascension. You can't carry those old negative feelings. They're too heavy. You have to let go of them. That's why the time is right now.

Barb: How do I let go of them?

Mike: You are doing it.

Barb: Do I just go into my private closet and . . . when I feel them again, just grieve and release? Let it all go?

Mike: I'll tell you. Remember, remember all those days of Camelot, and as you remember them, you can do your crying and your releasing. Just let it happen, and it will gradually straighten itself all out.

Barb: I love you. (Softly crying.)

Mike: You were picked for that role as Guenivere because of your great spirit. You're a great soul. That was quite an honor. You did a great job. Your purity of heart. . . .

Barb: I felt like I had failed.

Mike: No. Your purity of heart was the center, the key to Camelot. Everything that Arthur and Merlin did wouldn't have worked without your purity of heart. That's why Merlin picked you.

Barb: And he did pick me.

Mike: Yes.

Barb: I miss him.

Mike: He says every time you caress a flower or pat a tree, you're back with him.

Barb: He taught me so much. He taught me that there was life in all things, and it was all connected. And there is only the Oneness. And he taught me to hear the stars sing. (Crying softly.) And he taught me to hear the animals, the plants. He taught me how to listen, to hear. He taught me about the crystals, all of the rocks. He taught me . . . and he taught me how to see into man's heart, to know what their intentions were, regardless of what they said. And he taught me the wisdom of silence. (Crying softly again.) To be silent, which was very hard at times. To know what was going to happen, but to be silent. He taught me to know the life in the water and the fire, the air and the earth. And that which we couldn't see. The ether and spirit. And then there was the priest. . . .

Mike: What did he teach you about the priest?

Barb: He let me learn on my own.

Mike: (Laughing.)

Barb: (Laughing.) And that's where a lot of the wisdom of silence came in. He let me learn on my own. He taught a lot by saying nothing.

12

Linda as Morgana
May, 1994

Linda and I went to high school together in Tulsa, Oklahoma. Today she is a 54-year-old veterinarian in Houston. We renewed our friendship at a recent high-school reunion. Then, while on vacation in Orlando, she and I went out to dinner one night. During the course of our visit together, I mentioned very briefly my Camelot project. She almost leaped out of her chair, asking me to regress her and find out if she was at Camelot. "I am a full-blooded Cherokee, so I have always assumed that my interest in the mystical arenas of life was due to my Native American heritage. But I sense a connection here as well." She was right.

Mike: We'll make the trip together. Are we through the doorway yet? Okay, we're through the doorway. You just tell me what you're seeing, what you're experiencing. What are you feeling?
Linda: I'm riding a horse.
Mike: What kind of horse is it? What color is the horse?
Linda: The horse is chestnut color.
Mike: Okay. And how are you dressed?
Linda: I have on a long dress. It's green and white. It's green at the top and white at the bottom.
Mike: Describe your hair to me.
Linda: My hair is real long; real long and dark.
Mike: Uhhuh. Kind of brown. It's flowing out behind you as you ride. I see that. It's a nice sunny day.
Linda: It's beautiful.
Mike: Yeah. Are you riding with anybody else?
Linda: I think I'm riding by myself. I don't see anybody else.
Mike: How about behind you? Are there some horses behind you?

Linda: Yeah.

Mike: Two or three other horses. You're up ahead of them. You have raced on ahead. I see you beginning to slow your horse down a bit and the others now pull up even with you. Can you tell me who you're riding with?

Linda: He says his name's Arthur.

Mike: Is he *the* Arthur?

Linda: He tells me yes.

Mike: And who are you?

Linda: My name's Morgana.

Mike: Are you a friend of his, or a relative of his?

Linda: I'm a friend.

Mike: Okay. How old is Arthur?

Linda: He looks like he's about twenty.

Mike: Okay. What does he look like?

Linda: Oh, he has beautiful blondish brown hair. And he looks very strong.

Mike: What color are his eyes?

Linda: His eyes are blue.

Mike: Yes, I see that. Deep eyes. Very pretty eyes. His hair's kind of long.

Linda: Yes.

Mike: Is he the king?

Linda: He's the king.

Mike: And why are you with him?

Linda: I'm his friend.

Mike: Okay. What else would you like to tell me?

Linda: He doesn't want me to ride by myself.

Mike: Okay.

Linda: I love to be outside.

Mike: What's happening now?

Linda: I'm inside the castle, in a great big room with lots of people at tables.

Mike: Is it perhaps the Great Hall?

Linda: I don't know.

Mike: Look around the room. Do you see the Round Table?

Linda: Yes.

Mike: Are there knights sitting around the Round Table?

Linda: Yes.

Mike: What does the Round Table look like?

Linda: It's real thick wood.

Mike: How many people can sit at the Round Table?

Linda: Twelve.

Mike: You can see that? It's about that size? So it's not a very large table?

Linda: It doesn't look very big.

Mike: So the other knights sit at regular tables?

Linda: I guess they're knights sitting at the other tables. There's other people sitting all around.

Mike: Okay. How are they dressed?

Linda: They have tunics on.

Mike: Are they brightly colored or drab?

Linda: They look like leather.

Mike: Leather tunics, okay. So this is not a feast or anything? This is like a regular, just like a regular meal at the castle? Like a working meal? How is the room lit? Do they use torches, or do they have windows open? How do people see?

Linda: There's torches. There are plates of food.

Mike: What does the food look like?

Linda: Big plates of meat. And goblets. Beer.

Mike: Any vegetables or bread?

Linda: There's bread. I didn't see any vegetables.

Mike: Okay. Are you seated?

Linda: Yes.

Mike: Where are you sitting?

Linda: I'm sitting at a table by the King's table.

Mike: Okay. Who's seated at the King's table?

Linda: There's two people sitting at his table with him.

Mike: And who are they?

Linda: Gawaine.

Mike: Gawaine. Yes, okay.

Linda: I don't know who the other one is.

Mike: Okay. Is he a man?

Linda: Yes.

Mike: Does he appear to be a knight?

Linda: Yeah.

Mike: Okay. And who are you seated with at your table?

Linda: Some other women.

Mike: Okay. Is the Queen there?

Linda: The Queen's here.

Mike: Is she seated with you?

Linda: She's sitting at the end of the table.

Mike: And where are you seated at the table?

Linda: I'm sitting next to the end.

Mike: Okay. Is the Queen younger than you are?

Linda: She's about my age. She has blond hair.

Mike: How do you feel about the Queen?

Linda: I don't know how I feel about the Queen.

Mike: Do you like her?

Linda: I don't dislike her. I just feel tight in my chest when you ask me.

Mike: Are you perhaps jealous of her?

Linda: Maybe I'm jealous of the Queen.

Mike: Okay, then perhaps you love Arthur?

Linda: Yeah, I love Arthur.

Mike: Have you loved him for a long time?

Linda: Yeah.

Mike: How does Arthur feel about you?

Linda: I think he thinks I'm his friend. I think he loves me. He doesn't want anything to happen to me. But he doesn't, he's not . . . he doesn't love me like he loves the Queen.

Mike: Okay. But you love him?

Linda: Yes.

Mike: Have you two been lovers?

Linda: I think so.

Mike: Are you lovers now?

Linda: Yeah, I think so.

Mike: Okay. Does the Queen know?

Linda: I don't think she knows.

Mike: Okay. Look around the hall and see if you see the knight you know as Percival. Is he there?

Linda: Percival. . . . Percival is at the Round Table.

Mike: Can you see him?

Linda: Uhhuh.

Mike: What does he look like?

Linda: He has dark wavy hair.

Mike: How do you feel about him?

Linda: He's smiling at me.

Mike: He seems to be very understanding, now, isn't he?

Linda: Ummmmm.

Mike: Is he, like, your confidant?

Linda: I just asked him and he said, yes, he's my confidant.

Mike: Because the King trusts Percival, does he use Percival to keep in contact with you? Does he escort you to your secret meetings with Arthur?

Linda: Yeah.

Mike: So the King does trust Percival quite a bit. I believe seeing you is very important to the King. I've read in some books that Morgana was a priestess. You're a druid priestess?

Linda: Yes.

Mike: What does that mean? What does a druid priestess do? What do you do?

Linda: I have visions.

Mike: How do you have your visions? How do you do that?

Linda: I just go inside my head, and I have visions.

Mike: And you take those visions to the King?

Linda: Yes.

Mike: And that's how you help him?

Linda: Yes.

Mike: You help him to rule his empire by giving him visions? Warnings and. . . .

Linda: I want to keep him safe.

Mike: Yes, okay. And that's kind of your job there?

Linda: I think so.

Mike: Okay. What else do you do as a priestess? Do you do any rituals, or any. . . .

Linda: Yes, rituals and prayers.

Mike: Rituals and prayers. Do you do any magic?

Linda: Yes, I do magic.

Mike: What kind of magic do you do?

Linda: I use herbs.

Mike: You use herbs for your magic? Tell me about it.

Linda: Sometimes I eat herbs, and sometimes I burn them and smell the flames and smoke.

Mike: To make things happen?

Linda: Yes.

Mike: Inside your head?

Linda: Inside my head.

Mike: Okay. Do you ever use magic to try to make things happen to other people, to help the King?

Linda: Only good things.

Mike: Yes, of course. Doing God's work.

Linda: Doing God's work.

Mike: What kind of things do you do? Give me some samples of that kind of magic.

Linda: To make good things happen?

Mike: Yes.

Linda: Sometimes I dig up roots, and sometimes I dig up plants.

Mike: If, for example, the King has an enemy in a far area that's causing him trouble, can you do anything to help the King?

Linda: Yes, I can ask the spirits and all the little people to help protect him and they will. They just come out of the mist and keep him safe.

Mike: Okay. Who are the little people?

Linda: Just my little friends.

Mike: Okay. Where did you learn all of this about being a priestess?

Linda: I think I learned it from my mother.

Mike: Okay. Did you go to school? Did they have a. . . .

Linda: Yes.

Mike: An academy or school for priestesses?

Linda: Yes.

Mike: What was your mother's name? Do you remember?

Linda: My mother's name. . . .

Mike: It doesn't come to you?

Linda: No, it seems to me it starts with an "A." I don't know.

Mike: I think I read in some book that Morgana was Arthur's half sister.

Linda: (Almost a whisper.) He's my brother?

Mike: Yes, how does that feel?

Linda: I think that feels correct.

Mike: Did you ever have a child?

Linda: Yes, I did.

Mike: Was Arthur the father?

Linda: . . . Yes. (Begins to cry.)

Mike: Now it's okay to have some emotions. If you're just feeling some emotions, let's go ahead and bring them on up and talk about them. What happened to your child? Was it a boy or a girl?

Linda: It's a girl. No, it's a boy. He has longer hair, though.

Mike: What did you name him? Do you recall his name?

Linda: No.

Mike: What happened to him? Did you raise him?

Linda: I think they took him away from me.

Mike: Who took him away?

Linda: My sister.

Mike: Okay. Did Arthur have anything to do with that?

Linda: No.

Mike: Did Arthur know about him?

Linda: I don't think Arthur knew about him.

Mike: How do you feel about that? Them taking away your little boy?

Linda: Feels awful.

Mike: Is it a source of grief?

Linda: Oh, yes. But they tell me that I have other things I need to do for a while.

Mike: (Trying to console.) Yes, they feel that you're too important. Too important to Arthur. To his work, to your religion. Do you know where they took your son?

Linda: It's in a different castle.

Mike: Is he being raised by one of the other kings?

Linda: Yes.

Mike: Does he know that you're his mother?

Linda: Yes, he knows that I'm his mother.

Mike: Does he know that Arthur's his father?

Linda: . . . I don't think he knows that.

Mike: Do you ever see him?

Linda: I haven't seen him for some years. He's getting big.

Mike: And he lives a long way away?

Linda: Uhhuh. . . .

Mike: Is this other king raising him as one of his sons?

Linda: Yes.

Mike: Does the king know who he is?

Linda: Yes.

Mike: Could it be that that king's queen is your sister?

Linda: Yeah.

Mike: So he's being raised by your sister, who is the queen of one of these realms. How do you feel about your sister?

Linda: I think my sister thinks she's doing the right thing.

Mike: So she's doing it, but out of love and concern?

Linda: I'm not sure.

Mike: Okay. Think maybe she's doing it because she's ambitious?

Linda: I think she's jealous.

Mike: Okay. This gives her some power over you and Arthur.

Linda: I think she's jealous . . . for her son.

Mike: Who is your son's brother. Okay. All right. Do you ever use magic to help? Do you see your son?

Linda: Yes, I look in the fire and I can see my son.

Mike: Do you ever use magic to help your son?

Linda: Yes.

Mike: What kind? How do you do that? When he's sick, or needs some help?

Linda: To protect him from harm.

Mike: Okay. How does the king who's raising your son feel about your son? Is he a good father to him?

Linda: I think so.

Mike: Is he doing it out of love, or is he doing it for selfish reasons?

Linda: Selfish reasons.

Mike: Yes, selfish reasons. It gives him more power. But your son doesn't. . . .

Linda: I just can keep an eye on him that way.

Mike: Yeah, okay. Does Arthur seem happy with his Queen Gueni-vere? . . . Is that a hard question for you to answer?

Linda: I don't know if he is or not.

Mike: Are you pretty much dedicated to Arthur?

Linda: Oh yes.

Mike: Do you have any other men in your life?

Linda: Yes, I do. Friends.

Mike: I would imagine there would be a lot of men who would like to marry you. You're very pretty. You're the King's sister. I think a lot of them would probably petition the King for you.

Linda: I don't want to marry.

Mike: Huh?

Linda: I don't want to marry.

Mike: Okay, so you tell your brother that; you tell the King that.

Linda: Yes. I don't want to.

Mike: Yes, you want to stay where you are. So you can be close to him and help him. And you love him.

Linda: Yes.

Mike: He's your life. Is he older than you, or younger?

Linda: I think he's younger than I am. He's younger than me.

Mike: Okay. But you look younger than Arthur. You keep your youth, don't you?

Linda: Yes, I do.

Mike: How do you do that?

Linda: I drink special water.

Mike: Where do you get this water?

Linda: From a pool that's on an island.

Mike: Is that the famous island where the druid priestesses live? Avalon?

Linda: Yes.

Mike: Is the water naturally magic, or do you do some magic to the water?

Linda: It's special water, and then we do magic to the water.

Mike: So actually, you're quite a bit older than Guenivere, but you're not. You've stayed the same age with her, haven't you?

Linda: Yes, I guess I have.

Mike: Do other people know? They've noticed your extended youth, haven't they? They've attributed it to your powers as a priestess. . . . Tell me what you're seeing.

Linda: I'm in a lot of fog.

Mike: Are you on the island?

Linda: I'm on a boat, in the water.

Mike: Going to the island? Can you tell me where you are?

Linda: I'm on the island.

Mike: Were you in the boat alone?

Linda: Yes, I was in the boat alone.

Mike: Okay. Where are you going on the island?

Linda: Somebody's rowing the boat.

Mike: Okay.

Linda: I'm going to my home.

Mike: Do you spend a lot of time on the island?

Linda: Yes. That's where I love it the most.

Mike: Is it far from Camelot?

Linda: It's quite a ride.

Mike: Is it true that the island is in the other dimension?

Linda: . . . Yes.

Mike: So, only special people can get there?

Linda: Yes.

Mike: So no one else can see it, know it's there? It is still there, even today, isn't it?

Linda: It's still there.

Mike: You just have to know how to get there. When you get to the island, and you call for the boat, you have to do some more magic. To make the shift. Do you speak some words or do a ceremony, or eat some herbs, or how do you do that?

Linda: I speak some words, and I go through the mist.

Mike: And the island is there.

Linda: And the island is there.

Mike: Is it something that only the priestesses are taught?

Linda: Yes.

Mike: What would you like to show me on the island?

Linda: There's a circle of rocks . . . on the ground.

Mike: Okay. How big are these rocks?

Linda: Each one is about a foot around.

Mike: Are these on top of a hill, or in a valley, or. . . .

Linda: It's on top of a hill.

Mike: The highest spot on the island?

Linda: I think so. I think so. It's on top of a hill.

Mike: How big is the circle?

Linda: It's about 20 feet in diameter.

Mike: And how close are these rocks to each other?

Linda: They're about a foot apart.

Mike: Okay. Are they round?

Linda: Sort of round.

Mike: Sort of round. What color are they?

Linda: They're white. Whitish grey.

Mike: Okay. Why are you showing me this circle?

Linda: It's a special circle. It just seemed I should show you.

Mike: Do you do ceremonies at this circle?

Linda: Yes.

Mike: In the daytime, or at night?

Linda: Night.

Mike: Do you put a fire in the circle?

Linda: Yes.

Mike: Do you dance around the circle, or walk around the circle? Or chant?

Linda: We chant.

Mike: So you stand around the circle and chant. At night, with a bonfire in the center.

Linda: We have on cloaks.

Mike: Beg pardon?

Linda: We have on cloaks.

Mike: Cloaks. Okay. White?

Linda: Yes.

Mike: How often do you do this ceremony?

Linda: When the moon's full.

Mike: It sounds almost like the Indians and their Full Moon Pipe Ceremony. Same type of. . . .

Linda: The moon's very special.

Mike: Show me your house. What does your house look like?

Linda: It's made out of rocks.

Mike: Do you live there alone?

Linda: No.

Mike: Who lives with you?

Linda: Another priestess and a lady who helps take care of us. The other priestess is old.

Mike: Is she the senior priestess for the whole island?

Linda: Yes.

Mike: That must mean you have quite a bit of status?

Linda: She loves me very much.

Mike: Could she be your mother?

Linda: She tells me she is.

Mike: She's your mother.

Linda: She's my mother, my teacher.

Mike: Was she your birth mother?

Linda: She says no, she's my "mother teacher."

Mike: You were brought to her as a baby. Has she taught you to do things such as how to make yourself disappear?

Linda: Yes.

Mike: Can you make other people disappear?

Linda: Yes.

Mike: Can you change yourself into another shape? Like an animal or a tree, or something?

Linda: Yes, I can.

Mike: Can you do that to other people?

Linda: Yes, I can.

Mike: Okay. What else can you do?

Linda: I can do anything I need to do.

Mike: Okay. So, you're a very powerful priestess. One of the top ones. And your job is to help Arthur. Protect him.

Linda: Yes.

Mike: I would like to go now to. . . . Would you mind if we leave the island, or would you like to stay there for a while?

Linda: We can leave the island.

Mike: Okay. Tell me about Merlin. We haven't talked about Merlin. You're smiling. Do you like Merlin?

Linda: (Louder.) YES!

Mike: Is he your friend?

Linda: He's my friend.

Mike: Is he your confidant?

Linda: Yes. He teaches me a lot.

Mike: Good. Do you two ever do ceremonies or magic together?

Linda: Yes.

Mike: Spend a lot of time talking?

Linda: Yes.

Mike: I see you going to talk to him in the castle a lot. A lot of people talk to Merlin a lot, but. . . .

Linda: Yes, they do.

Mike: He cares for you very much too, doesn't he?

Linda: Yes.

Mike: Are he and Arthur close?

Linda: Yes, I think they're very close.

Mike: They spend a lot of time together. Did you ever go to Merlin's chambers?

Linda: Yes.

Mike: What did they look like? Are they in the basement?

Linda: Can't tell where they are. Blue.

Mike: Blue. The walls are painted blue?

Linda: It's blue. It looks blue.

Mike: Okay. Does he have tables and test tubes and things like that? And experiments that he works on, and books? What do you see around his quarters?

Linda: There's stacks of books.

Mike: Books, okay. What else?

Linda: There's lots of herbs hanging around.

Mike: Okay. What about a pointed cap? Does he ever wear a pointed hat that looks like a dunce cap? Do you ever see him with a pointed cap on?

Linda: He's smiling at me; he has on a pointed cap. (Laughter.)

Mike: Does he ever wear a crystal on his forehead, or a gemstone, like they show in some of the movies? Over his third eye?

Linda: Well, he has one on right now.

Mike: Okay, so that answers that question. Is it a crystal?

Linda: It looks crystal. It looks clear.

Mike: Okay.

Linda: He has on a blue cape. The purple-blue color of the sky.

Mike: What do Merlin's eyes look like?

Linda: They look like stars.

Mike: He has a real gleam in his eye, doesn't he?

Linda: Yes.

Mike: Would you like to stay there, or can we go on?

Linda: We can go on.

Mike: Okay. I would like to go now in the future to a period when Arthur announces . . . Arthur and Merlin announce that they're going to bring Christianity in as the official religion. Tell me about that experience, what it was like. How the people reacted, how you felt about it, and how Arthur felt about it.

Linda: I think Arthur's doing that because he thinks that's what he needs to do. I don't know that I feel good about it.

Mike: How do the people react to it?

Linda: The Queen's very happy. The people that are around me aren't happy.

Mike: Okay. How does Merlin feel about it?

Linda: Merlin says it's meant to be.

Mike: Do you feel that Merlin helped Arthur to accomplish this change?

Linda: He says he did.

Mike: Yes, okay. Good. Do you mind if we jump ahead a little bit more now? Okay, let's jump ahead to a period of time when the Bishop first comes to the court. Do you remember that?

Linda: Yes.

Mike: Did you meet the Bishop?

Linda: Yes.

Mike: What did you think of him?

Linda: I think the Bishop is evil.

Mike: What does the Bishop look like?

Linda: Has on red. Has a round face.

Mike: Is he tall, or medium build, or short?

Linda: I think he's short.

Mike: What kind of eyes does he have?

Linda: He has dark eyes.

Mike: What kind of hair does he have?

Linda: I don't think he has very much hair. He has on a hat.

Mike: How did things change at the court after the Bishop got there?

Linda: It feels very tense.

Mike: Why the change?

Linda: It's hard for people to change.

Mike: Well, the country's already become Christian. What changes is the Bishop making?

Linda: More laws.

Mike: Does Arthur have to approve these laws?

Linda: Yes.

Mike: Does Arthur approve them all?

Linda: He says he doesn't approve them all.

Mike: Okay. Mind if we jump ahead again? Let's move ahead about five years, and let's take a look at what's happening in court now.

Linda: There's fighting.

Mike: What kind of fighting? Okay, who's fighting in the court?

Linda: Looks like the knights are arguing.

Mike: Amongst themselves?

Linda: Yes.

Mike: How has that happened?

Linda: Something about the Queen.

Mike: About the Queen's honor, maybe?

Linda: About the Queen's honor.

Mike: What's happened?

Linda: Some people think she's not faithful.

Mike: Hummmm. Does this have anything to do with Lancelot?

Linda: That's what they say.

Mike: What do you think?

Linda: I think it's correct.

Mike: Have you ever seen the Queen and Lancelot together?

Linda: They love each other.

Mike: But have you ever seen them together?

Linda: I've seen them together.

Mike: They have been together. Romantically together?

Linda: I didn't see them romantically together.

Mike: Could it be that the Bishop has stirred this up, to use this to incite disharmony in the court?

Linda: The Bishop stirs lots of things up.

Mike: What do you think about those two? Could it be that the Bishop is taking Lancelot's infatuation with the Queen and using it to stir up trouble and dissention?

Linda: Yes.

Mike: Is that what's going on?

Linda: Yes.

Mike: I talked to Galahad, and Galahad told me that Lancelot's ego is such that Lancelot would fantasize about having relations with the Queen, but Galahad says it all amounts to nothing. What do you think about that?

Linda: I think that may very well be true. It's just easy to see that they love each other.

Mike: Is it? Could it be that the Bishop has exploited this situation in order to try to destroy Arthur?

Linda: Yes, that's very true.

Mike: Do you think that's what's going on?

Linda: I think that's true.

Mike: Okay. What else would you like to tell me about what's going on in the court at this time? Are you happy?

Linda: No.

Mike: Are you still seeing Arthur?

Linda: No.

Mike: Are you still Arthur's friend?

Linda: Yes.

Mike: Do you still counsel him?

Linda: Not so much.

Mike: Not so much. Why not? Does he not ask for your help as much?

Linda: He doesn't ask.

Mike: Why do you think that is?

Linda: He's trying to be a good Christian.

Mike: Oh, so they've got him pulling away from his old druid contacts? All right. How do you feel about that?

Linda: It's hard for me to understand.

Mike: Do you think that's why he stopped being your lover?

Linda: Yes.

Mike: Could it be that the Bishop made a fuss about it?

Linda: I don't think the Bishop knows.

Mike: Okay. How about some of the priests.

Linda: I just don't think they want Arthur to do that anymore.

Mike: They don't want him to what?

Linda: They don't want him to consult with me anymore.

Mike: Okay. They're just trying to isolate him from his friends. Do you think there's a conspiracy against the King at this time?

Linda: Feels like it, yes.

Mike: What would they be trying to accomplish?

Linda: Somebody wants to take the throne away from him.

Mike: Does Arthur realize that?

Linda: He knows it.

Mike: Do the knights realize it?

Linda: Yes, they know it.

Mike: How does Merlin feel about all this?

Linda: He says that we have to use our powers to see that it turns out right.

Mike: Okay. Is Merlin still close to Arthur?

Linda: I don't think Arthur is close to anybody now.

Mike: Okay. Is he close to his wife now?

Linda: No, I don't think so.

Mike: What's happened to Arthur?

Linda: He's struggling inside himself.

Mike: How old is he about now?

Linda: He's about forty.

Mike: Okay. Did Arthur ever take your special water to stay young?

Linda: Yes. When he was younger, he did.

Mike: But now he's stopped taking it?

Linda: No, he doesn't take it anymore.

Mike: I bet Merlin took this water too. That's why he stayed young so long. That explains a lot. That explains why he wanted you to have it. . . . Do you mind if we go to Arthur's death? . . . It's okay?

Linda: Uhhuh.

Mike: All right. Tell me how Arthur died?

Linda: Looks like he got stabbed.

Mike: Where did he get stabbed?

Linda: Got stabbed in the leg and in the side, the stomach.

Mike: Okay. How did that happen? Where did that happen? Was he down in the castle or the battlefield or where was he?

Linda: He was outside. I don't know if it's a battlefield, or some people just came up. I don't know.

Mike: Okay. Did you see him? Did they bring him to you? Or did you see him before he died?

Linda: No.

Mike: Did you see him after he died?

Linda: Yeah.

Mike: Okay. Did you help prepare him for burial?

Linda: No.

Mike: What happened? Where did the body go?

Linda: I don't know what they did with the body. He just came to me in spirit.

Mike: Ohhh. Okay. So, you weren't even allowed to see the body. Was the body brought back to Camelot?

Linda: Yeah.

Mike: What happened to all the knights?

Linda: I think the knights are killed.

Mike: Okay. And what happens then?

Linda: Arthur came to me in spirit when I was at the island.

Mike: Oh, so you weren't back at Camelot when the war was going on?

Linda: I don't think so.

Mike: And you stayed on the island. Did you ever go back to Camelot?

Linda: I don't think so.

Mike: Okay. Tell me what, as far as you know, what happened to Camelot after Arthur's death?

Linda: People just picked each other apart.

Mike: Who took over?

Linda: Arthur's son.

Mike: Your son?

Linda: Yes, my son.

Mike: Had he been living at Camelot with Arthur?

Linda: Yes.

Mike: Was he a friend of Arthur?

Linda: Yes.

Mike: Was he a friend of the church?

Linda: Arthur knew he was his son.

Mike: And the church turned him against Arthur?

Linda: I don't know.

Mike: Was he a Christian or a druid?

Linda: He's a druid.

Mike: Ohh, he is a druid. Okay. Was he allied with the church against your brother? Against his father?

Linda: They tell me yes.

Mike: So the church kind of manipulated him because they needed someone to take Arthur's place after they killed him?

Linda: Yes.

Mike: Does Arthur tell you that the church killed him?

Linda: Yes.

Mike: Does he warn you that they will persecute the druids now?

Linda: Yes.

Mike: That's his reason for coming to you? To warn you?

Linda: Yes. (Begins to lightly sob.)

Mike: Are you feeling some anxieties? What is it? . . . Go ahead, I've got some kleenex here.

Linda: I just feel isolated from those I love.

Mike: Such as. . . .

Linda: I'm supposed to stay on the island.

Mike: Do you ever see your son again?

Linda: No.

Mike: Does he ever know you're his mother?

Linda: I think he knows I'm his mother. Somewhere in his heart he does.

Mike: What happens to the kingdom when he becomes king? Do things go well?

Linda: It seems like they do on the surface, but. . . .

Mike: What is your son's name?

Linda: I don't know.

Mike: Does it start with an "M"?

Linda: I think so.

Mike: Could it be Mordred, or something like that?

Linda: That sounds right.

Mike: Okay.

Linda: My son's half-and-half.

Mike: Half-and-half what?

Linda: He's half good, half bad.

Mike: Okay. What happened to all the knights of the Round Table? Do they serve your son?

Linda: No.

Mike: What happens to them?

Linda: They're all gone.

Mike: What happened to Percival, your friend? Tap into your powers and tell me what happened to him.

Linda: He was killed in a battle.

Mike: The same battle that Arthur was killed in?

Linda: Yes.

Mike: Who killed him?

Linda: Mordred did.

Mike: Yeah. Soldiers fighting for the church, hunting people like Percival down. Do you see that?

Linda: Yes.

Mike: What happened to Guenivere?

Linda: I think she died trying to have a baby.

Mike: Okay. What happened to Camelot? Did Camelot stay the castle of the king?

Linda: It burned down.

Mike: Okay. And so that new king built a new castle somewhere else. Took another castle. What happened to Merlin?

Linda: Merlin still is.

Mike: Oh, he always will be. Is it true that he just went up, that he just passed into another dimension?

Linda: Yes.

Mike: Were they hunting him down?

Linda: Yes.

Mike: I heard that several days after the battle, they came to the castle to kill Merlin. And he just disappeared. They chased him through a tunnel, and when they got to the end of the tunnel, he was gone. Does that sound right?

Linda: Yes, that sounds right.

Mike: Okay.

Linda: He went through the fog and he was gone.

Mike: Anything else you'd like to tell me?

Linda: No.

Mike: How old was Arthur when he died? How old would you estimate?

Linda: I think he was fifty-six.

Mike: Fifty-six, okay. How much longer did you live?

Linda: I lived to be an old lady.

Mike: Did you ever become the High Priestess of Avalon?

Linda: I think I did. Yes, I did.

Mike: What happened to the other druids around the country after Arthur's death?

Linda: The church killed them.

Mike: Killed them all?

Linda: No. Some of them changed into other things.

Mike: They killed the ones they could catch?

Linda: Yes.

Mike: Someone told me that they hunted down everybody who had blue tattoos.

Linda: Yes!

Mike: That scared you when I said that! Did you have blue tattoos?

Linda: Yes.

Mike: That's why you had to stay in Avalon. What were your tattoos?

Linda: It was an "A."

Mike: Where was it? Why does that frighten you? . . . Why does that frighten you?

Linda: I don't know.

Mike: It was a tragic time for all the people, wasn't it?

Linda: Yes, it was.

Mike: How long did Mordred remain the king?

Linda: Too long, I think.

Mike: Okay. Was he still the king when you passed over?

Linda: Yes.

Mike: Okay. Tell me about your passing. Was it pleasant?

Linda: Yes.

Mike: When you passed over to the other side, who was there waiting for you?

Linda: Merlin was there.

Mike: Merlin was there. Was Arthur there?

Linda: Arthur was there.

Mike: Who else?

Linda: My mother was there.

Mike: Your "mother teacher"?

Linda: My "mother teacher."

Mike: Was it joyful?

Linda: Yes.

Mike: Did they explain to you that everything had turned out the way it had to turn out?

Linda: Everything turned out for the best.

Mike: Yes. You needed to hear that. Are you ready to come back?

Linda: Yes.

Mike: Thank you for very much for sharing this with me. This was a very nice experience. I appreciate it.

13

*Bill as Frederick
June 1994*

Background: Bill is a deacon of the Unitarian Church in Tampa, Florida. He is a 39-year-old advertising executive. He is married with three children. Bill always appeared to be very serious and somber about everything. He confided in me that he was very concerned that his serious and stern demeanor around his children was acting as a barrier. It prevented him from demonstrating his love for them as openly as he wished to. When I offered a regression to help him identify the source of these emotions, he readily agreed. Several weeks after the regression, Bill told me that he felt that his life was greatly changed. He was now more open and relaxed around his family, and his wife and children were much more content and relaxed around him.

Mike: When you're ready.
Bill: It's a heavy door. Well, I see a big hall, and I see a bunch of people. I am above the people, at an upper level, looking down from a few steps above. And it seems like there are a lot of people that are drinking and arguing. They are not fighting physically, but they are verbally having very heavy discussions.
Mike: Okay.
Bill: And there seems to be a big table. It's elevated. It may be King Arthur sitting there with a few other people. Eating.
Mike: Okay. Is this the Great Hall?
Bill: It must be.
Mike: Are there banners hanging around the outside walls? Can you look up and see banners?
Bill: Yeah, I see them on the wall behind where the King would be. I see white with red.
Mike: There are various colors.

Bill: Yeah. And there are some on the other walls that are deeper colors.

Mike: All right. Is everyone having a good time?

Bill: Well, it seems like they are partying, but they're. . . . I don't know why they're acting this way, to be honest with you.

Mike: They're very serious.

Bill: Yeah. And a little drunken.

Mike: And are you a little drunk?

Bill: No. I feel like I just walked in, and I'm trying to understand it. It feels disturbing to me that there's all this . . . arguing going on.

Mike: Can you sense who you are?

Bill: Well, it feels like I'm young. I have some kind of a white garment on. I have some of the . . . what's that stuff that protects you from getting cut?

Mike: Chain mail?

Bill: Yes. It's not armor. It seems like chain mail. But it's not exactly . . . it's almost like a fabric. With white. And I must be, I could be in my young twenties.

Mike: Okay.

Bill: I have like a . . . red cross on my chest.

Mike: All right. Are you seated at one of the tables?

Bill: I'm still standing, looking at all this stuff going on, and wondering why it is happening. And the King looks depressed. He's not very happy.

Mike: What does the King look like? His appearance? How is he dressed? What color hair does he have?

Bill: Well, he has got golden-brown hair, and he has got a long, full beard. And the King is moderately heavy. He has a very noble nose. I can't tell the color of his eyes. They look kind of brown, but it . . . there is a little tint of other color. He is handsome, and he looks to be in his fifties.

Mike: Okay. Is the Queen there?

Bill: It looks like the seat next to him, on his left, is vacant.

Mike: Okay. How about Merlin? Is Merlin there?

Bill: Yes, he is.

Mike: What does he look like?

Bill: Well, he is wearing a pointed hat. I can't place him exactly, because he seems to be moving. But he's got a pointed hat, looks like the hat is about two feet tall. And the hat is almost black, or navy blue, with stars all over it. And he has got very strong eyes, and he has got a kind of a whimsical charm to his face. He has got a white beard. It seems . . . not long. It seems trimmed more than the King's beard. White. He has got a kind of reddish white complexion. And his eyes are almost like a grey blue. And he seems to be happy or excited. The

King looks sullen, like he's disappointed about something, or like he has given up about something.

Mike: Can you ask somebody what's going on, or can you get a sense of what the issues are?

Bill: Sure. I asked one of the guys who is arguing, and he says that the King has given up. And they don't know what to do now. They are just trying to figure out what to do.

Mike: What has he given up about?

Bill: Evidently the crusaders are coming. And, rather than going to fight them to win . . . going into this thing, it's like we've already lost.

Mike: The crusaders. You mean, the Christian forces?

Bill: Yes.

Mike: They're moving against the kingdom?

Bill: They're on their way to attack.

Mike: Are they British, or are they European?

Bill: It seems like they're made up from a lot of different nationalities.

Mike: Why are they coming to attack you? I think that you all are Christian, aren't you?

Bill: Yes, some of us are. But it seems that they believe that we are the leftover stronghold of the old-world philosophies, and that they need to destroy us in order to have their energy be clean.

Mike: Is the Bishop behind this?

Bill: It seems to be.

Mike: Is it the Red Bishop; the guy who wears red all the time?

Bill: Who?

Mike: I don't know what his exact title is, but he is the bishop who has come into your court and has kind of taken over, and has pushed Arthur aside.

Bill: Yes, that's him. I don't know why Merlin seems to be so happy, but he seems to be so happy that he can't sit still. He is just moving all around, like he is really excited about something.

Mike: Can you speak to Merlin?

Bill: Sure.

Mike: Just go over and ask him why. I'd be curious to know.

Bill: (for Merlin) This is an important time of change, young man. There is so much excitement in here that I cannot sit still. For what we are about to go through is revolutionary and world changing. It is unfortunate that the lives of those here must go the way of those before, but to usher in this new age, it is necessary. You will all be back, to enjoy this at a different time. For what you have set in motion cannot be stopped.

The King feels forlorn, because he has taken it personally. Deep within, he understands the need for change. However, his personality does not want to go. Alas, the kingdom is lost, and the people here are fighting in spirit, out of frustration. It has been taught for them never to give up, and to give up is difficult. And so, drinking the night before the final battle is one of the few last remaining choices left. What good can it do to sit and wait and think about it sober? I think nothing.

My excitement comes from the fact that this change will revolutionize the consciousness on the earth. And it is yet but one of the many big changes coming through for the earth plane.

Mike: Beloved Merlin, who is this young man who is talking to you? In white? What's his name?

Bill: (for Merlin) Frederick.

Mike: Frederick. Is he a knight?

Bill: (for Merlin) He is from France. Or Gaul, as you call it. And he has come to help out with this change-over of energy. He seems to not be involved as emotionally as the others are, but he is only distressed that the time must move on. He has been a great warrior, and has fought in many battles with much success. And even though he is young, he has great wisdom and maturity about him. He will be going with us through this transition, and leaving this plane. But yet he will come back later to assist with future changes. He has been God-sent.

Mike: Okay, beloved Merlin, can you look around the hall and tell me if you see Percival?

Bill: (for Merlin) Yes, he is over here on my right.

Mike: What does he look like?

Bill: (for Merlin) He has a long center beard. He has grayish black hair, dark eyebrows, white complexion, muscular. He is wearing blackish armor with silver rivets.

Mike: Is he a nice-looking man?

Bill: (for Merlin) Very intense eyes.

Mike: Do you like him?

Bill: (for Merlin) Yes, but he is in a very serious mode right now. He is also contemplating the change. He is very warm-hearted, and a very good soldier.

Mike: Okay. The battle will be tomorrow?

Bill: (for Merlin) Yes.

Mike: Will we lose our beloved Arthur tomorrow?

Bill: (for Merlin) We have already lost him mentally. Yes, he will be lost at the battle. The battle will be in the early afternoon.

Mike: Is this the battle where he will be stabbed in the back?

Bill: (for Merlin) Yes.

Mike: What happens to all the knights of the Round Table after Arthur is killed?

Bill: (for Merlin) It seems that three remained afterwards, and when Camelot was destroyed, they had no purpose for continuing. And all the energy that was together, just dissolved. These three that were left, I just see them sitting at a table, resting, with nothing to do.

Mike: What happened to the others? Were they all killed in the battle?

Bill: (for Merlin) Yes. Some of them fought ferociously to save, to the best of their ability, what they could save. And these three, somehow, escaped the battle. Part of them feels that they should have gone with the others. They know not what to do now. When they realize that they cannot survive without Camelot, they will choose to join the others.

Mike: Do you have the names of the three? That survived?

Bill: . . . All I see are grey shadows.

Mike: Okay, that's fine.

Bill: (for Merlin) Percival seems to be one of them.

Mike: Okay. Were they killed a few days later? Up against the wall, by the. . . .

Bill: (for Merlin) One of them took his own life. And the other two were killed.

Mike: Yes. You were quite attached to Percival's family, weren't you?

Bill: Yes, there was a woman in his family. It may have been his sister, or a cousin. I felt like I was part of his family.

Mike: What happens to you, Merlin?

Bill: I'm sorry, I was speaking from Frederick's position.

Mike: Oh, okay. Excuse me.

Bill: And it's just this last part.

Mike: Okay, all right. Is Merlin gone? Can I speak to Merlin?

Bill: (for Merlin) Yes. I, Merlin, knew that my time was complete. And I chose to leave in spirit, for my work was complete. And although there was much pain physically, the job was complete. And I was finished.

Mike: In one of my visions, I saw some ruffians chasing you down a tunnel under the castle, and you just disappeared. Is that a correct scenario, or did you go some other way?

Bill: (for Merlin) I escaped from them, and shortly thereafter chose to move into the Light. But I have been with many of you since then.

Mike: Yes!

Bill: (for Merlin) Even the young Bill on your couch, I have been as a teacher to him also. As for you, I was the one, it was through my eyes that you saw the sword. It was given to you, courtesy of Michael.

Mike: Uhhuh. . . . It's very good to talk to you. I don't even know what to say, I have so many questions to ask of you. But as you know, I ask too many questions.

Bill: (for Merlin) That is part of the game of life.

Mike: Yes.

Bill: (for Merlin) You are performing many magical feats yourself these days.

Mike: Yes, with your guidance and love.

Bill: (for Merlin) There are many that need your help, and the work that you are doing certainly is beautiful. And it will not be too much in the distant future before this type of knowledge will be widely accepted. Although there are many souls who do chose to not stay around for the changes of consciousness, there are some who will be willing to seek their higher selves through your help. To choose to stay around for the changes. It is to test their life force to see if they really do wish to learn and become One.

Mike: Good. Okay.

Bill: (for Merlin) And fulfill their dreams. My mission is not clearly understood by many, since I have played more of a supportive role since the days of Camelot. But my spirit often intermingles with that of the Christ. And I often am not separate from Christ, but am one with Christ also. There are many different energies that emanate from Christ, and I am but one of them. Energies that come through to perform the magical healings, as some of you would call them. To work through all of you, to teach, and to be there to help you. You will always recognize me by my eyes. For they carry energy, and excitement, and adventure. And you know where to find me, of course.

Mike: Yes. Yes, I do. You certainly have taken me on a few adventures lately. Which I hope are not over.

Bill: (for Merlin) It is all part of the ride. And you were being rewarded, and you will be fulfilled in your dreams also. Does it not seem odd that so many of you are going through these challenges at the same time? There is a purpose and a reason behind it, for you are the forerunners of what is to come. And for success to happen, each of you needs to go through these experiences. First, so that when the masses are ready to go through, you will be there to guide them. You cannot teach what you do not know and do not experience first-hand. Simply remember though, that you are loved, and come from a place of love within. For in that, you will find the security and peace you seek. Even through these different experiences are often seemingly unpleasant, you can still go through them centered in peace and love, and remain who you are. It is only your outer sensations that are frustrated and confused and anxious. Your inner self knows all is fine.

Mike: Good.

Bill: (for Merlin) And with this I leave you until next time.

Mike: Thank you very much.

Bill: (for Merlin) You are quite welcome.

Mike: You know, Frederick, I forgot to ask him what happened to you. Would you like to go to the battle, the next day? Can you do that without feeling any stress?

Bill: Yes, I will go. I see myself fighting, even though it is overwhelming with the number of people in battle against us. I see Lady Guenivere standing above me, but I know that all is lost, and we are just simply going through the motions. I feel that I have no choice. I am against losing this way. It is overwhelming to go through. And I see myself being killed with a sword through the heart.

Mike: Okay.

Bill: The chest area.

Mike: There are too many of them on you at one time.

Bill: Yes, but I feel it is senseless to fight, so I might as well just give in and let it happen. I do not put up too big of a struggle.

Mike: How greatly are you outnumbered? Is it two to one, something like that?

Bill: It seems three to one, or four to one.

Mike: Okay. Where do these forces come from? From Gaul, from Germany?

Bill: Germany seems to be the big group. There are some also from Spain and from Italy.

Mike: All brought together to fight you?

Bill: Yes, there are also some from France . . . and some that are English mixed in. Rather than lose everything, they have chosen to change sides. They chose to change sides and move over. So some of them are friends, and we're fighting them also.

Mike: Okay. This has been a very interesting depiction of the final two days.

Bill: The battle seems to take place close to the castle grounds. It is where I perished. Not inside the walls. Out front. And it was very tight in the lines, neck to neck. It was very congested.

Mike: Ummmmm. . . . We haven't really gotten into the emotions which you felt during this period, which you may be carrying now.

Bill: Yes.

Mike: Could they be the same emotions which you are carrying in this lifetime now? I'm kind of listening to you, and guessing that now maybe you can help me to understand you better. Could you be carrying the same sense of . . . defeatism? A sense that. . . .

Bill: Yes, very much. I feel now like I did the day before the battle. That total loss is imminent, and there's so much that I wanted to do in life. But there wasn't a way out, and that I needed to keep these feelings within. I felt like I had this powerful warrior in me, but yet we were told not to win. The purpose of this battle was not to win. And it did not feel good.

Mike: Was it that you were not ready to die? Right?

Bill: I felt young and virile, and I loved life.

Mike: It was a great . . . loss, a great loss to you. Can you see how you have perhaps carried that feeling into the life that you have now?

Bill: Yes.

Mike: A fear that it might happen again?

Bill: Yeah. (Quietly crying.)

136

Mike: Go ahead and let it out, Bill. That's what it's all about. It's not going to happen this time. It's not going to happen this time.

Bill: I didn't want to die. (Sobbing.)

Mike: You have carried these tears for fifteen-hundred years. It's time to let go of them. You can't carry them with you into the new age. So we have to get rid of them now. You know, Frederick, if I may just talk to you a few minutes. Percival had the same feelings. He was very angry at Arthur, because he was also not ready to die. He lost his life, and he lost his family. But you know, when he went back and looked at this situation, from this lifetime, he saw things differently. Merlin put it to him very clearly. Merlin said, "Did you really want to live after Camelot? What was there to live for?" And he said, "What better way was there for a soldier to go, than in battle with these other soldiers? Life is eternal, you're going to come back anyway. You were just spared great grief and disappointment, by taking a soldier's death."

Bill: Yes, I understand.

Mike: But we didn't understand then, Bill. We didn't understand. But it is important for us to let those emotions out now, so please feel free to do it.

Also, I would like to repeat to you what Jesus told me about this. Because Merlin said it earlier when you were channeling Merlin to me. Jesus told me the same thing. He said, "The bringing of Christianity to that part of the world was the beginning of a new era. Unfortunately, the people who brought Christianity in were sacrificed in the process." And he said, "We are making amends for that now by bringing you all into another new age, another new era. Those of you who have prepared yourselves are being brought together. You are being taken into that other new era which is coming. This time you will be the winners. You will all have smiles on your faces. And it will be a happy ending." And Jesus said to me, "We like to see happy endings just as much as you do." So this lifetime is your payback, Frederick. You know what, it's all okay. It's all okay. So you can let go . . . of those feelings.

Bill: I choose to feel the warrior that I am.

Mike: Yes.

Bill: Victorious.

Mike: Yes. And we will all be victorious, going into this new age. The flow is on our side this time. We're taking our hits now, getting ready for it. Remember what Merlin said, "When we are into this new age, we're going to be glorious, magnificent."

Bill: I am in peace with that now.

Mike: Yes. You've made a big change. Just have that knowingness, and be about your business.

14

Barb as Guenivere July, 1994

Chapter 11 relates to you Barb's first regression as Guenivere. As I had mentioned, this first regression was a very emotional experience for her. Several months later she approached me to request a second regression. She felt that she had progressed in her emotional healing to a point where a second regression would help her. So we did it.

There are steps to the "recovery" process when dealing with affairs of the heart. The emotions we carry with us are like layers of an onion. As we heal, we strip away one layer to uncover the next layer. This definitely was the case here. In the first regression Barb was dealing with grief and heartbreak, which she had apparently later resolved. Because in this second encounter she got right down to the layer of her deep anger at Arthur.

Much of her anger seems to focus on that period when Arthur was bedridden for a year-and-a- half. This happened when Arthur was 49-years-old. It appears that Arthur had a nervous breakdown over his inability to deal with the Red Bishop. Arthur got ill, and laid in bed in a fetal position. The responsibility of running the kingdom fell squarely in Guenivere's lap. From all accounts, she did a great job of running things. But she, as we shall see, wasn't happy with having had to assume this mantle of responsibility. The following is the part of the regression which deals with this anger.

Mike: Tell me when you're ready. Let's go through the door, and tell me what you see.
Barb: Well, I see myself . . . I began to see myself immediately, as soon as you began to take me down the tunnel. I was dressed . . . it was a disguise. I was dressed as a boy. I wasn't a boy, but I was dressed as a boy. And I have gone to a place in the woods, to the cave. But I'm dressed as a boy. I'm not sure why.

Mike: What country are we in?

Barb: England. Britain.

Mike: Britain, okay.

Barb: Well, the cave is well-lighted. I like being here.

Mike: How come it is well-lighted? Was somebody there before you?

Barb: Well, yeah. . . . Merlin's there. He is not in the cave right now, but he's been there. He's around someplace, back in the depth of the caves. But he's not up front now.

Mike: And how old are you?

Barb: Hmmmm. . . . Fifteen, sixteen, somewhere in there.

Mike: And what's your name?

Barb: I'm Guenivere. I don't know why I'm dressed as I am. I see myself getting dressed. I've been told I can't do something, or I'm not supposed to do something. And so I'm running around, kind of scurrying, slipping in here and slipping in there as I build my disguise, and grabbing what I need. And running off. I'm in a hurry. I'm in a big hurry. It's important, for some purpose. I . . . I'd say I was very willful.

Mike: Why are you in the cave?

Barb: Because I was told I couldn't go there. And I decided I was going to go anyway. It's dusk or getting dark, and I know that I won't really be noticed. I'm trying not to be recognized so that I can slip out later.

Mike: Okay, who told you you couldn't go there?

Barb: Seems like Arthur told me I couldn't go. He had something private to do with Merlin. (Laughing.) And, I'm pissed off again. I'm definitely not staying home. I'm definitely not missing this, whatever it is. It's important. I think it's important that I be there.

Mike: So you're the queen?

Barb: Uhhuh.

Mike: You're already married?

Barb: Yes.

Mike: And they're having a secret ritual in the cave and you sneaked in?

Barb: Uhhuh.

Mike: Who else is there?

Barb: I don't see anyone right now. I'm not sure where they are. I think they're back in the cave, but I don't see them. But I'm a little unnerved right now. I'm beginning to wonder if maybe I . . . made a mistake in coming here.

Mike: Okay. You must be seeing something, or about to see something that distresses you. Are you there to witness the ritual?

Barb: I'm afraid I'm going to be seen, and I'm afraid to go back deeper into the cave. Because I really don't want to incur Merlin's anger, and I'm afraid he's going to be really angry with me. I'm not supposed to be here.

139

Mike: Okay. So you're waiting?

Barb: Well, I haven't left yet. . . . I'm trying to decide. . . . Okay, I am going to go back into the cave. I'm going to go. I'm going to find them. . . . I want to know what they're doing.

Mike: Okay.

Barb: There's several places they could be. The cave goes to the back, and to the left there is a tunnel and it's wider. . . .

Mike: It's like you're avoiding going further. . . .

Barb: Okay, so I go down this tunnel. (Big sigh.)

Mike: The bird is there I think.

Barb: Uhhuh. Yes, and this bird loves me, and I love him. And I'm so afraid he's going to start clucking to me and start sitting on my shoulder.

Mike: This is Merlin's black bird?

Barb: Yes, yes!

Mike: They're in a circle or something. In some kind of ceremony?

Barb: And Merlin isn't acknowledging that he knows I'm here. . . . I've just connected with him and he knows I'm here.

Mike: Sure. He's known all along.

Barb: But he's not acknowledging that. He's just aware of me . . . being there.

Mike: You didn't really think that you could sneak up on him?

Barb: No. (Laughs.) And he's telepathically . . . he's talking to me while he's doing something else. So I need to be silent and to observe. He's telling me that that which I see I will need to know, and for me not to forget. And I don't know what it is that I'm seeing. I don't see what they're doing.

Mike: Okay.

Barb: It has something to do with becoming invisible. It has to do with energy and. . . .

Mike: There's some secret words they say for that, isn't there?

Barb: Uhhuh. Yes, Merlin has about . . . he is holding a book in his hands, but he doesn't need the book. He has something else. He's holding a parchment of some kind. And he is teaching from whatever is written on that parchment.

Mike: I'm going to say a word to you. I'm going to ask you if you hear that word in the circle: "ven-a-tray-ah." (No answer.) I'm going to mention another word: "tray-ah-ven."

Barb: Yes, that sound is in the room. (Long pause.) Merlin is very good at dividing his attention while he's working. He is instructing, but then at the same time he is also telepathically communicating with me. And, he's telling me that it's important that . . . that I remember. And he's telling me that it is time for me to leave now, so that I'm not seen. And he's telling me that he won't answer all of my questions.

Mike: Can you tell if Percival is there?

Barb: I don't know. I know Arthur's there, because I know he left the castle to go there. But I don't know who else is there. They are all wearing hooded robes. . . . So I'm kind of backing away now. I'm leaving. I'm going back to my room, going back to the castle.

Mike: Are you still in telepathic communication with Merlin?

Barb: Yes.

Mike: Okay. Do you mind if I ask him some questions?

Barb: That's fine.

Mike: Okay. Merlin, is it time for me now to learn to do that invisible ritual?

Barb: (As Merlin) Yes.

Mike: Okay, I know the words. Is it simply knowing how to use the words?

Barb: (As Merlin) Yes. Knowing how to use the words, knowing the words, and energetically . . . as you repeat the words in a certain rhythm, you repeat them over and over again, and then that extra frequency, that frequency will . . . bring the shift. It's not simply the words, it's the rhythm and the force with which they're said. They're . . . they are emanated, as opposed to just . . . spoken. They must be spoken with intent, with power. But, with the intent and power . . . must also be a purity.

Mike: Is the rhythm . . . ven-a-tray-ah?

Barb: (As Merlin) Say it again.

Mike: Ven-a-tray-ah . . . ven-a-tray-ah . . . ven-a-tray-ah.

Barb: (As Merlin) That's very close, yes.

Mike: Okay, well, I'll work on that. It's like a chant.

Barb: (As Merlin) Yes. There is a specific rhythm to it, and it must come from deep within you.

Mike: Oh yeah.

Barb: (As Merlin) Not just simply spoken as one would speak in conversation. This is spoken from deep within.

Mike: All right. And then the other is . . . tray-a-ven . . . tray-a-ven.

Barb: (As Merlin) Yes.

Mike: Tray-a-ven. . . . Why is it so important? Other than escaping from my bill collectors, why else is it time for me to learn this?

Barb: (As Merlin) Because the remembrance of this ritual is not so important, but the remembrance of this will bring more to you that you do need to know.

Mike: Yes, I feel a. . . .

Barb: (As Merlin) So, this is only a part, this is like a key . . . this is like a key to bring into your conscious awareness more of what you do need to know and to remember.

Mike: Thank you, Merlin. . . . Barb, we went to this scene because it represents the emotions you wanted to deal with and release. I ask you now to explain to me what those emotions are, and how we should deal with them.

Barb: There is an issue of . . . stepping into power.

Mike: Did you want the power?

Barb: It's not a matter of wanting it. It's a matter of being able to use that which you are given. And that is the blending of the love and the use of the power. Without the power, you cannot use the other two. There has to be a blending, a balance. I had the power thrust upon me unwanted in that lifetime. So now in this lifetime I resist taking it again. It is therefore causing an imbalance.

Mike: Please explain?

Barb: It's as though the experiences of that lifetime have left me . . . alone. Have left me with a great feeling of aloneness. No matter where I am, there is a sense of walking separate and apart. Of not being free to fully embrace and connect. Not able to fully be at one with another person. There is always part of myself that is kind of held back. A part that is not shared, or released.

Mike: The loneliness of command, so to speak?

Barb: Yes.

Mike: And also, there is anger at Arthur.

Barb: (Deep sighs.)

Mike: Let's deal with the anger toward Arthur. I would like for you to try this: let's go back to the castle.

Barb: Okay.

Mike: Let's go to your favorite table. Now, you will please visualize that Arthur is sitting across from you. Where is that table located? Is it in the kitchen? Do you see him?

Barb: Yes.

Mike: You can love him and be angry with him too.

Barb: YES!

Mike: And I'm getting that you don't want to accept this truth. Let's go to the kitchen, because you're comfortable there. There is a nice big, heavy wooden table that you like. It's very non-threatening.

Barb: Yes, yes.

Mike: Arthur's sitting there, with a very pleasant, but strained, look on his face. He looks like a chicken who is about to have his head cut off, and he knows it. He is ready to take his lumps, because he loves you very much. And he says, "Okay, tell me." Now, tell him. Talk to him.

Barb: (to Arthur) This is not fair. I didn't want this. It's not fair. This is not fair. It's not FAIR!

Mike: Now get angry. Pound the table.

Barb: I just want to scream at him. (She starts screaming.) He is so, SO . . . HE IS SO POMPOUS. HE IS SUCH AN ASS. HE JUST . . . HE JUST WON'T LISTEN.

142

Mike: Say to him, "Arthur, you're an ass and you won't listen."

Barb: ARTHUR, YOU'RE AN ASS AND YOU WON'T LISTEN. YOU JUST WON'T LISTEN. Oh, he's such, he's so. . . .

Mike: Pound the table, pound the table. Pound the table here, pound the, pound the table. Pound the table.

Barb: He just, he just. . . .

Mike: Pound the table, pound the table in front of Arthur.

Barb: He just doesn't get it, he just doesn't get it.

Mike: Well, tell him.

Barb: It's like talking to a block of wood. HE'S A BLOCKHEAD. HE JUST DOESN'T GET IT.

Mike: He's in front of you now, so release it. Pound that table and tell him what a jerk he is and how unhappy he's making you.

Barb: But he's so pathetic. (Laughs.)

Mike: Yeah, and he's destroying your life.

Barb: He's, he's. . . .

Mike: He's destroying your love for him. Tell him. . . .

Barb: He's, he's just. . . . (Starts screaming again.) YOU'RE JUST . . . EVERYTHING I'M FEELING IS BEING TORN TO PIECES. BECAUSE YOU WON'T ACT, YOU'VE GOT TO DO SOMETHING. YOU CAN'T LEAVE ME TO DO THIS. I DON'T WANT TO DO IT. I DIDN'T ASK TO DO IT, AND YOU WON'T LISTEN WHEN I DO TRY TO DO IT. YOU JUST, YOU'RE SO STUPID. (Crying.) WHY WON'T YOU, WHY . . . WHY . . . ALL I WANTED TO DO WAS TO BE YOUR WIFE AND TO HAVE YOUR CHILDREN, AND I CAN'T DO EITHER ONE BECAUSE YOU WON'T LET ME!! I DON'T WANT THIS RESPONSIBILITY. WE HAVE A VILE MAN IN THE CASTLE WHO WILL DESTROY US ALL AND YOU LET HIM! AND YOU LET HIM STAY AND YOU LISTEN TO HIM. AND HE'LL STEAL MY SOUL IF YOU DON'T STOP HIM. . . . AND YOU WON'T DO ANYTHING. I HATE HIM. I HATE HIM. . . . AND I CAN'T DO ANYTHING ABOUT HIM. AND YOU ALLOW IT. (Very forcefully, but not screaming.) I'm not going to go in that chapel again. I will not do it. I don't care what happens. I won't do it. I don't care what happens to me. I don't care what you do. Go to the chapel. You be there if you need to. I won't go. (Very quiet.) I've done that battle. . . . Take yourself back to your bed and STAY THERE. I'm done with you, too. I'll do what needs to be done. But, I won't listen to you anymore.

Mike: Anything else you want to tell him?

Barb: (Big sigh.) I can just see him there, and he's looking at me and. . . .

Mike: Okay, I'm going to ask you to do something. I'm going to ask you to reach across the table and take his head, as if it actually were a football helmet. And take his head, and lift it over on your shoulders. Just imagine this. You're holding his head upon your head, just as if it were a football helmet.

Barb: Okay.

Mike: Now, tell me what you feel. It's not a good feeling, is it?

Barb: No, and that's why it's so hard to get angry with him. Because I have such compassion for him. And I know what he's feeling.

Mike: He's so sad.

Barb: Without even taking his head upon my shoulders, I KNOW, I see into his heart. And I see his sadness and I see his . . . bereftness, because he can't function in the way that he has functioned and the way that he wants to function. He just. . . .

Mike: Okay, I. . . .

Barb: He's doing the best he can do, but it doesn't relieve . . . me . . . of the burden.

Mike: He's inadequate for the challenge.

Barb: Yes. And I'm NOT inadequate for the challenge. I can stand in the strength and the power that needs to be wielded, and I can do that! I just don't want to. But I've had to. And it's going to have to be done for the sake of all. . . . I can't shake him.

Mike: I have Merlin here. Would you mind if he gave you a few words of. . . .

Barb: Please.

Mike: Merlin says that he created Arthur . . . molded Arthur . . . brought Arthur into existence for the specific purpose of doing what he's doing. And as flawed as things look to you, they are perfect in terms of the grand scheme. And Merlin asks me this question; it's rather rhetorical. He says, why isn't HE upset? Merlin says to you, shouldn't Merlin be the first one who feels betrayed? As Arthur turns to the Bishop, he abnegates his power, and lets his kingdom begin to crumble. Shouldn't Merlin be upset by this?

Barb: Yes.

Mike: And is he upset?

Barb: No.

Mike: Merlin says he's blessed with inner understanding of the natural order of these things. And he says unfortunately, it wasn't in the order of things for him to be able to mold you and the others the way he did Arthur. So you won't have a greater understanding.

Barb: Yes.

Mike: That's why he's here with you today, working on these issues. Because he's doing damage control on all of us. Fifteen-hundred years later. But he is now doing damage control, and saying, let's finally bring these things out, and get them resolved. So that we can all be the perfect, wonderful beings that we are, and go into the new age truly happy, and rejoicing. A new era that we're going to go into. . . . He said that he's not sure that this made you feel better, but it makes him feel better by telling you.

144

Barb: I understand.

Mike: He says that some of your anger is still there. He senses that perhaps it has to seep out over a period of time. He says you didn't get angry enough. But that's okay. Enough for now.

15

Greg as Arthur August, 1994

Background: This was a difficult regression for me. First of all, I didn't like this guy. This bothered me because I knew psychically that he represented a fragment or segment of Arthur. Arthur, the king I loved. How could this guy, who was a jerk, be a part of Arthur? Thus I was bothered. Why was he a jerk? I am really at a loss to explain my dislike of him. I did not know him. But I took an almost immediate dislike to him when we met to do this regression. Greg is a 37-year-old chef who works in one of the restaurants at Disney World in Orlando. He is good-looking. He is also pompous and self-centered. He considers himself to be a ladies man.

Another point of difficulty for me in this regression was that Greg had read a lot about Camelot. Normally this is a no-no. I try to limit my work to those who have not had their minds already programmed by existing literature or history. An Arthurian expert is not going to give me the type of pure Camelot story I seek. He is likely to let his preconceived concepts of what Camelot was like in books and movies influence his regression experience. But because I did not have many "Arthur" regressions, I was anxious to do this one anyway. I have attempted to edit out all questionable information which may not be truth.

As is evident from this regression, Greg was somewhat tortured by his Camelot past. It is as if he represented a "tortured" portion of Arthur's soul. I apologize for the anger and the few bits of profanity which creep into this work. I was tempted to edit it out. However, it is perhaps better left in, as a reminder of my conflict with this particular Arthur.

Mike: See the door?
Greg: Yes.

Mike: Ready to go through it?

Greg: Something is still fighting me.

Mike: Would it help if I opened the door?

Greg: I don't mind.

Mike: Okay, I'm going to take you by the hand.

Greg: I trust you.

Mike: I'm going to take you by the hand and I'm going to just open the door a peek. Okay, it is open. Now let's go through it. What do you see?

Greg: (Crying softly.)

Mike: Tell me what you see. I've got kleenex right here. Here is some kleenex.

Greg: (Big sigh.) I just see beautiful greenery. It's so green.

Mike: Yeah, it is. The plants and trees were greener then than they are now. It is a beautiful day.

Greg: I see nothing. It is a beautiful day. I see nothing but green trees. Why is it so upsetting to see it? I don't see it as much as I FEEL the green.

Mike: All right. Where are we going to go now?

Greg: To the castle.

Mike: What do you see?

Greg: My first vision is that I saw all the green. The second is that I'm at the castle wall. Huge, black, big walls. Big stone blocks making up the wall. That is all I see is a wall. Something's holding me back.

Mike: Walk along the wall. . . .

Greg: (Erratic breathing, deep sighs.)

Mike: Let's go inside the castle to the Great Hall. What does the Great Hall look like?

Greg: There is nobody there.

Mike: What does the Great Hall look like?

Greg: I see the Round Table, and just. . . . I see nothing but browns and grays.

Mike: Are you seated at the Round Table?

Greg: Nope. I'm just looking at it. Nobody is there.

Mike: Okay. Let's go to the night before your last battle. That is a way to shake loose some of these emotions.

Greg: (Two very forceful, fast deep breaths.)

Mike: Let's go to the night before your last battle, to dinner in the Great Hall. Do you see it now?

Greg: I love music so much. Yes, yes, yes, there are people all around the place.

Mike: What do you love?

Greg: I love music. I'm hearing music. I'm always lost in my own little world.

Mike: What kind of instruments are they. . . .

Greg: Flutes, flutes, flutes.

Mike: What is the atmosphere there, that night, the last night?

Greg: (Laughing.) Actually, it's frolicking.

Mike: Huh?

Greg: Actually, it's very frolicking.

Mike: It is?

Greg: And I'm just quiet. I'm just watching.

Mike: How are the other knights? Are they quiet, or are they frolicking?

Greg: I can't pick up on that. I'm lost in my own world. All I see is women with silk gowns. They're frolicking.

Mike: Okay, let's go to your. . . .

Greg: I don't pick up on the men at all. I just pick up on the women frolicking.

Mike: Let's go to your last time with Guenivere, when you said good-bye to her. How do you feel about Guenivere?

Greg: Not as good.

Mike: How do you feel about Merlin?

Greg: He's everything. . . . (Sobbing.)

Mike: What?

Greg: He is everything to me. . . .

Mike: All right. Tell me about your love for Merlin.

Greg: He is a part of me. He is not Merlin, he is me. (Erratic breathing.). . . . He is a part of me. He's my father, he's my brother, he's my lover, he's everything.

Mike: Do you feel sorry about the way that things have turned out with Merlin?

Greg: To me, Merlin is the earth. To me, Merlin is Mother . . . Earth.

Mike: Did you think that you disappointed Merlin?

Greg: Yes.

Mike: You have a lot of grief about that?

Greg: I did something wrong.

Mike: What did you do wrong?

Greg: I don't know.

Mike: Let us talk to Merlin. He is seated there next to you. Turn to him and talk to him.

Greg: I don't. . . .

Mike: Put your arm around Merlin. . . . Did you put your arm around Merlin? Put your arm around him. Got your arm around him?

Greg: No. I'm sorry.

Mike: Put your arm around him.

Greg: I respect him too much.

Mike: Put your arm around him.

Greg: Okay.

Mike: Reach over and kiss him. . . . What does he do when you do that?

Greg: (Laughing.) He smiles. . . .

Mike: Okay. Tell him, say I love you.

Greg: I love you, Merlin. He says that he knows that.

Mike: Tell him that he is your great love.

Greg: You are my great love.

Mike: I am sorry for those times I disappointed you.

Greg: I'm sorry for the times I disappointed you.

Mike: Now, what else do you want to tell him?

Greg: The time is soon upon us. . . .

Mike: Say, I die tomorrow.

Greg: He knows I die tomorrow.

Mike: Ask Merlin why you have to die tomorrow.

Greg: He says, "There's no such thing as dying."

Mike: Is that what he says?

Greg: Eternal life. . . . (Erratic breathing.)

Mike: I don't want your answer. What did Merlin tell you? Now what does Merlin tell you? Ask him, "Why do I have to die tomorrow, Merlin?" Ask him.

Greg: Why do I have to die tomorrow, Merlin? Cause it's. . . . (Starts crying.)

Mike: I want Merlin's answer.

Greg: My head is down, my head is down. I don't even want to look at him.

Mike: Look up. He is telling you to look up at him. We are changing the past. Merlin is not sad, is he?

Greg: No, he is not sad. He is smiling at me.

Mike: Yes, ask him why he's happy. Say, "Why are you happy, Merlin?"

Greg: Why are you happy, Merlin?

Mike: And what does he answer you?

Greg: (As Merlin) Because I have seen the future.

Mike: What?

Greg: He says, "Because I have seen the future." (Long pause. Heavy, erratic breathing.)

Mike: Do you see Merlin there now?

Greg: (Quietly.) No.

Mike: Where are you?

Greg: I'm back in the woods, in the trees.

Mike: All right.

Greg: I'm much more comfortable there. I'll be left alone.

Mike: How old are you?

149

Greg: I'm a little kid.

Mike: Okay. Where is your mommy?

Greg: Mother's never around.

Mike: Where is your dad?

Greg: Oh, Dad is never around. I'm all by myself. I'm just walking in the woods. I can't see my mother, I can't see my father.

Mike: All right.

Greg: I'm all by myself.

Mike: How old are you?

Greg: Seven-years old.

Mike: Seven-years old. Boy, that is young to be out in the woods alone. Okay, let's go home. Take me to your house, where you live. Take me where you eat your meals.

Greg: I see a cave. I feel more comfortable with the cave.

Mike: Okay, go in the cave.

Greg: It's a huge cave.

Mike: Okay. Is your mother there?

Greg: No.

Mike: Your father there?

Greg: Noooo.

Mike: Who's there?

Greg: (Laughs.) There are only two people. Just me and the old man.

Mike: Okay. What are you doing living with an old man?

Greg: There is only one person in my life. (Erratic breathing.)

Mike: What is his name? What does he call himself?

Greg: I shouldn't have been. . . . I'm not very good at this.

Mike: You love Merlin, don't you?

Greg: There are no names. We don't call each other names. I can feel him coming. He's the only person that. . . .

Mike: Okay, what do you do with this old man? What does he teach you?

Greg: (Heavy breathing; short gasps.) I don't want to be here in the cave anymore.

Mike: Tell me about the first time you saw Guenivere.

Greg: I'm sorry, Guenivere is irrelevant. (Laughing.)

Mike: Not to me, she's not. She wasn't irrelevant to you either. Tell me about the first time you saw her.

Greg: Michael, there's something fighting me. Something that I don't want to see.

Mike: I know, that is why we're doing this regression.

Greg: I'm trying to loosen it up. I can't.

Mike: Guenivere. . . .

Greg: Oh, there is no such thing as I can't.

Mike: Guenivere is not irrelevant. You are trying to block it. Tell me about the first time you saw Guenivere. Did you go to her father's house? Did she come to the castle? What happened? Who set the meeting up? Did her father set it up? Did Merlin set it up? Did you set it up?

Greg: I feel that a woman set it up.

Mike: All right. What kind of family did Guenivere come from?

Greg: Obviously she came from a very well . . . from a strong family. Her father was very strong. I can't see the mother. All I see is a strong father.

Mike: Okay.

Greg: Strong, strong father.

Mike: Was it politically expedient to marry her? Why did you marry her? Why did you pick her as your queen?

Greg: I didn't pick her.

Mike: Who picked her?

Greg: I don't know who picked her, but I remember looking at her. I was very much moved by her.

Mike: Why?

Greg: Her beauty.

Mike: What did she look like?

Greg: I've tried to see her so many times. I tried . . . black hair.

Mike: Skin?

Greg: (Shallow, fast breathing.) Very white, milky.

Mike: If you had to say that she looked like any movie star you have ever seen, who would you say she looked like?

Greg: Jean Simmons, Vivian Leigh. That type.

Mike: Good, great. Yes, okay. How did you feel about her after you got married?

Greg: Something is ripping me up inside.

Mike: You loved her, didn't you?

Greg: Of course I did. (Deep, gasping breaths.) Something is ripping me up inside.

Mike: Not all husbands, and not all kings, love their queens.

Greg: I'm trying to. . . .

Mike: Tell me about the first time you found out that she was unfaithful to you. Let's just jump right into this matter.

Greg: I don't mind if she fucks around. I love her. Sex has nothing to do with love.

Mike: Wait a minute. No, no, no, no. You're avoiding an answer. Tell me about the time that you first heard that she was unfaithful.

Greg: Of course. . . .

Mike: Tell me about it.

Greg: Of course it's going to hurt.

Mike: Yeah, that is why we're going to do this. Let's get into it. Let's get some of that hurt out into the open. Tell me about it.

Greg: Yeah, but it never does come out into the open.

Mike: But it does now. We're going to get rid of it. Believe me, I know. Because I loved her too. And I also carried that hurt. I didn't get rid of that hurt myself until this lifetime. Tell me about the first time that you heard that she was unfaithful.

Greg: I'm not he.

Mike: Huh?

Greg: I am not him.

Mike: What?

Greg: I am not him.

Mike: You are not who?

Greg: Who do you think I am?

Mike: You're not Arthur?

Greg: No, I'm NOT.

Mike: Who are you?

Greg: I don't want to be Arthur. (Crying.)

Mike: Who are you, then?

Greg: (Laughing, crying.)

Mike: You're some other king?

Greg: No, I am Arthur.

Mike: All right, enough of this foolishness. Tell me about the time when you heard, the first time that you heard that Guenivere was unfaithful to you. Tell me about it. Were you sick in bed?

Greg: I would never show it.

Mike: What?

Greg: I would never show it.

Mike: I'm not asking you that, I'm. . . .

Greg: I keep it private, to myself.

Mike: Who told you, how did you know?

Greg: A woman told me.

Mike: Who?

Greg: A woman.

Mike: Morgana. . . .

Greg: It wasn't Morgana.

Mike: Who was it?

Greg: She was insignificant. She was a young, a. . . .

Mike: I see like a chamber lady, who you knew and trusted.

Greg: YES, good.

Mike: A heavy-set peasant woman, who you trusted. Who you could talk to, very plainly and openly. And she told you. It hurt you very much, didn't it? Tell me about it, tell me how you felt. Let it out. Come on, let that emotion out.

Greg: There are very few people who feel . . . true love. You have to have the capacity to love. It is a spiritual love.

Mike: How did you feel?

Greg: Uh!!

Mike: Tell me about your feelings of betrayal.

Greg: Uh!!

Mike: Hurt. Come on, let that hurt and emotion of betrayal out. Let it out!

Greg: I won't let it out because I have to be strong. (Voice wavers.)

Mike: Hey, hey, hey. This is different now. You have been carrying that shit around for fifteen-hundred years. Now we're going to let it out. Tell me how you felt. Let it out NOW. Tell me how you feel! Tell me how you feel.

Greg: You can't just let that go overnight! It has been centuries. . . .

Mike: Let it go, yes. . . .

Greg: It has been centuries, that things haven't been the same way. . . .

Mike: Well, we're going to start. . . .

Greg: I'm a fanatic about love right now, and it is controlled. You have to learn to control. . . .

Mike: NO. You've been controlling it ever since, so that you wouldn't get hurt again. But I want you to tell me right now about the hurt. Tell me about how that hurt you, when you found out that she was unfaithful to you. Tell me about the hurt.

Greg: It taught me a lesson.

Mike: I don't give a shit about lessons. I want to know about the hurt. All that betrayal. You are carrying around all that betrayal with you, and it is killing you. Let's let that feeling of the hurt out. Now, come on. Let the hurt out. You are carrying all that betrayal.

Greg: What service, what purpose would it do? I've always been an equation, a man. What service would it do, what purpose would it do? I'm not her keeper.

Mike: I don't want to hear that stuff. I want to hear about your hurt.

Greg: Of course it hurts.

Mike: Tell me how it hurts. Move it up to the surface. I want the hurt to come out. Cry. Scream. Holler. Do you want some pillows to pound on?

Greg: Nope, cause I'm not that kind of person. And I never will be that kind of person. Because the point is, everybody has their own right to be and do as they wish. I am not her keeper. I will always say that to the end. . . . My true love, the truest love, is sharing her love.

Mike: All right.

Greg: If you truly understand spiritual love, it is not possessive and selfish. I will fight against that.

Mike: But, uh. . . .

Greg: If I feel hurt, if I feel upset in this, it is for myself, it is not for love. If I feel bad, it is not for love. It is for my own pettiness, my own selfishness.

Mike: All right, FINE! Now we're going to show some pity and self-ishness, and I want you to let out whatever it is that you have been holding all this time.

Greg: (Breaking up.) Merlin wouldn't want me to do that.

Mike: Yes, he does. He is here right now. He set this whole thing up. Who do you think brought us together for this regression? He wants you to get these feelings out of you now so you can heal. It's all over. It has been over for fifteen-hundred years. You've been carrying these feelings around. All of us. We have to heal them now. Let it out! It hurt, didn't it?

Greg: Of course it did.

Mike: But you are not showing it. I don't want to hear the intellectual crap. I want you to let your feelings out. Let those feelings out.

Greg: You're asking me to do something that I have avoided doing for lifetimes. . . .

Mike: Your wife cheated on you. You don't want to cry about it? Your wife betrayed you, and you don't want to cry about it?

Greg: NO, I don't want to cry about it!

Mike: All right then. You're wasting your time, you're wasting this opportunity.

Greg: (Panting.)

Mike: Merlin and everybody, your spiritual guides and the others, went to a lot of trouble to get you here, so that you could heal.

Greg: To self-pity myself is healing? If I truly love her, if I truly care for her, I would want her to run to him.

Mike: Ahhhhh.

Greg: That is the truest thing about love. If she loves and cares for another somebody, if I. . . .

Mike: Oh, that's bullshit.

Greg: I DID NOT choose her.

Mike: I'm not talking about. . . .

Greg: SHE DID NOT CHOOSE ME.

Mike: I'm not talking about Guenivere. . . .

Greg: She chose a love that she cared for somebody else, I will not. . . .

Mike: She didn't screw just Lancelot, she screwed a bunch of your knights.

Greg: YOU'RE RIGHT, she did! (Begins to shake.)

Mike: She screwed a bunch of them.

Greg: I love it. The truest thing that I love is. . . .

Mike: So why are you shaking, why are you shaking like a leaf?

Greg: I don't know. (Laughs, somewhat hysterically.)

Mike: It is because you're hurt and you won't let it out. You are carry-ing this hurt, you're carrying all this hurt around.

Greg: I loved, and this is what I feel, and this is what is. . . .

Mike: You're, I tell you what. . . .

Greg: I loved the concept of Guenivere. . . .

Mike: Yeah. . . .

Greg: I loved the energy of Guenivere. . . .

Mike: All right. But you got hurt.

Greg: Of course I did.

Mike: You keep saying of course, but you won't talk about it, you won't let it out. You won't let it out. Do some crying.

Greg: She couldn't help herself.

Mike: I'M NOT TALKING ABOUT GUENIVERE. I'm talking about you letting it out. Letting the hurt out.

Greg: I fell in love with the idea. I fell in love with the concept.

Mike: A bunch of us did. . . .

Greg: I made her something that she was not!

Mike: A bunch of us did that also.

Greg: I had to learn to accept what she was, and that is the truth.

Mike: A bunch of us did that. Many of us loved her, put her on a pedestal, and she couldn't handle that responsibility. She didn't ask for it. We know that now. I've been able to heal myself. Because you know what, I let my emotions open up, and I cried about it. And I screamed and hollered, and I got rid of all those stored up hurts . . . and you're sitting there in denial. You're denying. . . .

Greg: I AM NOT DENYING. I know exactly what it is. She was a concept. She represented a concept which I loved. Which I believe our love represented.

Mike: That is fine.

Greg: But it wasn't Guenivere. I DID NOT LOVE GUENIVERE. I love the concept of what Guenivere represented.

Mike: So, what has that got to do with releasing a hurt?

Greg: I accept it.

Mike: Good. Stay wounded. You're wasting your time here tonight. You're wasting my time. So just stay wounded.

Greg: (Panting.) So the only way to. . . .

Mike: All right. Let's move on. Let's go to the Bishop. Tell me about the Bishop. The guy who caused all the trouble in your court. Why did you let the Bishop do that?

Greg: He is just a stone. He is just a symbol. The main thing is for the people to choose.

Mike: So why did you let him take all your power away from you?

Greg: I could have destroyed the Bishop. I could have controlled everything. But the thing is in not controlling. It is in NOT controlling. People have to go for it for themselves. They have to live for themselves. Leaders are just representations, just a symbol.

Mike: What did you tell all the knights when they came to you, pleading with you to do something about the Bishop?

Greg: I told them, "I will not."

Mike: Why?

Greg: You can't do everything for the people. They have to choose for themselves. Each has their own destiny.

Mike: But you didn't let the people have a choice. You let the Bishop take over.

Greg: (Panting.) It wasn't the time. As with Jesus, it wasn't the right time.

Mike: Did you talk with Merlin about the Bishop?

Greg: No I didn't.

Mike: Why? He is the person you loved the most.

Greg: There comes a time when you have to choose your own path.

Mike: So, you left Merlin. Or did he leave you?

Greg: I left Merlin.

Mike: Do you feel that you betrayed Merlin?

Greg: (Panting.) I did not betray Merlin. I did what I believed is right. And that is what you have to do. You have to follow your heart. I will . . . not . . . do. . . .

Mike: So why did you get so disillusioned that you had to spend almost two years in bed? Why did you get so down and out? You let the Bishop do that to you, didn't you?

Greg: Guenivere. She took my heart. There is something else that bothers me. If you could just show me. (Laughing, shaking, panting.) I don't know. I didn't betray Merlin. He taught me to go my own way.

Mike: All right. Merlin taught you to go your own way. Okay. What else is bothering you? Guenivere took your heart, now what?

Greg: The people.

Mike: The people let you down?

Greg: The people. The people are everything.

Mike: They hurt you?

Greg: If I compare the people to Guenivere, Guenivere is but one kind of emotional hurt. That is the part that is human. But the people are everything.

Mike: Tell me about the people; the hurt the people have caused you.

Greg: Ohhhhh. . . . (Groans.)

Mike: You are thrashing around violently on the couch there, but you don't want to deal with this stuff. You're fighting, you're fighting, looking for excuses. . . .

Greg: BECAUSE THEY HAVEN'T CHANGED. The people have not changed.

Mike: See, we're not worried about the people. . . .

Greg: Jesus came. Jesus came, to set an example. But the people don't want to listen.

Mike: But see, we are not talking about the people. We are talking about YOU. We're talking about dealing with your issues. You keep trying to pass the buck. . . .

Greg: I'm not passing the buck. I never passed the buck in my whole life.

Mike: Talk about whatever hurt you. Whatever broke your heart, okay? How did the people hurt you?

Greg: (Laughs.) That one gets spiritual, and spiritual sounds . . . foolish. It wasn't the time.

Mike: I know that.

Greg: I have a hard time accepting the way things were at that time.

Mike: Look. Everything that happened was meant to be. Merlin knew that. That is why Merlin understood when you turned your back on him. It was all meant to be. But that is not the issue.

Greg: I DON'T UNDERSTAND many things. I don't understand why they set me up with Morgana. I love Morgana more than everything.

Mike: All right. Good, now we're getting somewhere.

Greg: SHE is my true love. I don't understand why they set it up in a situation again obviously so impossible. I put in my time with Jesus, as with this time. But it is so difficult. . . .

Mike: Okay, wait a minute.

Greg: I'm a dupe!

Mike: Let's talk about Morgana. Let's talk about your times with Morgana. Where did Morgana live? Did she live in the castle with you?

Greg: She spent a little time in the castle, but most of the time she was gone.

Mike: Where did she live?

Greg: Where? (Laughs.) In my heart.

Mike: All right. She was your soul mate. Morgana was your soul mate.

Greg: She was everything to me.

Mike: Okay. How did she feel when you got married?

Greg: She was ripped apart.

Mike: How many children did you and Morgana have?

Greg: (Sobs.) Only one.

Mike: Okay. Did you have a son?

Greg: Again, I . . . I'm having a hard time. Because I loved her . . . ever since I was a kid.

Mike: Tell me about Mordred. Did you ever spend any time with Mordred?

Greg: Yes, I loved Mordred. He was my son.

Mike: All right, tell me about it.

Greg: Mordred was my son. He was my blood. He would do anything for me. He would die for me, and I would die . . . (voice fluctuates) for him.

Mike: Okay. Did you have a daughter?

Greg: I can't recall.

Mike: All right. What became of Mordred when he grew up? Did he become a sorcerer, or a knight, or an administrator? What did he become?

Greg: What I feel was . . . a musician. But also, he was a knight.

Mike: He was a knight?

Greg: Yes, he was more of a knight. But he was a knight that was truer to what a knight should be.

Mike: Did you trust him?

Greg: Yes, I did.

Mike: Did Guenivere trust him?

Greg: Nope!

Mike: Why didn't Guenivere trust him?

Greg: Because he was my true love.

Mike: Is it not true, though, that Mordred betrayed you in the end? Lined himself up with the enemy, and betrayed you?

Greg: (Quietly.) I don't think that I want to accept that.

Mike: Okay. Isn't it true that Mordred actually arranged for the person that killed you? Mordred was your murderer?

Greg: (Laughing.) It's okay. It's okay. (Calmer.)

Mike: It's okay? You loved him that much?

Greg: I don't mind dying. It doesn't make any diff. . . .

Mike: Oh, that's not, that's not. . . .

Greg: I don't mind. . . .

Mike: You seem to skip over everything by saying, "It's all okay." Instead of looking at the hurt to the individual, or to you.

Greg: It's okay to hurt.

Mike: Tell me. . . .

Greg: There is nothing wrong with it.

Mike: Tell me about Morgana. When did you two first become lovers?

Greg: I can't marry her. The thing that sticks out in my mind the most about Morgana is our absolute oneness. I can be myself. She was me, I was her. When we were together, there was no . . . airs. I wasn't Arthur, I wasn't anybody. I was just me.

Mike: She loved you for who you were.

Greg: When we made love, we were animals. Pure animals. Pure nature. If I have to choose between the two things that mean the most to me, between "nature" and all the "power" . . . (Laughs.) Give me the "nature." I just want to be left alone. I don't want to think about Guenivere. I don't want to think about Mordred. (Laughs.) They rip my heart up. I just want to be left alone. . . . It is like I am in a mist, in a cloud. I am protected by the cloud.

Mike: I have a list here of some of the knights. I'm going to read through this list, and I am going to ask you to give me any comments you may have. If any of these names strike a bell, and you have any comments you wish to make. Agravaine?

Greg: I liked him.

Mike: King Bagdemagus?

Greg: Things are so dark.

Mike: Huh? Going dark?

Greg: Everything's so dark.

Mike: Bedivere?

Greg: (Laughs.) I liked him.

Mike: You liked him. Bors de Ganis?

Greg: I'm sorry.

Mike: Bors?

Greg: I like Bors. Anything with a "bor" I like.

Mike: Breuse sans Pitie?

Greg: No.

Mike: You didn't like him?

Greg: No.

Mike: What was wrong with him?

Greg: Couldn't trust him. He was flighty.

Mike: Flighty? Okay. Dinadan?

Greg: Very important.

Mike: Dinadan. Okay. Ector de Maris?

Greg: I look in my mind, and he is putsy.

Mike: Putsy. Okay. Gaheris?

Greg: Strong.

Mike: Strong knight?

Greg: Yes.

Mike: Good. Galahad?

Greg: Pure.

Mike: Okay. Did Galahad do a lot of spiritual work at the court, or was he a court symbol? How did you use Galahad?

Greg: He was a symbol for all of the knights.

Mike: Okay. A symbol of what?

Greg: Purity. I see light around him. A representation.

Mike: Good. Duke Galeholt?

Greg: Did he upset me?

Mike: He upset you? Okay. Gareth?

Greg: (Big sigh.) Something's fighting me that I don't want to listen to.

Mike: Okay. Gawaine?

Greg: I like Gawaine. (Laughs.) Even the sound "Gawaine" I like.

Mike: Kay?

Greg: Kay! I like him. My brother. I like Kay.

Mike: Good. Lamorak de Galis?

Greg: Some of these are foreigners, and I don't . . . foreigners I have trouble with. De Galis. No, I can't trust him.

Mike: Lancelot?

Greg: Of course.

Mike: What did you like about Lancelot? He was a foreigner.

Greg: Ohhhhh. (Panting.)

Mike: Let it out.

Greg: (Panting again, starts crying.)

Mike: Good. Tears finally come.

Greg: Ohhhhh. . . . (Crying.) Guenivere is a woman. They have their point and purpose.

Mike: You cared for Lancelot a great deal!

Greg: (More crying.) Ohhhhhh.

Mike: Let it out. Let that pain out.

Greg: I don't blame him.

Mike: Let it out. It doesn't matter.

Greg: (Still crying.) It doesn't make any difference.

Mike: You know what. It affected him also. His betrayal. It tore him up and it tore you up.

Greg: I know, I know, I know, I know. (Crying.)

Mike: He was greatly devastated by his betrayal.

Greg: Oh. Oh. (Heaving sighs. Panting.) I don't mean to sound demeaning to women. I don't even like to say men and women. I would rather talk about spirits. I don't even like to talk about mortal life.

Mike: Yeah.

Greg: Lancelot was my everything!

Mike: Do you want to talk about him some more?

Greg: I don't want to talk about him.

Mike: Okay. Lionel?

Greg: Good.

Mike: He was kind of austere, wasn't he? Wasn't he kind of a hard-ass?

Greg: Leave the name Lionel. . . .

Mike: Okay. King Pellinore?

Greg: Of course.

Mike: Of course what? A good guy?

Greg: He has been around me for a long long time.

Mike: How about Percival?

Greg: (Laughs.) Second to Lancelot.

Mike: Why?

Greg: Because I knew he would carry honor.

Mike: Was it true . . . that he was Merlin's son?

Greg: They are very, very, very, very close.

Mike: But you knew that. You and Merlin discussed that.

Greg: I don't know, but I do know that they were very, very close. I can see him with Merlin.

Mike: Sagramore le Desirous?

Greg: (Laughs.) I like Sagramore. Okay. I loved him.

Mike: Tristram?

Greg: Zero.

Mike: Zero? Ywaine? Accolon of Gaul?

Greg: These are knights I don't like.

Mike: Tell me. Which ones? How about Segwarides?

Greg: You are forcing me to think of knights that . . . this is giving me a pain right in the middle of my head. I don't want to think about them.

Mike: Why? Did they betray you? Did they betray you in battle?

Greg: They would never betray me in battle! Never in battle. Battle is purity. Going over to Christianity, that is what betrayed me.

Mike: Christianity betrayed you. Yes. Now we're getting somewhere. How did Christianity betray you?

Greg: Everybody has to make their own choice, as I had to make my own choice. Of course, you always have two choices. I am not going to make the choice for them. I can just present my view to them. It is like love. You present all the love you have to give. On the receiving end, if they cannot accept it, if they cannot understand it, if they cannot relate, then so be it. But the fact of the matter is that the seed of Christianity had to be planted.

Mike: Okay, let's talk about something else, something more pleasant. Let's talk about your sword. Excalibur.

Greg: NO! I don't want to pick it up. I don't want to think about it. (Panting.) They want me to pick it up, but I don't want to pick it up! Keep it there. Keep it there! I don't want to pick it up!

Mike: You don't have to pick it up. Tell me, how did you get Excalibur?

Greg: I have NEVER seen it in the stone!

Mike: Ah, well, that's bullshit!

Greg: (Laughs.) That's bullshit!

Mike: Tell me about it.

Greg: A woman gave it to me.

Mike: A woman gave it to you? Okay, who made Excalibur?

Greg: The only thing I know is that a woman gave it to me.

Mike: All right. Tell me. . . .

Greg: I don't remember. . . .

Mike: Okay. Why were you protected when you carried Excalibur? What was Excalibur's power?

Greg: It was connected. . . .

Mike: To what?

Greg: To the Light!

Mike: How was it connected? Did it glow?

Greg: It always glowed white.

Mike: Huh?

Greg: It . . . always . . . glowed . . . white! You could feel it.

Mike: Okay.

Greg: It was a part of me. (Heavy breathing.) I don't see it killing.

Mike: It didn't. . . .

Greg: I see a weapon. It didn't . . . I don't see it killing.

Mike: It didn't kill. It didn't kill. You never killed anybody with Excalibur.

Greg: I didn't.

Mike: Now tell me where Excalibur's power came from. What was the power of Excalibur?

Greg: (Panting.) Excalibur to me was not a sword.

Mike: What was it?

Greg: It was a cross.

Mike: Okay. What was its power? Why was it that you could not be hurt when you were carrying Excalibur?

Greg: The only thing I think of is that it was connected. It was a part of something. Part of the Force, part of the Power.

Mike: When you knighted somebody, you laid Excalibur on their shoulders. Why did you do that?

Greg: To give them the energy.

Mike: Ah hah. What kind of energy? Did Excalibur have energy, then?

Greg: Of course it did.

Mike: What kind of energy did it have?

Greg: You are asking me something that I. . . . There is something associated with Excalibur right now. Right now, in my heart, that I am trying to fight. And that is what I don't understand.

Mike: Okay then, I'm going to tell you. First of all, when Excalibur was made, Jesus and Archangel Michael put their hands in the molten metal. This was part of a special ceremony arranged by Merlin. And when they did that, they gave that metal the power of Love. And Excalibur's power was the power of Love.

Greg: Yes.

Mike: And when you held Excalibur, you were surrounded by an envelope of love. When you are surrounded by love, you are protected, and you cannot be hurt. So, that is what you don't want to remember. But it was the love, and love was the ultimate protection.

Greg: Why do I feel such a close connection with Archangel Michael and Jesus?

Mike: You were St. John. Arthur was a reincarnation of St. John.

Greg: Do you expect me to believe that?

Mike: Yep. You expect me to believe that you are Arthur. Good, I'll believe it, and you can believe that you were St. John. You needed that experience as Arthur. Now, I'm going to tell you some things to help put your mind at ease. Let me tell you what Galahad said when I regressed him. Galahad said that Camelot was not meant to be a constellation, which is permanent in the sky. Camelot was meant to be a shooting star. To exist only briefly. Because mankind was not ready yet for Camelot. Camelot was only meant to exist long enough to show mankind the way. . . .

Greg: (Crying.)

Mike: To show mankind what it could eventually become. It was to be an archetype. To show mankind the potential. Camelot set up a goal for mankind in terms of nobility and honor. And love. And Camelot is an ideal which has never been extinguished. Throughout history its concepts have periodically surfaced. But each time, mankind was not yet ready. So they were again extinguished. But they live on, in the hearts of mankind. They will always be there. And Camelot sets the standard for which we all strive.

What Jesus told me, and explained to me, was that Camelot was meant to be a difficult period. The people of Camelot were sacrificed to bring in a new era. Christianity had to be established in that part of the world, and Arthur was created for that purpose. And in accomplishing that purpose, he had to destroy himself.

Greg: He did not betray Avalon?

Mike: No. Everything. . . .

Greg: (Crying.)

Mike: You know what Merlin told everybody when they went to him and said, "Why are you letting this happen?" You know what Merlin said? He said, "It is the way of things. It is the way things have to be." So do you know what? Camelot was perfect. Camelot was exactly the way it was supposed to be. And now, it is time for those of us who have been carrying those emotions, those hurts and pains, to rid ourselves. . . . You see, I had to shed my own pains. Guenivere was my true love also. I had Guenivere on a pedestal. And I never knew or heard any of the bad things about her. And for me to accept that she was a fallen women was devastating. I was in bed two days, ill, after I heard the information.

Greg: Did Percival have a red beard?

Mike: I don't think so.

Greg: Then I was wrong. I thought so.

Mike: Could be, but I don't think so. I thought he was dark-haired. But he could have. . . .

Greg: I agree.

Mike: But anyway, you know what, it was all okay. And now it is time for us all to deal with these issues.

Greg: When is there going to be a gathering? Why have we returned?

Mike: Okay. I'll tell you why. The great spirit leaders up in heaven want us to come together again, and this time they want there to be a happy ending. Those of us who have struggled to grow spiritually, and have reached the proper level, now are coming together to go into the new age. This time there will be a happy ending for us all.

Greg: I sure hope that you are right.

Mike: Yes.

Greg: I sure hope you're, I hope you're. . . .

Mike: Yes, there will be a happy ending. Yes, because you know what! We are close to entering the next new era. Fifteen-hundred years later, mankind is entering into another new era, just like they did in Camelot. And this time, you were brought back to go into the new era, but this time you are going to win!

Greg: How is this new era going to come about?

Mike: It's happening now.

Greg: Do you know?

Mike: Yes.

Greg: Tell me how this new era is going to come about.

Mike: In two ways. The earth changes, and the new age. The vibratory rate of earth and its inhabitants will continue to increase until the magic moment. Then we are going to go into the Ascension.

Greg: Is it going to be peaceful, or sort of . . . cataclysmic?

Mike: Both. Depends on how you choose to view it. But, that is why all this is coming up now. And do you know why? In order to prepare yourself for this new dimension that we are going into, you have to get rid of all these old feelings. That is why they are being ripped out of you now. Because as your vibrations increase to match the increasing vibrations of the planet, you cannot carry that old negative stuff with you.

Greg: (Gasping.)

Mike: So you have to let it go.

Greg: I agree. There is pent-up . . . hurt. But number two, do you know what is going to happen in the future? I want to know what you see in regards to the organization. . . .

Mike: Wait a minute, wait a minute. Don't mess up my information here. We are doing a regression. . . .

Greg: I'm sorry.

Mike: And we're just about through with it.

Greg: Okay.

Mike: We will probably have to do this a number of times to let your emotional burden out gradually, because you are not prepared to release it all at once. But we made some pretty good headway tonight. We are beginning to crack some of these issues. And now what I'd like for you to do is to think about these issues. Think about releasing your hurt, because that's what it is all about.

By the way, you are not the only person who is Arthur. There are a number of people carrying fragments of the soul of Arthur. And from this discussion tonight, I think that you are a fragment of Arthur which is carrying much of the pain and grief. That is your cross to bear, so to speak. What you want to do is to work toward the releasing of the pain. You have made a pretty good start at it.

Arthur is a very special person. To the negative forces, it is important that you be blocked. And so they work hard to block you. Because when you release your pain, you release the pain of all the Arthurs. It affects all of the people that are here on this earth now carrying fragments of Arthur. Your soul progress will elevate all of them back up into the Light. So your work is quite important.

We all had pain. Galahad has suffered. And you know who has suffered? Guenivere has suffered. Guenivere suffered because of her betrayal to you. Percival suffered. Lancelot suffered. Merlin suffered. We all suffered. It is okay. And one by one, they are brought to me, and they lay on this couch, and they let it go. They release their suffering.

Greg: I have a question.

Mike: All right.

Greg: I am just trying to understand. I can't understand your term "fragmentation." It seems to me that there are two different things. A spirit and energy. I can't believe the spirit is fragmented, but I can believe the energy is fragmented. But how can that happen?

Mike: Here is how they explained it to me. They have given me, I guess you'd call it an analogy. Consider a soul to be as a squad of soldiers. And their squad leader (the oversoul) sends them off on various missions. He says to one, "You go get water." He says to another one, "You go get meat." He says to another, "You go get vegetables." He says to another, "You go get a horse." And they all go off on different missions. When they have accomplished their separate missions, they will rejoin, and then the squad will be complete again. The squad will also have benefitted; it will have the water, the meat, the vegetables, the horse. So, by splitting up into fragments, the squad was able to accomplish a more diverse range of things than it would have, had it remained whole.

That is what the different fragments of a soul, like Arthur's, have split up to do. They have gone on separate missions to accomplish sep-

165

arate experiences. It is all part of healing the whole. And I believe that you are the fragment of Arthur that is dealing with his sadness. . . . Which is not an easy thing to handle.

Greg: I wish that we didn't have to go through the coming destruction!

Mike: Let me ask you this. Do you think that you love this world more than God does?

Greg: Obviously not.

Mike: Okay. Do you think you can care for this world better than God can?

Greg: I guess not.

Mike: Then why are you worrying?

Greg: It's nothing.

Mike: You know who God wants you to worry about? You can't save the world, nor does God want you to. If you try to save the world, you lose everything for yourself. What you can do is save yourself. When you elevate yourself to God's level of consciousness, the effect you have on this world is awesome. That is how you can help save the world. That is what you need to work on. You work on your own spiritual growth and helping others to grow. Let God worry about the rest. All you have to do is do God's will. And that is what He has told us needs to be done right now.

Greg: All right. I am ready to come back now.

16

Jerry as a Page
August, 1994

Background: I first met Jerry when he moved to Orlando in 1991. He was a 34-year-old night watchman. He was a gifted channeller and psychic. He earned his living in the Orlando area as a night watchman and he also did psychic readings. After a few years, he moved to Nebraska. In the summer of 1994, he came back to Orlando on vacation. It was then that we did this regression. It was one of the easiest regressions for me. It was also very informative.

Jerry: Oh, there's some fear of stepping through the door.
Mike: Yes.
Jerry: There is a reluctancy to go through it.
Mike: Would it help if we admit that there's going to be some fears that come up, and perhaps some old bad memories to look at?
Jerry: Yeah.
Mike: But that you really want to bring them up because you are carrying those bad memories in your body anyway.
Jerry: Yeah.
Mike: So you really want to get rid of them?
Jerry: Okay.
Mike: All right. Ready?
Jerry: Yeah. (Deep breathing.) Well, it's like when I opened the door, I kind of just jumped into the . . . into the light. It's like I'm getting just flashes of the castle. I'm above the castle, and I'm looking down on it. And I'm seeing the front, and I'm seeing the people walk around in the castle. I see knights training in the courtyard . . . and I'm looking for myself, but I don't see myself there.
Mike: Look about you.

Jerry: Well, I see a person that is. . . . I see myself doing something like . . . I don't know. I see shining armor, helping the knights prepare themselves. I get the feeling that it is Galahad. That I'm handing him some armor that he is putting on, and I am helping him put it on.

Mike: Do you like Galahad?

Jerry: He's okay.

Mike: Why are you helping him?

Jerry: It was part of my duty to help Galahad, and . . . I get a feeling that it's not my normal routine to be there. But I was to be there that day to help him prepare to go out for. . . . Well, I don't know. I'm getting a feeling of combat.

Mike: Okay.

Jerry: But, I think that it's just less than combat. It is the ambiance of combat because they're going out to do their training. So when they went out to do their training, there was a lot of the ambiance of the real thing. But I don't particularly like him. He's okay, but I don't like him.

Mike: What does he look like?

Jerry: Well, I see him being big. And I want to say, I see him as I would see a gladiator. But not so much a muscle definition, but a very powerful, husky type of person. Not fat, but just big! He was a solid type of person. He has got a beard. He has always had a look of . . . kind of like a look of craziness across his eyes and forehead. But in his eyes . . . he has some sort of a special look in the eye. It was almost like a duality. It was . . . (big sigh) . . . it was like you could look in his eyes and see his soul, and you could see the love was there. But what was being projected was that of a knight. I can see both.

Mike: Is that why he was such a favorite in the court? Such a special man?

Jerry: He had a certain charm about him. I'd say, yeah, because of the charm. The charm that he had went with his abilities as a "great knight." He was able to have that charm, and still be the fearless knight. There was a balance.

Mike: Who did you think the best knight was?

Jerry: Well, I'm seeing somebody different, but I can't put a name on it. Well, I'm seeing somebody who is not a highly talked about knight that I assume to be the best knight.

Mike: Okay.

Jerry: And I can't see the name. I can see the face, but I don't see the name.

Mike: How old are you?

Jerry: Oh, I'm about sixteen.

Mike: Okay. Can you tell me something about your background? Who was your father? Who was your mother? Where did you come from? How did you end up at Camelot?

Jerry: Well, I'm seeing like a peasant person. I'm seeing a lady that I call my mother. But I don't see the father present. It's like, at that time as a child I didn't know who the father really was.

Mike: Do you know who the father is now?

Jerry: Well, I really . . . I really feel that the only father figure I ever had was Merlin.

Mike: What makes you feel that?

Jerry: Well, because as I got to be about ten or eleven, this druid priest would come and speak with the mother and talk to me. He was waiting for the right time to take me into the kingdom. I was to be a page, with the hope of becoming a knight later on.

Mike: Okay. When you became a page, did you have much to do with Merlin?

Jerry: Yes.

Mike: Okay. How often do you see Merlin?

Jerry: Every day.

Mike: Do you acknowledge him as your father?

Jerry: Yes, I do.

Mike: Does he acknowledge you as his son?

Jerry: He's patting me on the head and smiling. So I say "yes."

Mike: Okay. Is that just a secret between the two of you?

Jerry: It was a secret between the three of us.

Mike: I get the feeling that it was for your own safety. He had some enemies.

Jerry: And what I'm getting is that the mother was not my true mother.

Mike: She just raised you?

Jerry: Uhhuh.

Mike: Okay. Did Merlin ever take you to his chambers?

Jerry: Many times.

Mike: What did they look like?

Jerry: (Big sigh.) It was a room that looked almost hollow, like a cave. I see shelves that are along the front of the wall as you enter. And there is a table that is in the center of the floor. And over on my right, there is a bag that is hanging from the wall. Over on the left, there is a series of candles that are lit. There is also a candle in the middle of the table. It is . . . it is a medium sized room, but it seems so big to me. There are books on a shelf, a series of books. There are bottles. Also . . . wooden containers, on the shelves.

Mike: Does he ever teach you any magic?

Jerry: Yes, he taught me lots of magic.

Mike: What kind?

Jerry: . . . He called it, "The Magic of the Gods."

Mike: Okay. Did he teach you how to make yourself disappear?

Jerry: He taught me many things. Another druid priest would be there. Three other priests would be there. They were his closest friends. And they always treated me as if I belonged. They all showed me different things. . . . They showed me how to see the window of the soul. They taught me how to read the heart. And Merlin had a special type of ornament. . . . From it, people got the idea of the crystal ball. But I'm not seeing a crystal ball. It is something that is like a viewing glass. And he would help me look into it and see the future. And at one time, he showed me the whole . . . (big sigh) . . . he showed me the outcome of the Knights of the Round Table. He showed me their destiny.

Mike: What was that?

Jerry: (Big sigh. Begins to quietly cry.)

Mike: We've got kleenex here. I'm going to hand you some. Go ahead, release those emotions. It doesn't turn out well for Arthur, does it?

Jerry: It goes much deeper than that.

Mike: Okay. Tell me about it.

Jerry: . . . I'm checking now to be sure that it's okay to say what I have to say.

Mike: The chest is being unlocked. It's time to let it out.

Jerry: Let's go to the time that I was being shown the future of Camelot. The other druid priests were there, and they set me on this . . . stool. The three priests stood behind me, and Merlin was on my right side. And as I looked into the viewing glass, they showed me the wonders of creation. They showed me the creation of King Arthur, and the creation of Camelot. Camelot was to set a cycle in motion. It was to set an evolutionary stage that would create a momentum that would carry it on into the now. This information was very secret. If others knew of the secret, the momentum would not be created. That was the importance of the secrecy. If the knights were to find out, or anyone in the kingdom was to find out what was taking place, Camelot would not have fulfilled its destiny. So this work and knowledge became an underground effort of Merlin and the other druid priests. It was like they could see the heart of what was happening. And they were also counterbalancing the actions and energies of what the other priests in the kingdom were trying to do to take control.

Mike: Why did you start to get so sad?

Jerry: Because when I saw the viewing glass again, I saw what was taking place.

Mike: Can you share it with me?

Jerry: (Big sigh.) It's hard to explain, because when you looked into the viewing glass, it wasn't like a slide show where you would see one scene, and then another. It was . . . how do you explain it? It was as if you were to take a videotape out of its container and just pan it, you would view the whole thing at the same time instead of segments.

Mike: Uhhuh.

Jerry: When I looked into the glass, I saw where it started and I saw where it ended at the same time. And I saw everything in between. To see that just takes your breath away, because it's so much to take in at one time. You saw the beginning of the creation of the kingdom, all the way to the end of it at same time. So there were many emotions that hit me at once.

Mike: Let's move on. Can we go to the Great Hall? To one of the feasts? Tell me what that was like?

Jerry: (Big sigh.) Ohhhhh, well. From what I see in the Great Hall, it's like I'm seeing a room. In the middle of the room there is a huge aisle or corridor. I see it kind of being like an arched type of ceiling. And over on the left, I'm seeing a huge arch in the side of the wall. It is over what we would call a fireplace. And as I'm walking down the corridor, I'm seeing benches with rectangle tables. Each is almost like half a picnic table, with seats on one side. One after the other. People sat along the side of the corridor to watch the knights as they came down the corridor. At the end of the corridor was the Round Table. The Round Table is raised up. It is not at the same level as the other tables.

Mike: It is raised up?

Jerry: Yeah.

Mike: Does Arthur sit at the Round Table, or does he sit with the Queen when he eats?

Jerry: Well, there are different time periods. Sometimes he sat with the Queen, and sometimes he sat at the Round Table.

Mike: Do you see the Queen today? Is there a feast going on there?

Jerry: I'm seeing a glimpse of the. . . . I'm trying to put the scene together. Ummmm, something doesn't feel right in there. There's kind of a silence. . . .

Mike: Okay, let me ask you this. Would you like to stay there, or would you like to go on to another scene? Is there more that you want to tell me about the Great Hall?

Jerry: No, I guess not.

Mike: Ummmm. Tell me about Guenivere. She's the queen, right? Do you see her quite often?

Jerry: . . . Yes, I do.

Mike: What does she look like?

Jerry: She is very pretty.

Mike: What color hair does she have?

Jerry: It's kind of . . . I want to say brunette. But I'm seeing sunlight hit it, and it almost makes it a red color.

Mike: Is she nice to you?

Jerry: She was always nice to me.

Mike: Do you like her?

Jerry: I like her, but . . . there was something when I looked at her. It was hard for me to keep personal feelings out of what was going on, because I had already viewed what was going to happen. It was very difficult to deal with what was going on in front of me when I already knew what the outcome was going to be.

Mike: I see. It's almost as if you're telling me that you knew that it wasn't going to go well with her.

Jerry: Well, this was one of the lessons that I had to learn. I had to be able to see the future, and still be able to deal with the reality of the present.

Mike: What did you think of Arthur?

Jerry: Arthur was courageous in his own way, but he was a fool in another way.

Mike: Tell me about it. Merlin loved him very much, didn't he?

Jerry: Yes. We all did.

Mike: Okay. Tell me why you loved Arthur?

Jerry: Arthur had the courage to fulfill his destiny, even though he knew in his heart the outcome. And he let himself be blinded by the illusion to fulfill that destiny.

Mike: Okay. Why didn't you like him? What were his weaknesses?

Jerry: His main weakness was Guenivere. He did not want to see what was happening. He wanted to believe what he believed, and that was all.

Mike: Were some of the knights that way also?

Jerry: Most of them.

Mike: They respected her?

Jerry: Everyone had their respect, in their own way. Everyone had the concept of what they were there for. But each one had their own personal . . . emotions to deal with. Many people saw the knights as these perfect beings. And they weren't. They were pure of heart, but that didn't mean that they didn't have things to work out. They were human also.

Mike: Did you ever hear talk that Guenivere wasn't faithful to her king?

Jerry: Everyone knew that she wasn't. The King wouldn't admit it to himself though.

Mike: Did everyone kind of protect the King from getting hurt?

Jerry: In their own way.

Mike: What was your personal feeling about why the Queen would let herself be . . . so imperfect?

Jerry: She was the perfect one for the role that needed to be played.

Mike: Why was that? It was meant for that to happen?

Jerry: Yes.

Mike: Why do you think it was meant for that to happen?

Jerry: (Big sigh.) It had to happen because . . . the world was not ready for the completion of the Round Table. The Round Table and all that it represented of that time period was the mere planting of the seed. It was to create a consciousness, and to give that consciousness momentum for the future.

Mike: Okay. So everything was meant to fail now?

Jerry: Yes.

Mike: That's interesting. Guenivere loved her king very much.

Jerry: Yes.

Mike: I wonder why she felt it necessary to do what she did?

Jerry: Because of the person that she was, she could see beyond. And she was caught up in the beauty, the honor . . . of the representation of what the knights stood for. Arthur . . . Arthur was a very loving person. But he could not fully give her what she needed.

Mike: Physically, or emotionally?

Jerry: Both. At times, it was hard for him to focus on the love for her because of the demands that were made of him as a king.

Mike: Yeah. Okay. What I also hear you saying is that she was so caught up with the beauty of the Round Table Movement, but then also she was kind of pulled into the glamour of it all along with the knights.

Jerry: Yes.

Mike: Fascinated and captivated by that perfection. . . . Makes sense. Well, you seem to have some secrets that you don't want to . . . or maybe that you do want to unlock and let out this afternoon? . . . Yes, no, maybe?

Jerry: I'm scanning.

Mike: I can ask you some questions.

Jerry: Much of what I needed to let go of has already been released.

Mike: Okay.

Jerry: And . . . there WAS a lot of anger in me towards Merlin and the druid priesthood.

Mike: Why was that?

Jerry: (Big sigh.) Even though I had the honor of using the visual screen to see the beginning and the ending of the Round Table, when reality actually hit in the physical realm, it brought the realization of the truth of it. I was shocked and dismayed. My anger was . . . well, if you are the true wizards and priests, how come you couldn't change the outcome of the future once you saw it? . . . And so I was angry at them.

Mike: Have you released that now?

Jerry: Yes, I have released a majority of it.

Mike: Tell me about the Bishop when he came to court. What was that like? As a page, you must have been around a lot of the scheming that was going on?

Jerry: By being the page, by my connection to Merlin being kept secret, I was able to be the eyes of the druid priests and of Merlin. And when this bishop came, I was able to see things that other people couldn't see. I did not like him.

Mike: What did you think of him? What did you see that the others didn't see?

Jerry: Well I knew before I met him, that he was going to be the one that started the undermining of the Round Table.

Mike: Someone said that he came from the church court at Constantinople, where he was used to a lot of palace intrigue. So he started the same kind of intrigue in Camelot, where nobody was prepared for such a thing. Everything had always been very simple and honest and straight-forward.

Jerry: For some reason, I'm seeing that there is truth to that, but there is a question mark behind it. I'm sensing something phony about that.

Mike: Okay. What do you sense?

Jerry: I'm sensing that is what the Bishop wanted people to believe.

Mike: Ohhhhh. . . . That he perhaps really wasn't the powerful bishop that everyone thought, but that he was trying to BECOME powerful.

Jerry: Yes.

Mike: To become powerful by bringing Camelot under his control. He really didn't come as a powerful bishop. He just. . . .

Jerry: He came as the illusion of.

Mike: Yeah. The struggling person trying to make a comeback, so to speak. Oh, that makes sense, doesn't it?

Jerry: I actually see him being kicked out of some . . . some type of priest initiation.

Mike: At Constantinople. He was kicked out of there, sent out in disgrace. "Get rid of him, send him out to. . . ." When you send somebody. . . . It's like the Russians, when they send somebody to Siberia. They send the person as far away as they can send him.

Jerry: And he had the ability to see also. And he was, what we would call, misusing the power.

Mike: Let's go to the time that Arthur was sick. Do you remember that time when he was sick for a year or two?

Jerry: Uhhuh. It wasn't a year or two.

Mike: How long was it?

Jerry: Only for three or four months.

Mike: Oh, okay. Some people said he had a sword wound, other people say he was poisoned. Other people say he had a nervous breakdown. What was it?

Jerry: He was poisoned, and he was poisoned through a drink that was given to him by someone that the Bishop sent to him. And the other stories were rumors to protect the King.

Mike: Do you think they meant to kill him, or just to incapacitate him?

Jerry: They meant to kill him.

Mike: Who ruled the kingdom while he was sick?

Jerry: Well, the druid priests got together with Merlin, and it was actually them who ruled the kingdom through Guenivere. Guenivere was the "up front" person, so the people took on the idea that she was the one running the kingdom. It was actually Merlin and the druid priests.

Mike: Okay. I talked to her and she felt that Merlin abandoned her at that time and didn't give her much help. That he deferred to the Bishop. But it must have been behind the scenes that he helped her. Maybe the magic that he had taught to her helped her then?

Jerry: I'm seeing that Merlin and the druid priests were there, but what I'm seeing is that some sort of a potion was given to her.

Mike: By. . . .

Jerry: By the druid priests. To drink. Her feeling of abandonment was due to the fact that they were no longer standing right next to her daily. Because of the situation with the Bishop, they could not do so. The potion was a potion to give her the strength to gather or to accept the powers that they were sending to her. I see the four of them standing off in a wooded area. And I see a campfire. I was there. I see the four of them using their magic powders and chants to create a consciousness that was always in connection with Guenivere through the potion that she drank.

Mike: Okay. Where did all these stories about Guenivere and Lancelot get started?

Jerry: Ummmm. Just like any other rumors that get started. There are people who see something and what they see is not what they perceive. Truth gets twisted.

Mike: Do you think there was any truth to those rumors?

Jerry: . . . What I'm getting is no. There was a very deep love, there were times when they were alone that they did leave the castle together. Temptation was there. But it was from other knights. Because of what they did, they assumed that he did the same.

Mike: How about a knight named Lucan? Lucan the Butler. Does that ring a bell? Who was he?

Jerry: I'm getting Lu-ki-an.

Mike: Okay.

Jerry: I see him as being a very. . . . I see him as a quiet, yet rowdy type of person.

Mike: Do you see him as being one of those who was unfaithful to the King?

Jerry: (Big sigh.) I see him as being like the . . . I don't know what other word to use with it, but he was like the disloyal troublemaker. He had been Arthur's personal butler for many years. Arthur, out of a sense of loyalty, made him a knight. But in his heart he remained less than a knight. During his many years as Arthur's personal servant, he was witness to much that was personal and private in Arthur's and Guenivere's lives. Later Lucan disappointed himself by not being discreet.

Mike: Okay.

Jerry: It was through him. He told the other knights. . . .

Mike: That she was unfaithful?

Jerry: Uhhuh.

Mike: So he kind of was instrumental in her downfall? So to speak?

Jerry: She had already fallen.

Mike: Did you ever meet Percival?

Jerry: Yes.

Mike: What did you think of him?

Jerry: Percival was a very strong-willed person. He was very proud, and there was a lot of ego with him. But he had that . . . he had that love and the knowledge behind him. For you see, he also got to be in the chambers with Merlin.

Mike: Yes. He was a favorite of Merlin, wasn't he?

Jerry: Yes.

Mike: Do you understand why?

Jerry: . . . He was a relation to Merlin.

Mike: Did Merlin ever tell you that?

Jerry: Merlin only said that he was a relation.

Mike: When he lived at the Grail Castle, guarding the Grail Castle, did you ever go visit Percival?

Jerry: On three occasions.

Mike: Will you tell me about those visits?

Jerry: On each visit I had messages and potions to give to him from Merlin.

Mike: Was it a pretty castle? Or was it a castle? Was it a house, or what was it?

Jerry: I didn't like it. I didn't like going there.

Mike: Why was that?

Jerry: It just had an eerie feeling to me. I didn't see it as being beautiful. I viewed it differently. I saw what other people didn't see. I heard what other people said that they saw there, and what they felt there. But what I saw there was much torment and pain because I was seeing the future and I didn't like it.

Mike: Oh, because you were seeing the future.

Jerry: When I went there I couldn't see it for what it was at the time. I saw it for what it was going to be.

Mike: Because of Percival's death. . . . Did you ever see him fish off the wall? The castle was next to the ocean, wasn't it?

Jerry: I'm seeing water, but I'm not seeing an ocean.

Mike: Okay. Did you ever play with his children?

Jerry: There was talk, but not too much playing.

Mike: Okay, you were too much older to play with them. Did you like his wife?

Jerry: She was okay. I didn't know her that well.

Mike: All right.

Jerry: Merlin kept us separated.

Mike: I would like to go, if you don't mind, to the night before Arthur's last battle. I would like to go to the Great Hall where everybody was eating. Do you remember that night?

Jerry: (Big sigh.) Yeah.

Mike: Tell me about it. What was it like in the Great Hall that night?

Jerry: There was a wave of excitement. (Big sigh.) There was a solemnness that went through different phases of the evening. It is like I can see everyone around the Round Table standing with their arms outstretched. I'm seeing a huge glow of light come down from the ceiling, into the center of the room. I see the knights shining as if light had just covered all of them in pure essence. And the Light shines out through the whole room. Above the knights, I see Merlin's face. Merlin is giving them a blessing. And I see a tear drop from his right eye. Then there is silence.

Mike: Who were the people they were going to fight the next day? Who was coming to fight with them?

Jerry: I see it being a band of men. The evil priest went out to different . . . I want to say to different countries, and gathered a band of knights together and created an army.

Mike: What pretext did the priest use to gather these people to fight against Arthur?

Jerry: Well, the Bishop had used the idea that Christianity itself was weak. He proffered the thought that Christianity was weaker than the power of the Knights and the Round Table. He instilled the fear that if they were allowed to succeed, Arthur's movement would become the dominant factor of that time. It would eclipse Christianity. So he made it to be a power play between belief systems.

Mike: Was it also that the Bishop wanted to be able to persecute the druids, and that Arthur was protecting the druids?

Jerry: That's all part of the belief system.

Mike: Okay. But the underlying reason was that the church was threatened by the Round Table Movement? And its potential to be greater than the church?

Jerry: Yes, it was becoming too powerful for the Christians.

Mike: Okay. Were Arthur's people outnumbered by this force?

Jerry: I'm just seeing an ocean of people.

Mike: Okay. Were they from France and Germany?

Jerry: All over.

Mike: All over. All the Christian knights came, marching against Arthur. There was a solemn feeling the night before the battle in the Great Hall. Was it because they knew that they couldn't win against their fellow Christians? Why was there such a solemn feeling? Did everyone know they would die the next day?

Jerry: Everyone knew the odds. They knew what they were up against. . . . The solemnness was due to the fact that no matter how great the Round Table was, they knew it was coming to an end. But no one would speak of it.

Mike: Okay. Were you at the battle the next day?

Jerry: Not at the beginning.

Mike: Tell me about your experiences there. Where was the battle held? Was it far from the castle?

Jerry: Ohhhh, I see us about three miles outside the castle.

Mike: Okay. When did you get there?

Jerry: It was more towards the end.

Mike: The battle had been going on for some time?

Jerry: Yes, I was told to stay back. I stood with some of the druid priests and viewed the battle from a high place.

Mike: Where was Arthur?

Jerry: In the beginning?

Mike: Yeah.

Jerry: The Knights of the Round Table, when they went into battle, they formed a wing shaped formation. And they placed Arthur behind them. To honor him. To show their loyalty to him. To get to Arthur, well, you had to get past all of the knights.

Mike: Arthur was pretty old by this time, wasn't he?

Jerry: Well, it all depends on what you call old, for time periods.

Mike: Too old for him to be going into battle. Sixty or 70 maybe?

Jerry: I don't see him that old. I see him more around 55 in that lifetime.

Mike: Okay. Tell me about Arthur's death. How did it happen? Were they winning or losing the battle?

Jerry: They were losing.

Mike: How long had the battle been going on?

Jerry: The knights, the knights had lost at the beginning of the battle. From what was seen from our position on high, they didn't have a chance. And they were swarmed, they were swamped. It was only by the magic of the druid priests and Merlin that . . . kept it going, kept giving it the push.

Mike: Okay.

Jerry: But the . . . (big sigh) . . . but the druid priests and Merlin all had to withdraw their power because of the interference that they were bringing into their own karma.

178

Mike: Yeah. Interfering with destiny.

Jerry: Yes. And that's what I couldn't understand.

Mike: Yes. So how did Arthur die? Were you close to Arthur when he died?

Jerry: No, but I saw Arthur on the ground. He was already badly wounded. And I'm seeing . . . I'm seeing a sword or some sort of object stuck through the left side of his body.

Mike: Okay. Was he struck down by the enemy?

Jerry: No.

Mike: Who dealt him the death blow?

Jerry: One of the knights.

Mike: Can you see which one?

Jerry: . . . I can't tell for sure. With all the confusion, I can't tell which one it was.

Mike: Okay.

Jerry: Actually, I can't tell you who it was. It was done by one of the knights, because he was the one of the three that were left. It was done out of loyalty to the kingdom. Arthur was killed by one of the knights. Better that he be killed by the hand of a knight of love and peace, than to be slaughtered by the enemy.

Mike: Why can't you tell me who it was?

Jerry: It is to be revealed later.

Mike: Did you see Percival in that battle?

Jerry: Yes.

Mike: What happened to him?

Jerry: (Big sigh.) Percival was one of the three that were remaining. And Percival knows who the knight was that slew Arthur. After Arthur's death, all three knights went down.

Mike: Was it Percival that did it?

Jerry: What I'm seeing is that all three knights had the same idea at the same time.

Mike: So it doesn't matter.

Jerry: One of the other knights. . . .

Mike: Did it. It doesn't matter now. Arthur wanted it that way, didn't he?

Jerry: Yes.

Mike: What happened to Excalibur?

Jerry: Excalibur was lifted by the priests.

Mike: The druid priests?

Jerry: The druid priests. Lifted out and taken to a safe place.

Mike: Is it still there?

Jerry: It is not in this dimension.

Mike: They took it back where it came from.

Jerry: I've had enough.

Mike: Okay. Anything else you want to tell me?

Jerry: No.

Mike: I was wanting to ask you what happened to you after Camelot.

Jerry: That will have to be for another time.

Mike: Do you want to come back through the door, or just come back?

Jerry: I'm coming back now.

17

Fran as Guenivere
September, 1994

Background: Fran is a 26-year-old woman from Jacksonville, Florida. I met her while I was attending a seminar in Daytona Beach. She was so beautiful that it took my breath away. When she heard about my Camelot project, she asked to be regressed. So, with her boyfriend in attendance, we did this regression in her hotel room the afternoon of the same day that I met her.

Mike: Can you tell me what you're experiencing as we go through the door? How are you feeling?
Fran: I am relaxed, but I don't see anything yet.
Mike: Have you gone through the door?
Fran: The door is open.
Mike: Okay. Shall we step through? . . . What do you see now?
Fran: I don't see anything. I hear children playing.
Mike: Okay. Let's go toward those voices. Do you see them now? Where are they?
Fran: In a little open space, in a circle, dancing and playing.
Mike: In the woods?
Fran: No.
Mike: Where?
Fran: They are by a castle.
Mike: By a castle. Okay. Who are those children?
Fran: . . . They are the children of the knights and the people of the castle.
Mike: All right. Are you one of the children?
Fran: No!
Mike: Why are you watching the children?
Fran: I don't know.

Mike: Where are you?

Fran: I'm outside, at a distance, watching.

Mike: How do you feel, watching the children?

Fran: They make me happy.

Mike: Okay. Are any of those children yours?

Fran: No!

Mike: How do you feel about that?

Fran: I would like some. I would like a child.

Mike: You would like a child. Okay. Are you married?

Fran: I'm. . . .

Mike: Are you married? (No response.) You don't know?

Fran: I don't know.

Mike: You don't know?

Fran: I'm . . . blank.

Mike: Okay. Are you in love with anybody?

Fran: Yes.

Mike: Are you a man or a woman?

Fran: Woman.

Mike: Okay. Tell me about who you are in love with.

Fran: He is . . . the God of Vision. He is very idealistic. He will sacrifice himself for whatever he believes in.

Mike: Uhhuh.

Fran: He is very compassionate toward that vision. Very charismatic. People are drawn to him. Everybody loves him.

Mike: And you love him?

Fran: Yes.

Mike: And you are going to be with him now?

Fran: No.

Mike: Where are you headed?

Fran: I'll just go in the door.

Mike: Go in the door to the castle?

Fran: Yes.

Mike: Okay. Take me to your chambers and tell me what your chambers look like.

Fran: There is a bed in the far corner, and some straw. And then a bag with feathers over the straw.

Mike: Okay. That is the bed?

Fran: Yes.

Mike: Is it comfortable?

Fran: Uhhuh.

Mike: Okay. Do you sleep there with the man you love?

Fran: (Big sigh.) Sometimes.

Mike: Okay. Where do you hang your clothes? . . . What other kind of furniture is in the room?

Fran: A wooden chest. With flowers engraved on the front.

Mike: Okay. All right. Do you have many clothes? (No response.) Okay. That doesn't seem to interest you. Tell me what it's like when you are with the man you love.

Fran: It is lonely.

Mike: It's lonely? Why?

Fran: Because he . . . he can't, he doesn't understand . . . human love. He thinks that he has to do everything for everybody else. And what he wants, or what would make him happy . . . he can't have both. He can't do his mission in life, and be happy too. He is . . . it's like he is love, he is so perfect. But he doesn't give any sign of feeling that way, other than the way he feels about everything, everybody else, and the country.

Mike: Does he tell you that he loves you?

Fran: No.

Mike: Never says that to you?

Fran: No!

Mike: Do you miss that?

Fran: Yes!

Mike: Is that why you feel lonely?

Fran: I would just like some sign that I'm as important as everything else. Just a little sign. Anything.

Mike: But you know that he loves you?

Fran: No!

Mike: You don't know that?

Fran: No! He loves everything else.

Mike: Has he ever told you that he loves you?

Fran: (Big sigh.)

Mike: It's okay to feel emotion. This is a deep hurt!

Fran: He's told me, but it doesn't feel like it is true.

Mike: This is interesting, because I thought that Camelot was the Court of Love. I thought that everybody loved everybody else here.

Fran: It is love, but not like a . . . man would love his wife . . . love.

Mike: Ohhhh.

Fran: He loves the country, he loves the people, he loves the knights, and the children, and the country . . . and the country, and the peace. And bringing about this peace is what is his top priority. And if anything else gets in the way, it will get left behind.

Mike: But don't you get plenty of love from everybody else? Don't all the knights adore you?

Fran: Yes.

Mike: Isn't that great comfort for you?

Fran: No.

Mike: No, it's not?

Fran: It helps.

Mike: It helps! How about Merlin? Doesn't Merlin love you?

Fran: We have fun together!

Mike: What do you do with Merlin?

Fran: We talk. He teaches me.

Mike: What does he teach you?

Fran: Oh, some small things. Some . . . how to make small children feel better if they are hurt. Some more important things. Maps, warfare . . . leadership things, as well as medicine.

Mike: He teaches you those things?

Fran: Ummhumm.

Mike: Oh, that's nice. I somehow sense that he always finds time for you, when you wish to be with him.

Fran: He has got time for everybody.

Mike: Okay. Is that part of his magic?

Fran: Possibly.

Mike: Did he ever teach you any magic?

Fran: Some potions. I don't know that I would call them magic. (Big sigh.) Some . . . oh, not really mind reading, but just how to be more in tune with people. But I don't think it's magic.

Mike: Take me to the Great Hall when everyone is having a meal. Is that where you have your meals?

Fran: Ummhumm!

Mike: Now you are smiling. That brings good thoughts?

Fran: It is a happy place.

Mike: Yes! Tell me about . . . what goes on in the Great Hall?

Fran: Ahhh. . . . Music, talking. Just everything good. Everybody is happy, everybody loves each other. Ohhh.

Mike: Where do you sit?

Fran: By Arthur!

Mike: Okay. Where does Arthur sit? Is there a head table?

Fran: No.

Mike: Okay. Is there a table that is raised up a little higher than the others?

Fran: It's . . . it's . . . I don't think it's higher. It's . . . round, with a hole cut in the middle. With a fire, in the middle.

Mike: Well, okay. So that is where you sit with Arthur?

Fran: Ummhumm.

Mike: And who else sits with Arthur? . . . You are smiling! Does Merlin sit with him?

Fran: Sometimes.

Mike: Is that table you are talking about? Is that the Round Table?

Fran: It is a round table.

Mike: Is there another round table there?

Fran: I don't know.

Mike: Okay. What does the Great Hall look like?

Fran: Tall ceilings. On the walls there are torches. It is well lit, brick . . . brick type of walls. At the end there is a burgundy curtain over the archway.

Mike: Okay. What kind of food do you eat? What kind of food do you eat in those days?

Fran: Little chickens. Potatoes.

Mike: You don't recognize anything else?

Fran: I think it's pheasant. It's like little chickens. That's all I see right now.

Mike: Okay. How many meals a day do you eat there? Do you eat breakfast, lunch and supper? Or just once a day, or. . . .

Fran: Just once there.

Mike: Once a day. Okay, okay. And is that one of your favorite times of the day?

Fran: Ummmm, it's the happiest time.

Mike: Okay. They tell me that all the knights adore you. Is that true?

Fran: . . . Yes. Most of them, I think. Some I don't know as well as others.

Mike: At the tournaments, do they all try to please you . . . and win for you?

Fran: Yes.

Mike: Is it true that your brother has become a knight? Does that sound familiar?

Fran: I think he is just trying.

Mike: He's in training at the time. Okay. What would you like to tell me about how it is going in your life right now? What feelings and memories would you like to share with me?

Fran: I would like to help more. I would like to . . . be able to make a change. To help get to the end that Arthur wants. But . . . I believe in him, but I don't always believe his goals are possible. I think he needs . . . I see him working and spending all this time for something he may never attain.

Mike: Have you been married very long? How many years have you been married?

Fran: Four.

Mike: Four. And how old are you?

Fran: Twenty-six.

Mike: Okay. Are you a Christian or a druid?

Fran: I am a Christian, but I have attended the druid ceremonies.

Mike: When did you become a Christian?

Fran: For as long as I can remember. I was in a Christian household.

Mike: Okay, but you respect the druids?

Fran: Yes.

Mike: Has Arthur become a Christian?

Fran: He is a little of both. He believes in Jesus, but he also believes some of the ways the druids believe.

Mike: Has he brought the priest to the court yet?

Fran: No.

Mike: No. Okay. I would like to jump ahead in time, if you don't mind, to the time when Arthur does make Christianity the official religion of the court, and brings the priest. You wince when I say that. Why is that?

Fran: I don't know.

Mike: You have a distressed look on your face. Why is that?

Fran: I can't go forward. It's. . . .

Mike: Do you have a block?

Fran: Yes, that gives me a bad feeling!

Mike: But wouldn't it perhaps be a good idea for us to take a look at those. . . . I don't want to make you uncomfortable, but one of the purposes of our visit is for you to be able to feel your emotions, and to release them. And I have a crying towel right here. Tell me about your sadness. . . . Merlin is here and he says he is going to come down, and sprinkle some of his magical dust. Remember his magical dust that he used to use? He is going to sprinkle some of his magical dust on you, so you won't be fearful. He is doing it now, from head to foot.

Fran: (Big sigh.)

Mike: So you can let those feelings out and express yourself. He also smiles at you, very gently. He has great, deep love for you. And he says that perhaps you kept those feelings bottled up for too long. And, this would be a good time to release them, while he is here to help you. Tell me what happened when Arthur announced that the court was going to be Christian. Is that what he did?

Fran: Yes.

Mike: He did. How did everybody accept it?

Fran: People do whatever Arthur wants them to do.

Mike: He is very popular and powerful right now. Okay. Did all the knights. . . .

Fran: He is very good at motivating. People would come around . . . oh, everybody, if Arthur thinks that it is right.

Mike: All right, they will do it. So everybody became a Christian. Did that please you?

Fran: Yes!

Mike: How did Merlin handle it?

Fran: Merlin accepted it, because he knew it was meant to be.

Mike: Good. Are you and Merlin still friends now?

Fran: Yes.

Mike: Yes, yes. He is a better friend than ever, now, isn't he?

Fran: He is lonely. He is lonely too.

Mike: Yes, that is one of your bonds of friendship.

Fran: Yes. Arthur is away from both of us, more and more.

Mike: Yes, yes. Doesn't Arthur bring a priest into the court about now?

Fran: (Big sigh.) I don't know. All I can see . . . in a side room, I see two people arguing. I don't know what they are arguing about. I think it is Mordred and Morgana. And they are very upset with each other. But I don't know why.

Mike: How do you feel about Mordred?

Fran: I wish he was not here.

Mike: Does Arthur love him?

Fran: Yes!

Mike: Does he love Arthur?

Fran: He . . . he wants more recognition from Arthur. He feels like he doesn't get the respect he deserves, and nobody thinks of him as Arthur's son.

Mike: Okay. Could that be what he and his mother are arguing about?

Fran: I don't know. They are shaking each other?

Mike: Okay. How do you feel about Morgana?

Fran: . . . Hummmm . . . I . . . don't want her . . . to be here.

Mike: All right. What is she doing in the castle? Does she come to visit?

Fran: Yes.

Mike: At will?

Fran: Yes!

Mike: Very often?

Fran: Yes!

Mike: Okay. Why is it you don't wish her there?

Fran: . . . She doesn't belong there.

Mike: Okay. Tell me about the priest now. Could they be arguing about the priest? Or could they be arguing about the Bishop? Has the Bishop come to the court yet?

Fran: I don't see him.

Mike: Okay. How about if we jump ahead in time to when the Bishop arrives at the court. You are wincing again. Unpleasant memory?

Fran: I don't know. I. . . .

Mike: Tell me, when I mention the Bishop, tell me what thoughts you have.

Fran: I just feel bad.

Mike: You feel bad?

Fran: I feel angry.

Mike: Can you picture him in your mind, what he looks like?

Fran: No.

Mike: No, you don't want to picture him?

Fran: No!

Mike: Okay, how about when Arthur was sick. Do you remember when Arthur was sick?

Fran: Yes.

Mike: How was he sick? Why was he sick?

Fran: He ... I don't ... it was more a spiritual sickness.

Mike: Why was he spiritually sick?

Fran: He had ... he had lost hope.

Mike: Okay. Who ran the kingdom while he was sick? Was he able to run the kingdom?

Fran: He didn't have the will to.

Mike: So, who ran the kingdom? ... Did you run the kingdom?

Fran: I had a lot of help.

Mike: Who helped you?

Fran: The knights were there. They helped.

Mike: Which knights?

Fran: Gawaine.

Mike: Gawaine? Good.

Fran: Gawaine would always help everybody.

Mike: How about Galahad?

Fran: Galahad you could go to more for discussion and debates, but for physical help, you went to Gawaine.

Mike: How about Lancelot?

Fran: (Big sigh.)

Mike: You seem to hesitate. I thought he was the King's best friend?

Fran: Yes.

Mike: So, does he help you?

Fran: ... Yes!

Mike: How do you feel about Lancelot?

Fran: He gives me strength.

Mike: Okay. Good. Any of the other knights? Who are the knights who are the closest to Arthur? The ones you could depend upon at this time, when Arthur was sick?

Fran: Lancelot, Gawaine, Kay, Percival. . . .

Mike: Okay.

Fran: Gaheris. He was younger, but you could depend on him.

Mike: Okay. Those were the ones that you counted on. That's nice. How long was Arthur sick?

Fran: Years? I don't know how long.

Mike: Somebody said a year-and-a-half. Does that sound about right?

Fran: Long time.

Mike: And just about the time he got well, Lancelot left him? Do I have that correct? (No response.) You are nodding yes. Okay. Why did

Lancelot leave? (No response.) You don't know? Does it make you uncomfortable to talk about that?

Fran: Yes!

Mike: Yes. You would rather not talk about that?

Fran: No!

Mike: Okay. Does it make you sad to think about it?

Fran: Yes.

Mike: Okay. What is happening to Arthur's dream?

Fran: It is falling apart. It's crumbling.

Mike: How do you feel about that?

Fran: Like he is losing everything, and there is nothing I can do to help him.

Mike: Okay.

Fran: There is nothing anybody can do.

Mike: Do you still love him very much?

Fran: Yes! But I don't think he realizes it.

Mike: In his own pain, perhaps. . . .

Fran: I don't think he could ever know.

Mike: Tell me about Arthur's last battle. Who were they fighting? Does that bring pain to you to think about that? Hummmm? Seems as if you are holding back some tears on me, aren't you? Afraid you will let loose with them?

Fran: There is just a wall that I can't get through.

Mike: See where you are holding your hands . . . on your stomach? That is where you are holding all that grief. And that is why Merlin is here to help you. It will be so good to give that grief up! . . . I would like you to go to the last battle. Tell me how . . . how did you find out that Arthur had fallen?

Fran: I knew before he went that he would die!

Mike: Yes, and he knew also, didn't he? How did he say goodbye?

Fran: I told him I was so sorry, and I hoped . . . I wished it would have been different.

Mike: Uhhuh.

Fran: And that I could have made everything all right.

Mike: Is that part of the feeling that you are carrying? Suffering because you couldn't make it all right for Arthur?

Fran: I couldn't do anything for him. I couldn't help him. But I never felt like he wanted my help enough. That he wanted to do it, he felt like the burden was all his. And he felt so alone, even though everybody was with him. And that when everything fell apart, he bore all the grief. And he . . . he just never understood that the people were there to share it with him.

Mike: Okay.

Fran: And that we could have helped him if he would have let us.

189

Mike: Okay.

Fran: And he wouldn't let you.

Mike: I would like for you to go to the day after the battle. And you are seated in your chambers. Imagine yourself there. And Merlin comes down, out of the sky, out of the clouds. And he takes you by the hand. . . .

Fran: (Big sigh.)

Mike: And he lifts you up. And he takes you up to the Light. Because he wants you to see your beloved Arthur and his knights.

Fran: Fighting?

Mike: No, the fight is over. They are up in the Light now. They are with Jesus. And he lifts you up, and it's like, you go past this cloud. And suddenly you are there. And who is waiting for you, with a big smile? Can you see him? There is Arthur, and in a semicircle, around him, are all of the knights. In their shining armor.

Fran: No.

Mike: Yes.

Fran: No. (Whispers.) They would blame me for it!

Mike: No! They are all happy and smiling. And you know what they do? They take their helmets off, and they toss them in the air, and they cheer for you! Our lovely lady, our queen. And Arthur gets down on one knee, and kisses your hand. The most gallant knight of all. I can feel their warmth for you. I can feel their love for you. And they want you to see how happy they are. Look at the happiness on their faces. They are all united again. And this is forever. See that happiness?

Fran: (Big sigh.)

Mike: And now, somebody pulls out a throne. A golden throne, and they escort you over to it. And they put you on the throne. And they start coming by, one by one, to pay homage to you, and to tell you how much they love you. And how important you are to them. And the first one to come is Arthur. And he is weeping great tears. He tells you how much he has always loved you. He says, "I loved you the first moment I saw you. I've always loved you, and I always will."

Fran: (Softly crying.)

Mike: "And you brought me such happiness." Yes, he's telling you that. Accept it, accept it. He is speaking from the heart. And he says, "When everything else around me was dismal, I could always come to you. And feel young again, and feel light and cheerful."

Fran: (Still crying.)

Mike: And he says, "Don't you remember when we played in the woods? Don't you remember that? You remember! Do you know what that did for me? You were my strength, you were my inspiration. And you helped me so much with my dream." And he kneels once more, and he kisses your hand. And I see all the other knights lined up to do the same thing. To come up, and kneel before you, and. . . .

Fran: But. . . .

Mike: Go ahead!

Fran: It all ended, and all love was lost! (Sobbing.)

Mike: Do they look as if their love is lost?

Fran: I don't understand! Because love was the only important thing that was there, and then it all . . . when everything else fell apart, it was gone too!

Mike: But that is what they want you to see now. It is not gone! They have it now, up in heaven. And it will be there forever. The knights are still walking past you, one at a time. They have their helmets in their left hand, cradled in their left arm. And they are walking up, kneeling to you, saying things to you, kissing your hand. And most of them are crying, crying with the love that they have for you. And the joy that they feel. And they want you to understand how happy they all are now. And now Merlin steps forward, and he takes you by the hand. And he gently escorts you off the throne. And all the knights are standing there, and they wave goodbye to you, as you slowly fade from view, as Merlin takes you back. Back to the castle. And now you are back in your chambers, but you have had a chance to see that Arthur and all his men are happy, and they are okay.

Fran: (Stops crying, big sigh.)

Mike: Now, tell me what happens to you after. . . . Do you stay living in Camelot?

Fran: No. I go live by the sea.

Mike: Pardon me?

Fran: I go to live by the sea.

Mike: Okay. Where do you go live? Is it a house, or a mansion, or a manor house, or what?

Fran: A little church.

Mike: Okay. Do you live by yourself?

Fran: I have one helper. She's a . . . novice. She's learning.

Mike: Are there men there to guard you?

Fran: I am protected, but I don't see the men.

Mike: Okay. And how do you spend your time there?

Fran: I watch the sea. I watch the waves.

Mike: What do you think of?

Fran: I hope for another chance. . . .

Mike: Another chance for what?

Fran: To redo the dream and to make it work.

Mike: Okay. Aha, Arthur's dream has become your dream! Yes? You smile at that!

Fran: It probably always was! (Slight laugh through the tears.) I just couldn't see it.

Mike: (Laughing.) Yes, yes, yes, yes! I would like to go forward in years now, to the point where you make your transition, to your death. And without feeling any discomfort, tell me how you pass over.

Fran: Peacefully, in my sleep.

Mike: Okay. Peacefully, in your sleep. And what happens to you then, after you. . . . Describe to me what happens.

Fran: I finally feel peace. I feel light, like one of the birds flying over the ocean. I feel like I'm forgiven.

Mike: Okay. Forgiven for what? Do you feel that you have failed at something?

Fran: I felt. . . .

Mike: How did you fail?

Fran: I failed Arthur by being selfish.

Mike: Okay.

Fran: Because I wanted more attention, instead of seeing his dream of what was important.

Mike: All right. Where do you go now? You are light, you are up with the birds. Are there some angels there, taking you on to the Light?

Fran: Yes.

Mike: Okay. Tell me what happens? Where do they take you?

Fran: They welcome me and hug me.

Mike: The angels do?

Fran: Yes.

Mike: Okay. And where do they take you now? Don't they take you back to Arthur and the men there, again? Don't they take you into the castle that Arthur and his men have created? Isn't there Camelot all over again?

Fran: I just see peace.

Mike: Okay. And who do you see there? . . . You are not seeing anything?

Fran: No.

Mike: Okay. Are you blocked from seeing it? I see Arthur, and I see all his men. Once again, they are still there! And they are still happy, aren't they?

Fran: Ummhumm!

Mike: And who is going to be with them now? You are going to be with them now! And is this a temporary thing? No, it's permanent. You are shaking your head "no." That's right. This is permanent. Can you accept that now?

Fran: Yes.

Mike: You are going to be with Arthur forever. And you know how many times he is going to have to tell you that he loves you?

192

Fran: (Laughs.)

Mike: All of eternity. And all of those knights who love you? Do you know how much time they have to show their devotion and love to you? And to forgive you? They have all of eternity. See, forgiveness is not an issue with them, it is only an issue with you.

Fran: They were never mad.

Mike: No, no, no.

Fran: The knights weren't.

Mike: No, no. They have only love for you. They only felt your pain. They felt, they wanted to help you with your pain. But they always loved you. Can you accept their love?

Fran: Yes.

Mike: Now. Let's see, where do we need to go from here? There is something else we wanted to do. All right, now I would like for you to imagine that you are Guenivere the little girl. Once again. Can you imagine that, like maybe five, six-years old? Can you make that switch, to go back and be Guenivere the little girl?

Fran: I think so. (Very quiet, small voice.)

Mike: Okay. Now you are in a cabin, and it is winter time, and it is real cold outside. And there is a fireplace at one end of the cabin, a nice big stone fireplace. It has got a nice, big, warm fire in it. And there is a rocking chair . . . in front of the fire. And there is someone sitting in that rocking chair. And they have got you in their lap. And that someone is Arthur. And Arthur has that little girl. He is the grown man, and you are the little girl. How does it feel to be in his lap? Do you feel a little stiff and uncomfortable?

Fran: Yes.

Mike: Yes, I see you. You are a little stiff and uncomfortable. He reaches out, and he puts his arms around you. How does that feel? Tell me how it feels?

Fran: I don't understand why he is there.

Mike: How do his arms feel?

Fran: Comforting.

Mike: Yes. And now, he reaches out and kisses you on the forehead. And pulls you to him. And as he pulls you to him, you feel his body warmth, you feel the love that he has for you. How does that feel? . . . And you still feel a little stiff and cold, and you have got these warm arms around you. And you feel the love coming from Arthur. That feels good, doesn't it?

Fran: Safe.

Mike: Yes. And now Arthur says to you, "Now I can tell you how much I love you. And now I can tell you that I will always protect and love you. And I will always make you feel loved. I am going to be the father to you, that you didn't have as a little girl. Because your own father didn't give you enough love, the right love, did he? No. And that caused you great pain. And then you grew up and married a man much older, and he didn't give you the love either. And that caused you a great loss, didn't it?" Yes, you are nodding "yes."

Fran: Yes.

Mike: Okay. So now, Arthur says to you, "I'm here to make up for that. I'm going to be your father. And I'm going to give you all the love that your daddy didn't give you." And he starts rocking the chair, and he holds you in his arms. And he starts singing little lullabies to you. How does that feel? Can you relax a little bit and accept that love? You are still tense and tight. You need to relax a little bit. This is for real, and he's giving you all of the love you ever wanted from Arthur. He is giving it to you now. And all the love you ever wanted from your father, Arthur's giving to you now. Doesn't that feel good?

Fran: Yes.

Mike: Can you accept it?

Fran: Yes.

Mike: I see you starting to warm up a little bit. And I see you find a spot on his shoulder where your head fits, and you snuggle up against him. Oh, that feels good! And now that little girl is getting all the love she ever wanted. Doesn't that feel good?

Fran: But . . . he's not IN love with me.

Mike: He says he is.

Fran: It's different.

Mike: What makes you think that?

Fran: It's not, like . . . how you love a wife.

Mike: No, no, no. You are not a wife. You are a five-year-old little girl. And Arthur's telling you that he is there to be your father, and to give you all the love your father didn't give you. And that is what we want to give you right now, all the love your father didn't give you. Can you accept that?

Fran: Yes.

Mike: Okay. How are you feeling now? Are you feeling warmer? I see you warming up, inside. And getting quite relaxed. I don't understand those songs he's singing to you. They are Gaelic or something. But he's just rocking in front of the fire, and holding you, and kissing you. So that little five-year-old girl feels absolutely loved and protected. What do you do now? Do you fall asleep? I see you with your eyes closed, snuggled up against his chest. No one has ever done this before for you, have they?

Fran: No.

Mike: Now you have gotten the love that you never got. From your daddy. And it's been given to you by your beloved Arthur. And Arthur smiles, because now he knows when you grow up and become his queen, you will be more understanding. And you will be able to forgive him easier. Because you will already have gotten the love

194

that you so desperately sought. The love that he overlooked and failed to give to you. Can you feel that now? That when you come to Arthur, you are going to be a more complete person. Full of love, all the way through. Tell me what you are thinking?

Fran: How can you change what has been done?

Mike: Because the past only exists in our memories. Did you see the movie, "Back to the Future"? That is what we are doing, we are going back in the past, and changing the past. Because it only exists in our minds. So when you change the past, guess what? You change the present and the future. So this is a real change. We are changing Guenivere, right now. And you know what, now Guenivere realizes that that emptiness she felt in her heart wasn't really from Arthur. It was from her father, when she was a little girl. Can you remember that now? But that has been changed. Now that little girl is getting all the love, and all the comfort and all the kisses. And being told she is loved. So that she is complete. And she is going to grow up a complete lady. Feeling very loved. Can you see that happening? Can you accept that? How do you feel now? . . . Feeling his love?

Fran: Yes.

Mike: Feeling the warmth?

Fran: Ummhumm.

Mike: His nice arms around you. . . . Okay, I'm just going to leave you two there, rocking in the chair, in front of that fire. And the warmth you are feeling from the fire, too, is love. And you stay there as long as you would like. Until you receive all of the love you want and need. You may come back when you wake up from your nap in front of the fire with your beloved Arthur.

18

Tad as Sir Kay
September, 1994

Background: Tad is a 34-year-old bachelor. He lives in Orlando. He is a big, gentle and very sweet person. The kind of man that is big and strong enough to wrestle a bull, but yet wouldn't harm a fly. As this regression unfolded, I realized that this Kay has not changed much since Camelot. He is still honorable and noble. The battle scenes in this regression came to me very vividly, and it was as if I was there. A neat experience.

Mike: Please open the door, and I will go along with you to enjoy the experience.
Tad: Okay, I am outside the castle. It is very lush, with trees around us, and we are right outside of the castle.
Mike: Yeah, there are trees close to the castle. We are off to one side, right?
Tad: Right. I went through a small doorway. It is a little private entrance.
Mike: Does the door have a rounded top?
Tad: Exactly!
Mike: I have seen that doorway. It is a side entrance.
Tad: A secret entrance.
Mike: Yeah, yeah.
Tad: And the trees are around it, covering, hiding it.
Mike: Yeah, and there are some vines growing on the wall.
Tad: Yes.
Mike: Yeah, I have seen that also.
Tad: I am looking down at my feet, and I'm seeing leather shoes, but they are not like the shoes that we wear today. I'm also seeing some kind of a grey mesh material. I don't know what it is. It may be pants or . . . but it is a grey mesh.

Mike: All right. What do you see now?

Tad: Oh, I am just looking at the castle. It is huge. It is white, tinged with grey. The sky is blue and the trees are green. I am with somebody. I am with you.

Mike: All right. Who am I? What do I look like?

Tad: You are a knight.

Mike: Okay.

Tad: You are younger than me. If I had to describe the color of your hair, I would say it would be like a dark brown, almost black.

Mike: All right.

Tad: I hear the name Percival, but I don't know if that is you.

Mike: Just now you heard Percival?

Tad: Yes. I asked who you were, and they said Percival. I don't know if that is correct.

Mike: Who are you?

Tad: . . . I asked, you know, what my name was, and they said, "Sir Kay."

Mike: All right. You must be a knight then?

Tad: I'm a knight.

Mike: How does it feel to be a knight?

Tad: There is a lot of authority. It feels like a task that you have to uphold . . . and honor.

Mike: Okay. Could you take me to the Great Hall for one of your meals, and describe to me what it is like there?

Tad: Okay. I am seeing that on the walls there are shields mounted, with many different types of shields; different colors, different designs.

Mike: Could it be that each knight hangs his shield on the wall?

Tad: Yes! I'm seeing yellow and red. . . .

Mike: Is that your shield?

Tad: Yes! It is. I'm seeing like a dragon on the shield. I don't know for sure if that one is mine, but it feels like it is.

Mike: All right. Yellow background, with a red dragon?

Tad: You said a yellow dragon?

Mike: No. A yellow background with a red dragon.

Tad: Right.

Mike: Okay. Where are the banners? Are there any banners in the hall?

Tad: There are banners. They are hung higher up.

Mike: Okay.

Tad: This hallway is huge, and the ceiling is very high.

Mike: All right. What is going on in the banquet, or banner hall?

Tad: Well, there are a lot of people there. There is eating, talking, and festivities.

Mike: What kind of tables are they seated at?

Tad: It is somewhat like a round table, but it's not a table. The tables are in a circle. The people are sitting with their backs toward the wall.

And in the opening, in the center of the room, is where people will come and talk to them, or entertain, or make speeches.

Mike: So the tables are arranged in a circle, so everyone can see equally the entertainment?

Tad: It is not like . . . it is not the Round Table.

Mike: No, it is just a circular formation of tables. Where is King Arthur sitting?

Tad: To the right of me.

Mike: All right. How do you feel when you look at King Arthur? What kind of emotions do you have?

Tad: Good!

Mike: Do you love him?

Tad: Yes!

Mike: Tell me about your feelings of love for him.

Tad: Pride. I look at him with awe. That he brought a lot of people together.

Mike: Do you see Merlin in the hall?

Tad: Yes.

Mike: How do you feel about Merlin?

Tad: I love Merlin.

Mike: Is the Queen there?

Tad: The Queen is there.

Mike: How do you feel about the Queen?

Tad: . . . I love her too.

Mike: Why did you hesitate?

Tad: It is a different type of love.

Mike: Okay, tell me about your love for the Queen.

Tad: It is a fatherly type of love.

Mike: Okay.

Tad: That is the way I feel about Arthur, also.

Mike: You have a fatherly love toward him?

Tad: Uhhuh.

Mike: Okay. Did you ever go out in combat with Arthur? Do battle against enemies?

Tad: Uhhuh.

Mike: Tell me about some of those battles. Do you remember them? What was it like?

Tad: The horses were draped with colorful blankets. It was like a parade, when we left the castle. And there were just a few of us. The power that each one carried was like a giant vibration, you know. For anybody that came towards us, it was like the energy that we had around us, they weren't able to even invade our space. They would see us, and feel the doom that they were to encounter.

Mike: Your enemies, you are talking about your enemies?

Tad: Right. They would take a look at us, and they would be afraid.

Mike: What gave you that power? Was it magic, or was it just your power as knights?

Tad: It was our power as knights, but it was also kind of like magic too. From what Merlin has taught us. He would put a vibration around us. People would see things in us that they would be afraid of.

Mike: Okay. It made you appear fierce and foreboding?

Tad: Taller and bigger.

Mike: Taller and bigger. All right. Who are you going to fight?

Tad: I got . . . Norsemen.

Mike: Norsemen. Okay.

Tad: Whoever they are.

Mike: All right. Can you describe the battle to me?

Tad: (Big sigh.) . . . We are coming out of a clearing. And they are on the other side, lined up on the other hill. And they have a lineup, and we have a lineup.

Mike: Okay. How many men are on their side, and how many men on your side?

Tad: I got around fifty.

Mike: Okay. And how does the battle start?

Tad: Each side is taunting the other. . . .

Mike: Uhhuh.

Tad: . . . To make the first move.

Mike: And who makes the first move?

Tad: We made the first move.

Mike: Okay. . . . What did you do?

Tad: We shot arrows. And then, the ones on horses, we on horses went in through.

Mike: Charged them on horses?

Tad: Uhhuh.

Mike: What kind of weapons were you using; sword, or lance, or mace? What were you using?

Tad: I was using my sword.

Mike: Okay. What were the other knights using? Could you tell?

Tad: Some of them were using swords, and some were using maces.

Mike: Okay.

Tad: The lance, we had the opportunity to use the lance. But we were just going in with. . . . I went in with sword.

Mike: Okay. What happened when you hit the other line? How did it go?

Tad: Well, they didn't think that we were going to come. And we came. We won.

Mike: How many of you were on horseback?

Tad: About twenty.

Mike: Okay. So twenty of you on horseback charged fifty of them?

Tad: No. I am saying that the fifty that I was seeing on top of this hill, lined up, weren't on horses.

Mike: All right. Were any of them on horses?

Tad: Right. But they were down below, behind the top of the hill.

Mike: Oh, okay. So their horsemen were down below? So you hit their lines of foot soldiers first, with your horses?

Tad: Right. The ones that shot the arrows aimed at certain spots in their line. This opened up places in the line so that we could go through.

Mike: Oh, okay. So you rode your horses through where the men had been knocked down by the arrows?

Tad: Right.

Mike: They concentrated the arrow fire in a couple lanes?

Tad: Right.

Mike: And then you rode your horses through those lanes?

Tad: To get to the other people.

Mike: To get to the mounted soldiers in the back?

Tad: Yes.

Mike: Oh, okay. So you could stop them so they couldn't attack your soldiers?

Tad: Right.

Mike: And so who did you fight? Did you fight foot soldiers or mounted soldiers?

Tad: Mounted.

Mike: And you caught them by surprise?

Tad: Right.

Mike: Were they on their horses?

Tad: They were on their horses.

Mike: Okay. Did they have a chance to get their weapons out?

Tad: Yeah, they had a chance to get their weapons out. They were fighting.

Mike: All right. Tell me how your fight went. Who was the first person you ran into? What did he look like?

Tad: He had a black beard.

Mike: Uhhuh. Did he have full armor on?

Tad: Yes.

Mike: Where did you hit him, and where did he hit you?

Tad: We were hitting shields. Swords against the shields.

Mike: Okay. Each of you blocked the blows with your shields?

Tad: Several times.

Mike: Okay, and then what happened?

Tad: I got him in the neck.

Mike: Okay. He couldn't get his shield up fast enough?

Tad: Right.

Mike: All right. He went down?

Tad: Right.

Mike: Then what did you do? Went after the next one?

Tad: Went after the next one. I was helping somebody else.

Mike: Yeah. You spun around to your right and helped somebody else.

Tad: Yeah, I was helping Lancelot.

Mike: He had his hands full.

Tad: They wanted him.

Mike: The enemy wanted him?

Tad: Yes!

Mike: So they had two of them. I see two soldiers fighting Lancelot.

Tad: So I freed up one.

Mike: Yes. Yes. And what happened there?

Tad: I got my man again.

Mike: Okay. Very quickly this time?

Tad: Uhhuh. He wasn't expecting it.

Mike: Yes. You kind of caught him by. . . .

Tad: I got him from the back.

Mike: Yeah, yeah. Cause he was concentrating on Lancelot. Yeah, okay. What did you do then?

Tad: Then there was another one.

Mike: Uhhuh. You turned your. . . .

Tad: But after that, it wasn't that much longer until it was done.

Mike: Okay. Tell me about the third one.

Tad: I went for him too.

Mike: All right.

Tad: He had . . . he had like this ball, with chain.

Mike: Yeah, yeah. What did you do to him?

Tad: He went to bring up his ball and chain, and I stuck him . . . in the belly.

Mike: Okay. He was pretty scared, wasn't he?

Tad: Right.

Mike: He was kind of in the back. He was like one of the last ones you went after?

Tad: Right.

Mike: Okay. Yeah, all right.

Tad: And he was swinging his mace backward, and that is when I took my sword, and I just "keeled" him.

Mike: Okay. So, ah, what happened to the battle then? You destroyed all the mounted soldiers?

Tad: Taking prisoners.

Mike: Of the foot soldiers?

Tad: Uhhuh.

Mike: You came up behind them, and they gave up?

Tad: No. Our foot soldiers were doing battle too.

Mike: Oh, okay. Your foot soldiers had followed behind you, and had attacked their foot soldiers?

Tad: There was a massive battle in the middle of their line.

Mike: Okay. Did you do any more fighting?

Tad: No.

Mike: Was Arthur in this battle?

Tad: No.

Mike: Who was in charge of your forces?

Tad: I don't know. I like to say that I had some call in it, but I don't think I was in . . . charge of it.

Mike: What I sense is that all the senior knights kind of collectively decided what to do.

Tad: Yes!

Mike: Yeah, okay. What did you do with the horses, and the swords, and armor and everything?

Tad: We collected them.

Mike: Okay.

Tad: Arrows and. . . .

Mike: Picked up everything! What are you going to do with the prisoners?

Tad: Give them the opportunity to come onto our side.

Mike: And if they don't?

Tad: . . . I see a dungeon.

Mike: Put them in a dungeon. Okay. Do most of them agree to join you?

Tad: Yes.

Mike: Is this how Arthur built up his own forces?

Tad: Right.

Mike: And replaced his own battle loses?

Tad: Right. Most of them did it eagerly.

Mike: Pardon me?

Tad: Most of them did it . . . they were eager to join.

Mike: Yes, okay. Good. I sense it was almost with eagerness that they lost the battle. That they could join the greater force. They were part of a rag-tag, kind of rebel group.

Tad: They felt the magic.

Mike: Yes, and they liked to fight. They wanted to be part of it. When they joined your forces, did these men bring their families, or did they marry within your people?

Tad: Some brought their families.

Mike: Okay.

Tad: Some had no families. . . . And some made families.

Mike: Did they speak the same language that you did, or did they have to learn your language?

Tad: Again, some knew the language. Or knew, somewhat, part of it.

Mike: Uhhuh. I would like to ask you about the sword that Arthur carried. Excalibur. Can you tell me about that sword?

Tad: I am seeing . . . I am seeing, like a blue stone in the handle. And I don't know if it is just. . . .

Mike: Like in the butt of the handle?

Tad: Yes. Some type of a blue stone.

Mike: All right. Did he ever let you carry the sword?

Tad: . . . It was Arthur's sword.

Mike: Okay. Where did you live? Did you live at Camelot?

Tad: Yes.

Mike: Did you have a wife?

Tad: Yes.

Mike: Did you have children?

Tad: Yes.

Mike: Tell me about your children.

Tad: I had a daughter. Anne.

Mike: Anne. Okay. . . . Did you love your wife?

Tad: Yes.

Mike: Okay. Tell me about her.

Tad: . . . She was a jolly person, who liked to laugh. Lots of humor. When we were serious, she would always be poking fun.

Mike: What was her name?

Tad: Katherine.

Mike: Okay. If you were to be able to give a message to the people of the modern world some fifteen-hundred years later after your life, what would you want to tell them about your experiences as a knight of the Round Table?

Tad: To have courage, and fight for what you believe in. And always be clear in your thoughts and your actions.

Mike: Yes.

Tad: Clear, as in thinking. And clear, as in purity.

Mike: Tell me about purity. Did the knights have purity?

Tad: Yes!

Mike: How did they get purity?

Tad: Purity was in heart. Purity was in having good thoughts towards others, and God. Never self-indulgence. Purity was not being vain about yourself, but thinking of others before you. You know what I mean?

Mike: Yes.

Tad: Not being greedy. God came first. Before you.

Mike: Yes. Okay. The younger knights, they were all trained by Merlin? As you taught them how to fight with swords and lances and other weapons, weren't they also trained by Merlin?

Tad: He would teach us . . . he would teach us how to bring the power within ourselves. He would make us feel that we were invincible.

Mike: Okay. How did he do that?

Tad: By unlocking our heart. (Big sigh.)

Mike: How did he do that?

Tad: Unlocking our heart would be to find the secrets that lie within ourselves, and the many mysteries. . . . The secrets that we would use to build a shield around ourselves.

Mike: So that you KNEW you were invincible!

Tad: . . . He would do strange things.

Mike: Such as?

Tad: He would make words come out of different things.

Mike: Like inanimate things?

Tad: Like a voice coming through.

Mike: Could this be used to terrorize the enemy?

Tad: He would pick up a sword, and would wield it around, and the sword would speak. And he taught us how to make our swords speak. And as we would wield our swords around, the people that we were doing battle with, they would hear these swords speak, and that would freak them out.

Mike: Hmmm. I guess it would. No wonder you could defeat them. Yeah, okay. Changing the subject a bit, were you at the Round Table when the Bishop arrived at the court, and started causing all the trouble for Arthur?

Tad: No.

Mike: You had already passed away?

Tad: Yes.

Mike: At what age did you pass away?

Tad: I was in my sixties.

Mike: Okay. Can you tell me about how you passed away?

Tad: Well, I was old. But I died in battle.

Mike: Would it cause you discomfort to describe that to me?

Tad: No.

Mike: Could you tell me about that last battle?

Tad: . . . All battles are basically the same.

Mike: Was it just like the other one?

Tad: Sometimes they would try to come up from behind. Sometimes we would try to come up from their behind. This time, it was just coming together and fighting. And I took a sword in the side.

Mike: How did you let that happen? How many men were you fighting?

Tad: I was fighting one other, but another one came up from my blind side. . . .

Mike: Okay. He got you on your blind side. That was always a danger, wasn't it?

Tad: Yes.

Mike: Was the enemy force larger than your force?

Tad: No.

Mike: Who were they?

Tad: People that came from Scotland.

Mike: Okay. Were you on horseback?

Tad: I was on horseback.

Mike: Okay. Were some of them on horseback?

Tad: Yes.

Mike: Were they raiding down into your country?

Tad: Uhhuh.

Mike: As you were dying, how were your thoughts? What were you thinking?

Tad: My thought was . . . "Damn, why did this happen?" I wasn't expecting it. I was sorry that I was going out, but then, happy that . . . happy that I was going out with a sword in my hands, still.

Mike: Yes, yes. Did you think of Arthur?

Tad: Arthur was the king. . . . I thought of him.

Mike: Were you sad for Arthur at that time?

Tad: I wasn't sad for Arthur.

Mike: Was Arthur a happy person, as near as you could tell?

Tad: He was a happy person.

Mike: Okay.

Tad: We were close.

Mike: Were you like a father to him?

Tad: Yes!

Mike: Had you acted as his father?

Tad: Yes.

Mike: Did you help raise him?

Tad: Uhhuh.

Mike: Was he like your son? In your own heart?

Tad: Yes.

Mike: Did you have another son?

Tad: No! (Choked up.)

Mike: Okay, just a minute. I'll get you a box of kleenex. I sense deep suffering there. Your stomach is heaving. Is there grief about Arthur? Tell me about your feelings about Arthur.

Tad: I believed in Arthur!

Mike: Okay. That makes you very unhappy? I sense panic, in leaving Arthur.

Tad: It was a panic in the battle, in leaving the body. Wondering if Arthur would be all right.

Mike: Yes. Who was going to take care of Arthur, without you there? Right? Yes! Tell Arthur how much you love him. You never got to say goodbye.

Tad: (Crying.) That is what hurt!

Mike: Okay. I tell you what, Arthur is in front of you now. He has placed himself in front of you as you are dying. Now, tell him what you didn't get a chance to tell him before.

Tad: I love you, Arthur! (Crying.)

Mike: Tell him everything.

Tad: With all my heart and my. . . . (Crying too hard to finish.)

Mike: Yes. Let your grief out.

Tad: Merlin was helping him too.

Mike: Merlin was helping Arthur? Do you love Merlin for that?

Tad: Yes! Merlin please come to me, too.

Mike: Tell Merlin how you feel.

Tad: (To Merlin) Watch over him! He needs you!

Mike: You are saying to Merlin, "He needs you." Merlin says to you, "Dear old friend, I knew that your time was near. And I knew that this was the best way. This was the way you wanted to go."

Tad: (Crying.) Yes.

Mike: Merlin says, "Understand how much we love you. How much your devotion and loyalty and love has meant to us."

Tad: He has come to me in this lifetime, too.

Mike: Yes. Yes. "Because of that devotion, loyalty and love which you gave them then," he says, "you are greatly honored by both of them." Is there anything else you wish to tell them?

Tad: I will always be with you!

Mike: Yes, and he says they will always be with you! For eternity. Great, noble, honorable and reliable. Sir Kay. They could always count on you. They used you as a template, to set the standards for what their other knights would be, or could become. And in this, you will always be honored.

Tad: I am honored.

Mike: Yes. And Merlin also says, "It is time for you now, to accept who you are. And accept your greatness. And once again, become the knight." . . . He shows a bunch of knights standing in a line, and you are bigger, and taller, and more brilliant than all the rest. Because of your heart, and your fine qualities. And you will always be honored for that.

Tad: (Deep breath.) My shield still hangs there!

Mike: Yes, forever, forever! Forever! It still hangs on the walls of the Banner Hall. On a wooden peg.

Tad: I wish to let go of this . . . pain!

Mike: They are here to help you lift it up. Just release it! It is being released as we speak! Arthur and Merlin are appearing in front of you now, so that you will release your grief. . . . They have done just fine. They want you to know that they are okay. And the worry that you have carried for them, you don't need to carry anymore. Everything is fine. And Camelot did what it was supposed to do. So, can you release all that . . . worry and grief?

Tad: Uhhuh. Camelot is in my heart.

Mike: Yes, yes. And the angels come down now, and they lift that worry right out of your stomach. It is a great big bulge. And they lift that worry out, and they put it on a royal litter, in honor of you. Of the royal person you are. Because of your royal heart. And they proudly carry it off, up to the White Light. Which they say is Camelot! And all that grief now is gone. Is transmuted into the Light. And they ask you, now, to rejoice with them. And be happy. Everything was done, with great honor, great dignity, and great devotion. And you should now only be filled with wonderful memories. You led the perfect life. A brave knight, valiant to the end. With a perfect ending. . . . How are you feeling now?

Tad: (Big sigh.) Good.

Mike: Anything else you would like to say? Or are you ready to come back?

Tad: Yes.

Mike: Let's go find that doorway!

Tad: Okay.

19

Jackie as Arthur
September, 1994

Background: I wish that all of the regressions were as easy for me as was this one. Jackie was easy to regress, saw everything vividly and effortlessly, and proceeded smoothly through the healing aspect of the session.

Jackie is a 52-year-old housewife from Atlanta, Georgia. She was visiting in Orlando. When a friend of mine mentioned my Camelot project to her, she immediately requested a session. She told me that she had experienced flashbacks of a Camelot-like experience off and on for most of her life. She was anxious to explore this phenomenon further.

Mike: So, if you are feeling comfortable, I would like for you to open that door and go back to your lifetime at Camelot. If it is okay with you, I will go with you.
Jackie: Yes.
Mike: Okay. Ready to open the door?
Jackie: Uhhuh.
Mike: Let's do it.
Jackie: Okay. The door is open.
Mike: All right. What do you see?
Jackie: A hallway.
Mike: All right.
Jackie: And it is very bright and well lit.
Mike: Okay.
Jackie: And it leads into the main throne room.
Mike: All right.
Jackie: It has marble floors. . . .
Mike: Yes.

Jackie: Gold throne. . . .

Mike: Uhhuh.

Jackie: Red velvet drapes. There is a page there, with a trumpet. He has got a blue shirt and pants that are trimmed in gold. There is nobody on the throne.

Mike: Okay.

Jackie: It is empty.

Mike: And what are you going to do?

Jackie: I don't know why I am here.

Mike: Do you want to go sit on the throne?

Jackie: Yes. I'm going to sit on the throne.

Mike: How does it make you feel?

Jackie: Big. Tall. Powerful.

Mike: All right. Are you. . . .

Jackie: But humble.

Mike: Huh?

Jackie: Powerful, but humble.

Mike: Do you feel that you are a man or a woman?

Jackie: Man.

Mike: Okay. Where else would you like to take me in the castle?

Jackie: Out to the garden.

Mike: All right. How do you think King Arthur would feel if he had seen you sitting on his throne?

Jackie: I don't have any feeling about that.

Mike: Okay. Do you know who you are?

Jackie: No. . . . (Hesitates.)

Mike: Do you feel that you are King Arthur?

Jackie: Yes.

Mike: Okay. Tell me about the garden. Let's go out to the garden.

Jackie: The garden is very beautiful. Has a lot of herbs. And there are a lot of columns. Like marble columns. There are grape vines. Or something that looks like grape vines. And all kinds of arbors. And very green grass. And a lot of shrubbery. There is a little stream running through it.

Mike: It must have taken some special engineering to get that stream running through your garden.

Jackie: Yeah, I guess it did.

Mike: Who arranged that? Did you plan that?

Jackie: Merlin.

Mike: Merlin planned that? Oh, okay. You depend on him a lot, don't you?

Jackie: Uhhuh.

Mike: How do you feel about Merlin?

Jackie: He is good. Mischievous, but good.

Mike: Does he help you a lot?

Jackie: Oh yes.

Mike: Whose idea was it to create Camelot, the Round Table, the movement of the knights, and all that? Was that your idea, or Merlin's, or a combination thereof?

Jackie: Humm. I'm not sure. I think it was a group of people that started everything. But they're not here.

Mike: Okay. I get the feeling that there is some anxiety on your part in going back and visiting this lifetime. Are you feeling a little anxiety?

Jackie: A little bit.

Mike: I would like to please let you understand that there's a lot of love here for you. And the whole point of going back, as Arthur and Merlin have both told me, the point of going back and making this visit, is so that you can heal.

Jackie: Uhhuh.

Mike: So everything that we are going to do today is going to be with the objective of healing any of the old hurts that you might be carrying with you.

Jackie: Uhhuh.

Mike: Okay. They tell me that the camaraderie and love around the Round Table, and the fellowship of the knights, was really awesome.

Jackie: Yes.

Mike: Who created that? Did you create it?

Jackie: I can't take credit for it, because all people together, working together, they are the ones that created it.

Mike: Okay. Who selects the knights?

Jackie: Well, three of us.

Mike: Who are the three?

Jackie: I'm not sure.

Mike: You and Merlin?

Jackie: Yes.

Mike: And who else?

Jackie: I'm not sure.

Mike: Is it the Queen?

Jackie: She . . . helps.

Mike: How do you feel about your queen?

Jackie: I love her.

Mike: How long have you been married?

Jackie: Five years.

Mike: Five years. Has it been a good marriage?

Jackie: Very good.

Mike: Are you expecting to have children?

Jackie: . . . Yes.

Mike: Okay. You hesitated.

Jackie: I wasn't sure.

Mike: Okay. How did you pick Guenivere as your queen?

Jackie: She came to me in a dream.

Mike: Okay. And did the dream show you where to find her?

Jackie: I don't remember.

Mike: All right. You kind of had a wife before Guenivere, didn't you?

Jackie: Yes.

Mike: Who was that?

Jackie: (Big sigh.)

Mike: That is all right. Don't feel any anxieties. We just want to talk about these things and let them out.

Jackie: I loved her too.

Mike: I know. Do you still love her?

Jackie: Yes.

Mike: Wasn't it kind of a cruel trick, twist of fate, that she was your sister?

Jackie: Yes.

Mike: Does she feel disappointed about the way things turned out?

Jackie: Yes.

Mike: Have you been able to make her understand that you did what you had to do?

Jackie: No.

Mike: Okay. Have you tried to . . . tried to talk to her?

Jackie: Yes, I've tried to talk to her.

Mike: Do you still see her?

Jackie: Sometimes.

Mike: Where do you see her?

Jackie: In the caverns.

Mike: Are there caverns close to the castle?

Jackie: Yes.

Mike: Who brings her there?

Jackie: Her aides.

Mike: Where does she live now?

Jackie: Up on the other . . . hill.

Mike: Okay. Does it distress you to talk about this?

Jackie: A little bit.

Mike: You had some children, didn't you, with her?

Jackie: Yes.

Mike: How are they doing?

Jackie: They are okay.

Mike: Your son, what's his name?

Jackie: Hmmm.

Mike: Mordred?

Jackie: Yes.

Mike: Do you love him?
Jackie: No.
Mike: Why not?
Jackie: He is not honest.
Mike: Okay. How about your daughter. Do you love her?
Jackie: Very much. She is very beautiful.
Mike: Yes. She's going to grow up to be a priestess like her mother, isn't she?
Jackie: Yes.
Mike: And do very nice things for the people?
Jackie: Yes.
Mike: Do you still carry love for Morgana?
Jackie: Yes.
Mike: So you love your wife, and you love your . . . your . . . Morgana?
Jackie: Yes.
Mike: Let's talk about some of the knights. Tell me about Lancelot.
Jackie: He has got a big ego.
Mike: But isn't he your best friend?
Jackie: Yes, he is. But he would like to be king.
Mike: Yes. They say he came from a humble background in France. Is that true?
Jackie: Yes.
Mike: It is interesting that, coming from a humble background, he would think that he should be king of a land that is not even his country.
Jackie: I think that it has something to do with his birthright.
Mike: Okay. Like perhaps he was robbed of a birthright back in France?
Jackie: Yes.
Mike: So he thinks he should be king somewhere, and he happens to be here.
Jackie: That's right.
Mike: I sense some disappointment when you are talking about Lancelot.
Jackie: Yes. I expected more from him. I expected him to be, and act as if he were my very best friend. But he didn't always behave that way.
Mike: Could you be more specific?
Jackie: Well, he had a tendency to go behind my back with the younger knights of the Round Table, and try to cause dissension.
Mike: Yeah. Did he ever cause any problems with your wife?
Jackie: Oh, yes. He loves her! He loves her very much!
Mike: Does that cause you any pain?
Jackie: Yes.
Mike: Are you disappointed in him?

Jackie: Very much so.

Mike: Are you disappointed in your wife?

Jackie: Yes. They should not be together.

Mike: Yes. I sense a great heaviness in your heart.

Jackie: Yes, because I love them both. And they betray me.

Mike: Okay. What does Merlin say about that? Have you discussed this with your good friend Merlin?

Jackie: Yes. He says that they will have to pay for it, again and again, until they learn.

Mike: Tell me about some of your other favorite knights. Who were some of the other favorites? Galahad?

Jackie: Yes, he was good. He was trusting. Trustworthy.

Mike: Okay, how about Gawaine?

Jackie: He was just always there for me.

Mike: Big and cheerful guy, wasn't he?

Jackie: Yes, he was.

Mike: And he was dependable?

Jackie: Very dependable. He was always there.

Mike: But did he have the spiritual depth of Galahad?

Jackie: No. He did not.

Mike: How about Lionel?

Jackie: Hmmm.

Mike: More pain?

Jackie: Yeah. I don't seem to want to talk about him.

Mike: Okay, we won't talk about him. Lucan the Butler?

Jackie: There is more pain with him too.

Mike: Could it be because of the betrayal with your wife?

Jackie: Yes. He was right in the middle of it.

Mike: Yes.

Jackie: He helped. He felt he was doing the right thing, though.

Mike: How could that be?

Jackie: Because he didn't know any better. He was a romantic himself.

Mike: I sense that he came from a coarse background.

Jackie: Yes.

Mike: And he was not good knight material. He had been your personal servant for many years. Although out of your generous heart you eventually made him a knight, he just wasn't up to it.

Jackie: No, he wasn't knight material.

Mike: Yeah.

Jackie: Sometimes I'm too kind. I get too kind.

Mike: One of the knights was telling me about, and I forget his name, but he was a young knight and you sent him out alone to fight the Black Knight. Remember that?

Jackie: Yes.

Mike: Why did you do that? Why send your youngest, most inexperienced knight out to fight the Black Knight?

Jackie: Because he needed it. Because by doing this, he would overcome all his fears. And be able to take all the challenges that were in store for him.

Mike: Yes. He also had a pure heart, didn't he?

Jackie: Yes he did.

Mike: That is what is good.

Jackie: And he was trustworthy, and a very good, enlightened person. When you looked at him, you could see the light around him. Very bright and very shiny. Some other people didn't like that, seemed to be jealous of him.

Mike: Okay. The Bishop. Why in the world did you give the Bishop all your power?

Jackie: Because I was tired. Tired of fighting.

Mike: Battles, or intrigue around the castle?

Jackie: Intrigue around the castle.

Mike: The thing with Guenivere and Lancelot took a lot of your. . . .

Jackie: Yes, it took a lot of my energy. It made me not care about this plane of existence any more.

Mike: They say that you took sick for a year-and-a-half, or something like that?

Jackie: Yes. I was ill.

Mike: Were you poisoned?

Jackie: Yes. Arsenic.

Mike: Who did it?

Jackie: Not sure.

Mike: Could it have been the Bishop?

Jackie: Probably. He had the opportunity.

Mike: How old were you about the time you took to the sickbed? How many years? Can you remember?

Jackie: About . . . fifty-two, I think.

Mike: Fifty-two? Okay. And you died when you were about fifty-seven?

Jackie: Yes.

Mike: Fifty-seven. That is what I have been told. There was a knight named Pellinore.

Jackie: Yes.

Mike: How was he?

Jackie: He was okay.

Mike: He was okay. He was idealistic?

Jackie: Very much so.

Mike: What about Percival?

Jackie: He was good. And happy. He was happy. Very happy.

Mike: I talked to him, and he was very confused as to why you assigned him to guard the Holy Grail, at the Grail Castle.

Jackie: Because he was the most trustworthy of all.

Mike: You weren't just trying to get him to settle down and become a family man?

Jackie: Well, that too.

Mike: Why would you do that? Was there some secret about Percival?

Jackie: Per . . . ci . . . val was Merlin's . . . son.

Mike: So, you did this for Merlin?

Jackie: Yes. Merlin wanted that.

Mike: Okay.

Jackie: And Merlin always gets his own way.

Mike: One way or another, right?

Jackie: Right!

Mike: Did you ever go to Merlin and talk to him about your disappointments with Lancelot, and Guenivere, and the others?

Jackie: Yes, but he said everything will work out for the best. Sometimes we must experience what we must experience. And that is all part of growing.

Mike: The people loved you very much.

Jackie: Yes, I tried to be good and kind.

Mike: It is a shame they haven't been able to pay you back. So that you became discouraged.

Jackie: Perhaps they don't have the opportunity. There is too much interference from others. They don't know what they should be knowing and doing.

Mike: I'm fascinated about the way you used Merlin to help train the knights, so that they would be spiritual warriors as well as martial warriors. That was very clever.

Jackie: Well, that is a practical way of doing things.

Mike: Where did Merlin get all of his great powers?

Jackie: From another universe.

Mike: Okay. In this lifetime that you're living as Jackie, what are your plans as far as using the knowledge you gained as Arthur? What of your experience do you use in this lifetime?

Jackie: Well, I know I can help a lot of people. I've been a natural born healer for many, many years. I have only really come to realize it probably in the last ten years. But I do love all people, and I want to bring peace and joy to everyone.

Mike: I sense some heartbreak. What are we going to do about that heartbreak?

Jackie: Well, I'm working on it.

Mike: May I help you?

Jackie: Uhhuh.

Mike: I have got my hanky here if you want to cry.

Jackie: Uhhhh.

Mike: We do a lot of that in these sessions.

Jackie: Yes.

Mike: I would like to go back to the throne room.

Jackie: Yes.

Mike: I would like for you to sit on the throne again. Here is some kleenex. I would like for you to sit on the throne.

Jackie: I'm there.

Mike: And now I would like for you to call Guenivere in.

Jackie: (Big sigh.) Okay, she's here.

Mike: I would like for you to ask her to kneel in front of you.

Jackie: (Whispers.) She is kneeling. She says that she is sorry. She says that she loves me, and she says she is so sorry. (Starts crying.)

Mike: Can you feel her pain?

Jackie: Oh yes!

Mike: She just wasn't strong enough.

Jackie: No, she wasn't. And she says that she did not mean to hurt me.

Mike: It wasn't her dream. Camelot wasn't her dream. It was your dream.

Jackie: Yes, it was my dream. It is my dream.

Mike: It was superimposed on her, and she tried her best to do her part.

Jackie: But she wasn't strong enough.

Mike: She wasn't strong enough. Can you take her in your arms?

Jackie: Yes!

Mike: Can you feel the weakness in her chest?

Jackie: Yes!

Mike: Can you feel the pain?

Jackie: Yes, in her heart and in her throat.

Mike: Yes. So, who did Guenivere hurt?

Jackie: She hurt herself too.

Mike: Yes, yes, yes. Just hold her tightly. Can you give her your love?

Jackie: (Crying.) Yes. . . . My hurt is gone, now.

Mike: Yes. That feels better, doesn't it?

Jackie: Yes. That needed to be done.

Mike: Yes. You have been waiting a long time to do that.

Jackie: Yes.

Mike: Would you like to ask her to sit beside you now?

Jackie: Yes, I would. Ohhhhh.

Mike: Now she is really your queen again.

Jackie: Yes, she is. She is still so beautiful! (Crying.) And she is happy, too. I'm happy now, too. I have peace now.

Mike: Are you ready for the next person?

Jackie: Yes.

Mike: I've got them lined up to see you.

Jackie: Yes.

Mike: Let's bring Lancelot in. How does he look as he comes down in front of you?

Jackie: He looks very humble.

Mike: He is ashamed, isn't he?

Jackie: Yes, he is very ashamed. He is also crying. (Sobbing.) He also was weak, but I understand. I understand. It's okay, it's okay.

Mike: And who did Lancelot fail?

Jackie: Himself!

Mike: Yes, not you.

Jackie: Yes, he failed himself.

Mike: Can you take him in your arms?

Jackie: Yes. That feels better. That feels better, this pain. . . .

Mike: The pain feels better too?

Jackie: Yes, it is gone now.

Mike: He has waited a long time. . . .

Jackie: Yes, he has.

Mike: For you to forgive him.

Jackie: He has waited a long time.

Mike: Now he is free of his burden, he can release it.

Jackie: Yes he can.

Mike: He says he wants to ask for another chance to show his greatness.

Jackie: Yes, I will give him that chance.

Mike: And now he says that he understands why you were the king, and why he was not meant to be a king.

Jackie: Yes.

Mike: Only when he has mastered these challenges will he truly be "king" material.

Jackie: Yes.

Mike: Okay. I see him going over and sitting down at the side. He is still crying.

Jackie: Yes.

Mike: He is so relieved. He has tears of joy.

Jackie: Yes. We all feel better.

Mike: Who would you like to bring in now? Lucan?

Jackie: Yes.

Mike: What would you like to tell him?

Jackie: I don't know. There doesn't seem to be as much pain.

Mike: No, he didn't know any better.

Jackie: Yes. He is just a common person.

Mike: You tried to make a sow's ear into a silk purse.

Jackie: Yes. It is not his fault.

Mike: Actually, I see you telling him, please excuse me. . . .

Jackie: Yes.

Mike: For trying to do for you what you weren't ready for.

Jackie: That's right. He wasn't ready.

Mike: Yes. There is somebody else waiting out there to see you. It is Merlin.

Jackie: Oh, my friend. My good friend.

Mike: Yes.

Jackie: Yes. Have him come in.

Mike: Yes, he is coming in. Merlin the Great.

Jackie: (Chuckling.) He is not walking . . . he is skipping in.

Mike: But he still has some pain.

Jackie: Yeah. Yes, he does.

Mike: His feelings were hurt.

Jackie: Because he felt I should have confided in him more.

Mike: Yes. Despite all his greatness, he is also a man.

Jackie: And he has feelings. I am sorry that I hurt him.

Mike: Tell him.

Jackie: I'm sorry I hurt you.

Mike: Please forgive me.

Jackie: Please, please forgive me.

Mike: Now you take the great wizard in your arms.

Jackie: Ahhhh, yes.

Mike: How does that feel?

Jackie: It feels good.

Mike: He likes that too.

Jackie: Yes, he does. Yes, he says that we will be together again. And again. And again.

Mike: I see him reaching inside himself, grabbing a little black . . . gob of hurt.

Jackie: Yes, yes.

Mike: And flinging it to the universe. Now he is truly Magnificent again.

Jackie: He is.

Mike: Yes.

Jackie: I didn't realize how much I hurt him.

Mike: That is okay.

Jackie: I guess, being king, sometimes you forget that other people have feelings, too.

Mike: Yes.

Jackie: I think that I was so busy with my own hurts that I didn't see the hurts I caused others.

Mike: I would now like to bring Morgana into see you. Will you. . . .

Jackie: Yes.

Mike: Here she comes. She looks very elegant.

Jackie: She is always beautiful. Very beautiful.

Mike: I am going to escort Guenivere to a side chamber for a minute.

Jackie: Yes, please do.

Mike: I'm going to escort her to the powder room.

Jackie: Yes.

Mike: I take her out. . . .

Jackie: Okay.

Mike: So you can talk with . . . Morgana. She throws herself at your feet.

Jackie: She also is begging forgiveness, but I need to beg her for my forgiveness too.

Mike: Do it!

Jackie: I'm sorry too. For all the hurt I've caused you, by not being able to understand you.

Mike: Tell her you're sorry that you weren't able to be everything for her that she wanted you to be.

Jackie: Yes. I'm sorry I wasn't able to be for you what you wanted me to be. I tried.

Mike: But I always loved you.

Jackie: I have always loved you. Always.

Mike: What is she doing now?

Jackie: She is kneeling, and she is crying.

Mike: Yes.

Jackie: She is crying, and she says that she loves me too. And always will.

Mike: Can you two forgive each other?

Jackie: Yes. I forgive her, and she forgives me. We will be together again.

Mike: Yes. . . . Now I'm going to set another chair up right next to your throne. Guenivere is on your right, and I am going to set a chair up to the left.

Jackie: Yes.

Mike: And I'm going to place Morgana there.

Jackie: Yes, she belongs there.

Mike: Queen for a day.

Jackie: Queen in my heart for a lifetime. (Crying.)

Mike: I'm going to bring Guenivere back in now. And I whispered in her ear that everything is okay. And so she graciously . . . she kind of does a curtsy towards Morgana, and she sits down. And now, I bring in Mordred. He is hesitant to approach the throne. Can you beckon to him?

Jackie: Yes.

Mike: You will have to command him to come forward.

Jackie: Please come, son.

Mike: Now, what would you like to tell him?

Jackie: (Big sigh.) I would like to tell him that we need to make amends. That I will forgive him for what he has done to me.

Mike: Say, I forgive you.

Jackie: I forgive you.

Mike: And what does he do?

Jackie: He is bowing. He is down on one knee. And he says he forgives me also. I have also hurt him. And now he comes to me, and I hug him, and he hugs me. And the hurt is gone. The hurt is all gone, for him and for me. There is no more hurt.

Mike: Would you like for him to stay there, or to leave?

Jackie: He may go.

Mike: Okay. Would you like to see the Bishop?

Jackie: Yes.

Mike: Here he comes, in his red robe.

Jackie: Yes.

Mike: What would you like to tell him?

Jackie: I would like to ask him why? Just . . . why?

Mike: What does he say?

Jackie: He says that greed, and money, and other people . . . have gotten to him. But he is sorry. He feels I wasn't understanding of him. I'm not quite sure what he means by that.

Mike: What would you like to do with the Bishop now?

Jackie: Well, we need to make amends.

Mike: Okay.

Jackie: We need to forget and forgive. To go on with life.

Mike: How would you like to do that?

Jackie: A handshake will do.

Mike: Okay.

Jackie: Not a hug.

Mike: Yes, not a hug.

Jackie: I have a feeling that if he were hugging me, he might be stabbing me at the same time.

Mike: (Laughs.) I think we have a little work to do there still. But at this time, that is enough.

Jackie: Uhhuh.

Mike: He would like to tell you that he will spend a long time making amends for what he has done. And in that, he is gravely sorry. He says that he has also hurt you more.

Jackie: Uhhuh.

Mike: But he has also hurt himself.

Jackie: Yes. We will all learn together.

Mike: He says that somebody had to do what was done. And he is really sorry that it fell upon him because of his weaknesses.

Jackie: Yes. We all have weaknesses, unfortunately.

Mike: There is one person left who would like to speak with you. I wouldn't . . . we wouldn't want to keep him waiting.

Jackie: Who is that?

Mike: Jesus.

Jackie: Oh no, we don't want to keep Jesus waiting.

Mike: He comes in the door.

Jackie: Oh yes.

Mike: And he stands in front of you.

Jackie: Yes! He is coming over to hold me. . . . I am also holding him. He tells me to forgive and let go. That my experiences will make me a better king. And him being King of Kings, he knows.

Mike: He knows of your pain.

Jackie: Yes, he knows of all my pain.

Mike: And he has been there.

Jackie: And he suffered with me.

Mike: Yes. What does it feel like when Jesus hugs you?

Jackie: (Crying.) It feels wonderful. . . . Wonderful. It is a wonderful feeling. He loves me very much. Like he loves everyone. It doesn't matter to him that I am a king. He loves me anyway.

Mike: He is very sorry for your hurts.

Jackie: Yes, but he said I had to have them. I had to have the experience. . . . He says it is time for him to go.

Mike: Okay. What is happening now?

Jackie: Oh, he is gone. . . . He didn't walk away, he just left. Everyone else seems happy.

Mike: Yes. I hear a commotion in the courtyard. I think that all of the other knights are out there.

Jackie: Yes, they want to have a celebration.

Mike: Yes. May I open the door?

Jackie: They are ready. Yes, let them in.

Mike: Here they come. What a noisy bunch.

Jackie: (Laughs.) Yes, they are noisy. You would think that they were still on their horses.

Mike: Oops, somebody has pulled aside some side curtains, and here come the butlers with food and drink.

Jackie: Look at all that food, and drink. All that wine.

Mike: Oh boy. They are shoving all the tables back out of the way. . . .

Jackie: Right! Right! They want to dance.

Mike: There is going to be a party!

Jackie: We're having a party. A big celebration. Everyone is happy now, everyone is content.

Mike: And it is the Camelot of old. The magical Camelot.

Jackie: Camelot. Yes. And everyone gets along. It is wonderful. Just wonderful. . . . Even my loves are talking to each other. (Laughs.) Across me, behind me, in front of me, everyone is happy. . . . Everything will be okay now.

Mike: How do you feel?

Jackie: Light. Very joyous, and wonderful.

Mike: Yes.

Jackie: And peaceful. And ready to dance.

Mike: Good. Shall we come back now?

Jackie: Yes, I guess that it is time.

~ 20 ~

Brenda as Sarah (wife of Lionel) September, 1994

Background: Brenda is a 51-year-old veterinarian from Deerfield Beach, Florida. We met at church, and had been friends for about three years when we did this regression.

This is one of my favorite regressions. I like it because of the interesting perspective it gives of the personal traumas surrounding the last battle. I also like it because of the insight it gave me into the background of Percival's battlefield duel with the knight Lionel. Lionel had at one time been one of Percival's close friends.

Mike: Let us go back to your life during the time of King Arthur and Camelot.

Brenda: I'm starting to breath so rapidly.

Mike: Don't be nervous.

Brenda: No, I'm not. I'm just wondering why it all began.

Mike: Why what began?

Brenda: My breathing. Why I started breathing very rapidly. I was very relaxed before, very secure.

Mike: You must feel nervous about going back to that time period.

Brenda: I think so.

Mike: I have a feeling you don't want to confront Lionel.

Brenda: May be. I felt such comfort and such peace as we were walking through that tunnel.

Mike: Have you opened the door yet?

Brenda: Yes. And now I'm alone. I don't have you there with me.

Mike: Oh, I'm coming with you.

Brenda: (Heavy, rapid breathing.)

Mike: I'm right by your side.

Brenda: Okay.

Mike: Hold my hand.

Brenda: (Calming a little.) I got the same feeling. I am afraid to meet him.

Mike: Afraid to meet who?

Brenda: Lionel.

Mike: Okay. Let's skip Lionel. Take me to the castle and show me King Arthur. Show me some scenes around the castle. Or we could start with your childhood, whichever you feel more comfortable with.

Brenda: No. I felt the security. I like the castle. I like the people, the other women that I was with there.

Mike: You used to live there?

Brenda: Yes. I feel very comfortable inside it, yes.

Mike: You lived there!

Brenda: I . . . I . . . (breathing heavy.) I just feel myself in a room with the other women, chatting and talking and being with them. Sharing the things that we do during the day. But I don't have the same relaxed feelings this time.

Mike: Things are different. You are ready to look at some different issues. How would you describe your feelings this time?

Brenda: I'm kind of fearful of him.

Mike: Fearful of who?

Brenda: Of Lionel.

Mike: Okay, let's talk about that. He is cruel to you, isn't he?

Brenda: Yes, my whole body is shaking.

Mike: He is mean to the children too?

Brenda: He must be, because I'm just shaking all over.

Mike: What is Lionel's problem?

Brenda: Lionel loves himself. And he uses everyone around him. Lionel wants to be at King Arthur's side, and he is going to do everything he can to try to get there, no matter who he has to step on. Because I've heard him talking. About what he wants to do. And yet I can't do anything about it. I'm fearful for my life.

Mike: What does he want to do?

Brenda: He will kill anybody, he will, to get where he wants to be. There is some event coming up that he's going to be going to, but the other knights. . . . (Hesitates.) Do the women ever go out with the men, on any of the events that would be out away from the castle? There is some reason that I am so afraid for my life.

Mike: Do you think that he will kill you?

Brenda: I'm not sure!

Mike: Are you afraid of him, or are you afraid of other people?

Brenda: I'm afraid of him. I'm afraid for our children. He seems so mean, so. . . . I've never seen him this way before. So angry, so hostile.

Like somebody has threatened him. It is near the time when the table is going to be . . . broken apart. I had security before I met him, security when I was with you. But I don't. . . . I feel alone now. Totally alone.

Mike: What about the table being broken apart?

Brenda: This may be it! (Heavy breathing.)

Mike: Do you mean the Round Table being broken apart?

Brenda: Things are slowing down. . . .

Mike: Let me ask you this; has Lionel gotten involved with the Bishop?

Brenda: Maybe so. (Sudden rapid breathing.)

Mike: Does it bother you when I mention the Bishop's name?

Brenda: Yes!

Mike: It makes you fearful, and you are shaking!

Brenda: Yes!

Mike: You're twitching. Tell me about the Bishop.

Brenda: I see the two of them talking together. I am fearful that something is going to happen, something harmful to the people that I know and that I love . . . and the community here. I am also fearful for my children.

Mike: Are you fearful that Lionel is betraying the other knights?

Brenda: I think this is it, because I have a bond with the people. Because I love them more than I love Lionel.

Mike: You are breathing heavily, and your chest is heaving up and down.

Brenda: I am afraid.

Mike: You are very fearful.

Brenda: I am.

Mike: I have the kleenex here. It may be that this is coming up at this time so that you can release this fear that you have been carrying. Let me ask you this. Has Lionel joined a conspiracy with the Bishop against Arthur and the Round Table?

Brenda: (Heavy rapid breathing.) I'm fearful! I'm not fearful to cry. I'm fearful with anger, fearful with hurt! Fearful with . . . what can I do to protect those that I care for in this. . . .

Mike: What is he going to do? Tell me!

Brenda: He is going to kill somebody!

Mike: He is going to kill somebody?

Brenda: He so wants to get there, he is going to kill somebody to do it.

Mike: Who is he going to kill?

Brenda: I can't, I can't see that yet.

Mike: Is he going to kill Arthur? . . . Okay, you shook, you jumped, when I said that!

Brenda: I know. I can't stop shaking.

Mike: He is going to kill Arthur!

Brenda: (Sharp intake of breath.) I can't see that, but it's somebody, somebody. Yes.

Mike: Why did your body jump when I said that?

Brenda: I know. Oh God!

Mike: Do you love Arthur?

Brenda: Oh yes.

Mike: And you love Camelot!

Brenda: Yes. YES!

Mike: And your husband is going to be betraying them all, because of his ambition?

Brenda: Oh save me. What can I do to save my friends? I don't know what to do. He has betrayed me too. The man that I thought I loved, only loves himself. Only loves himself!

Mike: The spirits are giving me a message here, that the Bishop, a clever manipulator of people, spotted your husband right off. As someone who he could turn, in his work against King Arthur. Preying on your husband's vanity . . . and blind ambition.

Brenda: I have nobody. I have nobody.

Mike: Merlin is here, and he is saying that your husband has the role . . . he is the Judas. . . .

Brenda: (Sharp intake of breath.)

Mike: . . . Of the Court. Of the knights. He has a role to perform. Merlin understood that all along. It was not an error of judgment in selecting him. It is that he was picked, because they knew he would become a Judas. He is a very good-looking man; he is very vain. And his vanity is his undoing. By the way, what is your name? If you can stop shaking for a minute?

Brenda: Sarah kept coming to me.

Mike: Sarah?

Brenda: Sarah.

Mike: Sarah. Okay. I am going to go ahead and let you continue with this deep breathing, and this nervous twitching that you are doing, because I believe that we are bringing this emotion up so that you can release it. Certainly we don't want you to carry this with you anymore. And that is part of why God was here with you tonight, earlier, before we started. We both sensed His presence. And it was for this great releasing that you are here tonight. You have been carrying these emotions with you for too long. He hopes that, when this evening is over, and we have pieced it all together, you will understand . . . the wisdom and beauty of what happened. But you certainly were not in a position to see it at that time. It is now time to set the record straight. It is all over. But it had to happen. You need to know that. Did you ever go to Merlin to talk to him?

Brenda: I don't think so.

Mike: Did you know Merlin?

Brenda: No.

Mike: Okay.

Brenda: Only through you.

Mike: All right. Was I your friend?

Brenda: Yes!

Mike: Was I Lionel's friend?

Brenda: I thought you were MY friend.

Mike: Okay.

Brenda: I felt a comfort, an understanding with you.

Mike: Okay. Tell me what happens next.

Brenda: Lionel leaves.

Mike: By himself?

Brenda: Yes!

Mike: Leaves the castle?

Brenda: Yes!

Mike: Where is he going?

Brenda: He is going to meet the Bishop.

Mike: Is he going to meet the enemy forces and lead them to Camelot?

Brenda: (Sharp intake of breath.) Ye . . . ye . . . Yes!

Mike: You're twitching. You jumped when I said that.

Brenda: Yes!

Mike: Your legs twitched.

Brenda: I want to tell somebody, but I don't know who to go to. So I find Percival. I can tell him everything.

Mike: So what does Percival say?

Brenda: (Breathing heavy, fast.) You're helping me. I tell you all. I tell you everything. That is why I felt such warmth in your hand, as you held my hand while we were walking down the tunnel. I felt such peace, and I didn't want to let go. I am just tired. (Breathing slowing down.) It is going away.

Mike: What is going away? Your fear?

Brenda: Yes.

Mike: Good. You told Percival. What did Percival do?

Brenda: He was able to tell . . . Arthur.

Mike: Yes. It did not really make much difference though, did it?

Brenda: The die was cast.

Mike: Okay. What happened then?

Brenda: I just grabbed my little girl. I just clung to her. I want to stay within the castle. I asked you, "Where can I go? What can I do? Where can I go within the castle?" I am fearful of Lionel coming back. I am just holding on to my daughter and . . . not knowing where to go. I want to lock myself in my room. I am just walking around, not knowing what to do. I have told you, and I know that you are going to do what you can. You said that you will come back, and let me know. I said, "What if Lionel comes back, what will I do?" I keep asking over and over, "What if Lionel comes back?"

Mike: What do I say?

Brenda: And you just said, "Faith. Just believe. Believe that you will be protected. Just pray. The spirit within will guide you." You try to reassure my little girl, also. You try to stroke her and help her, so she won't feel the fear which is inside of me. You told me that you would come back. I feel that it will work, and that I will be secure there. But if I die, I don't want to die in the hands of Lionel. I want to die in the castle, knowing that I am with those that I love, and those that love me.

Mike: I have a feeling that we told you that we would not tell anyone that it was you who reported this information. So the word would not be out that you had told us. Lionel would have no way of knowing if he did come back. But, however, we still would protect you.

Brenda: Suddenly I'm calm. But my eyes have started to twitch. I can't even hold my hands up.

Mike: I sense that there is a great . . . smile. A sad but nice smile on Arthur's face, knowing of your love and devotion to him. That was a nice supportive act, that you did in that very, very difficult time of crisis. Arthur needed that. So what you did was very, very wonderful. And there is a lot of thanks here, right now. Merlin is here, Arthur is here. God is here. They all thank you very much for what you did for Arthur. You gave him the ultimate gift. You gave him your love and support in his time of trial and . . . desperation. And for that you are a really blessed person. Lionel, he just did what he had to do. Somebody had to do it. Now, can you tell me what it was like when the knights went out to fight? When did they go out? The next day?

Brenda: (Big sigh.)

Mike: Was it in the morning?

Brenda: Yes. Before the sunrise.

Mike: Did you get up with your children and watch the knights go off? On their horses?

Brenda: Yes.

Mike: Arthur's army was camped around the castle?

Brenda: I just clung to my daughter, as we looked out the window. She senses me, she knows, she feels my every emotion, and she was there. We watched. . . .

Mike: Did the knights have to go far to fight, or was it a few hills away?

Brenda: I see them drifting away. I can't envision the action. I just see them going. Just leaving the castle. In fact, my eyes are twitching. My forehead is twitching. I just see them off. . . . I just go out, in reluctance, out to them. As they leave. . . .

Mike: And that was in the morning. When did you first hear word of what was happening at the battle?

Brenda: It is not coming to me yet. I don't know. I can't feel. . . .

Mike: That is okay. Where would you like to go now? What scene would you like to go to?

Brenda: I want to know if they came back! Did they come back? Who came back? Did Percival come back?

Mike: You tell me.

Brenda: I feel that he did.

Mike: Who else came back?

Brenda: My face is twitching again, like when you were talking about Arthur. Did Arthur come back? I don't know. I can't see any other faces, I can't tell. I feel that you came back, and you were there to reassure me. And tell me the story. It was reassurance, but yet it wasn't. But you were there, and a few others were there with you. I don't want to go too far beyond here. I'm caught now, I can't. . . .

Mike: That is okay.

Brenda: I can't go any further.

Mike: Go wherever you'd like to go.

Brenda: I just feel that I am with the women, gathering around in the castle. I am feeling the protection of the castle, and those that came back. You came back. I know that. I can't see where we go from here. I don't know where we go, I just feel the. . . . I'm not frightened anymore. Now Percival is gone. Did he get killed out there? I'm not nervous anymore. I'm not shaking.

Mike: He went to his destiny.

Brenda: I'm calm. (Very quietly.) I'm calm.

Mike: He and two other knights went out. . . .

Brenda: Yeah. . . .

Mike: To fight, and die.

Brenda: (Still talking very quietly.) He is gone. He is gone. My eyes are twitching.

Mike: He did not want to live without Arthur . . . and the Round Table.

Brenda: My eyes are. . . . I'm free. I'm free. Oh my God, (deep sigh) . . . I'm free. I'm free.

Mike: Because Lionel is dead.

Brenda: Yeah.

Mike: Percival told you that, didn't he?

Brenda: Yes!

Mike: Who killed Lionel?

Brenda: (Very quietly.) You killed him.

Mike: Yes.

Brenda: You killed him!

Mike: I did!

Brenda: (Deep sigh.) Finally! I just want to, I just want to. . . .

Mike: Huh?

Brenda: Just reach out to you. You saved my life, you saved my daughter's life, you saved our lives.

Mike: As I saw things, Lionel and I just found each other on the battlefield. (Laughs.)

Brenda: Oh, God!

Mike: (Still laughing.)

Brenda: My eyes are twitching. My head is twitching. Ohhh. . . .

Mike: My good friend Lionel had never seen me deal with someone who had betrayed my Arthur. He was very powerful. He was very good in battle. Normally, he could best me. He was amazed that it turned out differently. I had the power with me. God graced us with a little bit of justice in the midst of all that injustice that was going on. Because the injustice had to happen, but. . . . It was a little play within the big play, and justice was done.

Brenda: Justice was done.

Mike: What happens to you and your daughter now? The Bishop comes back to the castle. Does Mordred show up?

Brenda: Mordred?

Mike: He is one of the knights who also sided with the Bishop, that came back victorious.

Brenda: I get nervous again with Mordred.

Mike: Yeah.

Brenda: I get nervous again.

Mike: I sense that Mordred showed up at the castle with the Bishop who was leading all of their forces. They camped in the fields around the castle, announcing that they were now in charge. And I also believe that I see all of the families packing up their belongings, very hastily, and departing. They were given safe passage.

Brenda: Yeah, that is what I was afraid about. That they would be harmed. But they will be safe. I was wanting to protect them. I was hovering with the women. Just wanting to be with them. Feeling the security of being with them.

Mike: Do you sense safe passage when you all leave?

Brenda: Yes! With the women and the children.

Mike: Yes.

Brenda: (Big sigh.) I can not see where we go. I don't know where we go. Do you lead us out?

Mike: I'm not there.

Brenda: You're not there? Okay.

Mike: I see you going to a house. A house with a thatched roof. Nice-sized, cozy house. A moderately sized house. It belongs to his family or your family. I sense that his family was a family of substance. Both of your families were families of substance. And so you go to that house, and you raise your children. And you, and your children, have a quiet and peaceful life.

Brenda: (Quiet, calm.) Uhhuh.

Mike: You are completely severed from all connections with Camelot and the court and what happens in the politics from then on. You became a bit of a recluse, actually. You were concentrating on your families, and your children. Does that feel right?

Brenda: Yeah. I felt the security of just being with my children.

Mike: Yes.

Brenda: We talked about that in my last regression. But I didn't know where I was.

Mike: In your last regression you spoke of your deep love for Lionel.

Brenda: Yes, I did, but. . . .

Mike: It is coming up quite differently this time.

Brenda: That's right. It was a codependent type of a fearful love.

Mike: Well, I also think it was perhaps a different phase of your life, too.

Brenda: Yeah.

Mike: I think that it was in a period of your life when he was the wonderful knight to you. He was very handsome, and charming, and dashing, and was a great father. And husband. But later his . . . darkness took over.

Brenda: I feel secure now, with just my daughter and family around me. I keep saying daughter.

Mike: I see a blonde little girl.

Brenda: Yeah. Beautiful little girl. Full of love, and compassion and. . . . I see us laughing and being together and sharing. But I can't see her, as I said before, I can't see her as a grown woman.

Mike: I would like to share something with you that I am being shown now. I am on the battlefield. I am fighting, and off to my left, oh, maybe fifty yards away, is Lionel. He is, of course, on the other side, fighting. And we catch a view of each other, at about the same time. We start heading for each other. We have to fight our way through. Each of us has to fight his way through seven or eight of the enemy, so we can get to each other. It seems to be something that each of us knew would happen. And he senses, something within him senses, that I know all about. . . . So, it is a great clash when we come together. Now we are both quite exhausted, with all of the fighting that we have already done. But I see us really smashing into each other, putting great dents in our shields. And then . . . he trips over a stone. He trips over a stone. The armor is such, the light armor that we are wearing, is such that it is hard to get up. And I get him in the stomach, with a straight downward thrust of my sword. I now see Merlin, who is winking at me and saying that no one ever said that he had to fight fair.

Brenda: (Laughs.) I thought that. . . .

Mike: (Laughing) . . . that the stone was Merlin's.

Brenda: Yes.

Mike: Merlin says that he is merely protecting his son. (Really laughing.) And he says, "Lionel may have had a role to play, but I certainly didn't have to reward him for it." And so he said . . . oh this is funny . . . that the stone materialized out of nowhere, and tripped Lionel. And that was that.

Two men immediately came at me from the right, and I had to divert . . . I couldn't even get my sword out of Lionel fast enough. I had to pick up something, and fight them off. Then get my sword, and get back to my lines. I had gotten out of the lines to fight Lionel.

Brenda: But you were still able to ward off the two that were coming for you?

Mike: Oh yeah. Yeah.

Brenda: Because I felt, when you were showing me about the coming together, I just felt that there was a protective shield. It was almost as if, I, in another life, was out there protecting you. It was almost as if I was standing between you two, protecting you.

Mike: The lines were not straight. The lines were bent. So I actually had gone behind his lines to get at him. And he had to fight through a number of our soldiers to get at me. So when the fighting was over, I was behind enemy lines.

Brenda: (Laughing.) And that's when. . . .

Mike: And two of the enemy realized that. In the commotion, of course, most of them didn't see me. The two of them who saw me said, "Yeah, we'll get this one." And they swung around to get at me, so I had to stop running. I literally just swung my shield around, swung it around, caught both of their sword blows. Then I picked up something. I think it was Lionel's sword.

Brenda: Yeah, sure. Merlin had it right there. . . .

Mike: Actually, I think I used Lionel's sword. I don't think I had gotten my sword out of him.

Brenda: It was there for you. It was put there for you.

Mike: Yeah, yeah. And, oh, I did get my sword back, but I had to hustle. I had to rush back to the lines.

Brenda: Yeah, you did away with him. He was the Judas. He was the Judas.

Mike: Interesting. Especially interesting that I met him in this lifetime.

Brenda: In this, yes. And for me NOT to have met him. . . .

Mike: Now I understand why you were not meant to meet him.

Brenda: That's right.

Mike: I always thought that it was peculiar that you two, going to the same church, could never seem to meet each other.

Brenda: That's right.

Mike: But it wasn't meant to be.

Brenda: It wasn't meant to be. I'm FREE!

Mike: Yes.

Brenda: I'm free.

Mike: Yes. And he is still punishing himself by being crippled in this lifetime.

Brenda: Yes. Yes.

Mike: He is not ready to forgive himself.

Brenda: And you're reigning . . . supreme.

Mike: Merlin says, "Well, not exactly. He has had his bad moments." Merlin says, "I know, I have been there with him through all of them." (Laughing.) Oh, that's good!

Brenda: When you told me about the battle, my eyeballs were twitching, my head was throbbing.

Mike: And now?

Brenda: Ohhhhh. . . .

Mike: "Now," Merlin says, "do you feel better?"

Brenda: (Laughs.) Yes!

Mike: It was good to get that emotion out, wasn't it?

Brenda: Oh God. That was a black spot that has been inside of me for a long time.

Mike: Yes, yes. Yes, you have been working it up to the surface . . . and now it is time for it to go.

Brenda: Yes it is.

Mike: It ties in with your business and personal frustrations. . . .

Brenda: Everything. . . .

Mike: It was a lot of your fears. You will be a very different person now.

Brenda: Oh yes. Because every time other emotions would try to surface, the fears were. . . .

Mike: Real strong confirmation on that. You just changed your life.

Brenda: Oh! (Deep sigh.) How can I thank you?

Mike: (Laughs.) Merlin says. . . .

Brenda: (Laughs.) Don't answer.

Mike: Merlin says, "Don't thank him, because he is trying to get his GOD WORK done so he can get his money." (Still laughing.) Because God told me that after I finish doing this Camelot work, then I could have my wishes come true. So Merlin says that I am just trying to rush through getting my "God's work" done.

Brenda: To get your money. Okay. Is Brenda going to get her wishes now?

Mike: He says, "It will be a lot easier for Brenda to get her wishes now."

Brenda: Okay.

Mike: And he says, "If you ever think that things are not working out right, go to God and remind Him that you are the one who warned Arthur." He says, "Use your chit." He is saying it laughingly, and he says that you are not doing anything in this lifetime that you did not ask to do. All of your hardships are self-imposed. Because you, being you, want to grow as fast as possible. So he is joking about having to remind God. But he says, "God, of course, already knows it. But it may be that, every now and then, you need to remind yourself. That you are the heroine."

Brenda: Yes, I need to lighten up. Lighten up.

Mike: Merlin says, "Actually, the information you gave to Arthur was very helpful. Although the die was cast, and the roles had to be played out, it gave Arthur and his men some understanding of the timing and the scenario. So, it eased a lot of their anxieties. You fed them some good intelligence, in other words. Which helped them with their plan. It made things easier for them."

Brenda: Is there someone in this lifetime for me, whatever is remaining in this particular time around, that I can share the love with? That I have within, that is so overwhelming, that I want to give to everybody?

Mike: "Well," he says, "you just took your block away."

Brenda: So now I'll be opened up to. . . .

Mike: He says, "Your block was that you were fearful of it happening again to you."

Brenda: Ah hah!

Mike: He says, "God was not keeping that man away from you. You have been. Your fear! Fear of this. . . ."

Brenda: Just like I knew.

Mike: Yeah. So do you think that you have gotten rid of your block?

Brenda: Now I'm open.

Mike: I was watching your face during the regression. It was changing tremendously.

Brenda: Uhhuh.

Mike: Boy, your face was changing.

Brenda: I was there.

Mike: Severe emotions. Yeah. Coming up. Very deep.

Brenda: God, it was. Ohhh! I have never experienced anything like that before, Mike.

Mike: As a matter of fact, the spirits are saying to heal and seal Brenda's aura, balance her chakras, and fill in all the holes in her aura. Also fill her with love. There is a big hole in your aura right now. You have got your hands on your stomach. There is a big hole right in your aura, right there.

Brenda: Yeah.

Mike: Big hole there. Amazing how you instinctively put your hands right on it.

Brenda: Really.

Mike: A great big hole, and they are filling it up with love. Merlin has one last message, and it is a message of understanding. He says, "Those of us who stood by our principles and our ideals, and perished by them fifteen-hundred years ago, are able today to . . . bask in God's love and rewards for having done that. And those who failed themselves fifteen-hundred years ago, are still punishing themselves for having done so." He says, "So many of us in this lifetime on earth have said to ourselves so many times that the good guys don't get ahead, while the bad guys get ahead." I know that I have done that! And Merlin is smiling at me and saying, "Do they? I will put that misconception to rest." And he says, "Lionel was brought into Mike's life, and now you will also see him. And you will see him with his infirmity, so that you will understand that the person who Lionel betrayed is Lionel."

21

Angela as Merlin
September, 1994

Background: I had attended a party in Palm Bay, Florida, hosted by my good friend Caroline Connor. Caroline is a very gifted psychic and medium, thus it was no surprise to me to meet many other spiritually tuned and gifted people at the party. Angela was a 54-year-old lady from Ft. Myers, Florida. She was a fashion designer. We hit it off immediately. She had a great sense of humor and wit. Less than an hour after meeting, we borrowed the use of one of Caroline's bedrooms, and we did this regression while the rest of the party continued on uninterrupted.

Mike: I'm opening the door. This door doesn't creak.
Angela: True. My favorite kind of door.
Mike: I see the door open wide enough for us to get through. Are you ready?
Angela: Yes.
Mike: Okay.
Angela: I have apprehension though.
Mike: I know. That's why I'm with you. (Jokingly.) Merlin says you have two choices. He says if you stay in that tunnel I'm probably going to try to kiss you. . . .
Angela: Oh, fun.
Mike: So, you'd better go through that doorway. I'll kiss you on the other side anyway.
Angela: That's encouragement. I see blackness except for three stained glass windows. In an arch.
Mike: Of a church?
Angela: I don't know. They're very pretty. Light is coming in through them, but it doesn't light anything in the room . . . much.
Mike: Can you see yourself?

Angela: No.

Mike: You can't see yourself?

Angela: I'm seeing in front of me.

Mike: All right. Do you have any idea where those windows are?

Angela: It's my room.

Mike: It's nice to have stained glass windows in your room.

Angela: My room has many things. I was seeing a high-backed chair with arms, that was carved and upholstered, and then I started seeing other things in the room. It's like a laboratory. It's a fun place.

Mike: What do you do in this laboratory?

Angela: Play!

Mike: Do you ever play turning lead into gold?

Angela: Easy.

Mike: Easy. (Mischievously.) Can you tell me if I'm supposed to ask secret questions like that? I get in trouble when I ask those questions. Merlin doesn't like it. Do you make potions?

Angela: I'm watching . . . arc . . . ing. Right now, I'm watching arcing. Making electricity.

Mike: No kidding. You are making electricity?

Angela: I must be. Somehow.

Mike: Is that part of your technique for making gold?

Angela: I don't know why I'm doing it, other than it's fun.

Mike: Are you a playful person?

Angela: Yes.

Mike: They say you have a twinkle in your eye. Is that true?

Angela: When there's a scheme.

Mike: Do you help to train the knights?

Angela: That wasn't a lot of fun.

Mike: Why not?

Angela: At least that's what I feel. It was sometimes difficult.

Mike: They were a mixed lot, right?

Angela: Right. Some were stupid.

Mike: Uhhuh.

Angela: Difficult.

Mike: I talked to one knight one time, and he said that you considered him one of the dummies. And there were only a few simple things you would teach him. And that the other knights dared him to sneak into your laboratory one time and get something, and he accidently broke something. He said that he lived in great fear after that, because he knew that you knew all.

Angela: (Laughing.)

Mike: Do you remember that?

Angela: I remember his fear. (Still laughing.)

Mike: And you used to really toy with him?

Angela: He was fun.

Mike: Yes, yes.

Angela: That wasn't very nice.

Mike: The knights also told me that you read to them from big books, large books, about leadership and things like that.

Angela: They're in my room.

Mike: Where did you get those big books?

Angela: I feel like they're always with me. I don't know where I got them.

Mike: Another thing that intrigues me is that I hear that you have a potion to keep yourself young.

Angela: True.

Mike: (Teasing.) And I'm no longer a spring chicken, and I'm trying to figure out how to get that potion from you. Are you going to tell me how to make that potion?

Angela: (Also teasing.) Not this time.

Mike: All right. I didn't want to hear any stories about formulas with alligator gizzards and things like that, anyway.

Angela: No, modern chemistry has refined all that.

Mike: Okay.

Angela: You can easily get it.

Mike: All right, but you won't tell me how?

Angela: Not just yet.

Mike: Okay. They also tell me that you used to take some of the knights into a cave at night, as part of their training program. One time, Guenivere sneaked in the cave. That was the story I heard. Do you remember that night?

Angela: I remember playing in the cave because they had to overcome their fears.

Mike: You were teaching them how to disappear and make themselves invisible?

Angela: You can't disappear if you're afraid.

Mike: Okay. Isn't that one of the secrets to the powers of the knights, that they had no fear?

Angela: Yes.

Mike: How did you make them fearless?

Angela: They had to overcome their fear of me.

Mike: Oh, okay.

Angela: Then we are one.

Mike: Okay. I also have talked with Guenivere, and she told me that she really loved you very much. And that she spent many fond afternoons in conversation with you.

Angela: She's very intelligent.

Mike: Did you enjoy your time you spent with her?

Angela: I feel very comfortable with that thought. Yes.

Mike: Did you help to select Guenivere as Arthur's queen?

Angela: I cannot answer that cause I don't remember that. It was more like a group decision.

Mike: Okay. Who got the idea for the Round Table Movement, and the concepts of idealism for the knights?

Angela: It was a physical manifestation of what was taking place on another plane.

Mike: I also heard that you helped to train Morgana in much of her magic, much of her skills that she had as a priestess.

Angela: We worked well together. She was very intelligent.

Mike: At some levels, you loved her very much, didn't you?

Angela: Yes. She feels like a part of me. But she was very . . . she was very beautiful. She was very soft, she was very kind, and she was very deceptive.

Mike: Deceptive, you say?

Angela: Yes.

Mike: Was that a good quality or a bad quality?

Angela: To get what she wanted, it was a good quality. To the person she took it from, it was a bad quality.

Mike: I always felt kind of sorry for Morgana. With her being a soulmate of Arthur, and yet also being his sister, so that their relationship could never be complete. Wasn't that a bit tragic?

Angela: No.

Mike: No? She thought it was tragic.

Angela: She doesn't now.

Mike: Okay. She did then.

Angela: When you're in the middle of unhappiness, it's so. But then it's over, and you've learned. She got what she wanted. She's very wise and very powerful.

Mike: What was it that she had?

Angela: The powers.

Mike: Okay. She had children by Arthur. Weren't there two of them?

Angela: Children?

Mike: Mordred and Elena?

Angela: I don't know.

Mike: Okay. Tell me about the knight Mordred. You know him, don't you?

Angela: I don't know. No. Right now I'm seeing a real weird thing that looks like an iron horse.

Mike: All right.

Angela: A horse made of iron.

Mike: Is it dark?

Angela: No, it's silver.

Mike: What is your guess as to what that means?

Angela: We were talking about Morgana. It is perhaps something that relates to her and her powers?

Mike: Uhhuh.

Angela: And this is what I see when I see . . . and talk . . . and think . . . of Morgana. The iron horse represents her pride. If she had children, they were not her pride.

Mike: Hmmmm. Okay, all right. But Arthur loved his son, didn't he? His son Mordred?

Angela: Arthur . . . Arthur was a very loving man. He did love many. He was affectionate to all of the small people, which were his children. Now, I'm seeing a small boy that isn't particularly happy. His father touches him, and puts his arm on his shoulder. But the boy looks up without affection.

Mike: Hmmmm. He's already been turned against his father.

Angela: He's not looking at his father with any strong love. He is only a small boy, perhaps five years old.

Mike: Do you think this is the first time he has met his father?

Angela: Possibly, because he does not have any emotion as he is looking at his father. It's just . . . this big person touching him.

Mike: They say you can see inside the heart of a man.

Angela: That everybody can do.

Mike: Okay. When that little boy was grown, and had become a member of the court, were you ever concerned about what was in his heart?

Angela: I'm seeing the man. The man is dark and empty.

Mike: Who was it who corrupted him? Was it the Bishop?

Angela: The man is a very fearful person. Anybody can tell him something, because he's afraid of everything. There is a bishop there . . . and there is a woman. An older woman there. I don't know if it's his mother . . . or his wife. They are talking on both sides of his head, trying to influence him.

Mike: Tell me about this bishop. Why did you permit this bishop to have such great power?

Angela: To play the stage. To play the play.

Mike: Okay. Was Arthur hurt when you began to withdraw from the court? Was it to make room for the Bishop?

Angela: I did not withdraw. Arthur withdrew.

Mike: Yes, so he could become the complete Christian. Were your feelings hurt when he did that?

Angela: Yes.

Mike: Did you fault Guenivere for influencing him, about his swing toward Christianity?

Angela: I think so. I have a split feeling on that answer. I don't really know how to answer it.

Mike: Tell me both sides of it. Tell me both sides of the split. Because I know that it is complex.

Angela: It was to be done. It was to happen, and I knew this was to happen. The loss is not easy. Change is not easy, because there was so much fun, and then there was no more fun. Guenivere was so wonderful, and then so NOT wonderful. So the change was not happy, even though it was to happen. And I knew this. I know this.

Mike: What did you do to occupy your time after you withdrew from active participation in the court?

Angela: I spent much time traveling. I helped others, and I taught others, and I learned more. Or I remembered more. I see the circle. I'm going full circle. This is the circle around the earth . . . like the sun dial. So I traveled the sun . . . with the sun.

Mike: One question I have, something I've never understood. It seems like such a tragedy for two soulmates such as Guenivere and Lancelot to be put in such a difficult position. As the Queen and the best friend of the King. Seems to me that it was setting up tragedy to occur. Was that part of what was meant to be?

Angela: They chose to learn those lessons. Many times this happens, and each time it has a different outcome. If they accept it, they don't re-experience it. If they don't accept the lesson, they come back and do it again. They will do it again.

Mike: What, in this particular case, should they have accepted?

Angela: That they were not to be lovers this time. They were to be like sister and brother this time, and to help one another and complement one another. To help Arthur and the others. There were so many things for them to do.

Mike: Yes. So in other words, they came in to face this great temptation.

Angela: Yes.

Mike: And overcome it.

Angela: Yes.

Mike: Okay. Thank you. That helps me understand a lot more. One question. In my research . . . I can't quite understand how the Bishop was able to convince a large army of Christians from Europe to come over and attack King Arthur. Can you tell me how he did that?

Angela: When people believe they are doing God's will, they do many stupid things. What they perceived to be the Christian thing. . . .

Mike: Another question. I was talking to one of the knights named Percival, who thought it was kind of a dirty trick that you and Arthur sent him to guard the Holy Grail. He felt lonely and isolated at the Grail Castle. Why did you do that?

Angela: Percival was very trustworthy. I feel softness in my heart toward him. There was no need for him to be lost.

Mike: Okay. Is it true that there was a mist hiding the Holy Grail?

Angela: We can do that. We can make things hidden. And we always hide it in the open. When it's in the open, no one sees it. The mist is golden. I'm looking at it. But maybe that's because I am looking at it, and someone else would see it in another light, or not see it. Because it is not available for everyone to see.

Mike: Why could Lancelot not find the Grail?

Angela: Greed.

Mike: What kind of greed?

Angela: The greed of being number one. To be "the one that finds it." To Be, was his greed. He did not have a pure heart.

Mike: Yes. A pure heart was necessary in order to see through the mist. Did you put the mist back around the castle after Percival was gone?

Angela: I see the mist only in two layers now. Again, no one would see the castle unless they were supposed to. I don't think I replaced the mist, because there was no need.

Mike: Yes. Is it true that Percival's wife buried the Grail, after Percival's death?

Angela: I'm watching it being carried. I have the feeling that it is being hidden in the rocks. It is not a cup.

Mike: What is it?

Angela: It is very light. Bright. Light. The person that is carrying it is shielded from it, and is carrying it. It is this large. (Gestures with her hands.)

Mike: Is it the plate that Christ ate on?

Angela: No, it is not a plate, unless it's bent.

Mike: Does it have anything to do with Jesus?

Angela: It is older than that.

Mike: Who placed it there in Britain?

Angela: The Light Beings. It's from the Pleiades. It is more spiritual than physical. Maybe that is why I only see it as Light.

Mike: I want to jump to the subject of Excalibur. What happened to Excalibur after Arthur's death?

Angela: I see it in many places. In the bottom of a lake, or river. I see it in another dimension. I see more than one. I believe that it is in all of us. There's more than one.

Mike: Okay. Did Excalibur ever appear as a golden sword? Or was there a golden sword that Arthur also carried?

Angela: The gold was on the handle. The blade was steel.

Mike: Uhhuh. After Arthur was defeated, what happened to you?

Angela: I just faded away.

Mike: Is it true that the Bishop sent out a gang of men to murder you?

Angela: That's right.

Mike: Can you tell me the details of your fading? You were a bit mischievous about that, weren't you?

Angela: I don't know, but it feels like it was fun.

Mike: Did they chase you down a tunnel? I want to make sure I have my stories straight.

Angela: They were very frightened.

Mike: Yes.

Angela: That was a lot of fun. That was more fun than the knights had at their exit.

Mike: (Laughs.) And when they got to the end of the tunnel, there was nobody there?

Angela: That's right. I just faded away. First I was very bright, and then I faded away.

Mike: Right in front of them?

Angela: Right in front of them.

Mike: Oh wow. They lost no time in spreading the word.

Angela: They had to find their way out.

Mike: Did you make that difficult too?

Angela: Uhhuh.

Mike: I hear the Bishop had a fit.

Angela: That was fun.

Mike: (Laughs.) And the entire invading army was shaken by that story. Because they had just experienced the most savage fight of their lives, and then this, your mystical exit!

Angela: Uhhuh.

Mike: You seem very happy with yourself about that one. That was style.

Angela: As I said, the bigger the scheme, the more the fun. They were very confused. I'm not supposed to take such glee in doing such a thing. But it is fun. It's one of the things they keep reminding me of.

Mike: Who is they?

Angela: I call it my higher self.

Mike: Okay.

Angela: Because we are all one. And you can do the same to me, and it wouldn't be much fun for me.

Mike: You know, I made the mistake of joking with you before, and that is biting off more than I can chew.

Angela: There's always someone better, to make us realize that we're not all-powerful. Unless we're together.

Mike: I can joke around with Merlin, but boy am I going to get it back in spades. I know it's coming.

Angela: Oh, we will see what it will be.

Mike: Do you have anything you would like to tell me about? Go ahead.

Angela: I'm seeing a kite coming to you with a long tail . . . and it just might be your fun.

Mike: Huh. You like doing that, don't you?

Angela: (Laughs.)

Mike: You KNOW I can't stand messages like that.

Angela: That's probably why he showed it to me.

Mike: Do you have any messages or anything you'd like to tell us? Or any other messages, or information I didn't cover you'd like to tell?

Angela: Well, Merlin and Angela are not fully awakened.

Mike: Huh?

Angela: So there's many things to be remembered. And since I am conscious, I don't remember many things.

Mike: You really enjoyed your life as Merlin.

Angela: Yes.

Mike: Thank you very much for sharing your experiences with us.

Angela: I am still reminded about not being nice, too.

Mike: (Laughs.) Are you ready to come back?

Angela: Yes, reluctantly.

Mike: Okay, but before we go, let's spend a little more time here. (Teasing.) Let's talk about turning lead into gold. Oh, that's right, I am not to ask that question. Can you give us a potion for losing weight?

Angela: That also is available here.

Mike: Have you given me that formula yet?

Angela: Possibly.

Mike: I don't think so. I don't think so.

Angela: It is all in the affirmation. The formula combination for both the perfect weight and agelessness.

Mike: Hmmmm. Perfect weight. That's the key. Affirm for perfect weight. You just told us the secret. Good, I got that. Perfect weight. Yes, yes, yes. I hope my perfect weight's not 300 pounds! Now, are you ready to come back?

Angela: Yes.

Mike: Shall we go find that doorway?

Angela: Okay.

Mike: Take my hand again.

Angela: Yes.

Mike: Cause I love you very much.

Angela: I love you also.

Mike: Let's go through that doorway.

Angela: You were a fun knight.

Mike: I'm still fun.

Angela: Yes. One of the smarter ones. Ah, you pretended you weren't.

Mike: (Laughs.)

Angela: Yes, you were smart.

Mike: I was just a country boy. Those are the ones you have to look out for.

Angela: That's right.

Mike: Are we through the door?

Angela: Yes.

~ *22* ~

Richard as Bedivere
September, 1994

Background: I had known Richard for about five years. He is 48-years-old. He works part-time as a salesman, part-time as a marriage counsellor. He is a regular within the metaphysical crowd in Orlando. He struck me as a person who was deeply searching for something, perhaps seeking love, but not certain what he was seeking. I felt that I knew him a lot better after listening to his regression. And I now understand his search.

Richard: I am through the door. Now, do you want me to talk or just. . . . I don't visualize very clearly. I see kind of colors and shapes, sometimes it comes through but not a lot. But I'm more kind of kinesthetic.
Mike: All right. Tell me what you're experiencing.
Richard: Okay. I have a sense of light, I have a sense of rocks. I have a sense of a kaleidoscope of crystal-like energies, swirling around; lights across this dome-shaped thing. I don't sense any movement or us. I am just kind of looking down this. . . . I just see shapes, colors. Everything is kind of nondescript. Like under a subterranean kind of thing.
Mike: Like you are in a cave?
Richard: Yeah. Kind of like a cave-like effect. And, I just had a flash of a possible suit of armor. It's hard for me to hold things distinct. Everything happens so quickly, it's hard for me to see anything in particular.
Mike: Are you feeling some anxieties, or. . . .
Richard: The anxiety would be only a sense that I'm supposed to see something in particular that I don't. That would be the anxiety. Nothing that I'm aware of. Nothing that I'm afraid of other than that.
Mike: Can you take me to the Great Hall?
Richard: Presuming that I know where it is.

Mike: Well, when I mention the Great Hall, can you see yourself in the Great Hall?

Richard: Well, the Great Hall suggests to me just a very spacious thing. I saw a round table and then I swirled up. I saw a big candelabra, full of light. But I'm thinking that would . . . well, they could have had candles around it. And just a sense of spaciousness, but no particular clarity about it. I seem to be hovering kind of above, with big pieces of wood on the ceiling.

Mike: Beams? You're kind of up there with the beams?

Richard: Beams, yes.

Mike: It's an overhead view?

Richard: Uhhuh.

Mike: All right.

Richard: And the idea of jester comes into mind. Of, somehow, association with a jester.

Mike: Okay. Go ahead.

Richard: Just that, again, it's an overview from the top. Again, I get this view, looking down, there are people milling about. Sort of an overview of men walking about, but again, no clarity about it.

Mike: How . . . they're in the Great Hall? Is that where you're seeing them walk about?

Richard: Yes.

Mike: Are there other tables besides the Round Table?

Richard: I get a sense of benches. . . .

Mike: Yeah, exactly.

Richard: Benches along . . . again, I only get flashes of these things. I don't stay with pictures very long.

Mike: Is Arthur there?

Richard: I have a sense of. . . . Yes. Although I don't see him, I get a sense of red-beardedness.

Mike: All right. Tell me, how do you feel about Arthur?

Richard: Little fear. Also appreciation, respect.

Mike: Tell me about your fear.

Richard: What is the fear? First thing that comes is not being sure I would please him.

Mike: Yeah. Not being able to fill the bill.

Richard: Yeah.

Mike: Measure up.

Richard: Yeah.

Mike: Okay. Is this your first trip to the Great Hall?

Richard: Feels like it.

Mike: And why have you come?

Richard: Uhhhh. . . . Well, I have been brought there. Let's see. I got a dual thing.

246

Mike: Okay, give it to me.

Richard: I got both that I had been there before, and that it was like a coming again, a being invited again.

Mike: Are you there to petition the King to become a knight?

Richard: Hmmmm. That sounds like a possibility.

Mike: Who has brought you there?

Richard: Well, I had a feeling it was you. We went there together.

Mike: Who am I?

Richard: Another knight, an older knight. A knight who has been there and kind of. . . .

Mike: Okay. We're speaking that he is perhaps sponsoring you?

Richard: Yeah. Showing me the ropes, giving me some information about. . . .

Mike: If I were to ask you to guess at your name, what would be a. . . .

Richard: It's really strange, I mean. . . .

Mike: That's okay.

Richard: I've been hanging this name around in my mind a long time. I got this Bedivere thing. I don't know why, or if that's actual, or if it's just been hanging around in my head a lot.

Mike: Bedivere?

Richard: Yeah.

Mike: That's a pretty weird name. Were there any knights named Bedivere?

Richard: I think so. I think there was a knight named Bedivere.

Mike: (Checking a nearby list of knights.) There was a knight named Bedivere, yes. Okay, tell me about your home life, Bedivere. What kind of family did you come from? Were you rich or poor?

Richard: Rich.

Mike: Okay.

Richard: I am well attired. Dressed in furs. I am big. That's interesting.

Mike: All right. And you're being sponsored by one of the other knights, who is maybe me?

Richard: Uhhuh.

Mike: Okay. Looking around the castle, or the Great Room, do you see the Queen?

Richard: Uhhh. Yeah. I have a kind of sense, a sense of. . . . I see things kinesthetically, rather than say, pictorially. Yeah, very beautiful. Very impressive, loving.

Mike: How about Merlin?

Richard: Yeah. He looks like the magician, that old picture of Merlin that I have.

Mike: I see this other knight getting up and speaking in your behalf. And I see you very nervous.

247

Richard: Uhhuh.

Mike: And I think he made some jesting comment to the group, and to Arthur about your "noble birth" and the wealth you come from. And this, this is . . . I'm picking this up very strongly. You are not understanding the humor and the camaraderie in the hall. That there is a lot of teasing. He makes a derisive remark that you came from the elegant background that most of them did not come from. And at that point there's great clamoring, and they're pounding their mugs on the table and they're saying, "Throw him out!"

Richard: (Laughs.)

Mike: And you're scared to death.

Richard: (Smiling.) Yeah, not very comfortable there. Kind of scared.

Mike: And Arthur went along with this joke. He says, "I don't know, I don't want to bring somebody into my court who makes all my knights who came from humble backgrounds feel uncomfortable." He says, "What do you think, men?" And then they're all shouting, "Throw him out. Send him back home." And you're really sweating it out.

Richard: But, I'm also feeling kind of accepted by it, too.

Mike: Sure. You sense that you are . . . at your expense, they're having a great big joke.

Richard: Yeah, and actually it's kind of a bluff and kind of a game and kind of friendly at heart.

Mike: Yeah.

Richard: I'm actually warming up, and feeling. . . .

Mike: Yeah, cause as this goes on you realize they're putting you on.

Richard: Yeah, right.

Mike: They're overplaying it.

Richard: It's a game.

Mike: And so you finally start smiling, and then they realize you're no longer intimidated. Now they all start cheering, and they stand up and they all hold up their mugs.

Richard: Uhhuh.

Mike: A toast for you, and you're really overwhelmed with this acceptance.

Richard: Yeah, and it feels real good to feel a part of that wonderful group.

Mike: Yeah, and this other knight escorts you over to a table, and seats you with all the other "would-be" knights.

Richard: Uhhuh. I just got a warm feeling come up under my feet, and I am filled up with acceptance and belonging. I feel good.

Mike: Did you realize your life would never be the same? You've sensed a type of love you've known before and you're pretty excited about this.

Richard: Yeah.

Mike: Now, tell me about your training.

Richard: Training? What do I get for training? Archery comes to mind.

Mike: How did you do archery training?

Richard: I see a target, and I see a. . . . I see helmets too, and I see crossbows. Mostly I see the target and I see farmland and I see shooting at a target. Both archery and crossbow.

Mike: Okay. All right. Which were you best at? The longbow or the crossbow?

Richard: Longbow.

Mike: Were you pretty good at it?

Richard: Yeah. Very good.

Mike: Was this your favorite weapon?

Richard: Sword comes into mind. . . .

Mike: All right. Tell me about your sword, your training with your sword.

Richard: I see this blade. Very long, strong, powerful blade. And, I am getting a sense of muscle, and hacking and practicing that way.

Mike: What do you hack at to get this muscle?

Richard: Some kind of wood, or trees, or kind of like a . . . stuffed benches.

Mike: Is it vertical or horizontal, what you whack on?

Richard: Horizontal. This way. (Indicates horizontal with his hand.)

Mike: Horizontal? You whack on those? That is to build up strength?

Richard: Uhhuh. I have a sense of burliness.

Mike: I sense your muscles building as you do this. Tell me about your other training, your spiritual training. With Merlin.

Richard: Uhh. Now, there's a love there.

Mike: Tell me about that love.

Richard: Well, first before I get any pictures. . . . It's just, I have a connection even now in this life with Merlin. You know, it's just this . . . St. Germaine, Columbus, all the incarnations of Merlin, I have this most appealing, deep-seated love and connection with him that is just an undercurrent in my life. Because I don't focus on it a lot, it keeps on recurring, reminding me that there is that bond. There is that connection that at various times comes up strongly . . . then is forgotten. And it reappears again, and is forgotten. So, I get just this golden energy. It is kind of moving energy, golden energy. It is thinking like birds or falcons. Again openness, nothing clear.

Mike: Where did Merlin train you? Out in the fields, or in the classroom, or in the chambers?

Richard: Well, the first thing I got was this openness, out in the woods.

Mike: In the woods. How did he train you? Did he read to you, or lecture, or have you do things?

Richard: I have a sense of that we talked and walked.

Mike: What did he teach you knights?

Richard: Hmmm. Let's see. I'm drawing a block on that.

Mike: All right. Does that cause you some pain and discomfort?

Richard: Some slight embarrassment someplace, but really just a. . . . You know, I really just accept it.

Mike: Okay. Let me see where the embarrassment comes from. Did he teach you about God?

Richard: I'm not remembering very much of the teachings.

Mike: All right.

Richard: I'm. . . . Mostly remembrance of the love, and a lot of it exists through to present times. Not just to this particular session.

Mike: All right. How about magic? If I suggest he taught you magic. . . .

Richard: Something in me leaps and says YES.

Mike: Does that feel good when I suggest that he taught you magic?

Richard: Yes. It does.

Mike: Can you tell me what kind of magic he taught you? Or why he taught you magic?

Richard: My guess is it's for the power it gives us in battle. Our ways of being a warrior. But again, I'm not as close to this as . . . there's something. . . . When you said Magic, something within me said, "yeah." Something got excited.

Mike: Good, that's good. Now, I'd like you to take me on one of your favorite battles, one that went well for you. Can you do that?

Richard: Well, we'll open up the door, and see what happens. Huh. I get . . . that's kind of strange. First I got a picture of armor on horseback. Big . . . big, on horseback. But, right away, it shifted and I was on a wagon train, which was really kind of like pioneer days, which was really kind of strange. . . .

Mike: Let's go with the horseback, the armor.

Richard: All right. So I get a sense of a black horse. I get a sense of being very big and heavy in the saddle, and the horse rearing up. And I'm kind of static and stuck in that frame. I don't move to any of the warfare yet.

Mike: All right.

Richard: Once again, the fear comes in. Freezing . . . or blocking me from finding the picture. Something is resistant.

Mike: We'll get into that. I'm sensing what it is. Show me the first man you killed.

Richard: I just had a picture of a sword. A picture of water. I have a picture. Maybe the water was after. . . . But, I'm blocking.

Mike: A stream?

Richard: It's like a lake. It's like clear, with reflections in it. Well, now I see a stream too. I'm not sure. I didn't get a clear picture, although I did get a sense that there was a killing. I didn't get a sense of the actual killing . . . it was like after. Again, something was blocking it.

Mike: Okay. Why do you think you might be blocking this? Shame?

Richard: Yeah, and maybe even repulsion. Possibly. Even to this day and this lifetime, blood makes me queasy.

Mike: Well, we'll get into that. There were various types of knights. There were cheerful knights, there were somber knights. There were knights who loved to fight, and there were knights who loved the magic. How would you describe yourself as a knight? How were you known by your fellow knights? What kind of reputation did you have?

Richard: I get . . . I'm really kind of surprised. I am big and burly, and I am a fighter.

Mike: And they loved you, and you had a good reputation. They considered you real solid.

Richard: Yeah.

Mike: When you were at someone's side, they felt very comfortable.

Richard: Yeah.

Mike: Let me also suggest something to you. You were very dedicated to God.

Richard: Yeah. Yes.

Mike: Okay. You fought for God.

Richard: Yes.

Mike: All the people you killed, you killed while in God's service.

Richard: I guess I believed they were infidels or against the faith.

Mike: Yes. Okay. Now, tell me what happened when the Bishop came to court. Remember when the Bishop arrived?

Richard: I got this funny kind of hat.

Mike: What color was the hat?

Richard: Black.

Mike: How was he dressed? How was the Bishop dressed?

Richard: Robes.

Mike: What color?

Richard: I'm losing the picture again, but I get a sense of brown or black.

Mike: Okay. How do you feel about the Bishop?

Richard: Kind of cold.

Mike: All right. Tell me about some of your memories in court, of standing around watching the Bishop while he was doing his thing in court.

Richard: There's this kind of repulsion kind of thing. I'm not clear.

Mike: During the last years of the court, Arthur was sick for a while. Remember that?

Richard: No, I don't have any memory of that.

Mike: All right. Tell me about how, toward the end . . . the last few years of the court, you felt more and more responsibility.

251

Richard: Yeah, and there is a concern for Arthur. There is a love and concern for his well-being, and there is a sense of responsibility. I don't know exactly how, but just to provide support and caring. I get a readiness to die. I was going to battle to die.

Mike: Yes, we'll talk about that in a minute. That was the last battle. But what I'm sensing is that you took on a great sense of responsibility for what was happening to Arthur.

Richard: I feel that as you say it, but I don't get any understanding about it.

Mike: Okay. How does that feel? Does that feel right?

Richard: Yes. It does.

Mike: Okay. There was also the growing horror in your chest and in your stomach that you were being betrayed by the God you love. Being betrayed by the men who represented the God you love.

Richard: Hmmm. I don't have that. I'm not catching that.

Mike: That doesn't register?

Richard: No, I'm not catching that.

Mike: Was your loyalty torn in two directions? Your love for Arthur versus your love for the church?

Richard: Yeah. I guess the confusion. I don't know. If I go back and see . . . because I said that I felt resistance toward the Bishop.

Mike: So you were loyal to Arthur, not the Bishop?

Richard: Okay. Loyal to Arthur. I guess I'm not loyal to the Bishop.

Mike: Let's go to the Great Hall the night before the last big battle. Tell me what you see.

Richard: Ummm. . . . I really have to leap at things, cause if I don't, I lose the trail.

Mike: If you don't get it, you don't get it.

Richard: Okay. I got a sense of the lights, and again that regal color and . . . quaffing and drinking and a cheeriness. Maybe it's a forced cheeriness to bring up everyone's energy.

Mike: Someone is here telling me here that you did go to Merlin to talk to him about your concerns.

Richard: That feels, that feels right.

Mike: Tell me about that visit with Merlin.

Richard: It is coming in that there is a pull that I don't understand between the two. Merlin was that person of centeredness and wisdom. Yeah, that feels right, that I would go and see him.

Mike: What did he tell you?

Richard: Just to follow my heart. Do what comes to me. Don't think about it.

Mike: Okay. The last battle, who were you fighting?

Richard: I don't know.

Mike: All right. That's blocked?

Richard: Yeah.

Mike: Okay. Can you go to the last battle?

Richard: I get duskiness and people wounded, the clamor of battle.

Mike: Where are you? In the lines, or on top of the hill?

Richard: In the lines comes to my head. I guess really hacking it out.

Mike: Yes. Do you outnumber the enemy, or do they outnumber you?

Richard: Oh, I think they outnumber us.

Mike: How do you feel as you're fighting?

Richard: Really staunch and just don't care. Just, just INTO IT!

Mike: Where's your king?

Richard: In the back.

Mike: Is he fighting?

Richard: No. I think he's down.

Mike: How did they get to him? Did they get through your lines?

Richard: No, I think he was stabbed from the back.

Mike: All right. How does that make you feel?

Richard: Well, hurt in the heart, but really angry. And just. . . .

Mike: Fighting even more.

Richard: Fighting even more.

Mike: Yes.

Richard: (Starts crying.) Really hurt, and really mad. Really furious.

Mike: There you go, Richard. Let it out. Why are you crying?

Richard: The loss of Arthur. Just the waste of it all, just the waste. So much effort, (still crying), sunk, oh God, now, for nothing.

Mike: You've been waiting a long time to get that out, haven't you?

Richard: I guess so. . . . It's just the tiredness of it all. The tiredness of it all.

Mike: How did you go down? How did the battle end?

Richard: (Sighing.) I guess I did go down. I don't remember. I. . . .

Mike: You were numb by then.

Richard: I don't even know what happened. I get a sense of being hit in the back of the head by a mace, a big. . . .

Mike: They had gotten around behind you by then?

Richard: Yeah. But it's again, vague. Just exhaustion, sadness, and just. . . .

Mike: I sense you standing there in the midst of your fallen comrades, as an island in the ocean, and being surrounded by the enemy. You, bulky and stalwart, at the end, in the end, just clubbed.

Richard: And battling it out, and overwhelmed and hit from behind.

Mike: Tell me what happened then.

Richard: Uhhh. I get a sense of water. Just kind of sinking underwater. (Laughs.) Like sinking down and being attended by feminine energies. Being comforted and taken home.

Mike: When you get home, who's there? Who do you see when you get there?

Richard: Couldn't see the feminine energy, but the. . . . Morgana comes, the name Morgana.

Mike: Morgana. Okay. Why Morgana? Were you a favorite of hers?

Richard: We had a deep love and connection. I already felt that in the regression today. (Begins crying again.) This is a profound connection and love that I have with Morgana.

Mike: Okay. Morgana comforts you. And helps you make the transition. Does she take you to the Light?

Richard: Yeah. I go. . . .

Mike: What happens when you get to the Light?

Richard: My heart still needs healing. A piece of (crying) . . . a piece of my sadness comes with me. My heart needs healing and the Light. From that frustrating and sad . . . all that beauty lost . . . and the frustration. So, I need to be soothed and comforted, in my heart. My heart is full of a sadness for those still left down there. And Arthur.

Mike: All right.

Richard: All our effort, lost.

Mike: Where are you now?

Richard: I'm resting and being healed in the Light, and Morgana is. . . .

Mike: I would like for you to turn around and look. Someone is standing behind you.

Richard: I think you know who it is.

Mike: It is Arthur. And the other knights.

Richard: They're all here. (Crying.) It's my heart that knows that. You know I don't see things very well.

Mike: They're right there. And you know what, they're all smiling.

Richard: Yeah, I know you are right. My heart knows that you're right about that, and I'm glad that you told me. Because this is truth.

Mike: And Arthur says to you, "Dear faithful and loyal knight. Don't grieve anymore. We're all fine. We're where we're supposed to be."

Richard: Yeah.

Mike: Now Arthur says, "It's all okay. It all turned out okay. We just didn't understand."

Richard: Yeah. You'll have to explain it to me. These are tears of happiness.

Mike: Yes. . . .

Richard: Yeah, it's good to be with you.

Mike: The other knights . . . are raising a cheer for you.

Richard: (Wailing, speaking to Arthur.) I . . . always loved you, your loving heart. I always . . . I hope I was always worthy for you. I hope . . . I hope . . . I hope I didn't let you down. I didn't want to let you down.

Mike: They're all waving their swords, their shields. And they're saying, "You're the greatest, you're one of the greatest. Your strength, your camaraderie, your support, your loyalty. You were the greatest.

Don't carry any of those feelings. And we're all together again, and we'll always be together."

Richard: Yeah.

Mike: They say, "And we'll always be part of the Round Table."

Richard: Yeah, we will. Always, we are. That feels good.

Mike: And Arthur . . . (crying) . . . Arthur pulls out his straight sword . . . and lays it on your wound. And you feel the love.

Richard: Yeah.

Mike: And I have a sense of Jesus standing in the background, watching this reunion of these good-old-boys.

Richard: Yeah.

Mike: And I see him smiling, and I see him saying to himself . . . "I'm not needed here right now." It's as if he is not wanting to interrupt this reverent moment. And you feel the love of Excaliber passing through you, and healing your burdens and your grief.

Richard: Yeah.

Mike: And filling you with its love. All feelings of inadequacy, all worries of whether or not you served properly, are just released and gone. And you know that you and your comrades are united in your hearts forever in that great love.

Richard: Yeahhh. Well, we're ready for . . . (laughing) more of the battles, or whatever it is. We're ready for it.

Mike: Yes. Yes, yes, yes, yes. The style of things will change, but in a way, it won't.

Richard: Yes. This is good.

Mike: How do you feel now?

Richard: Well, I want to give you a hug.

Mike: You want to come out now? Okay, you're back out?

Richard: Yeah, I'm already out. And I feel great.

~ 23 ~

Candice as Guenivere
October, 1994

Background: Candice is a 29-year-old housewife from Longwood, Florida. She has cancer.

Body, mind, and spirit are one. There is an emotional aspect to every illness. I believe that today's modern doctor, treating an illness as a completely physical phenomenon, sometimes misses the boat by not understanding this concept. I had already discovered that all illness can be traced back to some emotional trauma, or traumatic experience. Sometimes it is even a past-life experience. By using a regression, we are able to go back to the experience itself which has caused the emotions to be locked into the body, address the experience, identify the emotions, and release them. I, for the most part, relied upon my psychic abilities to determine what emotions were there, and where they came from. This caused my work to be only as good as my psychic ability. Then I made a breakthrough. I discovered that I could place the person in a light trance, and ask the person to "take us back to the point in time where you picked up the emotions which are causing you to have cancer (as an example)." The person being regressed would then take us to the experience, whether in this lifetime, or another. We would then identify and release the emotions. This has proven to be a very effective technique.

I had acquired this new knowledge a few months prior to Candice's visit. I explained everything to her, and she agreed to do a regression to look for the emotional source of her cancer. Unaware of my other Camelot regression work, she took us straight to Camelot. Lo and behold, Guenivere's guilt was manifesting as cancer in this portion of Guenivere's soul.

That Jesus himself came forward to participate in healing this Guenivere's emotional hurts is also very special.

Mike: Just look up and tell me what you see.

Candice: I see myself on a balcony.

Mike: Uhhuh. And what do you look like?

Candice: I'm young, and I'm very beautiful.

Mike: What color is your hair?

Candice: Kind of a reddish blond.

Mike: Okay. Where is the balcony?

Candice: It is on a castle, overlooking. . . .

Mike: Who are you looking for?

Candice: I'm looking for a man.

Mike: Who?

Candice: I can't tell if he is my husband, or . . . or my lover.

Mike: Okay. Let's have him show up.

Candice: My, he has very dark hair and a dark mustache.

Mike: How do you feel about him?

Candice: Oh, I love him very much.

Mike: Does he love you?

Candice: Yes.

Mike: Does he get up on the balcony with you? What happens?

Candice: He sees me, and he just waits. But, I'm leaving now, and I'm going down some long stairs. I want to be with him. And I run out to him. And I'm in his arms.

Mike: Where is this? In the castle?

Candice: No, this is outside.

Mike: Okay. Are you in the woods?

Candice: No, there are cobblestones. It's like a market.

Mike: Aren't you afraid somebody will see you?

Candice: A little. But I want to be with him. He is saying to me, "You know that we should not, we should not meet like this." And he sits me down by a fountain, and I think he is going away.

Mike: How does that make you feel?

Candice: Angry and sad.

Mike: Okay.

Candice: But he says he will be back soon.

Mike: Okay. You are seated by the fountain. I see Jesus coming up. He sits down next to you on the fountain. And he says to you, "Sweet Guenivere, things have now changed so that I can tell you what has been happening. Please understand that it is not my job to interfere with the people that I love. But," he says, "great unfairness was done to you. Merlin taught you to be able to look into the hearts of men, and he also taught you to look into your own heart. And you have great anguish in your heart because you love two men. You love your king, you love Arthur." Isn't that true? How do you feel about Arthur? I'm asking you now.

257

Candice: I respect him.

Mike: Okay. And Jesus says, "People who are jealous of you, as the queen, have done things to you. They have used their black arts, they have used black magic and potions on you. To make you to be unfaithful to your husband, to the King. And as a result of that, you carry a great fear and guilt. Of being unfaithful." And he says, "I'm here now to explain to you, that all of that is being changed. So that it never happened." How does that make you feel?

Candice: It makes me feel good.

Mike: Yes. Do you feel a heaviness from your heart being lifted?

Candice: Yes.

Mike: Okay. Jesus has explained that you were powerless against that spell that was placed over you. It made you do what you would not have otherwise done. It made you go against your own free will. Because you would not have been disloyal to your king. Jesus smiles, and gently he says, "It's okay to love Lancelot . . . just as you love the other knights." He says, "Look at how these knights all loved and adored you." And he says, "Is there a knight out there who would *not* lay his life down for you in a minute?" And you know that is true. They all would. And he says, "Your love for Lancelot is wonderful. But keep it noble. Keep it . . . aligned with the ideals and perfection of Camelot." And now he pats you on the hand and escorts you back to the castle. Now how does your stomach feel? How do you feel inside? Are there any changes?

Candice: I guess I feel a little nervous right now.

Mike: Tell me about it.

Candice: As I walk back into the castle, it is like a nervous, exciting feeling.

Mike: It's almost as if your anguish is over. Because there was an anguish there, wasn't there?

Candice: Yes.

Mike: And the excitement of the love, caused by the love spell, covered up the anguish. But the anguish was there, and was going to be there, and be there for a long time. And now you don't have to have that anguish. You can have your love for Lancelot, just as pure as your love is for the other knights. And that is the best love of all. You know that. A love that is completely pure, just as the ideals of the knights of the Round Table are pure.

I see you stepping up the stairs, a much freer woman. And Jesus is standing at the bottom of the stairs. He calls up to you and says, "Also, you do love Lancelot truly. And this way, you spare Lancelot the agony of betraying his king. And this is the truly great love you can give to him." And I sense that you now have an understanding and a peace in your heart which will make you very happy.

Candice: Hmmmmm.

Mike: What are you doing now?

Candice: I'm out on the balcony, looking out. Out into the land, and thinking. . . .

Mike: What are you thinking?

Candice: I'm thinking that . . . that I must go to my husband. That I want to love him.

Mike: What is happening now?

Candice: I was out on the balcony, and my husband comes to me. It makes me feel good.

Mike: I sense he is greatly relieved too. Because he knew what was going on.

Candice: Uhhuh.

Mike: And out of honor, he did not speak of it. And now, all the love can be pure, as it originally was meant to be.

Candice: Umhummm.

Mike: What is happening now?

Candice: We're still out on the balcony, in each other's arms. Now he leads me back into the castle, and he sits me down. And he kisses my eyes, and then he kisses my lips. He strokes my hair, and rubs his fingers up and down my neck. And I put my arms around his waist . . . and we just hold each other. I begin to speak, and he tells me not to. He puts his finger to my lips. Why do my arms feel so heavy right now?

Mike: I don't know. Perhaps because you have released such a heavy burden. I feel that you and Arthur are reunited now. Do you feel that?

Candice: Yes.

Mike: How do you feel about that?

Candice: Good. I want his love, and I want to love him.

Mike: What is happening now?

Candice: We are in the room, and we lay down on the bed, and we just hold each other.

Mike: Okay. . . . Are you still holding each other? Is a great healing taking place?

Candice: Yes.

Mike: (Very long pause.) What's happening now? Still laying on the bed holding each other?

Candice: Yes.

Mike: Okay, just keep laying there as long as you wish.

24

Earl as Lancelot
November, 1994

Background: Just as Merlin and Arthur chose knights from all types of backgrounds, so too, do the people coming for the Camelot regressions come from far-ranging backgrounds. Earl is 28-years-old, and rides a motorcycle. He works as a common laborer. He is a very charming fellow, who projects a personality of being somewhat of a rascal. He was brought to me by his girlfriend, who just happened to be a Morgana. That Earl's relationship with his girlfriend had some difficulties is not surprising, given this Lancelot's relationship with Arthur's sister.

Mike: Have you opened the door?
Earl: Yeah. I think I'm looking at a long table with lots of people sitting there.
Mike: Yep! That is probably the Great Hall. Is that where you are?
Earl: Yeah, but see, I'm getting . . . not real clear pictures, just that I'm in the hall.
Mike: All right. Tell me what all the people are doing?
Earl: Eating.
Mike: How are they dressed?
Earl: Tunics. It's not that clear.
Mike: Okay. Are the colors bright or. . . .
Earl: Bright!
Mike: Bright? Bright colors, okay.
Earl: Greens and reds.
Mike: Okay. What is their mood? Are these happy people or sad people?
Earl: Happy.
Mike: Happy. Okay. Can you look around the room, past the tables?
Earl: Seems to be torches and pictures on the walls, also some arms.

Mike: Okay. Are there some banners or flags hanging from the walls?
Earl: Yes.
Mike: Can you look around and tell me where the head table is?
Earl: The far end of the room, running along the wall.
Mike: Is this table higher than the others, raised up a bit?
Earl: Like, two steps.
Mike: Yeah, okay. Who is seated at that table?
Earl: Arthur.
Mike: What does he look like?
Earl: Seems to be a big man, with a beard. It's not that clear.
Mike: All right. Can you tell who is sitting with him?
Earl: There is a woman to one side, and some men to the other side.
Mike: What does the woman look like?
Earl: She looks very pretty.
Mike: What color is her hair?
Earl: Blond.
Mike: Okay. How do you feel about her?
Earl: Warm. Affection.
Mike: How do you feel about Arthur?
Earl: (Big sigh.) I think not good.
Mike: Can you elaborate about that?
Earl: I think maybe there is some envy there on my part. Some . . . it doesn't seem to be very clear.
Mike: Do you love the woman sitting with Arthur?
Earl: Yeah.
Mike: Have you ever been her lover?
Earl: I think so. It's not very clear, but it seems to be so.
Mike: How do you feel about that?
Earl: (Big sigh.) That we were meant to be . . . but weren't.
Mike: All right. Isn't she the queen?
Earl: Yes.
Mike: Don't you serve the king?
Earl: Yes.
Mike: Are you a knight?
Earl: (Big sigh.) Yes! I can't see myself too good, but, I have this sense, this feeling.
Mike: I think that you are one of the best knights, aren't you?
Earl: Yes, that's right.
Mike: Everybody looks up to you?
Earl: Right.
Mike: Aren't you the one who tells all of the jokes? The one who is very popular among the other knights?
Earl: Yeah.
Mike: Okay. What is your favorite weapon?

261

Earl: Spear.

Mike: Why?

Earl: I am very good at throwing, and I have a very good aim.

Mike: Okay, is the spear the same thing as the lance?

Earl: No, the spear is lighter and narrower. The lance is longer and heavier.

Mike: Okay. They say you are pretty good with the sword.

Earl: Yeah. I like the sword too.

Mike: Do you train the other knights, the younger knights?

Earl: Yeah, I have overlooked several younger men to make them good fighters. Kind of like a mentor figure to them.

Mike: They say you came from Gaul. That you didn't come from England. Does that feel right?

Earl: No, it doesn't feel right.

Mike: Do you feel English?

Earl: No. Feel more . . . it's not clear.

Mike: They say you came from a lineage in France that was royal. That you had a direct line to the king. How does that make you feel when I tell you that?

Earl: (Big sigh.) I feel like I come from very good stock, and have great value. I can't say that that rings completely true.

Mike: All right. I would like to go back to this feeling that you do not feel good toward Arthur. Do you resent Arthur?

Earl: I think there is some hatred there.

Mike: Can you tell me why?

Earl: The way he treats people; the little, the lower people within the ranks.

Mike: He doesn't treat them well?

Earl: No.

Mike: Do you feel that you would be a better king?

Earl: More fair and just.

Mike: Do you think the other knights like you more than they like Arthur?

Earl: I feel like I have the camaraderie with the other knights, and the closeness and the bonding. But the ramifications of following someone other than the king would be too great.

Mike: I see that you are smiling when you are talking about your relationships with the other knights. There is apparently great affection and love there.

Earl: Sure.

Mike: Yes. This thing about you being a lover with the Queen though, isn't that rather serious?

Earl: (Big sigh.) Dangerous.

Mike: Does anybody know about it?

Earl: I have a feeling that a friend of mine knows about it. A close friend of mine.

Mike: Who is that? Can you recall his name?

Earl: I venture to say . . . Michael. But I'm not one-hundred percent clear.

Mike: Is he a knight? I haven't run into a knight by the name of Michael.

Earl: He works on horses.

Mike: Trainer or something like that?

Earl: Uhhuh.

Mike: Okay. What in the world led you into a relationship with the Queen? Doesn't that jeopardize everything you stand for as a knight?

Earl: The connection is strong.

Mike: That is a difficult question I am asking you.

Earl: The bond, the knowing of one another. . . .

Mike: Is so strong?

Earl: Yep.

Mike: That you couldn't resist. Is that what you are suggesting?

Earl: (Big sigh.) Sexual attraction. Knowing. . . . Love for one another, can be felt by both.

Mike: The King also has a very beautiful sister, Morgana. How do you feel toward Morgana?

Earl: (Big sigh.) I'd venture to say we tolerate one another.

Mike: Okay. Why don't you like her?

Earl: She carries around some baggage. She's a little bit . . . she is heavy-hearted.

Mike: Why is she heavy-hearted?

Earl: She has been hurt.

Mike: Who hurt her?

Earl: I may have.

Mike: Were you romantically involved with her?

Earl: (Big sigh.) It's not very clear.

Mike: Okay. Who else may have hurt her? . . . I sense you don't want to talk about this?

Earl: I sense the same thing.

Mike: Okay. Take me on one of your battles. Tell me what it is like to be in battle. I'm very curious about that. Pick out one of your favorite battles and tell me about it.

Earl: (Heavy breathing.) We are storming out of the castle through open land. And there is an opposing force coming towards us out of the woods. And we meet them in the open. And I'm leading, and I run through the flank . . . taking people off of their horses, and through to the other end.

Mike: You are on a horse?

Earl: Yeah.

Mike: You start at one end and you roll up their flank, is that what you said?

Earl: I roll right through the middle of them, to the other side. And then I go back through.

Mike: Before the rest of your forces have reached them?

Earl: Yeah.

Mike: That is a pretty brave thing to do!

Earl: But I. . . .

Mike: You are smiling again. Are you good at that kind of thing?

Earl: Yeah, I like to charge.

Mike: I saw a lot of arrows coming at you. How do you keep from getting hit?

Earl: Shield.

Mike: It looked like every son-of-a-gun in that line was shooting an arrow at you as you came charging up by yourself. You are pretty foolhardy, aren't you?

Earl: Yeah. I still am.

Mike: Yeah. Do you use magic for protection?

Earl: I have, yes.

Mike: But that's not the main thing you rely on?

Earl: No, I rely on . . . on those who watch out for me.

Mike: Are you talking about your spirit forces?

Earl: Right.

Mike: Okay. As far as religion, who do you believe in? Do you believe in Jesus? Are you a Christian . . . or are you a druid?

Earl: A druid, I believe.

Mike: Okay. I'm sensing that you play at being a Christian, but you are still a druid at heart. Arthur is a Christian, isn't he?

Earl: Yes.

Mike: Anyway, let's go back to this battle. Tell me, you punch through their lines, and you come through their lines again, and then what happens? Were you using your sword? What weapon are you using?

Earl: My sword.

Mike: And your shield. Okay. Have you hit anybody yet?

Earl: I hit people going through, and then, back through again.

Mike: All right. How many have you hit so far?

Earl: Maybe 10 or more.

Mike: Okay. And where are the rest of your forces? Are they now catching up to you?

Earl: Yeah, they are engaging. The field looks broken up.

Mike: What I sense is that your reckless charge right up the center took the focus of the enemy off the rest of your troops. They were so busy shooting arrows at you that the rest of your troops were able to get right up on them.

Earl: Yeah. The opposing force broke up pretty quick.

Mike: Yeah. Who were those guys that you were fighting?

Earl: They look . . . scraggly. And uh . . . more nomadic. More. . . .

Mike: Like Norsemen, or Vikings or something like that?

Earl: Right. Big people.

Mike: The castle you came storming out of. Was that Camelot? Or was that another castle?

Earl: Very big wall around it.

Mike: All right.

Earl: With a tall, tall building within the castle grounds somewhere. Above the wall.

Mike: I sense this was not Camelot. I sense this was one of the other realms. Did you ever get wounded?

Earl: In the left arm. Stab wound.

Mike: Okay. You got stabbed. How did you get stabbed in the left arm? Tell me about that battle.

Earl: Might have been Morgana.

Mike: Stabbed you?

Earl: It's not clear.

Mike: All right. Did it happen in a battle?

Earl: Would have been an argument.

Mike: (Laughing.) Another smile, huh? One of the more serious battles!

Earl: Right! (Laughs.)

Mike: Opposing a woman instead of. . . . A couple hundred Norsemen are nothing compared to an angry lover, right?

Earl: Right!

Mike: I was talking to one of the older knights, his name is Sir Kay. He was telling me about some of the battles he participated in with you. Do you recall him? He is one of the older knights. I think he helped raise Arthur?

Earl: Broad-shouldered man?

Mike: Yeah.

Earl: Beard? Mustache?

Mike: Yeah. Very courtly, very dignified.

Earl: Gentleman.

Mike: Yeah, real gentleman. Arthur told me he kind of patterned the role that knights were to play after the example set by Sir Kay. Do you remember any of your battles with Sir Kay?

Earl: (Big sighs.) I have the sense and the feeling that riding with him made me invincible.

Mike: Good. I was talking with another one of the knights. Percival. I think that he was younger. I think you helped train him. What kind of knight was he?

Earl: Thin. Fast. Quick.

Mike: Was he a ladies man like you? Or was he more serious? It made you uncomfortable when I called you a ladies man?

Earl: Well, it's not clear.

Mike: Okay. He adored you. Percival adored you. Almost worshipped you.

Earl: He loved me.

Mike: Yes. Was that typical of the other knights? The younger knights? To feel that way about you?

Earl: I think I represented a figure that they could look up to.

Mike: When Morgana stabbed you in the arm, was she jealous about you and Guenivere?

Earl: Yes!

Mike: That was it? Did the wound heal okay?

Earl: No, it festered.

Mike: Okay. I'd like to go back and talk about this issue with the Queen. That seems quite serious to me. Doesn't that kind of threaten all of Camelot? One of the knights being involved with the Queen?

Earl: (Big sighs.)

Mike: Does that make you uncomfortable when I ask that question?

Earl: Seems to be a block there, to a degree.

Mike: All right. I guess what I'm suggesting, and I'm being rather blunt in my questioning you, but it seems to me that there is an issue here of betrayal of the King.

Earl: Yeah, but I love the people.

Mike: So that kind of makes it okay? You are holding your stomach now as if it is churning. And I think I'm stirring up some very strong feelings. Tell me, would it make you uncomfortable if we went to the time of your death? Could you tell me about how you died?

Earl: I have the feeling I might have been beheaded.

Mike: All right. But was it in battle?

Earl: No! In front of people!

Mike: Why were you beheaded?

Earl: For . . . my involvement with the Queen.

Mike: Did Arthur do it?

Earl: I think so. That's what comes to mind.

Mike: Tell me about the Bishop. The Red Bishop. Did he cause you much distress?

Earl: (Big sigh.) Seem to feel that he was aware of my interaction with . . . forces other than what he was familiar with.

Mike: Yeah, it was like he was going to use that information.

Earl: Yeah.

Mike: For his own. . . . Were you aware that he was plotting against Arthur to take the kingdom away for the church?

Earl: (Big sighs.) He was pulling and manipulating things behind the scenes.

Mike: Is he the one who spread the rumors about you and Guenivere?

Earl: I think so.

Mike: Did that cause you much pain?

Earl: Of course.

Mike: Did it cause Arthur much pain?

Earl: Of course.

Mike: What happened when Arthur found out about you and Guenivere?

Earl: Seems that he went into a rage.

Mike: Yeah. And what did you do?

Earl: It's not altogether clear.

Mike: Somebody told me you left the castle. Went into exile?

Earl: That sounds right.

Mike: Went out to the frontiers and fought. Stayed away for years. When I tell you that, how does it make you feel? Brings up a lot of grief? You are doing heavy breathing now. Is it bringing up old, uncomfortable feelings?

Earl: I have the sense that things were very dismal. Hard!

Mike: Yes. Did you miss Guenivere?

Earl: Yes!

Mike: Did you miss Arthur?

Earl: Yes!

Mike: You did have great love for him!

Earl: Right! That is why it hurt me, the way he treated people.

Mike: Yes, and you were older than most of the knights, and you could see what. . . . The rest of them just had blind adoration. You were able to see things, sometimes more clearly, about Arthur's failures.

Earl: I could see through him, to a degree.

Mike: Yeah. You know, we haven't talked about Merlin. What was your relationship with Merlin like?

Earl: Mentor relation.

Mike: Did you like him?

Earl: Yeah.

Mike: Did you love him?

Earl: Yes!

Mike: Did he love you?

Earl: Uhhuh.

Mike: What did Merlin teach you?

Earl: He brought me awareness of the forces that interact with us.

Mike: Did he ever teach you any magic?

Earl: Uhhuh.

Mike: What did he teach you?

Earl: How to cast spells. How to move energy. How to manipulate.

Mike: Did you ever go into his chambers?

Earl: (Big sigh.) Not sure.

Mike: Okay. Excalibur. Did Arthur ever let you carry Excalibur?

Earl: I have held Excalibur!

Mike: What was the power of Excalibur? Why was it so special?

Earl: Magical.

Mike: How was it magical?

Earl: Cast with. . . . The method by which it was made. The energy and the . . . crystals therein. The stones therein. The . . . blessings and energies contained within the making.

Mike: Okay. I've read something about a singing sword also. Have you ever recalled a singing sword in your travels?

Earl: That would whistle?

Mike: I don't know. Was that it? As you swung it, it whistled?

Earl: (Big sighs.) It seems, in my recollection, that the energy used to move it, as it moved, it would ever so slightly vibrate until it would hum and whistle, so to speak.

Mike: Okay. They tell me that you went on the Grail quest and never found the Grail Castle. Or the Holy Grail. Do you recall that?

Earl: Seems a little unclear.

Mike: Okay. Tell me about Galahad. He was about your age, wasn't he? One of the other senior knights?

Earl: Seems to be just a little bit younger.

Mike: Did you like Galahad?

Earl: We appreciated one another.

Mike: I heard that they sent Percival out to guard the Holy Grail at the Grail Castle. Did you ever go visit him there? Do you have any memories of that?

Earl: Seems hard to recollect.

Mike: Okay. I saw a vision of Arthur's final battle. And you were there. And you held Arthur in your arms as he died? Does that ring a bell? Arthur's last battle?

Earl: I have a vision of someone dying in my arms, but I can't. . . .

Mike: He has been stabbed in the back . . . just as the enemy forces attack you?

Earl: I see a wound in the solar plexus area.

Mike: Do you have any emotions associated with that? That memory of holding Arthur in your arms?

Earl: Grief. Sadness.

Mike: Yes. And in the vision that I saw, you were struck down, as you held Arthur. You were on your knees, holding Arthur. And you were struck down. That is the way you chose to die.

Earl: Yeah, I think I was beheaded then.

Mike: Yeah, they came up from behind with a sword. And that was the beheading.

Earl: Yeah.

Mike: You made no effort to even defend yourself. You just wanted to die with your king. It was a great reconciliation between you and Arthur, wasn't it.

Earl: (Big sigh.) I sense that he forgave me.

Mike: Yes, yes, yes. Now I would like to. . . . Before we began this regression, you and I agreed that we would go back to the source of your unhappiness in your lifetime now. As Earl. And so I would like for you now to go back and focus in on the emotions or the experiences which are causing your unhappiness in this lifetime. The major source of your unhappiness. We want to bring those emotions up, so we can embrace them and release them.

Earl: (Big sighs.) I have the sense that it has something to do with Morgana.

Mike: All right. Did you treat her badly?

Earl: I think I did.

Mike: Did she seek revenge on you?

Earl: She wasn't able to let go of some hatred.

Mike: What did she do to get even with you?

Earl: I have the sense that my leaving was a result of something with her.

Mike: Like your going into exile, and staying away from Camelot for years?

Earl: Yeah.

Mike: Okay. Let's go after the source of unhappiness. Is it something you did to Morgana? That is causing you to feel unhappy in your present lifetime?

Earl: (Big sighs.) I think my body is telling me. . . . Yes!

Mike: It's like you don't want to look at it. Let's go look at it. There is an incident. Let's go look at it. It's okay. You kind of need to give yourself permission to have this experience. To relive it. To embrace it. It is for your highest and best good, no matter what emotions it might bring up right now. Let's go ahead and bring them up, and look at them.

Earl: I think I was physical with her.

Mike: Okay.

Earl: I beat her.

Mike: Where were you when this happened?

Earl: I have the feeling that it was in. . . . I almost said "our" room. So I can't say whether it's her room or our room. It is not altogether one-hundred percent clear.

Mike: But it was a place where you met, and slept together?

Earl: Right.

Mike: Did you get into an argument or something?

Earl: I think she became aware of. . . .

Mike: Yes?

Earl: . . . Guenivere.

Mike: Yes. So why did you beat her?

Earl: I didn't want to be. . . . I felt threatened.

Mike: You felt kind of cornered, maybe?

Earl: Yeah!

Mike: All right.

Earl: And that's how I react, sometime. When I'm cornered now, I come out fighting.

Mike: Yeah, yeah. And she was pretty aggressive toward you, cause she was very jealous, wasn't she?

Earl: Yeah. And I've dealt with a Morgana, of sorts, in this present life. And it's been difficult also.

Mike: Why, specifically, the unhappiness? You beat up Morgana when she backed you into a corner about Guenivere. Because she was jealous. Why does this make you so unhappy? Tell me about your feelings. How do you feel inside, that makes you unhappy about this?

Earl: I felt sad and hurt that I hurt her. It's the feelings that I'm getting. But I also felt rage that she would not allow me to . . . interact, with trust. She held me too tight. I have the feeling that she didn't give me the room to breathe, which made me . . . move my eye about.

Mike: Well, I've been told that there were spells cast. By people using the forces of darkness. And that someone had put a spell on Guenivere, so that she would betray Arthur. How do you react to that?

Earl: Doesn't seem too unlikely.

Mike: Okay. Do you think it would have been necessary for someone to put a spell on you? Or would the attraction of Guenivere have been enough in itself for you to. . . .

Earl: Yeah.

Mike: You did not need a spell on you?

Earl: No!

Mike: Okay. (Laughs.) Could Morgana be the one who put that spell on you, or maybe it was Mordred? Or. . . .

Earl: Morgana!

Mike: Yeah. It was Morgana?

Earl: Yeah. I think I became aware of it. I could feel its interaction.

Mike: The spell on Guenivere?

Earl: Yeah.

Mike: And so, if she put the spell on Guenivere to be unfaithful to Arthur, why would she be angry with you? Maybe she didn't know that you are the one who would end up as the lover?

Earl: Sits right, but it's not altogether clear.

Mike: Okay. Excuse me for being indelicate, but. . . . I also heard there were other knights that Guenivere got involved with. Did you know anything about that?

Earl: (Big sighs.) Seems highly likely.

Mike: How did you feel about that?

Earl: "Angry" floated in real fast!

Mike: All right. It seems like a very, very difficult situation you have gotten yourself into. What I really hear you saying is that you were having a love affair with Morgana and with Guenivere at the same time. Yes?

Earl: Yes!

Mike: Ah ha! Was Guenivere aware of your affair with Morgana?

Earl: Yeah.

Mike: Was she jealous of Morgana?

Earl: Seems to be.

Mike: Wow! So you had two furious women?

Earl: Bad spot!

Mike: Bad spot! And the King lurking in the background.

Earl: Yeah.

Mike: So why your unhappiness? (Laughs.)

Earl: (Big sighs.)

Mike: Okay. So who did you love the most? Morgana or Guenivere?

Earl: (Big sighs.)

Mike: Tough question?

Earl: Guenivere. . . . But I think I loved Arthur very much too.

Mike: Yes. And how about Morgana?

Earl: Not as much.

Mike: Not as much?

Earl: Not very clear.

Mike: All right. We are still not getting at the point of your unhappiness. I want you to feel the feelings, and tell me what the feelings are.

Earl: Guilty.

Mike: Guilt! Okay. Guilt about what?

Earl: Guilty for . . . loving Guenivere.

Mike: Okay, now we are getting down to it.

Earl: Knowing that Arthur was somebody that I loved, and finding myself in a relationship that would hurt him.

Mike: You betrayed the code of honor of a knight, didn't you?

Earl: Yeah.

Mike: That didn't seem to bother you as much. I think you placed your love of Arthur even ahead of that!

Earl: Yeah!

Mike: Okay. Your guilt. How can we handle your guilt now, to release it? Would it help for you to say, "I betrayed my friend Arthur"?

Earl: I betrayed my friend Arthur. Knowing that . . . has caused me to carry the guilt to some degree . . . now.

Mike: I still see you in the room where you had your fight with Morgana. And you're just finishing strapping on your uniform, your metal armor. Or whatever it is you are wearing. And out of the corner, out of the dark corner steps Jesus. Can you see him there?

Earl: Yes.

Mike: And he talks to you. Jesus says, "My son, it is time that we set this straight. So you can release your feelings of guilt." And he says, "We placed you in a difficult situation. And it was hoped that you and Guenivere could . . . avoid the temptation of being together. And that was the purpose of your coming together in this lifetime. To be in such an impossible situation. But, you were human, and you did not." And, he says, "It's okay. I am the only one who can judge. And I do not judge you on this. I forgive you." And he moves his arm now, and he says, "Besides, this whole situation is very complicated. Because of the black magic, and the spells that are being thrown around." He says, "It is very difficult for everybody. I completely absolve you and forgive you." And I see you break into tears. And cry.

Earl: Yeah, I do too.

Mike: And you lean on your sword. You are just beginning to buckle it on, and you put it down in front of you, and you lean on it. And the tears come out of you, and the tears just stream down your face. And Jesus says, "Will you forgive yourself now?"

Earl: Yeah, Jesus is my friend.

Mike: Yes, he loves you very much.

Earl: I love him too.

Mike: Yes. . . . Can you forgive yourself?

Earl: It's hard.

Mike: Do it for Jesus.

Earl: (Beginning to break up.) I think I could do anything for him.

Mike: I see you kneeling before Jesus, and taking his hand.

Earl: (Deep racking breaths.)

Mike: Feeling his love. . . . And letting it into your heart. And letting him absorb the hurt, and the shame, that you have been denying. That you betrayed your Arthur.

Earl: Oh, oh. . . .

Mike: Let it out! Let it all flow out of your heart now. And it is absorbed into the wonderful love and the White Light of Jesus.

Earl: (Breathing so loudly Michael can hardly be heard.)

Mike: You are kneeling before Jesus the way you used to kneel in front of Arthur. And Jesus is your real King. Do you realize that now?

Earl: There is no other!

Mike: Yes!

Earl: (Crying.)

Mike: And your grief . . . and your sadness just flows out. Gradually emptying.

Earl: (Sighs are starting to slow down.)

Mike: Feel it flowing out?

Earl: It has been a long time.

Mike: Yes. And now Jesus beckons for you to stand again, and he says to you, "There has never been a minute of your exploits, where I wasn't there . . . watching." And he says, "I know who you are. And I'm very very proud of you. I love you even more than you love Arthur."

Earl: (Still crying.)

Mike: And Jesus continues, saying, "And you are the truly great one. In a way, there were some difficult strains put on people." And he says, "I could have made you the king here. In this life experience. But you didn't need the experience. Arthur did. And I made him the king. But you are truly a king and you know it. And that put you in a difficult situation. But you are my hero. And now you go forth knowing that you are my hero, whom I love completely. And everything is right between us. Please focus on and remember my love for you."

Earl: I feel like I'm getting closer to him.

Mike: Yes, yes. It's almost like you have been doing penance. You have been carrying those dark weights around in your heart all this time, which aren't necessary. And they have been lifted from you now. . . . I think it's time for us to leave. And, would you perhaps like to speak to any of the people? Would you like to speak to Morgana, or Guenivere? Or Arthur?

Earl: To say to them that I respect and love them for the part that they played in my growth.

Mike: Okay. I would like to go now to the scene where you are beheaded, holding Arthur in your arms. And I would like for you to go up to Heaven, go to that castle where everybody is waiting for you. . . . See it?

Earl: Yeah.

Mike: See the doors, the double doors?

Earl: Uhhuh! (Catch in voice.)

Mike: Open the doors and go inside. Open the doors, and who is standing there?

Earl: Arthur!

Mike: Yes, and all the other knights. And what do they do?

Earl: Cheer!

Mike: They cheer you, they cheer you! You are everybody's hero! Everybody loves you, Lancelot. Isn't that good? Isn't that great?

Earl: Uhhuh!

Mike: And you know what? That love is eternal.

Earl: (Big sighs.)

Mike: That castle up there is eternal. And you know what? Arthur and the knights are in eternity. And I look over . . . I look over to the side (beginning to cry), and I see Percival. With tears in his eyes. He is so happy to see you joined back with everybody again. He loves you so much. So there is no reason to carry anything other than glory and honor . . . and joy. Feel their love?

Earl: Yeah.

Mike: And back, behind the crowd. . . . In the back, seated up on a little raised area, there are two ladies waiting for you. You know who they are? It is Guenivere and Morgana. I would like for you to go approach them. Approach your Queen first.

Earl: (Big sigh.)

Mike: She holds her hand out. What would you like to tell her?

Earl: I have loved you since the beginning, and I always will!

Mike: Now, what would you like to tell Morgana? Leave Guenivere and move to your right, and approach Morgana. She is standing up, and she is in a beautiful dress. They are both dressed as queens.

Earl: They have been guiding me and helping me.

Mike: What would you like to tell Morgana?

Earl: Thank you for your inspiration. And your love. And your forgiveness.

Mike: And they both step forward together. And they each kiss you on the cheek, one on each cheek. And now everybody . . . all the knights start cheering again. And you turn around and you return to your friends. You all are together, forever.

Earl: As it should be!

Mike: Yes. Yes. Such love.

Earl: (Big sigh.)

Mike: Anything else you would like to say?

Earl: Thank you to my guides, for guiding me here. And to Jesus . . . my friend.

Mike: Your guides are smiling, and they are wiping their brows. And they are saying, "It's been tough up to now. It will be easier. The burden is lifted."

Earl: I know. I'm going to make them proud this time!

Mike: Yes. Yes. They always were proud. Make yourself proud.

Earl: (Big sigh.)

Mike: You're still the champion. You are still the hero. And you never were blemished. And now you know that. . . . I guess that's it!

Earl: Thank you.

25

Jake as Galahad January, 1995

Background: Jake is 43-years-old. He lives in Montana. He is a computer programmer. He had come to Orlando for several months to participate in a series of seminars. We met at one of the seminars, and became friends. I had picked up psychically that he was a Galahad. I had already regressed several Galahads, and felt that I already knew quite a bit about his life. This information helped me in doing the regression, especially since Jake did not easily identify himself at Camelot. His insights as a knight who was "slighted" by the King and Queen is interesting. Also fascinating are other revelations, such as Segwarides being the bastard brother of Guenivere, and the long time that it took for slain dragons to decompose.

Jake's manner of speaking in the regression was abrupt, choppy, and hard to follow. For the sake of authenticity, I have not significantly altered his manner of speech, although I found it at times difficult to follow and understand.

Mike: I'm going to go with you.
Jake: Ahhhhh. . . . What a beautiful sight! We're . . . on a vista. On a trail. Headed toward a greystone. Nice.
Mike: Headed toward a greystone?
Jake: A greystone. A castle-type building.
Mike: Yeah. Okay.
Jake: It does have its bunkers. It is out in a clearing. Very green, lush.
Mike: Are you walking, or are you on horseback?
Jake: I'm on horseback.
Mike: Who's waiting for you?
Jake: You and I are all I've got in my scope at the moment.
Mike: How are you dressed?

Jake: Hmmmm. I am wearing red velvet with . . . fur trim. Some armor. Light armor.

Mike: And the castle that you are going to? Does it have a name?

Jake: I don't see any indications of a name. I see a shape.

Mike: Is it your home?

Jake: It's more . . . rectangular, and has four . . . four towers on the corners. And the cutaways for the watchmen.

Mike: How do you feel about that place? Do you like it?

Jake: Oh, it must be home. It feels . . . it feels very live.

Mike: And what color is your horse?

Jake: He's a silver white steed. With a nice grey and silver mixed in.

Mike: Nice flashing mane. I see that. Very pretty horse.

Jake: Uhhuh.

Mike: What are you going to do at this castle when you get there?

Jake: Ummmmm. Hungry. Time for food. Going home.

Mike: Okay.

Jake: Dinner time.

Mike: Let's go to dinner time. Take me to where you eat.

Jake: It's a pretty good size table. Let's see. . . .

Mike: Are you seated with a lot of people?

Jake: Uhhuh. Sort of . . . off to the right of center.

Mike: What do they call it? You're eating in a big room, I see. What do they call this room?

Jake: I don't get. . . .

Mike: How about the Great Hall? Does that sound right?

Jake: Sure. I got confirmation from a person there.

Mike: You're eating dinner with some other men?

Jake: Some men, and a few ladies. And there are servants.

Mike: How do you feel about these people? These men and the young ladies that you are dining with? Are they your friends, or acquaintances? Do you feel good towards them, or indifferent?

Jake: Most are friends, and most are . . . most all belong there. There are a couple of guests from out of the area that just came in.

Mike: Is the King there?

Jake: I want to say to my left. About two or three seats.

Mike: Okay. You must be somebody important to be seated with the King. At the same table.

Jake: Uhhuh.

Mike: All right. Do you have a name?

Jake: Sir Gento?

Mike: Starts with a "G"?

Jake: Doesn't ring true.

Mike: That's okay. Is the Queen there?

Jake: At his right.

Mike: What does she look like?

Jake: (Big sigh.) Very pale. Dark hair. Elegant. Arrogant.

Mike: How do you feel towards her?

Jake: Cautious.

Mike: How do you feel towards the King?

Jake: Like a brother.

Mike: Like a brother?

Jake: Yes, there's a bond. Like a brother.

Mike: Is Merlin there?

Jake: I want to say he's sitting on the . . . left.

Mike: Uhhuh.

Jake: Of the King.

Mike: Yeah. On the other side of the King.

Jake: Uhhuh.

Mike: What does he look like?

Jake: He's got this deep . . . purple . . . that he wears.

Mike: How do you feel about him? What are your feelings about him?

Jake: One thing at a time. He's got a headdress of some type. He's got facial hair. And his eyes are always . . . piercing, but kind.

Mike: What color are his eyes?

Jake: They're dark.

Mike: And are you a friend of his? Are you friends with Merlin?

Jake: I'd say . . . a friend. Respected friend.

Mike: You mentioned me when we came up to the castle on horseback. Am I seated in the Great Hall?

Jake: Hmmm. . . . I'm going to go back to when we were on horseback, to identify you first.

Mike: All right.

Jake: Well, we weren't alone. There were some . . . a larger troop with us.

Mike: Uhhuh.

Jake: And I do see that similar purple . . . on that person next to me, on the left. So, it's not deep, deep purple. It's like sort of a royal purple. So, it might have been the same party that I saw in that color.

Mike: Were we friends?

Jake: Uhhuh.

Mike: We're back in the Great Hall now. Is the Round Table there?

Jake: It is elsewhere.

Mike: Can you tell me about the Round Table? What that's all about? What it means?

Jake: So, I'm trying to get my bearings. It's like I was . . . like I was looking down from a mezzanine or a balcony. On what was going on. Which allowed for, I guess there were 15, 20 people on that one main side of the big fireplace. And on this side, there's lots of room on the opposite side of the table, away from the King. Now, another part of the building. You're asking? Oh! Where is the Round Table? There is a dome type room. It's got three big fireplaces. So, now . . . in discussing things at the Round Table, it's like. . . . Everyone is sovereign, everyone is equal.

Mike: Uhhuh. Do you sit at the Round Table?

Jake: I don't . . . I can't focus on that one at the moment.

Mike: Okay. Is it true that they have 12 seats at the Round Table?

Jake: From its size, that looks like all that there would be room for.

Mike: All right.

Jake: It's quite a work of art, that piece of wood.

Mike: Tell me about it.

Jake: Fine grain on the top, rounded edges, ornate scallops around the bottom edge of the upper table parts. And then, below, some continuing . . . large legs that have an outward thrust and beautifully sculpted to the base. Lion type feet.

Mike: What kind of wood is it made of? Can you tell?

Jake: Dark, like oak. But, with lots . . . lots of character. It has some blendings with . . . very, I want to say . . . maple.

Mike: Do you know where they got the table, or who made it?

Jake: It was a league of artisans.

Mike: A league of artisans? Okay. Did Arthur have it made, or Merlin have it made?

Jake: It was made at the direction of the King.

Mike: The King. Okay. I would like to know more about the kinds of battles you've fought. First of all, what was your favorite weapon? . . . Did you like to fight?

Jake: It was a necessity.

Mike: All right.

Jake: Getting into that frame. . . .

Mike: Could you take me to one of your battles, and show me what it was like?

Jake: I have to really distance myself there. Too much pain.

Mike: Why is there pain?

Jake: It was a death.

Mike: Whose death?

Jake: It was a total defeat. It was the end of . . . me. There.

Mike: All right. Who was the enemy in this battle?

Jake: Trying to get around all the . . . pain.

Mike: Where does the pain come from? What part of your body?

Jake: Hmmm. . . .

Mike: Or is it emotional pain?

Jake: No! It was . . . it was a heavy sword. Several injuries, but what I'm trying to do is find, find the . . . identifying colors there.

Mike: You know, it's okay to feel that pain again. You might be able to release it. I know you said you're carrying that with you.

Jake: Okay.

Mike: What happened? Was Arthur at this battle?

Jake: (Big sigh.) I don't know. I don't know.

Mike: Where were you? Were you on horseback, or on foot?

Jake: On horseback. The first blow was in the neck, and it was . . . it was the debilitating one.

Mike: Did they get you from the front, or from behind?

Jake: Across. . . . It was deflected off of my chest, off my throat. Then. . . . That's all. I don't want to . . . back up.

Mike: All right.

Jake: Not a very big league . . . that we met. It was just enough, though. They were hiding, too.

Mike: Oh, it was like an ambush?

Jake: Uhhuh.

Mike: Was there a small or a large group of you?

Jake: Standard troop. Group. But we had been deceived. I'm seeing . . . plain, base blue. And white. At first it looks like a French symbol, but it's not. But it has that "fleur de lys" on it. (Big sigh.) That was the one that was the most devastating.

Mike: You died in that battle?

Jake: Uhhuh. And . . . to look back, or to go back, that was a long period of time that was covered. So if you see some other time or event to focus on. . . .

Mike: Okay. I would like for you to tell me about some of the magic that Merlin taught you.

Jake: Ummmmm. . . . Let's back up, then. Starting with the approach, let's see where the camaraderie is.

Mike: Okay.

Jake: I find this technique more clearing. Instead of jetting around, just go back to the entry point of the regression. So we're just clip clopping across the old drawbridge. There is definitely a moat there. So, let's . . . let's go off to see what the magician has to say. What is he teaching today? Hmmmmm. . . . Huh! My, quite an expanse. He has a beautiful den. He does have his . . . his quiet space. Very relaxing. Inviting. Scholarly. . . . He's talking herbs. He's showing some . . . not easily identifiable or specific stuff. Just so much of it that he's teaching. It's like it's going by, reels and reels of it. Probably spent good time together.

Mike: Uhhuh. Some of the other knights told me that Merlin taught them how to become invisible.

Jake: I guess on the use of a mirror and a candle. Understanding. Understanding the bending of light? It was like one of several things . . .

in his large den of things . . . around him. But this mirror, it's amazing. So his mirror technique . . . used the mirror to teach the bending of the light. Vanishing.

Mike: Were there some magic words you had to also say, or some special words? An incantation or something?

Jake: Just visualizing. I'm not seeing or hearing words.

Mike: Okay.

Jake: I'm not as . . . not as there as I could be.

Mike: I was also told that he taught the knights to appear as other things. Shapechange?

Jake: Hmmmmm. . . . Again, maybe it's a way of imparting the knowledge. The use of this candle, the light, and his little corner where he would conduct . . . initiation of the individual. And that initiate could now know some secrets.

Mike: I understand that he also gave you forms of protection. Magical protection?

Jake: Hmmmmm. . . . Certain gems. Crystals. Black tourmaline. Rose quartz. One other. . . . Azurite? Huh. It's hard to tell.

Mike: Okay. He also taught about how God would protect the innocent and those pure of heart.

Jake: Okay.

Mike: Weren't you famous for your purity? Your pure heart?

Jake: (Big sigh.) Oh, I would say that there was, from that status, from that individual person, being there, there was . . . no shadow of the complications with that. So, the purity of that would probably be seen as that way. With no encumbrances.

Mike: Tell me about finding the Holy Grail.

Jake: Huh. . . .

Mike: Do you recall finding the Holy Grail?

Jake: Uh uh.

Mike: No?

Jake: That was only passed along as information.

Mike: As what?

Jake: I only sense the passing along of information about its event.

Mike: Okay. Was finding the Holy Grail an important thing?

Jake: I sense . . . a turn in history.

Mike: Okay.

Jake: And the turn in history was explained . . . sort of after the fact of what was found. Sort of like, it was like, things were happening, and there was no other explanation. And so, these things got explained away because they were somehow affiliated or associated with this grail.

Mike: I've also heard that occasionally the knights were sent out to fight dragons. What did those dragons look like? Did you ever do it?

Jake: Hmmmmm. . . . I don't get a clear, there's nothing clear on that.

Mike: Okay. All right. Could they have been large animals, or even birds? Like Pterodactyls, left over from prehistoric times? Doesn't ring a bell?

Jake: I get an impression about that.

Mike: Okay.

Jake: Which does show a wingspread . . . and one that has been slain. It takes a long time for those stinking rotting things to die! Decay and go!

Mike: They were kind of nasty?

Jake: When they were killed, they just littered the countryside for so long!

Mike: Cause they were so big?

Jake: Stinking! Took a long time!

Mike: Okay.

Jake: Yep. There's too much there for it just to go away.

Mike: Did you ever fight one?

Jake: I don't personally see it!

Mike: Okay. I'm going to mention the names of some knights, and I'd like for you to just tell me your general impression as I mention those names. Gawaine?

Jake: Gawaine. The rumor about him for a long time . . . read like a lost child. He would disappear and reappear. In his early maturity, he disappeared. And was gone and . . . came back.

Mike: Like mystical? Disappeared?

Jake: Yeah.

Mike: How about Lancelot?

Jake: Hmmmmm. The brunt of the family jokes, as well as . . . causing, being part of the . . . broken hearts. The family rift.

Mike: Because of he and Guenivere?

Jake: Because of he and Guenivere and . . . other, let's say, wedges that came between them.

Mike: Between he and Arthur?

Jake: Well, I just see wedges. Their personalities and who they are. I don't know.

Mike: How about Percival?

Jake: Very loyal. He was, you could say, he was steadfast. He was predictable. Those are the main things that come to me.

Mike: Why did you feel uncomfortable around the Queen?

Jake: She has designs on . . . men, for her own desires.

Mike: Wow! So she was unfaithful to the King?

Jake: She wants to . . . tease that way, at least.

Mike: How about Lucan? There was a knight named Lucan?

Jake: There is a dragon man!

Mike: You didn't like him?

Jake: No. You wanted to know who was out fighting dragons!

Mike: Oh, he was out fighting dragons?

Jake: He was one.

Mike: Okay. How about Sir Kay?

Jake: I get a Round Table impression right off, with Sir Kay. And he, his turmoils, were most expressive there. He was very vocal at the Round Table. Very . . . "slam it on the table" kind of guy.

Mike: How about the one they know as the Red Knight?

Jake: Mysterious.

Mike: Mysterious? Did you like him?

Jake: He was aloof. Distant from people. There were some chums. Some brothers . . . he took. But, many people didn't have a close relationship with him.

Mike: How about King Pelinor?

Jake: Pelinor. I sense he wanted to create a better union between factions. But, someone caught on to his attempts, one of his . . . one of his confidants caused him great complications.

Mike: How about Mordred?

Jake: Mordred? I see dark, dark colors. Wearing black, reminds me of the Black Knight.

Mike: That reminds me. Acolon of Gaul? Remember him? . . . Or Segwarides?

Jake: Now, one at a time here. Acolon. He was a great jouster, what I sensed. What else he was known for doesn't stand out.

Mike: Segwarides. I think he was the Queen's brother.

Jake: Segwarides. French something-or-other involved. But . . . where does he fit?

Mike: Was he the Queen's brother?

Jake: Bastard.

Mike: Bastard brother?

Jake: Yes. He was a pain in the butt sometimes.

Mike: Okay. Can you be more specific why he was a pain in the butt?

Jake: I get this . . . losing? He acted immature and cantankerous and just. . . .

Mike: Was it because he was the Queen's brother? Did he try to act different? Take advantage of that?

Jake: Think it might have been the inbreeding.

Mike: Okay. How do you mean "inbreeding"?

Jake: Too close to the families.

Mike: Was it Guenivere's father's sister who was his mother?

Jake: Ohhh. . . . I don't recognize that. What I picked up was that the line was too close and left him . . . strange.

Mike: Tell me about the Bishop. The Bishop came to the court?

Jake: Hmmmmm. . . . An outsider with his own designs.

Mike: Uhhuh.

Jake: Trying to please the Pope.

Mike: Uhhuh. Okay. Did you like him?

Jake: He should have shot himself in the foot. He . . . he was . . . (big sigh) . . . he met the needs of the Queen and many other subjects they wanted to present him to. But he . . . twisted his role.

Mike: Okay. Let's see. Is there anything else you'd like to tell me about this lifetime? I have one more knight I'd like to ask you about?

Jake: Okay.

Mike: Galahad?

Jake: Adventurer. Out adventuring. Being an adventurer.

Mike: Did you like him?

Jake: Likeable fellow. Sure. He was . . . he was. . . .

Mike: I have another question for you. Are you Galahad?

Jake: I don't get a direct impression of that. I mean, as a visitor in that chapter in time, I think many of us can. . . .

Mike: I sense that Galahad had a lot of anger.

Jake: He was unsociable a lot because of that. That's what I sensed. He had anger about that, in whatever way. He was taking it out on his . . . duty.

Mike: Would you place your hand on your stomach please. Feel that anger? Feel Galahad's anger. Why is Galahad angry?

Jake: Feels displaced.

Mike: Is Galahad angry at his father?

Jake: Forlorn. Disowned. Possibly all of that.

Mike: I'd like for Galahad to feel his anger now. So he can release it. Tell me about your anger, Galahad. Why are you angry?

Jake: All that work. No recognition. Broken promises!

Mike: Who broke the promises?

Jake: King.

Mike: What promises did he break?

Jake: Oh, the promises of . . . being placed in his court, closely. And having the recognition . . . never took place.

Mike: He never appreciated you the way. . . .

Jake: No.

Mike: . . . He should have.

Jake: (Big sigh.)

Mike: Are you angry at the King?

Jake: And being cheated, and feeling cheated. Trapped. Cause I fell for some of the . . . the Queen's discussions, too. They seemed to play with me, like a toy. Toss me around emotionally.

Mike: You could never tell either of them how you felt, could you?

Jake: . . . Would not allow it.

Mike: I would like to change that, if we might. And I would like for us now to go to that special day, during the Equinox festivities. When the

King and the Queen have open court for all of the members of the kingdom to come petition them. And I would like for you to dress in your finest, as a knight. And I would like for you to go, and stand in front of them, and tell them exactly how you feel. Express your anger to them.

Jake: (Big sigh.)

Mike: Don't you worry about their feelings. Because this is your time to express your anger. Can you do that?

Jake: I think so.

Mike: I see you standing in front of them, very proudly. I think you're wearing some red again. And you have your light field armor on. Tell them how you feel. Which one do you want to talk to first?

Jake: The Queen.

Mike: Tell her!

Jake: My lady, you have not . . . done me right! You pulled at my heart strings. You told me mis . . . misconceptions. All sorts. All of these things. You pull at my heart. You confuse my mind. Inflame me against the direction . . . of the King. And I should never, would never have done those. And you know, this . . . this day, these are your . . . YOUR problems and not mine. I give them to you!

Mike: Yeah! Good. Give them to her!

Jake: (Big sigh.)

Mike: Yeah. Send them to her! What, what kind of look does she have on her face?

Jake: Surprise.

Mike: She's shocked, isn't she?

Jake: (Sharp intake of breath.)

Mike: She got caught! She feels the wave of energy . . . as you dump all that stuff back on her. Good!

Jake: (Sharp exhale.)

Mike: That makes you feel better, doesn't it? You've been carrying. . . .

Jake: And you, King. . . . (Loudly, forcefully.)

Mike: Yeah, tell him!

Jake: You caused me . . . great disdain. You have confused my mind in battle. You've caused me no . . . forthright . . . strength . . . to persevere. You've destroyed my lovelife too, by distracting my efforts and my energy. My allegiance. I stand by you, but I will not take ANY MORE. I will not take any more . . . of . . . this . . . playful stupidity! It's YOURS!

Mike: Is there anything else you want to tell the King? Because there is somebody here who wishes to talk to you.

Jake: Just a moment. . . . Now I've got a clear mind.

Mike: Okay, as you turn to leave the hall. . . .

Jake: (Huge sigh.)

Mike: In a simple robe, standing at the door. . . .

Jake: Who?

Mike: It's Jesus. Yes . . . go ahead, let it out.

Jake: Mmmmm . . . (starts to cry.)

Mike: And he says to you, "Beloved Galahad, beloved brother of mine. It has been so painful that they did not appreciate you. But," he says, "you know who has always appreciated your steadfastness and your loyalty? I have always appreciated you. I have observed, and not from afar. From up close." He says, "I honor you. Because YOU were key and instrumental in making Camelot a success. Your honor and your purity and your spirituality . . . were a threat to the King and Queen, and so they refused to acknowledge it. But," he says, "I hereby acknowledge and give you the recognition that you have always, always sought." And he says, "You truly are my brother. And you truly have manifested, in this lifetime, those great qualities . . . that I wanted to instill in all of my children on earth. You will ALWAYS be honored for that. Because the King and the Queen . . . they will be with you but a short time, and I will be with you forever."

Jake: (Big sigh.)

Mike: He says, "And I shall NEVER forget my great Galahad."

26

Mike as Percival
January, 1995

Background: Through the regressions of others I gradually learned about the last battle. I then regressed myself to check out my own memories of this special event. My good friend Jake (himself a Galahad) assisted me in doing this regression.

Mike: It is early in the morning. And I am in the stable at Camelot. (Big sigh.) It's the morning of the last battle, and we're up early. Must be about three o'clock in the morning. Camelot is so crowded that there is no room for all of us. Those of us who don't live at Camelot have no place to stay. Everyone has come back for the big fight. All the old knights have come out of retirement. Old soldiers, old pikemen. Old swordsmen. Everyone has come to show their loyalty to Arthur. And to fight with him in the last battle. So there is no room. I ended up sleeping with my pages, and my servants, in the stable. And so, they have candles set up. There is straw on the floor. It is the tack room, I think. And, they are dressing me for battle.

Jim: Are you anxious about the battle?

Mike: I am crying. . . . And they are crying.

Jim: Do you realize what is going to happen?

Mike: And . . . one of them is sharpening my sword. We are having a discussion about which sword to use. Apparently, I had two big swords. One is heavier than the other. And he's sharpening both of them. And he is putting a razor sharp edge on them, using a hand stone.

Jim: Uhhuh.

Mike: And we are all keeping busy, to hold back the tears. One of them is shining my armor, and one of them is brushing me off. He is placing the armor on me, very carefully. It is a bit of a ritual. I'm instructing them that once I leave for the battle, they are to take my other horses and . . . go back home. And that is why they are crying.

286

Jim: They love you?

Mike: Sure! And I am feeling . . . very sad for my family. (Starts crying.) I don't want to lose my family. Ohhhhhhh. . . . My two daughters and my pretty son. My two daughters who love to sit on my lap, one on each knee. Oh, they are so pretty. And my wife is so nice. I love my wife. I never had a family. I never had a family when I was growing up. And I finally have a family. (Crying.) I only had a family for this little while. IT WASN'T ENOUGH! It wasn't enough. I had such a nice wife. I love her. The castle is so nice. It is like heaven, it's like heaven.

Jim: You have waited a long time for your family.

Mike: Anyway, somebody blows the trumpet or something, and it is time for us to get going. And. . . . (Big sigh.) Now I'm at the battle. I am standing in the lines. They put the knights every so often. The knights are spaced, oh, about every 15 or 20 feet apart in the line. To bolster up the other soldiers. And. . . .

Jim: Kind of staggered.

Mike: So anyway. I'm agitated because one of my servants. . . . He's a serf, he's a serf! He has refused to leave. He is dressed in brown, coarse clothes. And he stands behind me with a spear. I don't know where he got that spear. He doesn't know how to fight! And, he refuses to go. He wants to stay, to guard my back. So, I give him some last-minute advice. And I show him how to put the spear in the ground. Since he doesn't know how to use it, I show him how to . . . dig a pocket in the ground, and put the base of the spear in it, and put his foot on it, and kneel down and just wait. And impale the people as they come bursting through the lines. Because they will have some momentum behind them.

And . . . (big sigh) . . . and I'm not angry at anybody. I'm sad. I have been here many times, in battles like this. So I know the feeling in the stomach, and I know the sound the enemy makes on the other hillside. And they make their appearance. And I know that. . . . (Big, big sigh.) Here they come. Most of our guys are pretty experienced. Everybody is pretty steady. But we are not up for this one. We are not up.

Jim: There is heaviness in the air.

Mike: So anyway, here they come. When they get up to our lines, they start really taunting us. They hate us! And they've been told all these . . . things about us, that we are such horrible people! They don't realize that they're just like us. We are all Christians! The truth has been twisted so much. And they, they strike us with a viciousness, and . . . here we go. I start to watch a few of our men go down. Men I've fought with before. And they hit somebody on my left. (Big sigh.) And I start to get angry. And I start to think about my wife and kids. And as I see the blood of my friends spill on the ground . . . I can't tell what it is that makes me angry.

287

Jim: Could it be the senselessness of. . . .

Mike: Oh, above my head . . . is Arthur's face. . . . And I know now that he is dead. (Crying.) Before, we were fighting for Camelot. And now I know Arthur is dead. And the rest of the men somehow know it too. And . . . it's like, suddenly everything changes. (Low, calm voice.) I'm not fighting for Camelot now. Camelot is gone. I'm fighting for these guys, next to me. These sweet, wonderful men. Young and old. I love these guys. (Starts to cry.) It's not fair for them to die. It's not fair. They did nothing. They did nothing. (Sobbing.) I want to save them all. Now I start fighting, now I start fighting. I'm going to save them all, I'm going to save them all. I don't want them to die! I step forward, I create a . . . I create a bow in the line. Because I want to draw them all to me.

Merlin must be here, because it is . . . something! I'm talking to my sword, and it just takes off, swinging horizontally. And they can't stop me! Boy, now I know, I see the power of magic. And we are empowered! We are empowered! I have to pull back because . . . the bodies are getting too high. So I pull back, and their whole line shifts a little bit. Now my light sword . . . that's the smart thing to do. Speed and agility is what it is all about now. With what is coming, it doesn't matter! I'm in a frenzy! I want to save all those guys! (Quietly.) I want to save them! . . . Someone has grabbed hold of my belt, and is pulling me back.

And, we have . . . broken up the attack for now. They have pulled back a bit, just pulled back about 20, 25 feet. So, I turn around. My servant is scared shitless. (Laughs.) He is as white as a sheet, but he's right behind me. His face is ashen. He is in shock. So I turn around, I go back to him. I'm covered from head to foot with blood. (Laughs.) And I say something stupid, like, "The first charge is always the toughest." Or something like that. I hug him, and I kiss him. He is stunned, now, when I do that. I turn around and I take a couple of steps back up to the line. (Big sigh.) One of the things that makes me so angry is that . . . they mutilated our wounded. They mutilated them! And I realize now that no one is to be left. We are all to be killed. And that really makes me angry! These men have done nothing wrong. They are not even being treated like . . . honorable foes. I know how to treat a foe. Especially a fallen foe. And . . . I'm angry at the injustice of it all. Such injustice toward all these great men. All of us pawns in a bigger game. . . .

Here comes a new charge. Oh boy, now it gets tough. (Big sigh.) Through the tired and exhausted foe that we have been fighting, comes a whole new wall of fresh men. Oh jeepers, we are tired! The guys we were fighting were tired, and now here are fresh ones. And now, we're really falling. You can't raise your sword. You just can't. You don't have the strength . . . too tired to fight these fresh ones.

And I do something . . . that Merlin taught me. And it's like I now have this singing sword. Merlin had been in plenty of sword fights, in many battles. He knew what it was like. He had taught us magic for this type of situation. It's like, I go into overdrive . . . and . . . not just fighting. My position shifts. I have a whole section of line I'm covering. The others next to me are too tired. There is now no one on . . . six feet to either side of me. I'm holding a line. A 12-foot gap in the line by myself. And, some of the other swordsmen, soldiers, have fallen back to keep anybody from getting behind me. And, my sword takes care of everybody . . . that comes up. I don't. My sword does. I'm hanging on to it. And, I don't even see them anymore, don't see who they are. I don't see them. I'm too tired for that. It is magic. . . .

I do see one of them. It is Lionel. He is one of our knights who has betrayed us. He's joined the other side. I knew that he'd done it. His wife had told me. Arthur knew it, that he had betrayed us. And I think that it is no accident that we see each other. I think they sent him over there, to deal with me. And I . . . my feelings are funny. I want to punish him, for breaking the code, for being . . . a fallen knight. I want to punish him for disappointing Arthur. So, he's like . . . fighting his way over to me. Half the problem for him is getting through his own troops. Because he's got to move through them as they are fighting along the line. And they are standing four or five men deep. And, I know he is coming . . . forward . . . to fight me. So, I start fighting my way toward him. I fight right through the lines. I'm behind their lines now. (Laughs.) That son of a gun. I never beat him in practice. He was big, strong. Powerful. (Still laughing.) And just as he got to me, just as he got to me, he stumbled over a rock. And I know that Merlin . . . I'm smiling. I know Merlin put that rock there. I see Merlin's face, with a big smile, flash above me. And I don't, there's no . . . ceremony to this. I just stick my sword in his stomach, like he's a cow. And here come two guys toward me, and so I jerk my sword out real fast. And I cut a spear in two, that one is trying to stick me with. And I swing back and hit the other one in the head. And then I turn around and run about 20, 25 feet back to where my lines are.

But half of us are down now. The enemy is all down also. So here comes a new, fresh wave of enemy. Actually, we're lucky. They didn't try to come around us. They're pretty stupid, actually. They could have easily come around behind us, and really caused us a lot of problems. Because they outnumbered us five to one. But they didn't. They wanted to beat us in a frontal assault. They had it figured to use successive waves, spaced about every 20 to 30 minutes. Oh, it's working. But, they're paying the price. This is the third wave.

There's nobody left. (Crying.) They killed my servant. They chopped him to pieces. (Wailing.) Everybody's gone. (Quietly.) Everybody's gone. . . . Oh, I've been covered with blood before, but never like this. It's all dried. It's . . . it's caulking up the joints in my armor.

My light armor. I don't really have much armor on. It's light, like just around my shoulders and chest. And, boy the blood smells. Alkaline. I don't like the smell of blood. There's nobody left to fight. I . . . I want to go home. . . . I'm so sorry . . . (crying). . . . I'm so sorry for all the men. . . . I'm so sorry for all the men. Ohhhh. . . . Sorry for them. . . .

Anyway, it's not exactly like we have uniforms on. . . . So, they don't know that I'm one of the enemy. And I'm so covered with blood. They can't tell who I am. Sure can't tell that I'm a knight. I don't look like a knight now. And, I'm pretty much dazed. The enemy, also dazed, sits and lies about, softly moaning and groaning in exhaustion. I start wandering back towards Camelot. Somebody picks me up. Somebody . . . the wagons or something, trying to haul some stragglers back to Camelot, or something. So I get taken back to Camelot. And I get back there, and everybody is crying.

Doggone. (Laughs.) My men didn't go back! They didn't leave! And they take me, and they start cleaning me up. And they take me and they lay me in the straw, and they bathe me. And I instruct them to get my armor, my gear cleaned up and my weapons. That evening, two other knights come to see me. I'm so stiff and sore I can hardly move. I'm laying down. And one is . . . Guenivere's brother. It seemed that Arthur didn't want Sedgwarides to die. To spare Guenivere, he didn't let him go to the battle. He left him in charge of something else, so he didn't go fight. And the other is Florence. A young knight who didn't get there in time for the battle. So we sit there, around a little fire, and we make a pact. We discuss our options. And it's not so much for Arthur or for Camelot, as it is because we are warriors. And we are tied, we have a bond with all those men back there on that battlefield. And, we don't want to leave them. I want to be with them. I love them so much. As much as I love my family. (Crying.) I want to be with them. I want to be with them. And so. . . . (Big sigh.)

A truce party has come in. Apparently the enemy hasn't recovered from battle either. And they've given the people in the castle three days, two days, something like that, to get out of there. Safe passage. Everyone is to leave Camelot that wants to leave. I don't think the enemy forces are in any shape to do anything. They're still too exhausted. So, one of my men goes out on horseback, and comes back and reports to me that there is a place that I know of . . . that has a. . . . It's an old castle. It's got a nice view, and it's got a wall. That would be a great backstop for us. I had asked them to go find us a place where we can make a last stand. And they did. And so we do it. . . .

And so the next morning, there we are, up again at three o'clock in the morning. And we've taken over this little area of the stables now. The three of us, and our valets and everybody. And they fix us up all over again. My armor is a little chopped up, dented, but boy is it shiny! And so, the three of us ride out, with our men. And there is no saying goodbye to Guenivere or anybody else. They all have such grief that they are dealing with. And they don't matter anymore. The only thing that matters is being back with the men. My comrades. And it's not even the other knights that I'm thinking of so much, as it is those men next to me in the line. Gee, I love those guys! Oh, I love them! So anyway, we eat a good breakfast. On the site. Apparently, we've sent somebody with a white flag. Warren's dead. We sent one of his men with a white flag to . . . tell them where we are. The last of the knights. You know, I still am having trouble getting angry at the enemy. Now, here they come. I want to call them bastards, but. . . . It's a parade. They've got banners. Spears, lances, all sticking up in the air. Four abreast, they march on horseback, right down the road. There they are, and just the three of us. . . .

We have sent our men off, and they have gone this time. They've taken off. (Laughs.) They're racing like hell to get out of there. . . .

The enemy could have probably picked us off with arrows, with archers. But, I think this is a group of men that didn't get to fight in the main battle. They're going to get to fight now. They are looking for glory. They're going to get a fight. So, I'm in the middle. Segwarides is on my left, and Florence is on my right. (Big sigh.) It's almost like a duel. Like. . . . (Laughs.) These . . . these cocky bastards. It's like . . . a few of them come up to do battle with us. Like about six. Instead of just hitting us all at once. It's like . . . who is going to get the honor, who is going to be able to say that he killed one of Arthur's knights. Everyone wants to kill a knight. And so we say, okay, you want to kill a knight? Here's your big chance. (Laughs.) These guys don't know crap about fighting. And, we're. . . . It's pretty grim, but we're kind of, we're kind of making wise cracks, as we slash them down. They have to come up and drag the bodies off. Because they can't do their foot work around us. They are stumbling over the bodies. So they have these servants come up . . . foot soldiers are dragging the bodies off. It's pretty grim humor. It's as if we've almost forgotten why we're there. But not really.

Ohhh. . . . Now they are coming at us en masse. They've given up doing it honorably! (Laughs.) They're changing their tactics. Now it's not who gets the honor of killing a knight. It's like . . . let's get those guys! And now, here they all come. We picked our spot pretty smart! They can't get at us. They can't all get at us. And we are chopping the hell out of them! We are chopping the hell out of them! These guys . . . aren't that good. They are a bunch of young dandies from Europe who thought they would. . . . They're adventurers! These guys aren't swordsmen, they're . . . these guys aren't combat trained, they're adventurers! (Laughing.) They can't get at us! We're laughing! They can't get us! And so now, they bring up the archers. And we know how to use our shields, but they've gotten somebody over to the side. And they catch . . . Segwarides in the neck with an arrow. And he goes down. (Big sigh.) And . . . I don't want to fight anymore. I would rather die with him. So, I just turn and put my arms around him. I catch him as he falls, and so they catch me in the neck with a sword. And I don't see what happens to Florence; just glimpsing that he is engulfed.

Now it's black. (Big sigh.) Ohhhh . . . (crying.) Jesus is here. Ohh-hhh. . . . Ohhhhh. . . . (Sobbing.) Ohhhh . . . (wailing.) He puts my head on his shoulder. I don't want to ever go back! I cry on his shoulder. I tell him, I don't want to ever go back there! I don't like it! I don't want to go. . . . Please don't make me ever go back there. Ohhhhh. . . . (Quieting down, then big sighs.) I'm tired, and I fall asleep in his arms. I don't want to go back! I don't want to go back! There's some kind of hospital, and I get sent to it to recuperate. Rest and recuperate. I don't want to go back anymore. I don't like it down there! Ohhhhh. . . . (Big sighs.) I don't have to go back for a long time! I don't have to go back for a long time! They may never ask me to go back! I know my friends have to go back. It may take a long time. (Speaking so quietly can hardly be heard.) I don't want to be hurt, I don't want to be disappointed anymore. I don't want to be hurt by my friends. I don't want to be disappointed. I don't want to see my friends suffer. I don't want to go back . . . for a long time. That's my sadness. That's my sadness! I don't want to lose any more men. I don't want to see them die. I don't want to be betrayed. I don't want to be hurt. I don't want to be sad. I don't want to not be able to take care of everybody else. (Big sigh.)

∽ 27 ∽

Doreen as the Bird Woman
April, 1995

Background: This is one of my more fascinating regressions. Doreen is a 42-year-old housewife from beautiful and quaint Mount Dora, Florida. She has three dogs, seven cats, canaries, and a parrot as pets. Her husband is a wealthy citrus grower. Doreen came to my home approximately a week prior to this regression. She was seeking a psychic reading to find out why she had an aversion to Jesus, and to organized religion. During the reading we found out that she had a Camelot connection, and this connection played a large role in why she disliked Jesus and his church.

So I was invited to dine with Doreen, her husband, and their three children at their home. After the dinner, we proceeded to regress Doreen, her husband, and one of the children. They were all at Camelot. Doreen was Gawaine's wife, David was Gawaine, and their son was Gawaine's son. These three regressions tell a wonderful story of love. That they are back again in this lifetime in the same family arrangement is, to me, a wonderful testimony to the wonder and perfection of God's system.

Hey, this book has it all. We have told of the violence, intrigue, and scheming. Now comes the sex! Doreen's account of her seduction in the woods by Gawaine a scant few minutes after their chance encounter left Doreen's children (who were sitting in the living room at rapt attention next to their Mom) blushing, as well as her husband flustered, and looking a bit guilty.

Doreen: I'll open the door. It's heavy . . . solid.
Mike: Tell me what you are experiencing.
Doreen: I want it to open to the right, but it is opening to the left.
Mike: All right.

293

Doreen: I'm uncomfortable.

Mike: You're uncomfortable?

Doreen: It's a little uncomfortable. Just a little resistance.

Mike: Okay. What do you see when you open the door?

Doreen: Ohhhhh. . . . (Big sigh.) Oh, it's beautiful! There's trees. (Deep breaths between words.) And hills. Oh, the sky. It's the prettiest blue! (Crying, laughing, sighing.)

Mike: Why are you crying?

Doreen: Oh, it's just so beautiful! I miss it!

Mike: What is so beautiful?

Doreen: The feeling! Oh, these trees! They are alive, they're singing!

Mike: Yes.

Doreen: Ohhhhh. Oh, there are birds. Oh, they just fly around . . . and land on you. Oh, it's like they hold your hand. Oh, there are animals everywhere! (Sharp intake of breath.) All kinds, and everyone gets along. Oh, it's like everyone has their place. (Still breathing deep and short, very emotional.) But there's this . . . oh, perfect total energy. Everyone is one with everyone, but everyone is different.

Mike: When you say everyone, are you talking about the people or the animals?

Doreen: Oh, the animals, the trees, the earth.

Mike: Yeah, things were different in those days, weren't they? Different energy? Kind of enchanted?

Doreen: Ohhhh!

Mike: Everything was an enchanted forest. Who are you?

Doreen: I don't know.

Mike: Are you a boy or a girl?

Doreen: No, I'm a. . . . I'm a girl.

Mike: How old are you?

Doreen: I think I'm kind of young. I have long hair, but I'm skipping around. And, I have on . . . it's not like a dress. It's more like . . . cheese-cloth. (Laughs.) That sounds kind of funny.

Mike: What's your name, little girl?

Doreen: I don't know.

Mike: Where are your parents?

Doreen: I have more of a feeling . . . I don't have an attachment to parents. It's more of a feeling of attachment to this area. Like I belong to the . . . Maybe the woods raised me, or something. I'm not really clear. . . .

Mike: You don't recall a mother or father?

Doreen: Well, there's this big hill. And there is this big place on the hill. It has like a reddish kind of roof. It's kind of in the distance, like I look at it and long for it. Or I look at it, and I know the pathway and I try to stay where I am.

Mike: Ummmm. I sense druid priestesses. Does this have anything to do with druid priestesses?

Doreen: I see bottles.

Mike: Are they your parents? Did they raise you?

Doreen: Do they wear a funny hat? I see a funny hat.

Mike: Man or woman?

Doreen: Oh, looks like a woman, but I don't know if I'm sure.

Mike: What does the hat look like?

Doreen: Ummmmm. . . . Kind of like a cheerleader's megaphone, with a thing hanging. . . .

Mike: Kind of like a what?

Doreen: Cheerleader's megaphone, with . . . something hanging from it. It's white.

Mike: Cheerleader's megaphone, you said?

Doreen: Yes, those things they yell out of.

Mike: Oh, yeah, megaphones. Looks like a pointed hat.

Doreen: Yeah, and it has this thing hanging.

Mike: Like the dunce cap.

Doreen: But it's not straight up.

Mike: A round, conical hat.

Doreen: But it's not straight up. There is a . . . very soft face.

Mike: If I told you the figure is a man, would that make any sense?

Doreen: Well, there is long hair, so I don't. . . .

Mike: What color is the hair?

Doreen: It's like the thing hanging off the hat. It's not grey, it's white. It's definitely pure white. Pure.

Mike: Could that be your father?

Doreen: Feels more like a teacher.

Mike: Okay. Could that be your teacher?

Doreen: I think this is one of my teachers.

Mike: What's his name?

Doreen: (No response.)

Mike: How do you feel about him?

Doreen: Oh, I love him!

Mike: Do you love him very much?

Doreen: Oh! Oh! And I respect him.

Mike: Yeah. He is a very busy man.

Doreen: I don't see much of him. I want to see more of him! But I know he has work to do. He's very important.

Mike: What is his name?

Doreen: Ohhhhh. . . .

Mike: Afraid to say it? Say it!

Doreen: I couldn't possibly have him for a father.

Mike: (Smiling.) He got around.

Doreen: I think I'm a little disappointed.

Mike: Why? Why are you disappointed?

Doreen: Well, I had such a feeling that he was so special, and you just said that he "got around."

Mike: Oh, I'm sorry.

Doreen: I'm uneasy with that. I don't like that.

Mike: Okay. Actually, I was only joking. I don't want to offend him either.

Doreen: He's laughing.

Mike: Yes.

Doreen: It makes me a little irritable.

Mike: Apparently you didn't inherit his sense of humor.

Doreen: Not in that area. I don't like that! (Begins to cry.)

Mike: Okay. Sorry. Don't cry. Don't cry! . . . Why do you love him so?

Doreen: I want him to stay special.

Mike: He is special. I love him very much also.

Doreen: I don't want him to disappoint me.

Mike: Okay.

Doreen: But he has so much to teach.

Mike: Yes. What does he teach you?

Doreen: Animal ways . . . and the magic of the forest. How to be a woman? How can he teach me that? Truths, great truths. Life is simple. It's a great truth. Feelings. . . . Go with your heart. Your heart doesn't lie. It doesn't deceive you, it doesn't trick you. He doesn't teach trickery, but he does PLAY with trickery. He's a trickster.

Mike: Yeah, he's got a funny sense of humor.

Doreen: I think I find that . . . conflicting, a little bit. I take the teaching seriously, and I haven't yet learned to . . . to trick with them, play a game with them. I don't think they are a game. I am taking them very serious. And he's playing. He's playing, he's having fun though. I'm not having that kind of fun. I like it, but it feels more serious to me. I don't play with it yet.

Mike: Okay. What do you think your job is? Why is Merlin training you like. . . . Oops, I said his name! Oh my goodness.

Doreen: That's his common name. That's okay.

Mike: All right. Why do you think he's training you like this? Do you have a special job?

Doreen: . . . Take care of his horse?

Mike: You know what he's telling me? He's telling me that when he's gone, then you are to take care of his animals. You are to be his link to the animal world.

Doreen: He has a beautiful horse. He has more than one horse. He uses them for different reasons. There is an all-black one, and there is an all-white one. And sometimes, he doesn't use the white one . . . just for . . . special purposes. Sometimes he disguises the white one, when he has to hide. And sometimes he uses the black one when he needs to bring the Light.

Mike: Why does he have to hide? Does he have enemies?

Doreen: I think he is cautious. I don't know if they are real enemies, but he is aware of dark forces. I don't know if they for sure know who he is. They are looking for him. They are looking. I don't know if they know how to find him. Maybe he even turns into an animal sometimes. I think he can be anything.

Mike: Yes.

Doreen: Yeah. He is sometimes different animals! (Laughs.) See, he is playing. I had trouble when he turned into animals. I couldn't tell him from a real animal. And that's when I got irritated with his games. Cause I didn't ever want to mistake him. I wanted always to be able to honor him. And he says it doesn't matter. I should be lighter and have more fun with that.

Mike: Did you ever go to Camelot to visit him? Where he lived?

Doreen: I see an area, but it doesn't . . . it's not anything. It doesn't feel like . . . there's hay around. There's hay, or. . . . I have a bucket in my hand. I'm helping with something. I don't know what I'm helping with, but there is hay. Merlin's horse is telling me I have to warn him. I have to go and get him, but he knows that. What? Why is the horse giving me a message? I think those things. . . . It's confusing me. Because he knows everything. It's uncomfortable for me. And of course, the horse is telling me not to be in my head, just to . . . do what I'm asked, and not to question it so. I have to go to this courtyard. I think it's a courtyard. Huh. There's a lot of stone around, and like some benches and bushes around. To look for Merlin. The walls are not solid white, but it's kind of a white, light light grey or white. I feel like I'm sneaking in here to get him, so maybe I'm not acceptable to be there. I . . . I'm not sure. But I feel like I'm sneaking to try to find him. Oops! He just popped out a window. (Nervous laugh.) So he's standing with me. He knew I was coming. Why was he there? Oh, HE summoned me, and the horse was really giving me the message to go to him! Now, I'm to go in the woods, to go and find something. I'm not sure if it's something, or someone.

Mike: Are you supposed to meet somebody?

Doreen: He said it's great . . . it's very important.

Mike: Who do you meet? (Starts laughing as he tunes into the scene.)

Doreen: I've never seen one of them before. Oh, my, a knight in shining armor. I know! (Sharp intake of breath.) He has a breastplate on, it looks like. I don't know what a breastplate is.

Mike: Does he have armor across his chest?

Doreen: Battle like, protection. Protection. And what a smile. Oh, his eyes!

Mike: Is he a big fellow, or little fellow?

Doreen: No, he's big! Bigger than me. And he's on his horse. Beautiful horse. I like his horse. He stops for me. I don't know if I knew . . . he was the one I was going to meet. But when I see him, I know it's the right one. He's the right person.

Mike: Merlin set this up, didn't he?

Doreen: He must of. It's just like him. . . . My heart is racing.

Mike: (Laughing.) You know why he did this? He told me that he wanted . . . he loved Gawaine very much. And to reward Gawaine for his loyalty and support, his steadfast loyalty and support of Arthur, he arranged for Gawaine to meet you like this.

Doreen: He loves Arthur as much as I love Merlin.

Mike: Yes. Yes.

Doreen: But he wants to . . . play in the woods. (Laughs.) That makes me uncomfortable.

Mike: Are you a prude or something?

Doreen: Yes, I . . . I must be. I've not had a man. I've not been taken before. A man's not had his way with me.

Mike: (Jokingly.) And he tries to mess around in the woods?

Doreen: Yeah!

Mike: (Feigning displeasure.) I thought this guy was a knight or something.

Doreen: I like him though.

Mike: You like it?

Doreen: I like him. There is a sense that it's all right.

Mike: (Smiling.) The kids may have to leave the room in a minute.

Doreen: He's very gentle. He's very gentle with me. . . . But he's very physical. He's gentle. (Whispering.) He's gentle. He has to be gentle with me. He just . . . lays me down. He is very easy with me. He's very honoring to me. He is a true knight! (Giggles.) He makes me feel good. I think I love this person. I know I love this person. It's the first time I've felt love like this. It's different than. . . . It's equal to my love for Merlin. (Big sigh.) Wait til I get ahold of him. (Laughs.)

Mike: Wait til what?

Doreen: I get ahold of him. Merlin!

Mike: Yeah.

Doreen: And he told me to save myself. (Laughs.)

Mike: (Laughs.) And then he set this up!

Doreen: Do you . . . can you believe that? I'm going to tell him. (Giggles.) There's a white dove . . . that's probably Merlin! (Really laughing.)

Mike: Of course. Didn't you say he could shapeshift?

Doreen: And he's even watching. Tsk, tsk, tsk, tsk. . . . And to think that I'm going to take care of Merlin's horse for a while.

Mike: Do you two get married?

Doreen: Yes, but it's very simple.

Mike: What's this guy's name, anyway? This knight?

Doreen: Oh, his name? I just know what he feels like. His name, his name. . . .

Mike: Well, that's okay.

Doreen: I'm not a very important social person. He's much more socially important than I am.

Mike: Do you go to live in the castle with him?

Doreen: Hmmmm. . . . I'm only seeing the inside. I don't know if that's the castle or not.

Mike: I want to ask you. . . .

Doreen: Before we were married, I was hiding in the barn. With his horse. I don't know if I was acceptable, or I . . . I think I was a little hesitant. I didn't want to go there. I wanted to go back to the woods.

Mike: Let me get this straight. This knight kept you in the barn?

Doreen: Hmmmm. . . . I took care of his horse. I didn't feel comfortable.

Mike: Oh, oh. Okay.

Doreen: No, I don't think he . . . kept me there. I think that was the way I could be close to him, and still be outside. I like it outside better. Yeah, I like it outside.

Mike: After you got married, to this knight, who kept you in the barn. . . .

Doreen: We married early though. I was young. I'm younger than him.

Mike: He must have introduced you to Arthur and Guenivere and all the other people in the castle. You must have gotten to know them. I'm interested in your impressions of them. What did you think of King Arthur?

Doreen: Pretty impressive cat.

Mike: Okay.

Doreen: There's a little bit of cockiness, though.

Mike: Do you trust Arthur?

Doreen: Nope! I don't think so.

Mike: What about his wife, Guenivere?

Doreen: Nope! . . . Nope!

Mike: How come?

Doreen: She's not pure.

Mike: Okay. How about Galahad? Do you remember Galahad?

Doreen: Galahad? Galahad? Does he have brown hair?

Mike: Yeah, I think so.

Doreen: Kind of stocky?

Mike: Yeah. Kind of shy, nervous around women. Unlike . . . your knight.

Doreen: Quiet. You have to talk to him.

Mike: Uhhuh.

Doreen: He has some hidden qualities. He's trying to protect some-one. I'm not sure who. I think I like him until Guenivere gets ahold of him. Cause he would like to be . . . in her esteem. You know. Recog-nized by her, and. . . . Ohhhhh, ohhhhh, ohhhhh. . . . I don't like that! It's like, she uses that power. She knows he would like that.

Mike: Yeah.

Doreen: And then she can get him to do things.

Mike: Uhhuh.

Doreen: And to . . . to check things. So she has a little spy.

Mike: Hmmmm. Um, let's see. How about Lancelot? What do you think about Lancelot?

Doreen: Lancelot?

Mike: About the same age as. . . .

Doreen: Is he tall and thin? Black hair?

Mike: Good looking?

Doreen: Oh, I don't think he's so good-looking!

Mike: All right.

Doreen: He doesn't have much inside.

Mike: (Joking.) They say that he is better-looking than your husband.

Doreen: He doesn't have as nice of eyes as my husband! His inside isn't as pure.

Mike: That is true.

Doreen: Beauty is skin deep. You see, I can see straight through a per-son.

Mike: You ARE Merlin's daughter. That's right.

Doreen: The exterior means nothing. It's just a shell. But Lancelot uses his shell to get into . . . doors. And . . . and GET things. Although on a very superficial level, I'm feeling . . . oh, I'm feeling very critical. I don't like that.

Mike: It's okay. I'm asking you, because this is kind of a historical investigation.

Doreen: I have a feeling that I'm . . . relentless. There is not much room for error with me.

Mike: That's okay. There is a younger knight by the name of Percival. Did you ever run into him?

Doreen: Is he laughing? Does he laugh a lot?

Mike: Yeah. (Tongue in cheek.) Got a great sense of humor.

Doreen: Quite the jokester?

Mike: Yeah, that's him.

Doreen: Has a belly laugh. Not aggressive, but more outgoing. Ummmm, more genuine, more sincere. He's glad he's where he is. He likes being there.

Mike: Where is that?

Doreen: He is in this room. But, but it's like he has . . . he's not trying to fight for recognition, or fight for being the best. He just is comfortable with his place. And he gets to be more powerful than the others because he is . . . easy with it all. And he just watches the others: this comes in, and this goes out. And he notices that. It doesn't leave an impression on him. But, it's like . . . oh, this one is after "what's her name" today. And, he's very at ease. More balanced, more balanced. Less ego, just more balanced. The others are working for goals. And some of them are self-righteous things. He doesn't have that. He is just having a good time.

Mike: Your father, Merlin. Does he ever comment about Percival?

Doreen: He's going to be teaching him . . . great powers.

Mike: Why do you think that?

Doreen: I think he's going to be handing over the sword to him.

Mike: What sword is that?

Doreen: The magic sword.

Mike: Why is that sword magic? You are talking about Excalibur?

Doreen: I don't know. It's funny shaped. It glistens. It can even dance by itself. It is . . . love, in a nutshell.

Mike: Yeah, but the power?

Doreen: It's the totality of love. It can do anything by itself. Merlin learned from that thing . . . his power. And he wants to pass it on. But only to people he's been told . . . that are pure. Not everyone can do this.

Mike: They say that your husband was one of the first knights to find the Holy Grail. Did you hear anything about that?

Doreen: Merlin told me that my husband did the deed.

Mike: Was your husband too modest?

Doreen: Well, yes. And he was told to keep it very quiet. It was a great honor. And sometimes I had to read his mind. He didn't just tell me things. I was lucky that I knew these things. Because . . . (laughs) . . . you couldn't get it out of him. If he gave an oath, oh . . . he wouldn't go against that, no.

Mike: Was Merlin proud of the fact that your husband found the Grail?

Doreen: Yes! There's a . . . freeing . . . something, and I don't know what that is. It's . . . freedom, of some kind. Something. Freedom. I don't know what that means.

Mike: Okay. Where did your husband find the Grail?

Doreen: I want to say . . . under a rock, under water? Seems like water is there, but seems like there is a rock there too. I don't know how you can have both, but there's a tree there too, cause he's on a limb.

Mike: If it's okay, I'd now like to jump a little bit ahead in time, to that time at Camelot where the Bishop became a problem. Began to destroy the harmony of the court.

Doreen: I'll say.

Mike: Yeah. How did you feel about that?

Doreen: I don't like him at all. Do away with him!

Mike: Why did Arthur let that happen?

Doreen: I don't know.

Mike: Who do you fault for all that to happen? Do you fault Arthur?

Doreen: No. . . .

Mike: Do you fault Guenivere?

Doreen: Yes, she did it!

Mike: Guenivere did it. So you dislike Guenivere?

Doreen: I don't necessarily dislike her. I don't like what she did.

Mike: What did she do?

Doreen: She hurt Arthur. She broke his heart. She broke a lot of people's hearts, I'm here to tell you.

Mike: She did, huh?

Doreen: A lot of people really loved her, and had her on a pedestal. She's going to have to wear that for a long time.

Mike: Have to wear what?

Doreen: The pain of breaking people's hearts. Having them trust and love so greatly, and then to break their hearts.

Mike: Did she disappoint Merlin also?

Doreen: A little bit. He still loves her. It doesn't change his love. He's real clear. No, no, no. I still have to learn this. . . . Arthur is devastated.

Mike: How do you feel about Lancelot?

Doreen: Oh, I don't like disappointment. I just don't like when people hurt other people. And I don't like any of it. No. None of it. No. No excuse.

Mike: How does your husband handle this . . . this change in the situation?

Doreen: He's mostly quiet. He's had a change in personality. . . . He is quieter than he was, more serious now.

Mike: But you can't do anything to change things, obviously.

Doreen: Uh uh.

Mike: He's taking it all on himself?

Doreen: He is wearing their pain.

Mike: Yes.

Doreen: And I'm frustrated, cause I see it all. And I can't do anything. . . . I'm pleading with someone. I'm pleading.

Mike: With Merlin?

Doreen: Uh uh. I'm pleading with Guenibaby. (Yes, she called her Guenibaby!)

Mike: Guenivere?

Doreen: Yes. I'm asking her to mend her ways. To help. She can turn things back around.

Mike: What does she say?

Doreen: She is laughing! She is telling me that I'm of nothing, anyway. I should go back to the woods.

Mike: She is that cruel?

Doreen: Ooooo. . . . I have to love her anyway. She just . . . wants her way. She wants to have all the POWER! She can never have all the power. Doesn't she understand? She wasn't intended to have all the power. It's really ill used, though. A woman's body, a woman's feelings. It takes away from the purity. It takes away from love. And she's trying to use Christianity, too. Oh! Hide behind that, will you!

Mike: You have no use for her, do you?

Doreen: I know deep down, she's good. But those kinds of ways . . . just destroy. Bring death and collapse. Take away beauty and purity. What I have no use for. . . . She knows, now that she has been told. She knows. And she knows she can correct it. And she still won't. That is what I have no use for! Not if it was . . . misguided, or . . . or . . . or she had no understanding. But I know now that she knows, and she . . . still . . . is going to use it to her ill-gotten good. For power! Oh. . . . That is a misuse of power and love. She can't do that.

And no one will listen to me. Merlin tells me it doesn't matter. They are not ready to hear that. Makes my heart very heavy. And my husband's heart is very heavy. He's just quiet. Merlin says it doesn't matter. I can talk to everyone, but . . . he really . . . understands more. My blabbering about it is not helping either! It is on its own course. This is what is meant to happen.

But we will take this knowledge with us. That won't leave. The times will change. He tells me it will be a long time before there will be another . . . (crying) . . . woods with those trees like that. The magic will be there . . . but from the destruction of Camelot, it is going to be a long time before everyone works together enough to bring it back to that perfect state. Where everyone was one with everyone. There will be glimmers, but . . . it will be a while. But, he will lead me, he knows that I will have flashes. . . . I'll know when I am in a spot that will remind me . . . of what I long for.

Mike: Did he ever tell you that the whole Camelot would come back together, some day?

Doreen: He said we were always together, yes. Yes! Yes! In every major history period! Absolutely! Yes, he says this!

Mike: Uhhuh.

Doreen: And he constantly reminds me that no one person is evil. But my greatest lesson is . . . that I'm blaming me, myself. For not being able to get through to them or something.

Mike: Merlin is here right now. And he is suggesting that, in this regression, we take a look at your dislike for the church. Also your dislike for Jesus. You felt the church was destroying Arthur and Camelot.

Doreen: They were afraid of me. That guy with the red hat. He had a red hat.

Mike: Yeah. The Red Bishop.

Doreen: The red hat. He saw me in the woods, working. I was doing some magic. So he banned me from the woods. From the trees. (Big sigh.) He was afraid of me. He said I was evil. (Very quietly.) He wants to punish me.

Mike: Did Merlin ever tell you that what was happening at Camelot was meant to be?

Doreen: Yesss. . . .

Mike: So what happened was okay?

Doreen: I feel like I'm wrestling with that issue.

Mike: He wants to ask you now if you can please forgive the church, and forgive . . . Jesus. Jesus and his church did not do these things. There were flawed people within the church. Just like there were a few flawed knights in Camelot.

Doreen: But that's the way he has always. . . .

Mike: Would you please forgive Jesus and his church?

Doreen: That's no big deal. What I haven't learned, Merlin says, is to forgive me . . . for being caught . . . in the woods. With my magic.

Mike: You blame yourself because you thought you could change things. And yet Merlin knows HE couldn't change the way things were, so. . . . So can you forgive yourself for not being able to change things? Can you do that?

Doreen: I don't think so.

Mike: He does. He says, you weren't supposed to change anything.

Doreen: But I didn't get to even TRY!

Mike: You weren't supposed to.

Doreen: Merlin sent the Bishop to find me? No. . . . No, he didn't.

Mike: How else could the Bishop know where you were? Just like Merlin arranged . . . to meet . . . your husband in the woods. . . . You really weren't supposed to do that magic.

Doreen: (Whispering.) But he wouldn't have done that.

Mike: Yes he did. He was doing the right thing. He knew that you weren't supposed to change things. You couldn't change what was going to happen in Camelot. None of us could change it.

Doreen: But you are supposed to try . . . when things aren't right. Merlin taught me that. He did. He taught me that. With love, you are to try. You are to do your best.

Mike: You can send them love. But you can't change their will. You wanted to change their will, didn't you?

Doreen: Maybe so.

Mike: You are not the only one who did that. Galahad did that. Many others.

Doreen: Why did it fail?

Mike: Because it was meant to fail. And, as Galahad said one time, Camelot was meant to be like a shooting star and flash across the sky. It was not meant to stay there in the sky like a constellation. Camelot couldn't last. The world wasn't ready for it. It lasted just long enough . . . to plant the ideals in the hearts of man. Merlin asks now if you've accepted that? Camelot was perfect. A perfect experience.

Doreen: Oh, it was.

Mike: So, please forgive yourself. . . . With the same smile. Everything was perfect. Will you please forgive yourself?

Doreen: I. . . .

Mike: And he honors you, and your husband, for the stalwart friends and supporters of Arthur that you were. What happened in Camelot was meant to be. And he wishes for you to have the same honor and respect for yourself that he has for you.

Doreen: I always wanted to be with him more.

Mike: That's why he enjoyed teasing you so much in my house when we did the reading a few weeks ago. He knew who you were. You didn't know the connection yet, and he was having fun at your expense.

Doreen: Does he have an owl?

Mike: Yes, it sits on his shoulder. And he was having fun with you, because he knew how great it was going to be when you remembered. He was trying to signal you how special he feels about you. You were truly a great person.

Doreen: He has a lot of love.

Mike: Can you say that? I was truly a great person . . . at Camelot! Can you say that?

Doreen: Inside my head.

Mike: Say it!

Doreen: I did.

Mike: For the recorder. I want to catch this for posterity. . . . Say it.

Doreen: This doesn't feel so easy.

Mike: Say it.

Doreen: I was a good person at Camelot.

Mike: I was a great person at Camelot. Say, Merlin says I was a great person at Camelot.

Doreen: Merlin says I was a great person at Camelot.

Mike: Merlin is very proud of me for what I did at Camelot. Say that!

Doreen: Merlin is very proud of me for what I did at Camelot.

Mike: My husband is very proud of me for what I did at Camelot.

Doreen: I am very proud of my husband for what he did at Camelot.

Mike: My husband is very proud of me for what I did at Camelot.

Doreen: My husband is very proud of me. . . .

Mike: I'm very proud of me for what I did at Camelot.

Doreen: I'm very proud of me. . . . Very, very proud of me.

Mike: Feels good, doesn't it?

Doreen: No.

Mike: Yes! Believe it!

Doreen: Uneasy.

Mike: I know, but believe it. And actually . . . what Merlin has shown me in the many regressions we have done, is . . . the truly tragic people, the truly unhappy people, are the ones who disappointed themselves at Camelot. The Gueniveres, and the Lancelots, and the Bishops. They are the people who are tormented. And people like yourself, who truly were noble and honorable . . . are to recognize that. And honor themselves now. . . . You don't like Jesus, do you?

Doreen: I don't think he is the only good person.

Mike: Okay. Can he come talk to you?

Doreen: Sure.

Mike: All right. He is standing right in front of you. Do you see him?

Doreen: Uhhuh.

Mike: May he put his arms around you?

Doreen: Okay.

Mike: How does it feel?

Doreen: Warm.

Mike: Put your arms around him. . . . How does that feel?

Doreen: Warm.

Mike: Just warm, huh?

Doreen: Uhhuh.

Mike: Can you feel a little more than that? Cause he says to me, "No matter what she does. . . ."

Doreen: (Laughs.)

Mike: "I will always love her. And no matter whether she believes in me, I believed in her."

Doreen: Oh, I believe in him. I just don't believe that. . . .

Mike: You are just sore at him, because you blame him for Camelot. That's what he knows. And he says, he honors you for what you did at Camelot. And with time, you two will sort out your relationship.

Doreen: You see, if you call him Merlin, I don't have a problem.

Mike: (Laughing.) Merlin is in the background, waving, like . . . don't do that, you'll get him in trouble with Jesus.

Doreen: Nah. . . . If you put Mother Nature there, I don't have a problem with her. What I have a problem with is always being told that there was just one way! One path! One path, one path, one path, one path. Narrow, narrow, narrow.

Mike: And is it Jesus' fault that you were told that?

Doreen: Well, it seems to me that he ought to get his message across the board better than the way it's gotten across! You know, shake the world. Do something!

Mike: I still have Merlin whispering in my ear, saying you are still sore about the way Camelot turned out, and you blame Jesus for it. And you shouldn't. And you blame yourself for it, and you shouldn't. Maybe with time . . . now that we've had this visit tonight, you can accept. . . .

As a matter of fact, what Merlin is saying. . . . He is asking a question. He's saying, "Who was really the queen? Who conducted herself as a queen?"

Doreen: I don't know.

Mike: You did! And Merlin is saying . . . in his eyes, you are a queen. By your deeds.

Doreen: I just did what he taught me. . . .

Mike: Now, is there anyplace else you'd like to visit while we are back there?

Doreen: I don't care to go anywhere else.

Mike: After your husband's death, where did you go live?

Doreen: It's darker. There's some rocks, but it's not very pretty. There are a lot of people around. Feels okay, but it's not PRETTY like it was.

Mike: You went back to the woods, with other people?

Doreen: Yeah, but they weren't all the same people that had the same touch before, in the woods. It's not the same feeling. But that's all right.

Mike: Did you have children? You and Gawaine?

Doreen: Yeah, I see children.

Mike: How many?

Doreen: I think there are three.

Mike: That is what I was sensing.

Doreen: But I feel like one is missing.

Mike: Three plus one. Four altogether. Maybe you lost one?

Doreen: I don't know how, but I feel like one is missing. They are good children. They're not so little any more.

Mike: No, they are big. They're grown.

Doreen: Well, some of their hearts are still little. You know, they like to. . . . I guess I'll always be a mother. But it's time they learn some of these things. I wanted to make sure I taught them before I left.

Mike: When Merlin left, did he say goodbye to you?

Doreen: (Begins to cry.)

Mike: Does that make you sad? You don't want to talk about it?

Doreen: (Whispering.) It's okay to talk about it.

Mike: How did Merlin leave?

Doreen: I'm seeing, like a fire. But he did tricks that way. I don't. . . .

Mike: Could the fire be when they burnt Camelot?

Doreen: Well, there's a lot of smoke. Maybe that's what it is. There is a lot of smoke. It's going to go on a long time. It'll last a long time. It smells. And the birds aren't singing.

Mike: Merlin is here now. And he is saying that he has been waiting a long time to be able to come through to you in this lifetime. And . . . he's hoping, that as a result of this regression, you will open your heart to yourself and to him, and let him in again. There is much love to be shared between the two of you.

Doreen: Uhhuh.

Mike: He says that you love his animals, just as you did before. If you'll just open up your heart and love yourself and love him. You can make a great connection. . . . Well, let's see. How about me? Was I back at Camelot with you?

Doreen: (Chuckles.) Quite a guy!

Mike: (Jokingly.) Merlin told me that I was a janitor, and I swept the castle.

Doreen: I don't think so! No, I think you were. . . . Well, the first person that popped up was that little guy who really loved . . . Guenivere. And, she manipulated you. She was unfair. The one who had the good sense of humor. I see you doing somersaults, and I. . . .

Mike: For her?

Doreen: Yeah. As a matter of fact, you are. . . . You just want her to notice you. It's like, why won't you notice that it doesn't matter if she has noticed you? But see, she used that evilly. I don't know your name, but you are this. . . .

Mike: (Laughs.) Schmuck!

Doreen: No! That's not your name. You're in the castle.

Mike: (Joking.) . . . They call me Sir Schmuck!

Doreen: You're in the castle. You're definitely in the castle. You're with my husband, and you are with King Arthur.

Mike: To change the subject a bit. . . . Merlin is now saying that you are his knight in shining armor. He asks, "When are you going to get back up on your horse?"

Doreen: I never rode the horse, Merlin!

Mike: Yes. But he says you're HIS knight in shining armor. He wants you to . . . feel it.

Doreen: I'll work on it. Maybe he could tap me on the head, or punch me, or something . . . as a signal. And I'll . . . keep my attention on it.

Mike: He is showing me what he is planning to tap you with.

Doreen: Okay. What is it?

Mike: It's a great . . . big . . . club!

Doreen: Okay. Where? So I'll know how to feel it?

Mike: On the head.

Doreen: On the head? Could he be a little more gentle? How about on the arm or something? Oh. Ask him if that is. . . . I had an owl that followed me for a couple of years. Kept dropping feathers til I got the message. Bet that was his owl. In the daytime, this owl came! When owls don't ever come around. Must have been his owl!

Mike: Well, he's saying maybe he's one of your pets right now.

Doreen: Ooooo. . . . Okay, I just want to have a signal. Can we work out a signal?

Mike: He's going to give you a shake.

Doreen: A shake? Great!

Mike: A shoulder shake or a twitch. . . . Shake.

Doreen: Great!

Mike: A twitch or a shake.

Doreen: All right. I'll work on it. You've got my word.

Mike: Ready to come back?

Doreen: No. I kind of like it there.

Mike: Okay, stay there. Stay there.

Doreen: Good. I'll bring the story back with me.

Mike: (Joking.) We'll just throw a blanket on you, and we'll go have a party in the kitchen.

28

David as Gawaine
April, 1995

Background: David is Doreen's husband (see previous chapter), and Peter's father (see next chapter). Whereas Doreen is an animated, very expressive and vocal person, David is laid-back, quiet, and pensive. Some things just don't seem to change, as it appears from these regressions that Gawaine's wife is also outspoken and expressive, while Gawaine is quiet and laid-back. I guess that perhaps our basic personality traits are somewhat fixed, from lifetime to lifetime.

An interesting tidbit is that the class distinction between Gawaine and his wife seems to crop up. Remember that Gawaine is of royalty. His father is a king. Gawaine's wife is "of the forest." Despite that he loves her, that she is the mother of his children, he refers to her as his "woman," almost as if he may be a bit embarrassed by the situation.

Mike: When you see that point of light, we'll walk toward it. And I have somebody whispering in my ear as we do this, saying: it's okay. It's okay for us to go back and visit. That it's perhaps time for all this information to come to you. And that there is nothing to be fearful about. And that the spirit ones that are watching, the spirit ones who are with us tonight, are very excited about this event. They assure you that you will enjoy it. Can you see the spot of light?
David: Yes.
Mike: Okay. Let's walk toward the light. Can you see where we are coming out?
David: Well, I'm sensing the light, but I don't really see where we are coming out.
Mike: Okay. I'm going to tell you what I see.
David: Okay.

Mike: I'm not really trying to lead you. I'll just tell you what I see. I see a courtyard. And I see a bunch of men . . . practicing . . . with swords. Like, training.

David: Uhhuh.

Mike: There's a lot of noise and shouting. A lot of aggressive. . . . Everyone's sweating, working real hard. Sunny, very sunny. But cool. You don't see that?

David: I can picture what you are saying in my mind. But I don't feel like I'm actually there.

Mike: All right. There's a large wooden post in front. Like the kind of vertical post they put in a horse corral, to tie the horses to when they break them.

David: Uhhuh.

Mike: It's about ten inches in diameter. And you have a sword in your hand. And you're whacking this post. The swords are dull. You are doing it to build strength. And you pick up your sword and whack the post.

David: (Big sigh.)

Mike: What does it feel like as you are doing it?

David: It feels like a release of a lot of energy.

Mike: Does it feel like something you have done a lot? A very well-practiced maneuver?

David: It feels comfortable.

Mike: Do you feel like you are there now?

David: No.

Mike: Okay. Let's go to the Great Hall where they eat their meals. Do you get any kind of image for that?

David: I can see a place with a real high ceiling.

Mike: Yeah, that's it.

David: Lots of wooden tables. And heavy wooden benches.

Mike: Yes.

David: Lot of . . . a lot of noise. A lot.

Mike: What kind of noise is it? What does it sound like?

David: It's like . . . people are laughing and talking with each other and having a good time.

Mike: A lot of gaiety, a lot of festivity in that hall! A lot of camaraderie. Do you see yourself there or do you feel yourself there?

David: Yeah, I sense that I'm there.

Mike: Can you look around the room and tell me where the flags are? The banners?

David: They're like on the wall. They're kind of angled out from the wall.

Mike: Yes.

David: And there's torches also, on the wall. Providing light in the room.

Mike: Those banners . . . are the knight's coats of arms, aren't they? Can you see yours? Can you look around there and see yours?

David: Yes.

Mike: Can you tell me what it looks like?

David: (Big sigh.) I don't see it real distinctively, but it has a black background with grey. . . . Some grey or silver type designs on it.

Mike: All right. That's pretty good.

David: As though it's some sort of metal.

Mike: All right.

David: Like a cross.

Mike: Good! Now, can you look around the hall and see if King Arthur is there?

David: I see someone who could be King Arthur.

Mike: Where is he sitting?

David: He's sitting in the middle of a long table.

Mike: Is it raised up above the others?

David: There are people on either side of him.

Mike: Okay. Do you see Merlin? Is Merlin there?

David: Well, I don't know if I'm seeing him, or if I'm seeing what my image of him is.

Mike: Tell me what he looks like. What is he wearing?

David: Like a robe.

Mike: What color?

David: Blue.

Mike: Yep! Does it have some designs on it? Any patterns, or. . . .

David: Just like . . . stars.

Mike: What color are they?

David: Silver.

Mike: Okay. That's it! You got it. And what does he look like?

David: (Chuckles.)

Mike: (Laughs.) Not at all like the cartoons, huh?

David: Um, he looks very wise.

Mike: Does he have a beard?

David: Yeah. He has white hair.

Mike: Does he look old, or young, or middle aged?

David: Well, he looks . . . both. He looks, he has a youthfulness about him, and yet he looks old.

Mike: Yes.

David: He looks wise, but he . . . he looks timeless.

Mike: He looks as if he has a lot of energy, doesn't he?

David: Uhhuh.

Mike: Like he can hold his own with anybody. Can you see his eyes? Tell me what kind of look he has in his eyes.

David: He has a lot of love in his eyes!

Mike: Yes. What color are they?

David: Blue.

Mike: Yes! They say it's like looking at the universe to look in his eyes. How does he feel about you?

David: I feel that he has great love for me.

Mike: Why do you think that is?

David: Well, I think he has great love for everyone. But, I don't, I'm not really sure. Maybe for some of the things that I have done.

Mike: How does he feel about Arthur? Does he love his Arthur?

David: Yes.

Mike: How do you feel about Arthur?

David: I have a lot of . . . love and respect for Arthur.

Mike: Why?

David: Because he's a great leader and he sees the way things should be, and he inspires us to help create that.

Mike: What made you follow him?

David: Because I sensed in my heart what he was saying was true.

Mike: Did you ever fight him? With practice swords or anything, when you were a younger man?

David: I don't remember anything like that. Other than just as part of some of the things that we do for training.

Mike: Okay. How does Arthur feel about you?

David: I think he . . . he loves me like a brother.

Mike: Why is that?

David: Because he trusts me. And he feels that I will do what he asks me to do. I will carry out his wishes, and . . . that, he knows that my heart is good.

Mike: What is your name?

David: It's as though . . . it's as though there is a little bit of a veil there yet. There are certain things I can see, but everything is not totally clear to me yet.

Mike: That's okay. We're still in the Great Hall. Can you look around and see if you see Lancelot? Tell me what you think of Lancelot?

David: Well, I. . . .

Mike: I know, because of who you are, you don't speak badly of anyone. But I'm asking you what is in your heart. This is kind of a historical investigation, so I think that it is okay for you to be real honest with me. Although you wouldn't normally do this, because of who you are.

David: Well, I don't really trust him.

Mike: Why is that? . . . He is a great fighter, isn't he?

David: Yes, but he's trying too hard.

Mike: How about Galahad? Is Galahad around here? What do you think of Galahad?

David: I can't really get clear on Galahad right now.

Mike: Let's see. I think that Arthur had three older knights that were his right-hand men. Galahad and Lancelot. The other one was Gawaine. Gawaine.

David: I think that's me.

Mike: Yes. Have you found the Holy Grail yet? They tell me that you found the Holy Grail.

David: (Big sigh.) . . . No.

Mike: Okay. Looking around the Great Hall, who is that young knight that Arthur uses for a lot of errands? Percival. Is Percival around there?

David: No, I don't see him.

Mike: Is Guenivere in the hall? Is she eating with the King?

David: Oh, yes, she is there.

Mike: What does she look like?

David: She is incredibly beautiful!

Mike: What color is her hair?

David: It looks silver to me.

Mike: Okay. How do you feel about her?

David: Right now I'm feeling a lot of love.

Mike: Good. She's a great symbol of the beautiful part of . . . what your movement stands for. What is the Movement all about? What is this Round Table thing? What do you all stand for?

David: We're trying to bring a sense of honor . . . and principles for living life.

Mike: Where is the Round Table? Is it there in the Great Hall?

David: No, it's in a separate chamber.

Mike: Do you sit at it very often?

David: Yes.

Mike: What color is it?

David: I want to say black.

Mike: Yes, it is. Real dark oak. So dark it's black. They tell me that Merlin teaches you knights magic. That you use magic to help you in your battles.

David: Uhhuh.

Mike: For protection. Can you tell me about some of the magic that he has taught you?

David: Well, real power is not physical. Real power comes from . . . the heart. And purity and honesty and belief in action. And from this purity of the heart, are different things that you can do in battle. To multiply your power and your efforts. Like make yourself appear in more than one place.

Mike: I've heard about that. Arthur told me about that one.

David: Yes. And allow your sword to work on its own.

Mike: Yes. Percival told me about that. Where you just kind of hang on to it and it does the fighting?

David: Yes.

Mike: Did you ever make yourself invisible?

David: Yes. I was just going to tell you that.

Mike: All right. (Laughs.)

David: (Laughs.) You can disappear.

Mike: That must do a job on them when you disappear in front of them.

David: Well, what's really wonderful about it, is that it's all really very effortless. You think of battle as being very strenuous and tiring and fatiguing. But when you use these techniques that Merlin has taught us, it's all really very effortless. It happens very . . . spontaneously.

Mike: I guess each knight must have a favorite weapon. Do you have a weapon that is your favorite?

David: Yes, the sword.

Mike: Okay. As an older knight, you've been in a lot of battles. How is it that you are always able to win?

David: Because I'm fighting for a cause I believe in. I have to believe in what I'm fighting for, in what I'm doing, in order for me to . . . succeed.

Mike: Can you tell me about one of your favorite battles? Or any battle that comes to mind? Give me some kind of illustration of what it is like?

David: . . . For some reason, I'm just having difficulty recalling.

Mike: That's all right.

David: It seems like we are always tremendously outnumbered.

Mike: Yes. And you still win.

David: Yes.

Mike: Tell me about your love life. Are you married?

David: I have one woman.

Mike: Tell me about her.

David: Well, she's very beautiful. Both inwardly and outwardly. She is what I would call . . . exotic. She's not someone from nobility.

Mike: How did you meet her?

David: (Slight chuckle.) I found her in the woods.

Mike: What was she doing?

David: Well . . . I don't know if you'd believe me if I told you.

Mike: Go ahead.

David: She talks to the animals.

Mike: Okay.

David: And the fairies.

Mike: Is she a druid?

David: Yes.

Mike: Are you a druid?

David: No, but I wouldn't mind being one.

Mike: Is she a priestess?

David: I don't know.

Mike: Okay. What attracted you to her?

David: Her spirit. Her heart. Her knowledge of things that I would like to know.

Mike: Did it take a long time to court her?

David: No.

Mike: She fell for you pretty quickly?

David: Well, we fell for each other.

Mike: Do you have any children?

David: Not yet.

Mike: Does she live with you there at Camelot?

David: Yes.

Mike: Are you from the nobility? (He squirms.) Does that make you uncomfortable when I ask you that?

David: For some reason, right now, I'm not really clear where I came from. I don't remember how I got here.

Mike: Tell me how you feel about your parents. Your mother and your father.

David: I don't really feel anything.

Mike: Okay. Tell me how you became a knight.

David: Because Arthur asked me to.

Mike: I sense that your father was of some prominence. . . . Anyway, we'll leave that for another time. There comes a time, at Camelot, when the Bishop arrives. The Red Bishop. Do you know who I am talking about? Can we go forward to that time?

David: I don't have a very good feeling about this person.

Mike: Why?

David: Because I think he is evil.

Mike: Okay. Did you ever tell Arthur that?

David: He doesn't see him the same way I do.

Mike: Did you ever talk to Merlin about it?

David: Yes.

Mike: What does Merlin say?

David: Merlin says that Arthur will have to learn for himself.

Mike: Uhhuh. I kind of get the idea that as the Red Bishop became more powerful in the court, it kind of hurt Merlin's feelings, and he withdrew. How do you feel about that?

David: I just don't understand. When Arthur had this very pure and honest knowledge, why would he be attracted to someone . . . like this bishop? Why couldn't he see the evil that was there?

Mike: Uhhuh.

David: Just like with Lancelot. Why couldn't he see the weaknesses, the shallow parts to them?

Mike: One of the knights is named Mordred. Do you recall him? I believe he was Arthur's son?

David: Yes, I think he is . . . unfortunately a misguided person.

Mike: Yes. How is he misguided?

David: Somehow I see him and this Bishop . . . and Lancelot, somehow connected.

Mike: Yes. Kind of a conspiracy between Mordred and the Bishop?

David: Well, I'm afraid Mordred was in such a . . . an effort to try to. . . . I don't know. In a way, it's like Mordred wants to get his father's attention, and yet, do him harm also.

Mike: How about Arthur's sister, Morgana? Does she fit into that?

David: (Big sigh.) I don't feel good about her, either. I'm not clear on how she fits in, but I don't have a good feeling about her.

Mike: Somebody told me that she is Arthur's lover. Is that your knowledge?

David: This is possible. It's hard for me to understand how someone like Arthur can be such a visionary, and yet still be attracted by these lesser things.

Mike: Uhhuh. Yes. To change the subject. Do you do a lot of your fighting on horseback?

David: Yes.

Mike: Where do the horses that you all ride come from? How did Arthur get those horses?

David: They came from Spain.

Mike: Okay. Did he import them specifically so you would have spirited, good quality horses for battle, for fighting?

David: Yes.

Mike: How many horses do you have?

David: I have three.

Mike: What is the color of your favorite horse?

David: White.

Mike: That's nice. They say you are a very big and powerful man. Is that true? How would you describe yourself?

David: I'm not really getting a clear picture of myself physically. It seems it is more my spiritual self that is coming through.

Mike: Could you be described as shy and unassuming?

David: Yes.

Mike: And very, very loyal?

David: Yes.

Mike: And very cheerful?

David: Uhhuh.

Mike: Always with a good word for somebody?

David: Yes!

Mike: You were a great inspiration for the younger knights, weren't you?

David: I tried to lead by example.

Mike: Did people ever use black magic against the knights? The dark forces?

David: Oh yes.

Mike: How did you protect yourselves from that?

David: Merlin taught us how to put an invisible shield around ourselves.

Mike: Okay. They tell me that Merlin doesn't age. That he stays the same age he is, because he drinks something. Have you heard that about his youth potion?

David: No.

Mike: I also heard that the young knights, when they go to training with him, go to his chambers and kneel in front of him while he reads from great big books. Have you ever experienced that?

David: Uhhuh.

Mike: What are those books?

David: It is timeless knowledge.

Mike: Where did Merlin get those books?

David: I don't think they came from any place on earth.

Mike: Okay. Where did Merlin come from?

David: (Chuckles.) That's a good question. I really don't know where he came from, but I'm just very glad he is here.

Mike: He appreciates you very much as a faithful and stalwart . . . friend and supporter of Arthur. Arthur is under a lot of pressure. How does your woman feel about Arthur?

David: She sees another side to Arthur from what I see.

Mike: What does she think about Guenivere?

David: She sees another side to her than from what I see.

Mike: It's almost as if you lack the capacity to see the bad side of people.

David: Well, I would say that it's more like I allow . . . the beauty and the strong points within the person to dominate in my view.

Mike: I would appreciate it if we could go forward in time to that point where you went on your quest to look for the Holy Grail. By the way, what was the purpose of these "quests" that Arthur sent everybody on?

David: It was always to strengthen an aspect of the knowledge.

Mike: Did he sometimes send you out to seek out dragons and things like that?

David: I don't remember that.

Mike: Did they ever send you out to search for the Holy Grail?

David: That sounds familiar to me.

Mike: You don't particularly recall it though?

David: No.

Mike: Okay. You must have killed a lot of men in combat? How do you feel about that?

David: Well, I feel as long as the purpose is, is pure. . . . It's the end that we are trying to achieve that dominates. I don't feel particularly good about it, and I don't feel particularly bad about it. I feel it's what had to be done.

Mike: Okay. Did you ever go over to Gaul? Did you ever leave the British Isles and go to Gaul?

David: It sounds familiar, but I'm not clear on what my experiences were there.

Mike: Some of the men from Gaul came over to Britain to become knights. Why was that?

David: For some reason they didn't have that opportunity over there.

Mike: All right. I'm also told that the knights came from all walks of life. Rich and poor, peasant and nobleman. Is that true?

David: Yes.

Mike: How were those selections made? Who determined who could become a knight?

David: I think this came from Merlin's guidance, as well as Arthur.

Mike: Uhhuh. How would the peasants be chosen? The ones who became knights? How were they chosen?

David: The word would come back when there was someone with some outstanding quality, that this person would be worth looking at. Then that person would be called forth.

Mike: Were you heavily involved in the selection and training of the people like that, who would become knights?

David: Yes.

Mike: What did you teach those knights in training? What part of the training did you get involved in?

David: I was more involved in preparing, not only physically, but preparing them mentally and spiritually. So that they would be well rounded . . . in not just the activities of battle.

Mike: Okay. I would like to . . . go to the last battle.

David: (Big deep sigh.)

Mike: Would it be okay if we went to the last battle? What can you tell me about the last battle?

David: Well, I have mixed feelings about it.

Mike: Tell me about it.

David: Well, it was something we had to do because destiny was pulling us in that direction. At least we were pulled in that direction because of the way things had gone. It was, on the one hand, a celebration or an honor of all that we had achieved, or tried to achieve. On the other, it was very sad, because it was the end of a great era.

Mike: Who were you fighting?

David: The Christians.

Mike: But weren't you a Christian at this time?

David: These were different people that had been brought forth against us.

Mike: Did they come from Europe?

David: Yes.

Mike: Who had the larger forces?

David: They did.

Mike: How much did they outnumber you?

David: It's hard to say. We were massively outnumbered.

Mike: Okay. You must have been pretty old at that time. I think that Arthur was fifty-seven at the last battle. And you were about Arthur's age, weren't you?

David: I would say so.

Mike: Did you come out of retirement, or were you just an older knight at that time?

David: It seems as I was among many who came back into being active, at this time.

Mike: Why would you do that, if you knew it was the last battle?

David: It was as though to honor all that had been. Camelot.

Mike: But didn't you know you were going to die?

David: Yes.

Mike: And you still volunteered to come back?

David: Yes, many did.

Mike: Why?

David: . . . It was the honorable thing to do!

Mike: Okay. Where were you in the battle? Were you on a horse, or were you in the lines? Were you guarding Arthur, or. . . .

David: I was on a horse.

Mike: Tell me how the battle started.

David: I don't remember.

Mike: Okay. Did Arthur get killed during that battle?

David: Yes.

Mike: How did he get killed?

David: He was stabbed.

Mike: Stabbed? In the fighting?

David: . . . No.

Mike: Who stabbed him?

David: Someone within the ranks.

Mike: One of his own men?

David: Yes.

Mike: Was he stabbed in the chest?

David: No. He was stabbed in the back.

Mike: Was it during the battle?

David: Seems as though it was before the battle began.

Mike: Okay. Did you see this happen?

David: No.

Mike: Tell me how the battle went. Do you remember?

David: Seems as though it went on forever.

Mike: Yes. And how did you fall? . . . Is that too painful?

David: . . . I think I actually died of a broken heart.

Mike: When Arthur died?

David: Yes.

Mike: Was Lancelot with him when he died?

David: Yes.

Mike: They had reconciled, hadn't they?

David: Yes.

Mike: When you died, how did you feel about leaving your wife?

David: (Starts to shake.)

Mike: Are you okay? Are you feeling your grief?

David: Yes.

Mike: Okay. I would like to take you past the point of death. To the tunnel. Up into the Light. To the castle. Do you know where I am talking about?

David: Yes.

Mike: And I'm going to fling open the doors for you. And who is standing there, in the castle? They are all there, aren't they? . . . Can you rejoin with Arthur now?

David: I'm only seeing my wife.

Mike: Okay. . . . Great love, isn't it?

David: Ummmmm. . . .

Mike: Is that who you are grieving for now?

David: Yes.

Mike: It is wonderful to have a love like that!

David: Ummmmm. . . .

Mike: That is eternal. She'll never leave you. . . . Where would you like to go now?

David: (Big deep sigh.)

Mike: Or what are you feeling? Tell me what you are feeling so I can. . . .

David: Ummmmm. . . . I think I realize I have a lot of . . . strong feelings about this whole time period. I don't know if I'm ready to be really clear about it yet. It's kind of foggy to me.

Mike: May I give you some of my personal observations?

David: Okay.

Mike: It's very healing for us to go back and experience all this. Because it brings meaning to our present life. It gives meaning as to who we love, and why we love them the way we do. It gives meaning to some of the things that have been in our breast all our life, things that we didn't understand. Such as the feelings of honor and nobility. Feelings of idealism. Feelings that many of the times you were the man out of synch with the rest of the world. Because you were from the Round Table. And the rest of those people out there weren't. And they don't even understand where you are coming from. And that's why it takes a while to process this information. And truly integrate the fact that you are a knight of the Round Table. And you always will be.

David: Sometimes it is not easy.

Mike: No! It wasn't easy then, and it's not easy now. Especially not easy now, cause we don't even know that we are knights. . . . Now you know. I think it will make life easier.

David: Well, sometimes it defies logic.

Mike: Yes.

David: Because you find yourself drawn to do things that, logically, seem to be the hard way to do things.

Mike: Yes. I think that this is probably a good time to wrap it up, and come back. Are you ready to do that?

David: Yeah.

Mike: And you can be with your woman who speaks to the animals again.

David: (Chuckles.) Is she here?

29

Peter as Gawaine's Son
April, 1995

Background: Peter is the 16-year-old son of Doreen and David. As you will recall, Doreen was Gawaine's wife, and David was Gawaine. Peter is a very loyal and dedicated son, eager to please his parents. Eager for his parents to be proud of him.

As this regression unfolded, I was amazed at the similarity between their Camelot lifetimes and their lives together today. Peter is a perfect reflection of Gawaine's son; a young man so eager to please, eager to be like his father, that he chose to show up at the last battle so that he could die alongside him.

When Gawaine's father, who was a sub-king in Arthur's realm, died, Gawaine was in line to replace his father as king. But Arthur, surrounded by treachery on many fronts, depended too greatly on his faithful and loyal Gawaine to let him go. So Arthur sent the grandson, instead of the son, to become the new king. This newly consecrated knight, still a teenager, was broken-hearted at this sudden and unwelcome change in his destiny.

Peter talks of his battle with a dragon. Such battles with dragons have crept up in a number of regressions. I believe that these "dragons" were perhaps the remnants of the dinosaur age, a few remaining dinosaurs left to scare the wits out of young knights before being finally exterminated.

Mike: Tell me when you see the point of light.
Peter: Okay.
Mike: See it?
Peter: Yeah.
Mike: Okay. Let's walk toward it. Tell me what's happening.
Peter: It's getting really bright.

Mike: Okay.

Peter: In my mind, I see a lot of trees, but I don't know if that's. . . .

Mike: That's all right. Just go with it. Don't fight anything, just move with it. Don't stop to think about it, just tell me what you are seeing. Trust your subconscious. Where are these trees located? In a field, or in the woods, or. . . .

Peter: They're like, right in front of me. Like, I don't know if I'm seeing my house, or a forest or. . . . I don't know what it is.

Mike: Tell me what you see.

Peter: I see real bright green. . . .

Mike: Yeah.

Peter: Trees, right in front of. . . .

Mike: It's like the grass and the trees looked greener in those days than they are now. They had a vibrancy that they don't have now. A more brilliant color to them.

Peter: Like on a real, real sunny day.

Mike: Yeah, exactly. Are there some children playing in those trees?

Peter: Now that you said that, I can picture children in them. I don't know if that's because. . . .

Mike: That's all right.

Peter: Okay.

Mike: Are you one of those children? Go to the child that is you. About four-years-old?

Peter: Yeah. I'm really high up in the tree.

Mike: Okay. Tell me what's on your mind, or what you are thinking.

Peter: I want to be the best. To climb up higher than everybody else.

Mike: Okay.

Peter: (Big sigh.)

Mike: What's the matter?

Peter: My heart just started beating really fast.

Mike: How come?

Peter: I don't know. I guess maybe I'm a little scared!

Mike: Of being up so high?

Peter: Oh. Yeah. I'm a lot higher than everybody else, and the tree is really, really big.

Mike: Aren't there some devas up there with you, or some fairies? Are they scaring you? This is something you got from your mom, your ability to see them. Right?

Peter: Yeah.

Mike: Are they your friends?

Peter: Yeah, they are helping me climb, so that I can be better than the rest of them.

Mike: What do they look like?

Peter: They are like, fairies. They have really bright wings. They are like silver, almost.

Mike: Uhhuh. How big are they?

Peter: As big as my forearm.

Mike: They are looking out for you, aren't they? They are protecting you?

Peter: Yeah, I think my mom sent them or something.

Mike: Yeah. So you don't have to be afraid.

Peter: Yeah.

Mike: Yeah. Tell me about your mother.

Peter: She loves to be in the woods and help out the animals. She's . . . her and my dad love each other a lot.

Mike: Do they love you?

Peter: Yeah, a lot.

Mike: Does your mom love you a lot?

Peter: Uhhuh.

Mike: Do you love your mother?

Peter: Very much.

Mike: Why?

Peter: Because she is very loving. She helps me a lot. She's just got a lot of love . . . that emanates from her. (Starts to cry softly.) It's like, when you walk up to her, you just feel engulfed in love.

Mike: Is that why you are crying?

Peter: I don't know.

Mike: Is it because you love your mommy so much?

Peter: Yeah.

Mike: Why is that making you cry?

Peter: I don't know. My eyes just started to water.

Mike: That's okay. I've done a lot of crying on that couch myself. That is what it's there for. How about your dad? How do you feel about your dad?

Peter: He's very powerful.

Mike: Is he a farmer? A merchant? What does he do?

Peter: I'm not getting a clear picture.

Mike: Okay. Do you love your dad?

Peter: Yeah. I also respect him a lot.

Mike: Does your dad love you?

Peter: Yes.

Mike: Does he spend a lot of time with you?

Peter: Yeah.

Mike: Is it because of your dad that you feel that you have to be the highest in the tree?

Peter: Yeah. I want to make him proud of me.

Mike: That is hard to do, isn't it?

Peter: Oh. . . .

Mike: Cause he's so. . . .

Peter: Yeah, he's very important. And I want him to spend as much time with me as he does with everybody else. But, he has to be gone a lot. (Crying.) I don't like that.

Mike: I know. You have a fear that you can't be as great as your dad.

Peter: (Big sigh.) Yes.

Mike: And that's why you are climbing to the top of the tree?

Peter: I want to be the best. I want to be. . . .

Mike: Just like your dad.

Peter: Well, I don't know. Yeah, I want to be. . . . Somehow I want to be . . . better.

Mike: Okay.

Peter: For some reason. I don't know why. I just have a feeling, like I want to be . . . better. The best.

Mike: That's going to be tough. He's a pretty great man!

Peter: Yeah, I know.

Mike: Okay. Did your dad ever take you to see Camelot?

Peter: (Big sigh.)

Mike: Tell me where you live?

Peter: Okay. I see . . . a stable. I don't think that's where I live. Maybe I spend a lot of time there?

Mike: Uhhuh.

Peter: I see my mom petting a horse. Maybe that's my horse. Maybe she's helping him so he'll be a better horse than the others. The rest of the horses. So he can run faster and help me. Because I use a horse a lot.

Mike: How old are you now?

Peter: Ummmm, I'm not four. I'm older. I'm 12, 13 maybe. (Big sigh.)

Mike: Okay. Still love your mom a whole lot?

Peter: Yes!

Mike: How about your dad?

Peter: I want to be more like him than I did when I was younger, even.

Mike: Good.

Peter: I love riding my horse a lot. I'm riding him now. I can feel . . . my heart's beating really really fast. I'm riding very fast.

Mike: Okay. Your mother is doing a lot to help you . . . be like your dad. Because she is getting the animals to help you. The horses and the other animals, they are in tune with you. And, she's got you in tune with nature. Are you a happy person now?

Peter: Yeah, I'm free! Riding. I like that a lot!

Mike: Have you started to learn how to use a sword?

Peter: Yeah. I used my father's sword one time. It was really big and really heavy. I could barely pick it up, it was so heavy.

Mike: Has he taught you how to fight with a sword? Given you some lessons?

Peter: I'm not real clear on that.

Mike: Okay. How about the bow and arrow? Has anyone taught you to shoot the bow and arrow?

Peter: Yeah. I'm really good at that.

Mike: Who taught you how to do that?

Peter: (Big sigh.) I'm not sure.

Mike: Okay. What do you plan to become when you grow up? You are getting pretty big. Thirteen years old.

Peter: I want to be like my dad. I want to be a powerful knight! (Big sigh.)

Mike: Okay. Let's go into the knight training program. What is it like to go into training to become a knight?

Peter: It's a lot of work. There's a lot of people around me. We are all using swords and hitting something.

Mike: Yeah. Hard work, isn't it?

Peter: Yeah, I'm real tired and real sweaty. But I've got to keep going. I've got to become real good.

Mike: You're in training with a bunch of other young men?

Peter: There's people around me.

Mike: Who is training you? Who is doing the teaching?

Peter: Some older person with a beard.

Mike: Could that be Merlin?

Peter: I don't know. It's a grey, it's a really dark grey beard. It's like he is just beginning to age, just turning . . . the beard is just turning. . . .

Mike: All right. Could it be an older knight?

Peter: Maybe.

Mike: Does your father help in any of the training?

Peter: I'm not getting a clear picture of that.

Mike: All right. I'm going to mention the names of some of the knights, and you tell me if you've run into them. Tell me your feelings about them. Galahad? Has Galahad helped train you?

Peter: That doesn't register.

Mike: How about Lancelot?

Peter: Does he have dark hair?

Mike: Yeah.

Peter: I don't know if he trains me, but I've seen him before.

Mike: What do you think about Lancelot?

Peter: Well, my parents don't . . . don't feel real strongly toward him. So they tell me not to get real involved with him.

Mike: All right. How about Sir Kay?

Peter: Maybe that's the older knight I. . . .

Mike: Yeah, it is.

Peter: Okay.

Mike: He trained Arthur. That's a real honor. To have him train you.

Peter: He knows a lot of stuff.

Mike: Yeah. What's your favorite weapon?

Peter: The sword or the bow and arrow. I'm not getting a clear picture.

Mike: All right. Do you like fighting on horseback?

Peter: I don't know if it's fighting. I love riding my horse!

Mike: Okay.

Peter: I'm very close to my horse.

Mike: You're shaking. What's the matter?

Peter: I don't know. Maybe I'm cold, or. . . . I don't know.

Mike: What's it like to be a knight in training? Are you having fun? Are you enjoying it?

Peter: I don't know if I'm enjoying it. But it's something that I'm making myself do. I have to be the best. Yet, I like doing it because I get to ride my horse a lot.

Mike: I'd like to look at another aspect of your training. Tell me, have you met Merlin?

Peter: I think he's in front of me right now.

Mike: What does he look like?

Peter: He's older. Right now, I can see his eyes. They are very deep, penetrating.

Mike: What color are they?

Peter: Blue, or purple, or something. I can't tell. They are just very penetrating.

Mike: What do you think about Merlin? What is your impression of him?

Peter: He knows a lot.

Mike: Do you like him?

Peter: I'm not getting a clear picture.

Mike: All right. Does he seem to like you?

Peter: I know he loves my mom, and I'm sure he loves me too.

Mike: Okay.

Peter: He loves everybody here.

Mike: What does he teach you, or what is he doing with you?

Peter: I can't really tell what he's doing, or what he looks like. I just see . . . his face and his eyes are just, so. . . . You see forever. And he can see into you.

Mike: Okay. That's the main impression you have of him. . . . I'd like to have you take me to the Great Hall for one of the meals. You sit with the other knights in the Great Hall, don't you? When you eat?

Peter: Yeah. My dad's up in front with some of the other knights. And I'm sitting here with my friends. Eating. Yeah.

Mike: What's it like in the Great Hall?

Peter: It's. . . . It's very loud, clanging of. . . . I don't know what the clanging is. Everybody yelling and laughing and. . . . We have a good time there.

Mike: Do you like it?

Peter: Yeah. Tell jokes, and sometimes we . . . one of the younger knights might have done something a little funny in training, and we pick on him sometimes. You know, we're not mean. We just joke about him. He has a good time with us, though.

Mike: Is King Arthur in the Great Hall?

Peter: Yeah. He doesn't. . . . It seems to me he doesn't talk to the other knights as much as he . . . he watches. He watches what everybody in the Great Hall is doing.

Mike: Okay. Where does he sit?

Peter: He sits right near my dad.

Mike: Okay. Is Merlin with Arthur? . . . You don't see him? Okay. How about the Queen? Guenivere? Is she with Arthur?

Peter: I . . . I don't. . . .

Mike: That's okay. What do you think of the Queen? Have you met her before?

Peter: I don't know if I've met her, but I know who she is. She's really, really beautiful. The King almost idolizes her in a way. Cause he loves her a lot. I guess. I . . . I don't know too much about that.

Mike: That's all right. Do you become a knight?

Peter: Yeah. I become a knight.

Mike: Tell me what the ceremony is like when they make you a knight.

Peter: All I can see is maybe the King tapping me on the shoulder.

Mike: What does he tap you with?

Peter: His sword.

Mike: What is the name of his sword? Is there anything special about his sword?

Peter: When he taps me, I feel a lot of energy. I feel powerful. Like a spell has been put over me. That I have love. A lot of warmth from that sword!

Mike: Right. Okay. You are a knight now. Do you enjoy being a knight?

Peter: Yeah.

Mike: Do you have a girlfriend? Someone you are in love with?

Peter: I'm getting a picture of someone with red hair.

Mike: Where did you meet her?

Peter: Maybe at the castle. I'm not sure.

Mike: Yeah. That's what I think. How do you feel about her?

Peter: She's gorgeous. I like her a lot. We have a lot in common. We think the same things.

Mike: Do your mother and your father approve of her?

Peter: They see that I am happy, and they like that. So, they approve of anyone that would make me happy.

Mike: Good. Do you ever go on any battles? Tell me about one of your battles.

Peter: . . . I'm getting a slight picture of a . . . green monster.

Mike: Of a what?

Peter: A green monster.

Mike: Okay. You were sent to kill a dragon or something?

Peter: I don't know if I was sent to kill it, or to make it leave. Or something.

Mike: What does it look like?

Peter: It's huge, and it's really scaly. It's got a lot of scales. It's really big.

Mike: Is it dangerous?

Peter: I'm not scared of the danger. I'm just. . . . I've never seen one before and it just seems a lot bigger than how it's been described to me. I'm kind of shocked by how big it is.

Mike: Are you by yourself?

Peter: I have my horse.

Mike: Okay. What do you and your horse do?

Peter: We circle it a couple times, to get a view of it, and to see how powerful it might be. We will have to fight it if it won't leave.

Mike: What happens now?

Peter: Well, I get closer, and then I start to get a little scared.

Mike: Uhhuh.

Peter: My heart's beating fast.

Mike: Which weapon are you going to use against it?

Peter: I think I'm going to have to use the sword. I don't think the arrow will work. My arrows aren't that big. So, I don't think an arrow will hurt this big, powerful dragon.

Mike: Okay.

Peter: (Big sigh.) . . . Um, I don't know. Maybe I see it get up. Like it's annoyed by me circling it. I've circled it a lot now. I think I know its weakness. Maybe its . . . its underside. Maybe I was taught that would be where you . . . where you would attack it. And it would be weak there, and that's where you should stab it if it won't leave. I'm just hoping that it will leave so I won't have to kill it. . . . But it won't leave, so I have to pull out my sword. And I have to stab it. There's red all over my sword now. Red, or. . . .

Mike: Does the animal try to scratch you or bite you, or what does it do? Does it attack you?

Peter: My horse is so fast, I just circle around and . . . stab it. I'm able to get away at a safe distance. Because my horse is really, really fast and keeps me safe.

Mike: Good. Your mother has trained that horse well.

Peter: Yeah. (Big sigh.)

Mike: What happens now?

Peter: I just see me riding. That's the main picture I get. I see me riding.

Mike: Do you think the dragon died?

Peter: I think so, because . . . because I pulled my sword out, and there was plenty of blood all over it. And I had to wipe off the blood, and I put it back into the sheath. And I got on my horse and we left. We just rode back.

Mike: What color is your horse?

Peter: It's brown. It's beautiful!

Mike: What is your horse's name?

Peter: (Big sigh.)

Mike: That's okay. Do you recall your name?

Peter: Um, it starts with a . . . a "B"? It starts with a B . . . B-R. . . .

Mike: That's okay, we'll get it later. What else would you like to tell me about being a knight? Can you tell me about any other battles?

Peter: I'm not getting a clear picture on anything.

Mike: Do you get married to this red-headed lady?

Peter: Hmmmmm. . . . I'm not sure. I think so.

Mike: Do you have children?

Peter: I think we have children, but I'm not sure.

Mike: What happens next in your life? That you would like to tell me about.

Peter: I think it is right after I get married. I have to leave Camelot. I have to maybe go somewhere. On a mission, or leave, or. . . . I don't want to leave. I like Camelot. I like being a knight. I don't want to leave.

Mike: Do you take your wife with you?

Peter: Yeah. Of course. I love her very much.

Mike: Is there a sadness about leaving Camelot?

Peter: (Big sigh.) Yeah!

Mike: I sense a great sadness. Is there a sadness that you won't get to become a famous knight like your father?

Peter: Yeah. I think that I want to, you know, be real close to him. And I have to leave, and I can't become as great as he is, or as great as he has become. I want to be powerful like that. I would like people to respect me that much, and. . . . I don't want to leave, I don't want to leave, I don't. . . .

Mike: Where are you going?

Peter: I have to. . . . I don't know where I'm going, I just don't want to leave!

Mike: Take me to where it is you are going to be living. Tell me what it looks like. Do you go see your grandfather?

Peter: (Big sigh.) I'm not getting a clear picture on that.

Mike: Do you know your grandfather?

Peter: Yeah, he was a powerful . . . king, maybe. I think he dies, and I have to take over his kingdom because my dad is so powerful to Camelot, King Arthur can't let him go. King Arthur says that my dad is important, but it's my responsibility now to go to . . . to go to this other place and rule in place of my father. I have to go there and teach the people to be spiritual, and make this kingdom . . . great, like Camelot, maybe. Maybe it's a kingdom in Camelot, I don't know. It's near there. It's not THAT far away.

Mike: Okay. What is it like running this kingdom? Does that make you a king? Do you become a sub-king to Arthur?

Peter: Um. . . . Yeah. I'm not, I'm not real clear over it. I know that I have an army, but it's not real big. It's not real great. I haven't had a chance to make it that great.

Mike: Do you do that?

Peter: I try to train as many men as I can, but I don't have that many . . . great men. A lot of them go to Camelot, go there and become knights or soldiers. So I don't have that many here in my actual kingdom.

Mike: Okay.

Peter: To train. But some do. And I'm very proud of them for what they do.

Mike: But you've helped them, haven't you?

Peter: Yeah, I teach them to be knights as good as I can.

Mike: Are you happy?

Peter: I miss Camelot a lot! I miss that place. I love it.

Mike: I sense a great sadness in you.

Peter: Yeah, I miss. . . .

Mike: A great sense of sacrifice.

Peter: Yeah.

Mike: Are you angry at your dad because he didn't come back, and you had to?

Peter: Um, I'm not angry. . . .

Mike: Are you happy with your wife?

Peter: Yeah, we have three children. I think we have three children. They're all. . . . I'm not sure if there are two boys and a girl, or three boys. And that's what keeps me from . . . that's what holds my sadness inside. I get a lot of love from them. I love them a lot.

Mike: How does your father die?

Peter: He dies with me.

Mike: Yes. Can we go to that last battle?

Peter: Yeah.

Mike: Tell me about it.

Peter: My knights aren't really well-trained yet. I . . . I haven't had time to teach them to be great. I haven't had time.

Mike: That's okay. . . .

Peter: Just not enough time!

Mike: That's okay.

Peter: And so, I have to go with my men to help Dad and the others, because there's . . . there's a lot of people opposing them. They have spears, and they try to stab us! I didn't do anything to these people. Why do they want to hurt me? . . . I have to help these knights, and . . . and I can't fend off all these people and help them, my knights, too. So, so I. . . .

Mike: Where's your dad? Is he in the line with you?

Peter: I'm not getting a clear picture on that.

Mike: All right. Are you with your men in the line?

Peter: Yeah. I have to go in between them, and help them, cause they're not good enough yet. They can't use the spells to help them with their swords, and protect them. They're not good enough, so I have to. . . . They try. They're real brave. But I still have to help them. And I can't fend the enemy off!

Mike: Who is this enemy you are fighting?

Peter: The church! The church has sent men to. . . . I don't know what church. . . .

Mike: Okay. Do you hate these men?

Peter: I don't understand. . . . I don't hate them. I just don't understand why they want to attack me!

Mike: All right. How are you dressed?

Peter: (Big sigh.) I'm not real clear in what I'm dressed in.

Mike: All right. How are your men dressed?

Peter: They have a light armor. They have a light armor on.

Mike: All right. Are you on your horse, or are you standing on the ground?

Peter: I think my horse gets stabbed, and I have to be on the ground.

Mike: All right.

Peter: Wait, maybe I'm on my horse. Maybe I'm on a different horse. Maybe my horse died, and I have to be on a different horse. I don't know.

Mike: How's the battle going?

Peter: Badly. My men can't handle all these men. They keep coming up, and they surround us. There are thousands, millions. A lot of them. It's not going very well. The first wave, we thought that was all. And then they hit us with another one. They just keep coming and coming. It seems endless. (Big sigh.)

Mike: Are you tired?

Peter: Yeah, I'm worn out. I can't handle all these people. The sword is moving automatically, but I'm still tired.

Mike: How is it moving automatically?

Peter: We were taught spells in knight school. How to make your sword move on its own. You just have to guide it. So that in long battles. . . . You can be worn out. . . . That's a weakness in a battle, being worn out.

Mike: So, what happens to your men?

Peter: Um, there's 14 of them, I think. There's only 14. Maybe more. But, some of them die, and I'm having to fend off. . . . More people come, so I have to fend off these extra people that are attacking me, and help my men with all the men that are attacking them. And, I go down. And I don't know what happens to them afterwards. I think, I guess they were just slaughtered!

Mike: How did you go down?

Peter: I was on the very end of the line. There was the second wave, and they . . . just came up on us, over a hill. I don't know. And I was on the end, and I just got stabbed!

Mike: Where abouts?

Peter: . . . Maybe, right here. My neck.

Mike: The right side of your neck?

Peter: Yeah.

Mike: Okay. What happens now?

Peter: I fall from my horse. Maybe they slaughter my horse, too. Maybe that's why I thought I was off the horse.

Mike: Why would they kill your horse?

Peter: They just kill everything. They don't care what it is, who it is. I think they think we are evil. I didn't do anything to them. I'm not an evil person! I'm a . . . good person. I think that red guy brought them here. That man is mean. He brought them all here to hurt us.

Mike: Where do you go now? You have been stabbed. What happens?

Peter: I'm not getting a clear picture on that.

Mike: Is it dark?

Peter: Yeah. Everything is dark now. I'm not sure.

Mike: Let's go through the darkness. Tell me where you come out.

Peter: I'm not getting a clear picture on where I come out. It's all still dark now.

Mike: All right. How do you feel about having died this way?

Peter: It's an honor to die in battle, because you are helping out your kingdom. But I don't think the people are going to survive afterwards. I'm worried about my men, my wife, my mom. Because I think everyone will die. All the soldiers will die. And what will they do to the women? My men will just be slaughtered. I can't help them out.

Mike: Okay. . . . Anything else you would like to visit in this lifetime?

Peter: Nothing is coming up that I want to visit.

Mike: Do you feel that you were a success in your life?

Peter: Maybe I was not as successful as my father, but . . . I think I had a good life. I had a good family. . . .

Mike: Okay. I have Jesus here. And he is saying to you that you carried from that lifetime a feeling that you didn't have a chance to equal your father and his accomplishments. But Jesus is saying, on the contrary, you equalled everything your father did and some. Because your father did everything he was supposed to do in his lifetime, and he did it well. And Jesus is also smiling and saying to you, isn't that also true of you? You did everything you were called upon to do in this lifetime, and you did it well. And Jesus says, it was HIS decision as to what you were called upon to do. You were called upon to do different things than what your father was called upon to do. But in your way, and your lifetime, you were every bit as great as your father.

Peter: (Big sigh.)

Mike: Can you accept that?

Peter: Yeah.

Mike: And he's stepping up, and he's got a great big ribbon, like the kind they give soldiers for bravery. And he's pinning it on your chest. And he's very proud of you. Can you see that?

Peter: Yeah.

Mike: See him pinning it on your chest?

Peter: Yeah.

Mike: And he tells you that you are the greatest among the great. And he says, his scoreboard and his scorebook are the ones that are important.

Peter: . . . Okay.

Mike: And he says that, now that you bring up the subject, he points out to you that your father HAD to be at the last battle. You did not have to be there. Do you know why you were there? Because you were great inside. You had the greatness inside.

Peter: I want to know what happened to my men.

Mike: Okay. Jesus takes you by the hand, and he lifts you up. And I see you going up into the sky.

Peter: (Big sigh.)

Mike: And coming out on a big, nice, open field, with a lot of green. And there are your men, all bivouacked. They have some tents set up, and they are up in heaven. They are together again, and all of Arthur's army is there, isn't it? Do your men look happy?

Peter: Yeah.

Mike: Do you want to go give them a hug?

Peter: I give them a pat on the back. They did a good job.

Mike: Yes. Yes!

Peter: I'm proud of them!

Mike: God and Jesus are proud of them too. . . . I want you to look at the love in the eyes of your men, for what you did for them. THEY were there because they loved you, and because of their respect for you. And they knew you tried to make them into knights, and they appreciate and love you for that.

Peter: . . . Okay.

Mike: And Jesus also points out, that as far as touching other people with the "movement," which was what Camelot was all about, you accomplished more than most. And your being brought back to your grandfather's estate to run things was Jesus' way of bringing Camelot . . . out to the various parts of England so it could be spread. And you did your job well. You did exactly what the plan called for.

Peter: Okay.

Mike: Can you accept that?

Peter: Yeah.

Mike: And that's why he puts that great big ribbon on you. You were every bit as successful as your father. And your father is very proud of you. And you two can love each other as equals. Which is what you want, isn't it?

Peter: Yeah. (Big big sigh.)

Mike: Feels good to be as great as your dad!

Peter: Yeah.

Mike: You always were, weren't you?

Peter: I guess now I know that I was.

Mike: Yes, now you can accept it. Jesus has got a big grin on his face as he steps back and disappears. Fades away. . . . I think we'll just leave you there with your men in the field. This is a good time to come back. Are you ready to come back?

Peter: Yeah.

Mike: Say goodbye to them. Okay?

Peter: . . . Okay.

Mike: Okay. You can come back anytime.

~ 30 ~

Stephanie as the Red Knight
April, 1995

Background: When I regressed Stephanie's husband Jake, he was a Galahad. Therefore, it was very interesting to me that Stephanie turned out to be a Red Knight. You see, Galahad and the Red Knight had a complicated love/competition relationship. Apparently, in this lifetime, Jake and Stephanie are working on the husband/wife facet of their love relationship.

I know Stephanie well. She is a 39-year-old Mary Kaye executive. This regression really rings true, because Stephanie has a huge heart of gold. And the Red Knight that I love and remember so fondly had a huge heart of gold.

There were three of us present with Stephanie when we did this regression. The part about the last battle was so touching and emotional that our sobbing (all three of us) almost drowned out the talking. Few moments have touched me as did those moments when the Red Knight was telling how he unexpectedly showed up at the last battle so that he could die with the only true friends he had ever had.

Mike: Do you see the light?
Stephanie: I see a little light.
Mike: All right. Let's head toward it. We're coming out of it now, aren't we? Where are we?
Stephanie: Hmmmmm. . . .
Mike: Can I tell you what I see?
Stephanie: Okay.
Mike: I see an open field, and I see a bunch of knights. It's a bright sunny day, and they are practicing swordplay. With their swords. They are out training. It's hot, sweaty work, and they are all hacking away at each other. They are using great big wooden shields, and dull

337

swords. And they are banging away at each other. Do you see that? . . . I see you. Boy, you are a tough one.

Stephanie: (Big sigh.)

Mike: You are flailing the hell out of some guy with your sword. No one wants to train with you because you are so strong.

Stephanie: But I am nice.

Mike: But you are nice? I don't think you could convince that knight that you are beating on right now that you are nice.

Stephanie: Hmmmmm. . . .

Mike: But you are nice. But you are also a ferocious warrior, aren't you?

Stephanie: Hmmmmm. . . . Tough!

Mike: Do you know what your name is? I've got your name. I can give it to you. Can I tell you?

Stephanie: Uhhuh.

Mike: You are the Red Knight! The famous Red Knight. How does that sound?

Stephanie: Sounds good.

Mike: Yeah! So tell me what it's like to be the Red Knight. Tell me some of your memories.

Stephanie: Challenging.

Mike: Challenging? Okay. How did you get to become a knight? How did that happen?

Stephanie: I don't know.

Mike: Let me ask you this. Do you know Merlin?

Stephanie: I must.

Mike: You must? Yeah, because in the message I'm getting, Merlin brought you to Camelot. Why did he do that?

Stephanie: He needed me.

Mike: He needed you? That's right, he did. He needed you because he was going to use you to teach the other knights a lesson.

Stephanie: (Starts to cry.)

Mike: That's okay. It's all right. Why are you sad? Is it because you want to be loved?

Stephanie: (Big big sigh.) I guess I needed to be needed.

Mike: Yes! You were needed. You wanted the other knights to love you, didn't you?

Stephanie: Hmmmmm. . . . They are afraid of me!

Mike: Yes, because you are so big and strong . . . and gruff. But that's not really who you are, is it?

Stephanie: No.

Mike: You are very gentle and soft inside. . . . So why do you think Merlin brought you there?

Stephanie: Protection.

Mike: Huh?

Stephanie: To help protect.

Mike: Sure. And to help teach the other knights. You taught many things. You know, I regressed a Galahad once, and he told me that you terrorized him. Do you remember that? Remember Galahad? That . . . little knight?

Stephanie: It's like David and Goliath.

Mike: Yeah. Yeah. And you know what, Merlin wanted you to do that. So you could teach Galahad. Because Galahad had to overcome his fears.

Stephanie: He helped me overcome some of mine.

Mike: Who did?

Stephanie: Galahad.

Mike: Galahad? Did you two become friends?

Stephanie: Uhhuh.

Mike: How did you feel about Galahad?

Stephanie: Protective.

Mike: Yes. Did you love him?

Stephanie: Uhhuh.

Mike: Why did you love him?

Stephanie: Gentle, but strong.

Mike: Yes. He had those great spiritual qualities. That made him so exceptional.

Stephanie: I miss him. (Crying.)

Mike: You miss him?

Stephanie: All of them.

Mike: You miss all of them?

Stephanie: Uhhuh.

Mike: I know. I know the feeling. All my life I've been searching for them, and didn't know it. And you have been too. All your life you have been searching again for that love. That you felt.

Stephanie: Surprised.

Mike: What?

Stephanie: I'm surprised!

Mike: That's all right. We have a lot of surprises when we do these regressions. (Laughs.) So, where did you come from, where did Merlin find you? Were you a rough woodsman, or. . . .

Stephanie: In the hills.

Mike: Merlin found you in the hills?

Stephanie: Pine trees.

Mike: Pine trees? Did you cut trees down?

Stephanie: House. Wood house.

Mike: And he asked you to come to Camelot?

Stephanie: Uhhuh.

Mike: Okay. Well, he was very clever. Very wise. After you got to Camelot, did you become good friends with Merlin?

Stephanie: (Big sigh.) Father figure. Guide. Something I was missing.

Mike: Did he ever talk to you about Galahad?

Stephanie: Yeah.

Mike: What did he tell you?

Stephanie: He needed . . . he needed protection.

Mike: Did he tell you to go pick on Galahad, to pick a fight with him?

Stephanie: I don't know.

Mike: You don't know? Did you ever pick a fight with Galahad?

Stephanie: Many times.

Mike: Why did you do that, if you loved him so much?

Stephanie: He had to learn from me.

Mike: He had to learn from you. That makes sense. What did he have to learn?

Stephanie: Common sense.

Mike: Okay. All right. How about to conquer his fears?

Stephanie: Ego.

Mike: Ego?

Stephanie: Ego was out of balance, I guess.

Mike: His ego is out of balance? (Jokingly, because there was a Galahad present in the room.) Some things never change.

Stephanie: Stupid sometimes.

Mike: Stupid? Yeah. Boy, there's some old patterns there. So you love him, and you want to help him.

Stephanie: (Big sighs.)

Mike: Tell me about the Great Hall, where you had your meals.

Stephanie: Big.

Mike: Yeah. Where were the banners? Where did they keep the banners? With all the knights coats of arms on them?

Stephanie: They were hanging on the walls, weren't they?

Mike: Was yours up there?

Stephanie: I don't know.

Mike: Was Galahad's up there?

Stephanie: Lancelot.

Mike: Lancelot's. Did you say Lancelot?

Stephanie: Uhhuh.

Mike: What did you think of Lancelot?

Stephanie: . . . Okay.

Mike: Could you beat him on the battlefield?

Stephanie: I can beat most people.

Mike: You can beat most people. Ahhhhh, so that's why Merlin needed you, huh? Okay! How did Lancelot feel towards you?

Stephanie: Envious sometimes.

Mike: Envious! Okay. Who was your favorite knight?

Stephanie: Hmmmmm. . . . (Laughs.) Hmmmmm. . . . Percival comes to mind.

Mike: (Laughs.) Why?

Stephanie: Humor, maybe.

Mike: Had a good sense of humor?

Stephanie: Not afraid of me.

Mike: Not afraid of you? What kind of a fighter was he? They say he wasn't very big or very fast.

Stephanie: He stood his own.

Mike: Stood his own. Okay. Did he like to fight with you?

Stephanie: Play.

Mike: Hmmmmm. . . . Did he tease you a lot?

Stephanie: Play.

Mike: How did you like it when he played with you?

Stephanie: Okay.

Mike: Okay. You liked that, huh? I think he saw through your gruffness, and saw the love inside.

Stephanie: Kind of like a brother.

Mike: Yeah, okay. Good. Good.

Stephanie: Funny.

Mike: He's funny? (Laughs.) I was talking to Merlin one day, and he confided in me that he was using you to teach Galahad. You were a very important lesson in Galahad's life.

Stephanie: Still am.

Mike: Still am? Okay, good. Do you still love Galahad?

Stephanie: Uhhuh.

Mike: Do you think that's where your love started, back in Camelot?

Stephanie: Maybe before.

Mike: Maybe before. I think so too. . . . Tell me about the King. How do you feel about the King?

Stephanie: Sometimes . . . not good feelings.

Mike: Why is that?

Stephanie: The trust isn't good.

Mike: The trust is not good? Hmmmm, that's interesting, because most of the knights are very envious of him. Or are very devoted to him.

Stephanie: Something gut feeling, something. . . .

Mike: How about the Queen? How do you feel about the Queen?

Stephanie: Good.

Mike: Okay? Did you ever meet Morgana, the King's sister?

Stephanie: I don't know.

Mike: The King had a son who was a knight. Mordred. Did you ever fight him? Ever practice with him?

Stephanie: I think I practiced with everybody.

Mike: Okay. Do you remember fighting with Mordred? Practicing with Mordred?

Stephanie: No.

Mike: How about the Queen's brother. Segwarides?

Stephanie: Huh! Tall?

Mike: Tall. Yep. Liked to ride horses. Didn't like to fight.

Stephanie: Kind of skinny?

Mike: Yep. Kind of shy.

Stephanie: Timid?

Mike: Yep. Timid, that's him.

Stephanie: Woosey.

Mike: What?

Stephanie: Woosey!

Mike: Woosey? Okay. Did you ever beat on him when you had a chance?

Stephanie: Picked on him.

Mike: Big time. (Laughs.) He was really terrorized of you, wasn't he?

Stephanie: Picked on him a lot.

Mike: Yeah. Yeah. Good for you.

Stephanie: Nice horses.

Mike: Nice horses? Who? Segwarides?

Stephanie: Yes.

Mike: Yeah. What kind of horses did you have?

Stephanie: I see a black one, long long mane. Very, very astute, and tall. Big.

Mike: Where did you get your horses? Did Arthur give them to you when you became a knight?

Stephanie: One I brought with me. From the woods.

Mike: What's your favorite weapon?

Stephanie: I see a long chain thing. . . .

Mike: Yes! Okay, the mace! Whatever you call that thing. The big black ball with the spikes on it, on the end of the chain, and the handle.

Stephanie: Uhhuh.

Mike: Wow! You must have been bad news with that thing.

Stephanie: Take some heads off with that.

Mike: Yeah. You liked that, huh?

Stephanie: Hurts, pretty bad.

Mike: Did any of the knights ever go to Merlin and complain about you, being too rough and too strong?

Stephanie: Hmmmmm. . . . Merlin laughs.

Mike: Yeah. Says he has his reasons?

Stephanie: It's good for them.

Mike: Yeah. It's his joke and your joke. He knows why you are there, and you know why you are there.

Stephanie: (Laughs.) It was very good for me.

Mike: Yeah. It was very good for you. Gave you a chance to learn love, didn't it?

Stephanie: Yeah. Knew love, just didn't know that kind of love.

Mike: How was it in the Great Hall when you had your meals? With the other knights? Did you enjoy that?

Stephanie: Good camaraderie.

Mike: Yeah. Anyone ever tease you, or play jokes on you, or anything?

Stephanie: Something in my beer?

Mike: Who did that? I'm almost afraid to ask?

Stephanie: Probably Percival.

Mike: Was it a bitter herb or something?

Stephanie: Something nasty.

Mike: Yeah. (Laughs.)

Stephanie: Bad tasting.

Mike: I think he made it a point to be sitting on the other side of the Great Hall when you tasted that. And everyone was waiting for you to taste it, right? You jumped up and spit it out?

Stephanie: Uhhuh. All over.

Mike: (Laughing.) I can see it now. But you know what, you loved it! Because it meant that you were being loved by the other knights, weren't you?

Stephanie: Sure.

Mike: Yeah. And a lot of them were afraid when that happened. They thought, what's this guy going to do?

Stephanie: They didn't always understand me.

Mike: Yeah, they didn't. But Percival did.

Stephanie: Yeah. Galahad was good.

Mike: Galahad was good? You two were buddies?

Stephanie: Yeah.

Mike: Did he sit with you in the meals?

Stephanie: Some . . . times.

Mike: Sometimes. Okay.

Stephanie: Sometimes I'd sit by myself. I'm messy.

Mike: You were messy?

Stephanie: Uhhuh. Sloppy. Everybody was sloppy though.

Mike: Yeah.

Stephanie: I don't know. Sometimes I'd be by myself.

Mike: I know. Because you kind of gave off this gruff exterior, like you weren't really friendly. But you really were, and you really enjoyed that . . . camaraderie in the Great Hall, didn't you?

Stephanie: Uhhuh.

Mike: Never had anything like that before?

Stephanie: Nope.

Mike: It was like the childhood you never had.

Stephanie: It took a while to get used to it.

Mike: Yeah. Sure. Cause you weren't used to that love.

Stephanie: Ummmm. . . .

Mike: Yeah, nice feeling. . . . So, how long were you a knight? For years and years and years?

Stephanie: Seems like long time.

Mike: Long time? What happened to you? Did you grow old and retire, or did you die in a battle, or. . . .

Stephanie: It doesn't seem like I was dead.

Mike: Did you just leave one day?

Stephanie: See the . . . pine trees.

Mike: Uhhuh. You went back to the woods?

Stephanie: Took someone with me. Maybe.

Mike: A wife, maybe?

Stephanie: No. I don't see that. I don't know who.

Mike: Was this part of your pact with Merlin?

Stephanie: That I could go home.

Mike: Yes. After you had done what you came to do.

Stephanie: If I lived.

Mike: Yes.

Stephanie: Maybe. I wanted to go home eventually.

Mike: Yes. His work with you was finished. Your pact was over.

Stephanie: But if he would need me. . . . If he needed me, I would be there.

Mike: Yes. Yes. Did you ever come out of retirement, to go back and fight again?

Stephanie: I remember fighting at something.

Mike: Was it the last battle? Was it Arthur's last battle? Did you come out of retirement to fight at Arthur's last battle?

Stephanie: Maybe.

Mike: Did Merlin call you down?

Stephanie: Yeah, he called me. But I don't know . . . what it was.

Mike: You had quite a connection to Merlin, didn't you?

Stephanie: Mentally.

Mike: Yeah. Do you remember the last battle?

Stephanie: Ummmm. . . .

Mike: I see you standing in the lines. And you had a sword that was twice the size of anyone else's sword.

Stephanie: Very heavy.

Mike: And I see that there is nobody standing six feet on either side of you. Because when you start swinging that sword, nobody wants to be around. (Laughing.)

Stephanie: Even the enemy was afraid of me.

Mike: Sure. They like, poured around you. They didn't pour ON to you.

Stephanie: There was too many sometimes.

Mike: Yeah. But you sure cleared a path, a swath, with that big sword. The enemy would split into a "Y" when they got to the lines, and they would all avoid you.

Stephanie: That must be why I didn't die! Maybe. (Laughs.)

Mike: How did you feel about that last battle? Were you proud to be there?

Stephanie: Important time.

Mike: You knew everyone was going to die, didn't you?

Stephanie: No.

Mike: You didn't?

Stephanie: Not everyone.

Mike: Not everyone? You knew most of the people would die? . . . Did you know it was the end of Camelot?

Stephanie: I guess I knew I wasn't going to be going home.

Mike: Okay. How did you feel about that?

Stephanie: Sad. Happy, too.

Mike: Why were you happy?

Stephanie: Conclusion.

Mike: Yeah, you were back. You were included again, weren't you? Is that what you mean?

Stephanie: No, I was done!

Mike: Oh! Conclusion. Conclusion of your life?

Stephanie: Conclusion of that time.

Mike: Yeah, okay. Do you feel that you had had a pretty good lifetime?

Stephanie: Still . . . needed some other pieces.

Mike: How did it feel to be there with all those men, that you loved so much, and you knew that they were all going to die next to you?

Stephanie: That was excruciating at times.

Mike: Yeah. Did you see Percival in the lines?

Stephanie: Everyone, I think.

Mike: Yeah. I see him coming to greet you. He's off to the right, about a hundred, a hundred and fifty yards. He can see you, because of a little hill that's there. He sees you standing there with your sword. He looks over his left shoulder.

Stephanie: He looks so small.

Mike: (Laughs.) You want to protect all your friends, don't you?

Stephanie: Can't do it!

Mike: No, neither can he.

Stephanie: (Crying.)

Mike: It's okay. It's okay. That's okay. Here they come. Here they come. (Crying.) What's it like?

Stephanie: Not good.

Mike: It's okay, cause it's all about love. It doesn't matter. It doesn't matter. You all are there for love. You are there because you love them.

They are there because they love you. It doesn't matter. And those waves of men that are coming, they can never stop Camelot. And what we did.

Stephanie: (Sobbing.) I can't help them.

Mike: I know. I couldn't stop them either. I couldn't save them.

Stephanie: I can only do so much.

Mike: (Sobbing.) I know. They're all dying. . . . See, I think the thing we had to learn was, we weren't supposed to save them. We weren't meant to save them. The important thing was, that you wanted to.

Stephanie: Ummmmm. . . . (Racking sobs.)

Mike: And the important thing is, the great love! The great love that we felt for each other, standing in the lines. As I look to the right and the left, at all those determined faces. . . . And you know what they were? They were determined to die together! Because of what we believe in. People like you came out of retirement. Didn't have to be there. But it was your chance to show what Arthur and Camelot meant to you. And that is awesome! Camelot was over, it was time for Camelot to be over. It would have been over, no matter what we had done. But the greatness is in the way you conducted yourself. And your love! And for that, you will always be honored! You will always be honored. And you'll always be with all the knights, and the King and the Queen. And you will always be part of Camelot.

Stephanie: The Red Knight.

Mike: What?

Stephanie: The Red Knight!

Mike: The Red Knight. . . . When the chips were down, he was right there. Out of love. Right to the end.

Stephanie: (Big sigh.) Commitment.

Mike: Yeah. It was a good feeling, wasn't it? Wouldn't have missed it for anything.

Stephanie: Had to be there.

Mike: Yeah. And I got so tired with my sword, there were so many of them. I did one of the things Merlin taught me, and my sword took over. And I just held on to it. And it just went from side to side to side to side. Otherwise, I couldn't have lasted either. Til there weren't any more left to fight.

Stephanie: (Big sigh.) I can't see anybody.

Mike: I know. I know. Everybody's gone. . . . Are you gone? I sense they got behind you?

Stephanie: I just feel lighter.

Mike: Yeah. They got behind you. You couldn't fight them from all directions. After the lines around you had completely collapsed, they surrounded you. And you went to join the others. And everybody is very proud of you. They always have been, and they always will be.

Very proud of you. . . . It's what you always wanted to be. You always wanted to be one of the greatest of the knights. And you always wanted to be loved by all of them. And that's what you accomplished in the last battle. Everybody loves you now. And everybody honors you for your commitment. And your love. Kind of neat, isn't it?

Stephanie: (Big sigh.)

Mike: It's interesting how we get things. We had to lose it to get it.

Stephanie: Yeah. . . . I keep doing that.

Mike: Not any more. Not any more, not now that you know who you are. And you know of your greatness. And you truly can accept inside how much you loved, and are loved. By all those people. It won't be that way now.

Stephanie: It's okay.

Mike: Yeah. Can I tell you what happened to Percival?

Stephanie: Commitment. . . .

Mike: He was so covered with blood, they didn't know he was the enemy.

Stephanie: (Laughs.)

Mike: He walked away, when there was nobody left. He walked away. But you know what? He wanted to be with you. And the next day, he went out and told them where he was. And they came. And they sent about one hundred men. Against him and two other knights. And the three killed most of them. (Laughs.) But he joined you on that day. So, the last of the knights joined the Round Table again. Because we wanted to be with you. That's where it was. That's where love was. We weren't going to be left behind. And you wouldn't have wanted to be left behind either.

Stephanie: No!

Mike: You wanted to be there. So, it turned out perfectly, didn't it? In the meantime, there's a whole lot of European . . . adventurers, who lived the rest of their lives with nightmares. That great big dude with his sword. (Laughs.) With the black beard.

Stephanie: (Laughs.)

Mike: You put the fear of God in those guys! So. . . . How do you feel now?

Stephanie: Better.

Mike: Where would you like to go now?

Stephanie: . . . I'm okay.

Mike: Ready to come back?

Stephanie: Yeah.

Mike: Okay. All right. I have a parting message for you from Merlin. He says he still has that same connection to you. If you will just honor it. And he still has that great love for you too. And you know that, don't you?

Stephanie: (Big sigh.)

Mike: And I have Jesus here. And he's talking, and he says that you have no idea the esteem in which he holds you and honors you. Because of the way you loved and protected his children. He considers you truly one of his favorite knights. That's quite an honor. And he says he's very anxious for you to love yourself as much as he loves you. And he sees that happening. And when you love yourself as much as he loves you, then the two of you can be much closer friends.

Stephanie: (Big sighs.)

Mike: Part of that is honoring your greatness. For you truly are great. . . . Yeah, the Red Knight!

~ 31 ~

Thomas as Lancelot
February, 1996

Background: As our list of Camelot regressions grew, I became frustrated that we hadn't yet obtained many good Lancelot regressions. Then I hit paydirt with Tom. Tom is a 43-year-old herbalist and athletic trainer in Orlando. He is gentle, a loner, and a ladies man. In short, a perfect Lancelot. I have known him for about six years, and he is a close friend. Now I realize why. Percival loves Lancelot very deeply, and I love Tom very deeply.

To me, this is a wonderful regression, and it tells a beautiful story; a wonderful love story. When we began this regression, I knew that Tom was a Lancelot. Tom did not know.

Mike: And we'll step through the door, and now tell me what you experience.
Tom: It's a big room.
Mike: Tell me about it.
Tom: Very high ceiling. It's got . . . arches. Floor of stone. I feel dizzy.
Mike: How do you feel about this room?
Tom: Seems like it goes somewhere else.
Mike: Okay. Let's leave the room. Where would you like to take me now?
Tom: To the right.
Mike: Okay. I would like for you to reach down with your right hand and tell me what kind of belt you are wearing.
Tom: It's leather with a metal buckle.
Mike: Okay. Now reach down around your legs and tell me what you are wearing there.
Tom: It's a long robe.
Mike: Okay. Now reach up around your chest and tell me what you are wearing.

Tom: It's cloth. It's like . . . leather. I feel very comfortable.

Mike: In those clothes?

Tom: In those clothes.

Mike: Okay. Where are you taking me?

Tom: I don't know.

Mike: What's your name?

Tom: John?

Mike: Okay. What is your job?

Tom: I live here. No . . . I come here. I work here.

Mike: Okay. What's your job? What kind of work do you do?

Tom: I come here all the time.

Mike: All right. I'm going to mention the names of some of the people, and I'd like for you to tell me your reactions to these people. Is that okay?

Tom: Yeah.

Mike: Galahad? What do you think of Galahad?

Tom: All show, no go.

Mike: Is he a personal friend of yours?

Tom: Yeah. He is cocky.

Mike: How about Gawaine?

Tom: Nice guy.

Mike: They say Arthur can always depend on Gawaine. Is that true?

Tom: Yeah.

Mike: What about Sir Kay?

Tom: He's older.

Mike: Yeah.

Tom: He had . . . grey hair?

Mike: Uhhuh.

Tom: Can depend on him.

Mike: Okay. Are you a knight?

Tom: I think so.

Mike: Why did you feel dizzy when we were in the Great Hall?

Tom: I still do.

Mike: Do you feel dizzy, or do you feel dizzy thinking about the Great Hall?

Tom: No, I just do. It's like. . . .

Mike: Are you distressed?

Tom: It's like my head hurts.

Mike: Okay. Tell me how you feel about King Arthur.

Tom: That's why I'm here.

Mike: Why?

Tom: Because of him.

Mike: Go ahead and say it. It's kind of painful, isn't it?

Tom: Yes.

Mike: That's okay. That's why we are here today. To get this emotion out. It's really okay.

Tom: Arthur's trying. We're trying. We're all trying.

Mike: Okay. What do you think about Merlin?

Tom: (Laughs.) He's . . . funny!

Mike: Do you like Merlin?

Tom: Yes!

Mike: Do you love him?

Tom: Oh yeah!

Mike: Does he love you?

Tom: I hope so!

Mike: What do you think about the Queen?

Tom: . . . It's Arthur.

Mike: What?

Tom: It's Arthur I care about.

Mike: Okay. You don't want to talk about the Queen?

Tom: I don't know. I don't want to say anything.

Mike: How about Morgana? Tell me about Morgana.

Tom: Black hair is all I see.

Mike: Do you love her?

Tom: . . . No. But I like her better than the Queen.

Mike: You love her better than the Queen?

Tom: I like her better than the Queen.

Mike: Yeah. Morgana's a really nice person, isn't she? Tell me, what do you think about Lancelot?

Tom: He's clever. He's smart. He knows.

Mike: Knows what?

Tom: Knows things.

Mike: And who are you?

Tom: (No response.)

Mike: It still hasn't come to you?

Tom: . . . There's a shield. It's supposed to be mine.

Mike: What's your favorite weapon, to fight with?

Tom: I don't like to fight!

Mike: But you are good, aren't you?

Tom: But I don't like to.

Mike: Can you take me. . . .

Tom: My arms are very strong. I . . . I don't like to fight, but I have to.

Mike: Can you take me on one of your battles? Pick a battle out, and take me there and tell me what happens. Tell me about it.

Tom: People are being hurt! (Big sigh.) I'm on my horse. They're on the ground. I see a small house. A woman. A child. They can't do that! I won't let them do that!

Mike: They're doing something to this woman and child in the small house?

Tom: They're killing them!

Mike: They're killing them? Who's doing it?

Tom: A man. He's got a. . . . (Starts breathing heavily.) He's got a pointed hat.

Mike: So what happens?

Tom: I'm getting closer. I . . . I have a sword. A long sword. And I hit him, and he falls.

Mike: Where did you hit him?

Tom: Across the neck. She's okay. And . . . the boy's okay.

Mike: Okay.

Tom: My horse . . . steps on him. He's dead.

Mike: So it's Lancelot to the rescue? (Author's comment: I kind of trick Tom by mentioning the name Lancelot to him.)

Tom: They're running.

Mike: The rest of them are running?

Tom: They don't want to . . . (panting) . . . they don't want to fight me. They don't want to fight me. No one else wants to fight.

Mike: How many of them are there?

Tom: There's two or three more. They're gone. This sword is heavy. (Still panting.)

Mike: Was this a peasant's house?

Tom: Yes, it's just a hut.

Mike: And you just happened to be going by?

Tom: Yeah. I was by myself. She's okay, though. And he's okay.

Mike: Is this the kind of thing Lancelot does all the time?

Tom: I don't like to fight. I don't want to see people hurt!

Mike: But it has to be done, doesn't it?

Tom: Yeah.

Mike: How's your relationship with the King these days?

Tom: It's good. He knows I go out. . . . (Still panting.)

Mike: You really got into that fight, didn't you?

Tom: Yeah.

Mike: Do you need a minute to catch your breath?

Tom: Yeah. I'll walk with my horse for a while. . . .

Mike: . . . Is it okay if I start talking to you now?

Tom: Yeah.

Mike: Okay. Why do you suppose you were dizzy when you were in the Great Hall? Is there something going on there that makes you uncomfortable?

Tom: My head hurt.

Mike: Is it that . . . the people in the Great Hall are talking about you? About how you dishonored Arthur, and yourself? How do you feel when I say that?

Tom: I'm not sure.

Mike: Okay. . . . So it's embarrassing for you to go into the Great Hall now. Where everybody's having their meals. Because you know that everybody knows. Is that why you feel uncomfortable there?

Tom: No. . . .

Mike: Guenivere spends part of her afternoon sitting on a stone bench out in her garden. Do you know the one I am talking about?

Tom: Yeah.

Mike: Why don't you go out there? She's sitting out there now. Why don't you go out and talk to her. . . . How does she react when she sees you?

Tom: She says I shouldn't be here.

Mike: Uhhuh.

Tom: She's getting up and going away.

Mike: Why do you suppose she is doing that?

Tom: I don't know.

Mike: Go ahead and sit down on the bench. There is someone else who wants to talk to you. Guenivere has left now, hasn't she?

Tom: Yeah, she's gone.

Mike: Are you seated on the bench?

Tom: Yeah.

Mike: To your left, if you'll look up, you'll see a man in a white robe coming.

Tom: It's Merlin.

Mike: Okay.

Tom: He's sitting next to me.

Mike: Okay. What is he saying to you?

Tom: (No response.)

Mike: Can I tell you what he says?

Tom: Yeah.

Mike: Okay. He puts his arm around your shoulder, and he says to you that he has enjoyed his relationship with you. As counter forces. And he says that you, the great warrior, took all those young men, inspiring them on the practice fields to acts of greatness in battle. And then he, catching them on the rebound, had to quiet them down and get them to go into their spiritual side. He smiles and says that sometimes you created quite a job for him, because of the great work that you did on the practice field. And the balancing act that the two of you have done has created warriors of great balance. Spiritual and martial balance. And he says he loves you as if you were his son. He's never told you this before. He says if anything, everybody thought there was a rivalry between the two of you, and he enjoyed keeping that feeling alive, because it was good for the movement.

But the two of you are here now, alone, as friends, and he can tell you that he loves you as his son. And he says he has great responsibility, and it's not always a good responsibility. There's a lot of sadness, because he is in charge of Camelot. Of seeing it through to the end. And he says Camelot is a reflection of the world. It can't be good all the time. And it has its own destiny and its own life. And he says that within the greatness of Camelot were sown the seeds of its eventual destruction.

He has wept many times in his chambers . . . for his other beloved son, Arthur. And he looks back at the hours, and the days, and the months, and the years he spent training Arthur. Pouring his heart and soul into Arthur, so Arthur would become like him. But he smiles and says it's part of God's . . . humor, he believes, that every father who does that is destined for disappointment. Because we cannot pass on our greatness to our children. It's something they have to earn. He says that he has learned this, just as every other father on the earth has learned it. Because Arthur truly was his son. And he says, Arthur has failed him, and has failed Camelot. And because so many people around Arthur love Arthur so deeply, they are blind . . . to see any fault in Arthur. And they are hurting themselves very deeply by taking on the guilt for those failures which are occurring now at Camelot.

He says that everything was very predictable when Arthur started to fail . . . his ideals. When Arthur began to become a womanizer, began to betray Guenivere. When he began to ignore the Queen, and basically abandoned her. Then a temptation for you and Guenivere was set up which was completely irresistible. And he views your love and infatuation for the Queen as an extension of your love for Arthur. He views it as an act of beauty. And an act of pure love. What he has to tell you right now is that . . . you are to forgive yourself. Because you did not betray Arthur. Arthur betrayed Arthur. In doing so, he betrayed every one of the knights. And so this guilt that you carry in your breast . . . is to be released. It's not necessary. . . .

Tom: What will happen?

Mike: Merlin says, "What will happen is what is supposed to happen."

Tom: What will I do?

Mike: Merlin says, "You just keep being Lancelot. You just keep being the life of the party. You keep being the great fighter. The great leader of the younger knights. The great warrior. And you leave the rest to Merlin and God. They will take care of everything." And he wants to see you start smiling again.

Tom: It's hard. . . .

354

Mike: It's okay. Think of his love. And think of his training that he gave you. Think of your spiritual side. Think of your heart. Think of your connection to God. Everything will be okay. You have not disgraced anybody.

Tom: (Huge forceful sigh.)

Mike: The people you think that are jeering at you . . . are suffering a great agony. And he says, "At this moment as we speak, Percival cries for you. Loves you so much he wished he could spare you this. They all do. Because see, it's not just Arthur's dream. It's your dream. And Gawaine's dream. And Merlin's dream. Everyone's dream. You all created it. Arthur couldn't have done it without you."

Tom: I'm scared. . . .

Mike: It's okay.

Tom: That it won't go on.

Mike: But it will go on forever.

Tom: (Big sigh.)

Mike: The lady and the little boy that you saved. . . .

Tom: Yeah. . . .

Mike: It's in their hearts forever. The men you fought. It's in their hearts forever. What you've done. And they will be better people in all the other lifetimes to come because of what you did. What they saw you do. You have affected tens of thousands of people.

Tom: (Deep sighs.)

Mike: And he says . . . Merlin whispers close to you so nobody will hear . . . he says, "You truly are Jesus' brother. And in your way, you are doing everything you can to be just like him." And he knows it. And Jesus knows it. And it's all okay. You've been magnificent. You'll always be brave Lancelot.

Tom: (Deep labored breaths.) I have to go!

Mike: Where do you want to go?

Tom: I don't know, but I have to go.

Mike: Okay.

Tom: I have to ride.

Mike: Okay. Which horse are you going to ride?

Tom: Mine. My horse.

Mike: Which one? What color is your horse?

Tom: It's white. (Still labored breathing.) Goodbye.

Mike: What?

Tom: Goodbye!

Mike: Okay. But . . . you got Merlin's message?

Tom: Yeah.

Mike: Everything's okay?

Tom: Yeah. But I have got to go.

Mike: You're the great Lancelot. You did a great job! Everybody loves you, Lancelot. What happened to you was very unfair. Unfair for you. You were a victim. It's okay! It's only because of your great capacity for love that you couldn't . . . you couldn't sit by . . . and watch the Queen suffer the way she was. You were just being the great Lancelot. It's okay. Everybody understands. And someday Arthur will understand. It's okay. There's nothing to be forgiven. Everything is okay. You are the only one who has to accept that now. Can you accept that?

Tom: Yeah.

Mike: Really accept that?

Tom: Yeah!

Mike: You're the great Lancelot?

Tom: (Still deeply breathing.)

Mike: You're the great Lancelot?

Tom: Yeah.

Mike: Everybody loves you. Say it. Everybody loves me.

Tom: Ohhhh. . . .

Mike: Say it!

Tom: Everybody . . . loves me.

Mike: Yes! Say Jesus loves me.

Tom: Jesus loves me.

Mike: Jesus is proud of me.

Tom: Jesus is proud of me.

Mike: I've done good work.

Tom: I've done good . . . work.

Mike: I'm proud of myself.

Tom: (No response.)

Mike: I'm proud of myself. . . .

Tom: (Deep labored breathing.) Ooofff. . . . (Tom, unable to say it, pops out of the trance.)

32

About Time

I experienced things about time during the regressions which I could not explain. For instance, during the regression of the knight Frederick, there was a point where I asked Frederick to go to Merlin and ask Merlin some questions. Frederick asked Merlin the questions. Merlin then proceeded to answer my questions, and Frederick relayed his answers to me. The direct and enlightening answers almost startled me, and left no doubt in my mind as to their authenticity. In effect, Mike Miller in the year 1997 was talking to the Great Wizard Merlin in the year 500-something. This kind of thing happened with regularity, and I began to sense that it is possible to bridge the time barrier. How do I explain this to the reader?

An explanation came to me when I attended the Global Sciences Congress annual Florida seminar in 1997. Global Sciences is an enlightening event which is held at several points around the USA each year. At this three-day event, speakers from a far ranging spectrum of interests bombard us with the latest in technology, spirituality, political awareness, etc. During the 1997 session, a survivor of the Philadelphia Experiment spoke to us.

A brief background sketch of the Philadelphia Experiment is that at the beginning of the Second World War, Nikola Tesla was hired by the US Navy to develop a way to make ships invisible to the enemy. This was a highly classified secret program. For those of you who are not aware of the fascinating scientist and inventor Nikola Tesla, he is credited with inventing many of the developments in technology which we take for granted today, such as alternate-current electricity and 3-phase electrical motors. Tesla took a new Navy destroyer, the USS Eldridge, and rigged it as a floating experiment. He placed large generators in the interior of the ship. He then wrapped large-diameter electrical cables around the hull of the ship, in effect making the Eldridge a large electrical coil. When electricity is run through the wires of a coil, an electrical field is created inside of the coil. This is how an electrical magnet works. His idea was apparently that when the generators aboard the ship energized the wires which surrounded the Eldridge, the electrical field which was created would make the ship invisible.

So far, so good. The US was at war. It was 1943. Great pressure was placed upon Tesla and his program to speed up the development of this secret weapon. Time schedules were forced upon Tesla which he could not tolerate. The plan was for a fully manned Eldridge to be used in the experiment. Tesla, without success, warned the Navy that it was too dangerous for the men who would be aboard the ship to proceed with a full scale test, and that more time was needed to perfect his invention. When he was directed to proceed anyway, Tesla resigned in protest. The experiment proceeded without him, with the people who had been under his direction now in charge of the program.

Tesla was right. His experiment did work. The destroyer was in the harbor in Philadelphia, closely monitored and observed by scientists and Navy officials in nearby ships. When the generators aboard the Eldridge were energized, the ship began to hum. Then as the generators were turned up to generate a higher voltage and electrical current, the ship began to glow. Then a haze formed around the ship and it disappeared.

What had happened? Tesla had proven that the time dimension you are in can be changed by changing your frequency. By placing the USS Eldridge within a large electrical field, and then increasing the electrical field, he had increased the frequencies of every cell and molecule in the ship, and the men aboard the ship. They had then "disappeared" from the present time dimension.

What Tesla had tried to warn the Navy about was that he knew how to make this happen, but he did not yet know how to control it. Thus the Eldridge, and the 140 men aboard her, went on an uncontrolled journey. At first they were projected to the year 3543 (showing up at Niagara Falls, N.Y.) Then as the frequency aboard the Eldridge changed, they were projected backwards, appearing at Salt Lake, Utah in 2043; Imperial Reservoir, California in 2005; Sebago Lake, Maine in 1997; Lake Mead, Nevada in 1983; and so on until eventually they returned to the Philadelphia Naval Harbor in 1943.

Most information about the Philadelphia Experiment remains highly classified. But the story has surfaced. A movie was made about it. Survivors who are now able to speak about it tell a fascinating story. The uncontrolled aspect of the experiment did prove to be dangerous for the crew of the ship. Most perished as a result of damages incurred in the dematerialization and rematerialization process. The survivors spent many years institutionalized as a result of their journey.

What did listening to this speaker tell about the Philadelphia Experiment do for me? Well, he explained to me that it is a difference in frequency which separates one time dimension from another time dimension. When Mike Miller, sitting in his study in Orlando, Florida, in 1997, wishes to speak to Merlin as he sits in the Great Hall at Camelot in the year 525, all Mike Miller has to do is adjust frequencies so that the time difference (barrier) is eliminated. How do I do that? I am not sure. But apparently our minds have the power to do this, especially when in the light trance state of a past-life regression. I believe that this is the truth that I stumbled onto while conducting these regressions.

It has led me to realize and accept that we can, using the awesome power of our minds, transcend time. Thus, I am able, at times, to be in both worlds; Camelot and now. And it is fascinating. I do it. You can do it. Try it, you'll like it.

33

Dana as Lancelot
February, 1997

Background: I met Dana one Saturday evening at a party. She was 40-years-old, and had just arrived in town from Alaska. She was a very spiritually tuned person. So it didn't take us long to discover a Camelot connection. She was still grieving from a recent divorce after 22 years of marriage. Her natural buoyancy and energy did not quite hide the sadness she carried within. I assumed that this sadness related to the divorce. However, as we found out, this sadness went back a lot further. . . .

Mike: Let's go through the door back to the time of Camelot. You step through the door. If it's all right with you, I'm going to follow along. And as you step through the door, tell me what you experience.
Dana: It's dark.
Mike: Okay. See any light at all?
Dana: It's a tunnel. Wait. There's a light in the distance.
Mike: There is light at the end of the tunnel?
Dana: Yeah.
Mike: Okay. I'm going to put my hand on your shoulder so we don't get separated in the darkness, and I'm going to follow you. Please lead me to that light. And tell me what you experience when you walk out of the tunnel. Where are we?
Dana: It's really bright. It's hard for me to see. We're outdoors. We're outside.
Mike: Yeah, we've come out in the woods. It is pretty in the woods, isn't it?
Dana: It's beautiful.
Mike: Is there a path right there in front of us?
Dana: Yeah.

Mike: What are we going to do now?

Dana: Let's take the path.

Mike: Okay.

Dana: I feel really nervous. Like I haven't been here in a really long time.

Mike: You haven't. Want me to lead the way?

Dana: Yeah. (Several big sighs, begins softly crying.)

Mike: There you go. We follow the path. We come to this little clearing, and there is a cabin there. Do you recognize that cabin?

Dana: Yeah.

Mike: Is that where you grew up?

Dana: I'm not sure.

Mike: Who's that old lady sitting in front of the cabin?

Dana: My mother.

Mike: All right. Before we go over and talk to her, I want you to take your right hand and reach around your waist and tell me what you're wearing for a belt.

Dana: There's a big buckle.

Mike: Okay. Follow the belt around. Is there a sword on the end of that belt?

Dana: Yeah. It's heavy.

Mike: So does that mean you're a man?

Dana: Yes.

Mike: Reach down around your legs and tell me what you're wearing.

Dana: Leggings. Very smooth ones.

Mike: Reach up around your chest and tell me what you're wearing.

Dana: Chain mail.

Mike: How about on your head? Reach up to your head and tell me what you're wearing.

Dana: Nothing.

Mike: Okay. Now let's go up to this old lady sitting in front of the cabin, and you talk to her.

Dana: She is my mother.

Mike: Yes.

Dana: She's very old.

Mike: Yes. She looks up. Does she recognize you?

Dana: Yes.

Mike: What does she do?

Dana: She cries.

Mike: Have you been gone a long time?

Dana: A very long time. (Crying.)

Mike: So let's explain to her what you've been up to, and why you went away. You tell her whatever your heart tells you to tell her.

Dana: I love her very much, and I didn't want to be away so long. But I had work to do. And I missed her very much. Now my work is done. And the dream is over.

Mike: What did she say?

Dana: She's just crying and holding me. She's glad I'm home.

Mike: She's been waiting a long time, hasn't she?

Dana: Yeah. She thought I wasn't coming back.

Mike: Did she know where you had gone?

Dana: She had an idea, but she didn't know for sure. I couldn't tell her.

Mike: Ahhh. . . . What country are we in?

Dana: France.

Mike: And who are you?

Dana: (Crying.) Lancelot.

Mike: Okay. She's been waiting for you so she could cross over.

Dana: I know. She's very old, and she's very tired.

Mike: So, I'd like for you to turn around, and look. . . . There's somebody standing behind you, watching both of you.

Dana: It's Percival! (Still crying.)

Mike: Okay. He says to you, "Permit me to escort your mother up so she can join us, and I'll take her to Jesus. I'll do that for you so you can take Mike back . . . back and show him Camelot."

Dana: It's hard for me to leave her again.

Mike: Oh, you'll be with her. You see, you and Percival have already crossed over, so you're taking her up to join you.

Dana: Okay. . . . (Stops crying.)

Mike: Now. Are you comfortable with the idea that you've just crossed over?

Dana: Yeah. That's right. It feels right.

Mike: Okay, let's go back to. . . . Let's go back to your death. If we could do that without too much discomfort for you. And tell me what is going on.

Dana: I feel really peaceful.

Mike: Before your death, how did you die?

Dana: I'm not sure.

Mike: Are you holding someone in your lap?

Dana: A little boy.

Mike: Hmmmm. . . . Do you love this person? How do you feel about this person that you're holding in your lap?

Dana: Love.

Mike: How would you describe your love for this person?

Dana: Complete.

Mike: Why are you holding this person in your lap?

Dana: Because I'm dying.

Mike: Is he dying?

Dana: I don't think so.

Mike: He's a grown man, isn't he? Is there a grown man in your lap? You have got his head in your lap.

Dana: It's confusing. It's hard to see.

Mike: Is there a lot of noise around you? As you're holding the man's head in your lap?

Dana: I can't hear any of it. There's a lot of noise and there's a lot of activity, but I feel like time is standing still. (Begins to cry.)

Mike: Yes. . . . Could it be a battle?

Dana: Yes. (Sobbing.)

Mike: What kind of battle is this?

Dana: It's hard for me to see because it's swirling around me.

Mike: All right. Who's that on your lap?

Dana: Arthur.

Mike: Yes. He is dying, isn't he?

Dana: Yeah.

Mike: What happened to Arthur?

Dana: He was stabbed.

Mike: So if there's a big battle going on, why are you holding Arthur? You're a knight. Why aren't you up there fighting?

Dana: (Crying, barely able to speak.) It doesn't matter anymore.

Mike: It doesn't matter anymore. That's what you said. Would you rather be there and die with Arthur, than to fight?

Dana: Yes.

Mike: Why?

Dana: Because it's over now. Our work is finished.

Mike: Arthur's not dead yet. Is there anything you want to tell him?

Dana: (Sobbing, unable to speak.)

Mike: Tell him you're sorry. Say, I'm sorry.

Dana: I'm sorry, Arthur.

Mike: I'm sorry I hurt you.

Dana: I'm sorry that I hurt you.

Mike: I didn't mean to.

Dana: I never meant to.

Mike: I love you so much.

Dana: I love you so much.

Mike: Please forgive me.

Dana: Please forgive me.

Mike: It feels good to say that, doesn't it?

Dana: Yes!

Mike: Something in your chest just left. A cloud of darkness around your heart is gone.

Dana: Yes. . . .

Mike: Your grief is why it was there. It's gone now, isn't it?

Dana: Yes. (Quieting down.)

Mike: Jesus has come down to reclaim Arthur. He's standing beside you, very gently waiting. I suggest we . . . let him take Arthur with him, up to the Light. And, if it's all right with you, let's go back to the castle. I'd like for you to say goodbye to Guenivere.

Dana: Okay.

Mike: Where are we?

Dana: Outside in the meadow.

Mike: Okay. Is she there?

Dana: Yes.

Mike: How is she dressed?

Dana: (Sobbing.)

Mike: You don't have to hold back the emotions, you know. It's okay. That's why we're doing this, to release those emotions. Release all that sadness.

Dana: (Stops sobbing.) I can't see how she's dressed. I can only see her face.

Mike: Tell me what her face looks like.

Dana: She's beautiful. She has beautiful blue eyes, and she's so sad.

Mike: Why is she sad?

Dana: Because of me. . . . (Starts sobbing again.)

Mike: So let's talk to her. What would you like to tell her?

Dana: I'm so sorry. I never meant to hurt you. I only meant to love. In the best way I knew how. Please forgive me.

Mike: And what does she say? She's crying, isn't she?

Dana: Yes. She said she already forgave me.

Mike: I heard her saying something about she'll love you forever.

Dana: I hear her.

Mike: Do you want to tell her you'll love her forever?

Dana: I can't.

Mike: You can't tell her? How come?

Dana: I can't make that much of a commitment.

Mike: That's all right. (Joking.) You are Lancelot!

Dana: I can tell her I'll love her for always.

Mike: All right. I would appreciate it if you would also tell her that what is happening is okay. That it is time for Camelot to be over.

Dana: It's hard for her to understand that.

Mike: Well, it's hard for all of us to understand that. But tell her that God's wisdom is greater than ours, and we must trust our God and our Jesus.

Dana: It's all part of the plan.

Mike: Yes.

Dana: This is the perfect . . . ending. Not what we expected, but the perfect ending.

Mike: Are you finished saying goodbye to her?

Dana: I want to tell her that I'll be with her again, and that we'll then never be separate. (Deep sigh.)

Mike: Now would you be interested in going to see Morgana?

Dana: Yeah, we can do that. (Huge sighs, repeated over and over.)

Mike: Let's go see Morgana.

Dana: We're inside. We're in a room with stone walls. Fireplace. She's beautiful.

Mike: Yes. What color hair does she have?

Dana: Black.

Mike: Is she on the Isle of Avalon?

Dana: No, she has come to see me. She has come to say goodbye.

Mike: What would you like to tell her?

Dana: That I did love her.

Mike: How does she react to that?

Dana: It is what she has waited to hear.

Mike: Anything else you want to tell her?

Dana: I'm sorry if I hurt her. I had to do what I had to do. It seems I say that to everybody.

Mike: It's all right. Tell her that you also paid the price.

Dana: Yeah, I did.

Mike: Paid the price.

Dana: I think she understands. She can't say that she forgives me, but I think she understands.

Mike: How did you hurt Morgana?

Dana: I loved her.

Mike: She loved you?

Dana: And I couldn't be with her . . . but I did love her.

Mike: Did you and Morgana ever have any children?

Dana: Yes.

Mike: How many?

Dana: Three.

Mike: Okay. Would you like to go say goodbye to them?

Dana: I didn't see them very much. I don't think they know who I am.

Mike: We don't have to if you don't want to.

Dana: No . . . it's okay.

Mike: Isn't one of them named Elena?

Dana: She is . . . the oldest?

Mike: I think so.

Dana: Yeah.

Mike: Let's go see her first.

Dana: She's mad at me . . . for leaving her, for not being there.

Mike: Where is she living? Where do you find her?

Dana: She's in a castle. Somebody else is raising her.

365

Mike: So how do you know that she is mad at you? Does she throw something at you?

Dana: No. She's very cold. But I can feel that she loves me.

Mike: Sure. So let's talk to her.

Dana: She doesn't want to talk to me.

Mike: You talk to her. Believe me, she'll listen.

Dana: I love you very much, and I'm very sorry that I wasn't around as you were growing up. You're a beautiful woman, and I'm very proud of you. And I ask you to forgive me, and understand me. (Crying.) She's crying.

Mike: This is very important for her. That's all right. It is much more complete now.

Dana: She's been waiting a long time for me to say this.

Mike: Why don't you also, if this feels right, tell her that you know you've hurt her, but you also hurt yourself.

Dana: I know I hurt you, but I also hurt myself. And it hurt me more not to be with you.

Mike: And I see what I've missed.

Dana: And I see what I've missed. . . . She says she loves me. She'll be okay now. There is a little boy, with long curly hair. He pretends he doesn't recognize me. He's polite. He's got a toy sword belted around his waist. He wants to be a knight. It's okay. He comes to me now and lets me hold him. I want to tell him that I love him very much, and I'm so proud of him. He's been like a little protector for his mom and his sister. It's okay. He's okay. . . . I feel like there is a baby, too. Still in a cradle. A little girl with dark, dark hair.

Mike: Pick her up and kiss her.

Dana: I'm almost afraid to. Morgana is here. It's almost like, I'm afraid she doesn't want me to.

Mike: Oh . . . but the baby needs to touch you.

Dana: Yeah.

Mike: Go ahead and touch her.

Dana: Oh, she's beautiful. . . . (Crying.) She smiles at me. She knows me. . . . Morgana picks her up, and puts her in my arms. I love these children. It's been really hard for me to be away from them. But I think we all understand now. I feel like they need to go.

Mike: Okay. Say goodbye. Let's go somewhere else. Where would you like to take me now?

Dana: The stables. I want to see my horse.

Mike: Yes, I've heard about this horse.

Dana: (Crying.)

Mike: What's your horse's name?

Dana: I'm not remembering.

Mike: What does it look like?

Dana: He's huge. Huge! Black. Beautiful. Very regal, very proud. He loves me as much as I love him. We're the same. I've never been able to relate much to people, but I can relate to this horse.

Mike: They told me that you guided your horse in battle with your knees. That you didn't even have to touch his reins.

Dana: He's very, very perceptive. We're one. We are one.

Mike: Yes.

Dana: We move as one. (Big sighs.) There are no edges. It's like, I can't tell where I end and he begins. It's funny that I could never experience this with any human. I experience it with my horse, the oneness. It's because he's not threatening. Wow. I know he can't hurt me and I know he won't hurt me. And I can be open with him, and he trusts me just as much. (Crying.) I feel like we're not going to say goodbye. I feel like we're both going to the same place. He's so beautiful. I want to ride.

Mike: Okay.

Dana: You can come with me, but I don't know if you can keep up.

Mike: I'll just wait here.

Dana: (Big sighs.) It's so fast and free. I've never felt so much freedom as when I'm riding. I want to be this free all the time. Feel this joy. . . . (Laughing.) We ran a couple of circles around you just to tease you. Okay, thanks. I'm standing beside my horse now, and I'm looking at you. Okay, where do you want to go now?

Mike: Well, I was going to ask you that, but don't you want to say goodbye to Merlin?

Dana: Oh, Merlin scares me a little.

Mike: Why is that? Because he knows?

Dana: Because Merlin knows.

Mike: Yes. So let's go down there and fess up, since he knows anyway.

Dana: Yeah. It's time, isn't it?

Mike: Where are we going to go to see him?

Dana: I'm thinking he's in the cave. He's doing his thing. He's got things boiling, and. . . .

Mike: Is that his cave, or his chambers?

Dana: Ahhh . . . feels like a cave.

Mike: Okay.

Dana: Yeah, I have to go in the mountain to see him. This is a secret, a secret cave. Very few people know where it is. The hillside is very green. It is very overgrown on the side of the hill. There is moss all around, and you can hardly see the entrance. Oh . . . he knew I was coming. He does know everything. . . . I'm a little nervous.

Mike: That's okay. He trusts me. That's a joke!

Dana: (Laughs.)

Mike: Want me to go get him?

Dana: No, that's okay. He's doing his thing. He knows I'm here. He's just . . . doing his thing, while waiting for me. I have to come to him. I have to walk in by myself. (Big sigh.)

Mike: Is he talking to you?

Dana: No. Not yet.

Mike: I can't see his face, can you?

Dana: No.

Mike: Okay. He's talking to me. Can I tell you what he's saying?

Dana: Yeah.

Mike: He says, "It's okay. I knew that you were coming." And he says, "As you know, I know everything. I even know who you really are."

Dana: Ohhhh. That's a scary thought.

Mike: And he says, "The joke is on you." He says, "You were always nervous about me because you didn't know who you are. But I know who you are, and I know why you're so special." . . . He has got a twinkle in his eye.

Dana: (Big sigh.)

Mike: And he says, "I also know that everything is okay. As a matter of fact, I've got a secret for you. My boss isn't Arthur. My boss is Jesus." And he says, "Jesus and I have known all along that this is the way it was supposed to end. So," he says, "you thought I was angry at you, didn't you?"

Dana: Yeah.

Mike: "I wasn't." He says, "That has been my joke on you, because you didn't come see me and talk about it." He says, "I might even have told you who you were, and why you were in this predicament. But," he says, "I'll tell you this. Everything is okay. And everything is as it should be."

Dana: You still aren't going to tell me who I am?

Mike: Merlin says, "Well, I'll tell you this much. What you did with the Queen was okay."

Dana: (Sobbing.)

Mike: "Because," he says, "I know the love bond between you two is so strong that you could not watch her suffer without trying to rescue her." He says, "You know that is what you were doing. I think maybe you thought you were punishing Arthur a little bit for not appreciating her enough." He says, "That is what you were thinking, wasn't it?"

Dana: Yes, sometimes.

Mike: "But," he says, "not really. You really were trying to rescue your queen." He says, "This isn't the first time you have seen her suffer . . . and you couldn't let her suffer again."

Dana: I could never let her suffer.

Mike: He says, "After all, it's really quite simple. Weren't you trying to be her knight in shining armor? Maybe you were."

Dana: I'm confused.

Mike: So. . . .

Dana: I feel like you're teasing me.

Mike: Merlin says, "Oh, but I always do. Besides," he says, "I'm teasing you because you never came to see me and talk about this. Until now," he says. "Do you think I'm going to make it easy?"

Dana: I feel like I've always been so serious.

Mike: He says, "I thought it was scared. Of me."

Dana: I didn't know if I was ready to hear what you had to say.

Mike: Merlin says, "So ask away now."

Dana: I'm ready now, Merlin. Please talk to me.

Mike: Merlin says, "Ask me. What questions do you have for me?"

Dana: Who am I really?

Mike: Merlin says, "My son."

Dana: Ahhhh. . . . (Sobbing, barely speaking.) I knew. I knew. Somewhere in my heart, I knew. And I've been struggling with that part of me for a long, long time.

Mike: He says, "Remember those early battles when I used to go along on a horse, and carry a sword?" He says, "Did you notice that I was pretty good with a sword?"

Dana: I was very impressed.

Mike: He says, "Yes. So, kind of . . . like father, like son. I was impressed too. And very proud of you. As a matter of fact, I've always been very proud of you." He says, "Even when people came to me in my chamber here, asking me to do things to you. I always smiled, because I knew I was very proud of you, and that I understood."

Dana: So what I'm hearing is that I am both magician and warrior.

Mike: Merlin says, "Oh yeah."

Dana: And I fought being the magician for so long.

Mike: "Yes. Kind of out of balance, actually."

Dana: (Crying.) Kind of way out of balance.

Mike: Yes. But he says, "You are one hell of a warrior. Imagine what it would have been like if you had been a magician too. We could have just sent all of those other knights home."

Dana: (Laughing.) . . . Can I do it now?

Mike: Merlin says, "Well, time is a funny thing. Yes . . . but it might not be now. It might be at the next Camelot. And," he says, "the interesting thing, my son, is that our work is not over. And . . . Camelot is not over. We have a lot more work to do, and we will do great works together again. And, Lancelot will ride again. And, I'll sprinkle some of my magic dust, and when he makes his great ride next time, he'll be, you'll be, on the same horse."

Dana: Yes, thank you. . . . I feel like a piece of my heart has been put back in place. Thank you.

Mike: "Ahhhh," he says, "I guess there's more of the puzzle I may as well explain." He says, "About Guenivere. Many of you knights were frustrated by the fact that Guenivere brought this guy Jesus in and crammed him down everyone's throat. How did you feel about this? When Christianity was kind of forced on everyone?"

Dana: I loved Jesus, I always have. But I didn't want to see the old ways totally wiped out.

Mike: Merlin says, "Yes, so your loyalties were divided?"

Dana: I thought they should be blended.

Mike: "Well . . . let's talk about how you love Jesus. And let's talk about how Jesus loves you. A long time ago, in another part of the world, when Jesus was a young man on this earth, he had a brother. This brother loved him very much. Do you know who that brother was?

Dana: Tell me.

Mike: Merlin says, "That brother was you. His name was Matthew. And that brother sacrificed greatly to help Jesus do his job."

Dana: (Crying.) It was great love. It was no great sacrifice.

Mike: "Jesus knows you feel that way, but he knows better. He knows that it was a great sacrifice. And so, when you came back this time as Lancelot, Jesus and I had this little understanding that we would make you invincible in battle. We were mirthful at times, that we had made you invincible. And sometimes we just pinched ourselves, and wished we hadn't done it."

Dana: Sometimes I wish you hadn't done it.

Mike: Merlin says, "That's why. Because by making you invincible, we created quite the knight. But, all joking aside, you were magnificent. And you were the inspiration the other knights needed. And, you see, some of the other knights, especially the younger ones, always thought that there was competition between you and me. They always thought you represented the warrior, and I represented the magician."

Dana: (Crying.)

Mike: "And I laughed, because I knew that within your heart you were a better magician that I was. You just chose not to honor it. Because you didn't understand. And I bit my tongue and bided my time. Because you had things to do, Lancelot. And it's all part of learning about love. And you need to understand about that little boy Matthew. In doing what had to be done to protect Jesus, Matthew left his mother when he was still a young man, and never saw her again. He suffered grievously for his mother for the rest of his life. Did he love his mother?"

Dana: (Crying.) Yes.

Mike: "Could you feel the love that he had for his mother?"

Dana: Yes. . . .

Mike: Merlin says, "Okay. That's part of our little joke on you. Because that little Matthew's mother came back to join us in this lifetime. And she's the Queen."

Dana: Guenivere?

Mike: "Yes. Now do you understand why you loved her so much?"

Dana: (Big sigh.) Yes. And why I protect her.

Mike: Merlin says, "Yes, and so how could you not love her when she needed love?"

Dana: It explains the purity of the love as well. But I also felt so guilty.

Mike: He says, "Yes . . . all because you didn't come and talk to me."

Dana: I can be pretty stupid sometimes. (Laughing.)

Mike: (Laughing.) Merlin says, "Not to worry, I wouldn't have told you anyway."

Dana: Pretty stubborn, huh?

Mike: Merlin says, "No, no. I wouldn't have told you anyway. I couldn't have told you. But I can tell you now. And we can joke about it. So you can now take all that guilt and toss it. And," he says, "my bosses, Jesus and God, tell me that our work is done. They tell me that we did our work magnificently, and it's now time for Camelot to go away. It would have been too easy to push a button and have us all vaporize. That's not the way to do it. So the forces were set in motion to bring Camelot to an end. But Camelot will never go away. We have done our work too well."

Dana: It will always be in our hearts.

Mike: Merlin says, "Yes, we've done our job."

Dana: It's in everyone's heart.

Mike: "Yes, and who's the greatest knight of them all?"

Dana: Lancelot!

Mike: "So, I'm pretty proud of you."

Dana: (Big sighs.)

Mike: "Can you be proud of him?"

Dana: That's a hard one.

Mike: Merlin says, "You'd better be. And I'll tell you what, it won't be too many more days til I will have another visitor; the Queen. And I can tell you that she and I will have a little talk, too. So you won't have to explain anything to her. She will understand. Arthur will have some people also explaining things to him where he is. So everything is all okay, isn't it?"

Dana: Yeah, it's all okay. All my guilt will now go away.

Mike: Merlin says, "Actually, now I'd like for you to visualize yourself up in heaven. You see, we've got a Great Hall up in the sky, ready for you all. And I'd like for you to see yourself up there, standing with your left hand around Guenivere, and your right hand around Arthur."

Dana: Yeah.

Mike: See that?

Dana: Yeah.

Mike: "Do Arthur or Guenivere have any problems with that?"

Dana: No.

Mike: "They both love you."

Dana: (Sobbing.)

Mike: Merlin says, "It's like, yeah . . . to me it kind of looks like the three musketeers together."

Dana: Yeah.

Mike: "A very happy scene to me. Actually, I hate to see them so happy up there while you are so unhappy down here."

Dana: I'm ready to be happy.

Mike: "And as far as this magician bit goes, I'll make sure you get plenty of chances to perfect that. I may even bring you back as a woman sometime; horror of horrors!"

Dana: (Laughing.)

Mike: "Of course, just so you will have to perfect the magician within you. Mystical power to the powerful warrior. And, then, when you have mastered both of these powers, we'll really get down to business."

Dana: Yeah, and we know who that woman is, don't we?

Mike: "Yes, yes. Old what's her name."

Dana: Yeah.

Mike: "Okay. So it's all pretty magnificent, isn't it?"

Dana: Yeah.

Mike: Merlin says, "Now, there's just one problem left. That darn Percival. He's so jealous of you. He's so jealous!"

Dana: Ohhh, he loves me.

Mike: "He loves you, but you got the Queen and he didn't. Boy, you're going to pay heck with Percival for that."

Dana: (Speaking directly to Mike.) You know what, Percival? You're going to get the Queen. She is really yours.

Mike: You trying to make me cry now?

Dana: Oh, wow. She is your true love.

Mike: "Well," Merlin says to you, "actually, I had all bases covered. Because Percival was there to give her a different type of love. The other kind of love she needed."

Dana: Yeah.

Mike: Merlin says, (jokingly), "Had Percival not, you two would have probably fought a duel a long time ago. And we wouldn't have wanted that. Although, there were times when I saw him reaching for his dagger. But, we constrained him."

Dana: We both just wanted to protect Guenivere.

Mike: Merlin says, "Oh no, I'm joking. He loved you so much."

Dana: I know, but there were times that we both just wanted to protect Guenivere, and if we perceived the other one hurting her in any way. . . .

Mike: "Oh yes." And he says, "Percival would have let his head be cut off for Arthur, and either arm. One arm for you and one arm for. . . ."

Dana: Guenivere.

Mike: "Guenivere. So, it's okay. It's okay. It balances out. Actually, we had a pretty neat plan, and I was privileged to know what was going on. So it was easier for me. How do you feel now?"

Dana: I feel very grateful that you told me all of this. Everything makes sense now.

Mike: Merlin says, "Well, now you know, the battle has been going on some time, and you know, we couldn't win that battle. It wasn't God's will for us to win it. So, the Great Hall up there in heaven is getting pretty filled up right now. As a matter of fact, I think they're having a big party. The ale is flowing. So unless there is someone else you'd like to visit, I think we ought to go up there and join the party."

Dana: Yes, I think that we ought to celebrate. It's about time.

Mike: He says, "Now, I am going to put on the disguise of a young knight, and I'm going to walk along behind you. Okay?"

Dana: Okay.

Mike: "So let's go up to the Great Hall. See the big doors? Push those doors open and walk in."

Dana: (Big, deep breath.) Wow. . . .

Mike: "Tell me what's happening."

Dana: It was real noisy, and everybody got quiet when we walked in.

Mike: "Yes. And they started cheering, didn't they?"

Dana: Yeah.

Mike: "Because they love you?"

Dana: Yeah.

Mike: "I disguised myself as a young knight because I wanted you to understand that they are cheering for you, not me."

Dana: Thank you.

Mike: "So you must have done something right."

Dana: (Laughs.)

Mike: "There's no reason to have any guilt, is there?"

Dana: Not anymore.

Mike: "Who's that coming up to kiss you? Isn't that Guenivere?"

Dana: It is Guenivere.

Mike: "And who's rushing up right behind her? Arthur?"

Dana: Arthur.

Mike: "So it's all pretty great."

Dana: Yeah.

Mike: "And who's that behind them? Percival!"

Dana: (Laughs.)

Mike: (Jokingly.) "My God, I think he's going to kiss you."

Dana: (Laughing.) Percival, cut it out.

Mike: (Laughing.) So, it's all okay, isn't it?

Dana: Yeah. It's all okay.

Mike: I'm going to leave you there with them. Because you know that you are always the life of the party. Even up here. Lancelot, always with his stories. And that merriment of yours, that friendship, that camaraderie. That is very real and that is very eternal. So we did our work well, didn't we?

Dana: Yeah.

Mike: It was a pretty darn good lifetime, actually. And a pretty darn good way to wrap it up.

Dana: And we'll all be back for a huge celebration. We're all coming back.

Mike: Yay.

Dana: We're all here again.

Mike: We'll be back until Camelot is here to last forever.

Dana: Yeah.

Mike: And then we'll be back for that Camelot too. But there will be no serfs and knights. We will all be knights. We'll all be knights.

Dana: Yeah. Everybody will be equal.

Mike: Yep.

Dana: And everybody will be joyous and happy.

Mike: Yes. Yes. So. . . .

Dana: Now I'm ready to come back. . . .

Mike: Okay. Come back anytime.

Dana: (Several deep breaths, laughs.)

Mike: That was good.

Dana: Yeah. I love you so.

Mike: I love you too. . . . Oh, that Merlin was cute. He was really clever.

Dana: I feel so alive. My whole body's itching and tingling. It's like. . . .

Mike: Your heart doesn't have that shield around it anymore.

Dana: Yeah, it's like the life has come back into it. It's incredibly wonderful. Thank you.

34

The Camelot Connection

It was Jesus himself who told me about the connection between many of the main characters in Camelot, and to his own lifetime here on earth. This information was very powerful. Also very intriguing. So, fascinated by this revelation, I set out to explore the connections. I regressed a number of the key Camelot players back to the time of Jesus. The connections are fascinating. Briefly, I ascertained that:

Merlin was Joseph
Guenivere was Mary
Arthur was the disciple John
Morgana was Jesus' sister Elizabeth
Gawaine was Jesus' brother David
Galahad was Jesus' brother Jacob
Lancelot was Jesus' brother Matthew
Percival was Jesus' brother James
Gaheris was John the Baptist
Tristram was the disciple Paul
Segwarides was the disciple Matthew
Mordred was Judas
Percival's mother was Jame's wife Sarah

In addition, Percival's wife Martha was the daughter of the Inn-keeper in Nazareth where Jesus was born. It was at her insistence that her father made room for Joseph and his family in the stables. Also, the youngest child in Jesus' family was Mary Martha, who came back as one of Percival's sisters. Jesus had an adopted sister, Ruth. Finding her as an abandoned orphan, he had brought her back from his pilgrimage to India. In Camelot, Ruth was the "Mother Priestess" at Avalon who raised Morgana. The page who rescued Excalibur at the last battle was the disciple Peter. The knight Pelleas was Elizabeth's husband, and

375

helped Elizabeth care for Mother Mary in her waning years. Sir Kay, the knight who raised Arthur, was the man known by Jesus as "Uncle." He was a lonely widower neighbor who spent much time helping Mary look after her young children. When Jesus was older, he took Jesus under his wing, caring for him on the caravan travels to Egypt and the Far East, during the "lost years" of Jesus. The knight Andred was a follower of Jesus, helping to establish the church after Jesus' death. He was one of the early Christians who went about bravely preaching the messages of Jesus, in the face of great danger from the Roman authorities. The knight Gringalin was a Roman soldier assigned the duty of guarding the body of Jesus at the tomb. He befriended Mary when she came to the tomb. Her anguish caused him to have tears in his eyes. Against orders, he let her into the tomb where she witnessed that Jesus had risen. The knight Pharien was the disciple Thomas. The knight LaVaine was the Roman Centurion in charge of the crucifixion of Jesus. He had great compassion for Jesus. He violated orders by giving Jesus a drink to ease his suffering. The vinegar-like substance he gave to Jesus was to numb the pain and to quench his thirst. He was in charge of removing the body from the cross, a job he conducted with reverence, treating Jesus' body with great respect. He was also very respectful toward the members of Jesus' family when they came to claim the body and take it for burial. He ignored orders to arrest all male members of Jesus' family when Jacob came with Mary and Elizabeth to claim the body.

Jesus' brother Jacob married a woman named Cora, who was cunning and deceitful. Her antics caused much distress for Mary and her family. After Jesus' death, the next oldest son, James, became the head of the family. Joseph had passed away years earlier. Cora became jealous and envious of the close relationship between James and his mother. Jacob was the next in line as head of the family, after James. Three years after Jesus' death, James was caught by the Romans while preaching in a mountain village. He was put to death. It was Cora who had told the Romans where and when the brother of Jesus would be found preaching the forbidden Christianity. So who was Cora at Camelot? Why the Red Bishop, of course! Cora was perfect for the role.

The Red Bishop had a younger assistant who participated with the Bishop in every step of the plot to overthrow King Arthur. During the time of Jesus, this man was a younger member of the Sanhedrin. Out of ambition and impatience for recognition, he was the one who agitated for, and promoted the execution of Jesus. Most of the leaders of the Sanhedrin (Jewish religious leaders) were elderly, wise, and not overly anxious to get involved in solving the "Jesus problem." Had this younger member of the Sanhedrin not agitated for the crucifixion of Jesus, it is unlikely that Jesus would have been put to death at that time.

One sunny afternoon in July of 1995, I was lounging in my backyard with my friend Jake and his wife. Jake is a Galahad, his wife is a Red Knight. (Definitely an interesting relationship, given the troubled relationship between Galahad and the Red Knight as revealed in the regressions; but that is another story.) We were casually visiting, and one thing led to another, and I regressed Jake back to the American Revolution. He told, very clearly and distinctly, how his printing shop in Philadelphia was used as a nighttime rendezvous spot for the patriots. He described the personalities of many of the key figures: (Patrick Henry was "a dangerous hothead.") He elaborated in great detail about the strategies of the early patriot movement. I was so fascinated that I almost failed to ask him who he was. As the regression was drawing to a close, I finally asked, "What is your name?" He replied, "Ben." I still didn't get it. After a half dozen more questions, I finally realized that I was talking to Benjamin Franklin! You could have knocked me over with a feather.

It made sense. Wouldn't Galahad, the most spiritual of all the knights, want to come back and help to rekindle the flame of Camelot? What about the others? I quickly grabbed (some refer to it as being "mugged") some other Camelot people and regressed them to the American Revolution. Wow. I found that it was another group reincarnation. Yep, they came back to do it again. The United States of America *is* the new Camelot! My discoveries:

Gawaine was George Washington
Gawaine's wife was Martha Washington
Lancelot was Paul Revere (who headed George Washington's spy network)
Percival was Thomas Jefferson
Guenivere was one of Thomas Jefferson's daughters
Percival's mother was Thomas Jefferson's wife
Mordred was Benedict Arnold (is there a pattern here, or what?)
The knight Frederick was Lafayette

Where was Merlin? "Ben Franklin" suggested to me that he was Thomas Brown, an apprentice printer who worked in Franklin's print shop. He stated that when the Declaration of Independence had been written in Philadelphia, everyone was afraid to sign it. Their signature on this document, so they feared, would bring death and confiscation of their property. Then an "unknown" man in the audience stood up, and made an impassioned speech. When he finished, one by one, the makers of the Declaration of Independence strode forth and signed it. According to "Ben", it was Thomas Brown who made the speech. Then he disappeared, to never be seen again.

This really gets intriguing when it was suggested that Thomas Brown was really Saint Germaine, visiting this new country incognito. Wasn't Saint Germaine the guy who lived for three or four hundred years? His life is well documented. Was it Merlin again, still using his youth potion? This guy Merlin really gets about. There is suspicion, if not belief, that he has incarnated as Nostradamus, Christopher Columbus, Sir Francis Bacon, as well as Saint Germaine.

When I saw the movie "Braveheart," I was deeply moved by the scenes in the battle lines, especially when the men stood in line, swords in hand, waiting for the battle to begin. I asked Merlin about the movie, and the effect it had on me, and he smiled. "Mel Gibson knows that he was William Wallace, and that is one of the reasons he made that movie," said Merlin. "But what Mel Gibson doesn't know is that William Wallace was a reincarnation of Lancelot. Guenivere was Wallace's wife, who was slain shortly after their marriage. The English princess who later became William Wallace's lover was Morgana. They were all trying to carry on their Camelot work." Then he continued with a smile, "Mel Gibson carries much of Lancelot's charm and presence. Is it any wonder that Lancelot was so popular with the ladies, as well as with the other knights?"

My main focus in this book has been to get the Camelot story out to you. But here and there, intriguing bits of information popped up. I did not have the time to be able to delve in any depth into these issues, but here are a few of the other fascinating tidbits of information that have surfaced:

John F. Kennedy was an Arthur
Bobby Kennedy was a Morgana
John F. Kennedy, Jr. is a Guenivere
Princess Diana was a Guenivere
Princess Diana's son Harry is an Arthur
John F. Kennedy Jr.'s wife is an Arthur

I have been told that Benjamin Franklin went to his grave deeply resentful towards the American people for not making him president. Our president Bill Clinton represents this segment of the Benjamin Franklin soul-energy. Buried within Bill Clinton is this old resentment from this past lifetime. At a subconscious level, he dislikes the American people. Thus possibly one reason for his many shenanigans. But the presidential experience has caused him such enlightenment, that he truly wishes now to become a good leader. He will defy the financial powers which rule the world, at much sacrifice to himself. Merlin says that it is all part of the plan.

Merlin may be toying with me on this one. But I choose to believe it. And I pass it along to you. He says that when John F. Kennedy, Jr. is in his late thirties or early forties, he will become President of the United States. So we will once again have Arthur and Guenivere leading us. But this time it is reversed. Guenivere is our king, Arthur our queen. At the same time, Prince Harry will have become the King of England. Arthur and Guenivere again reign over us. So maybe, just maybe, Camelot will be here again, and will last much longer this time. Are we now ready for Camelot to endure?